Sentiments & Activities

George
Caspar
Homans

Sentiments & Activities

Essays
in Social
Science

With a new Introduction by the Author

Transaction Books
New Brunswick (USA) and Oxford (UK)

New material this edition copyright © 1988 by Transaction, Inc.,
New Brunswick, New Jersey 08903.
Copyright © 1962 by The Free Press of Glencoe

Library of Congress Catalog Number: 88-4714
ISBN: 0-88738-725-X
Printed in the United States of America

Library of Congress Cataloging in Publication Data

Homans, George Caspar, 1910-
   Sentiments & activities: essays in social science / George Caspar
Homans.
     p. cm.
   Reprint. Originally published: New York: Free Press of Glencoe,
1962. With new introd.
   Bibliography: p.
   Includes index.
   ISBN 0-88738-725-X
   1. Social sciences.   I. Title.   II. Title: Sentiments and
activities.
H35.H66 1988
300—dc19   88-4714
                                             CIP

To the memory of

Elton Mayo

Her grasp of appearances was thus out of proportion to her view of causes; but it came to her then and there that if she could only get the facts of appearance straight, only jam them down into their place, the reasons lurking behind them, kept uncertain, for the eyes, by their wavering and shifting, wouldn't perhaps be able to help showing.

—HENRY JAMES, *The Golden Bowl*

Contents

Introduction to the Transaction Edition

I began the first edition of *Sentiments and Activities*[1] with a long "autobiographical introduction." I need no such thing for the present edition, since its place has been pre-empted by my book-length auto-biography, *Coming to My Senses*.[2] Thus I must write a new introduction of a different kind.

Some of the papers in this edition require no further comment. Such are, for instance, "The Strategy of Industrial Sociology" and "The Strategy of Small-Group Research." The advice they offer seems to me still pertinent, though like much advice, I doubt whether later researchers have taken it to heart. I can only re-emphasize my view that first-hand observation and interviewing are the place from which all good sociology takes off, even if it does not end there. What I shall comment on are papers of a different kind: they have had direct, specific, sometimes long-term consequences. They have had continuing histories.

My fieldwork in the Customers' Accounting Division of the Boston Edison Company (now its real name can be revealed), represented in this volume by "Status Among Clerical Workers," "The Cash Posters," and "Status Congruence," led me to think about status and distributive justice as American workers looked on them, which was remarkably like the way Aristotle did in the *Nichomachean Ethics*.[3] It seems strange, in view of the bloody struggles recorded in history over issues of dis-tributive justice, that so few modern sociologists or social psychologists had paid any attention to them.[4] But following these papers and a more general discussion in my *Social Behavior*,[5] a mass of observational and experimental work on the subject began to appear, until it became a major intellectual growth-industry, and, as the fashion is, was called "equity theory." It is not a distinct theory but a deduction from a more general theory of behavioral psychology.

The paper "Social Behavior as Exchange" has met the same sort of fate. Following my return to academia from the Navy in 1946, and after much field work on, and teaching about, the behavior of members of small groups, I became interested in finding more general propositions from which my empirical hypotheses about social behavior might, under given conditions, be derived. And when derived, explained: theory is explanation. My friend B. F. Skinner had long ago made me familiar with the principles of behavioral psychology. I wondered if I could begin to solve my problem by considering the situation—the basic social situation—in which the actions of each of at least two persons rewarded or punished the actions of the other, in accordance with behavioral principles. Such behavior might obviously be looked on as an exchange of actions. Naturally, research done with this approach came to be called "exchange theory" and, like "equity theory," became an intellectual growth-industry. Again, it is not a distinct theory but a set of deductions from behavioral psychology. But I must accept the responsibility for the mislabelling, for it was I who gave the paper its title. I believed in beginning small and, taking off from the basic social situation, I went on to explain in the same way in my *Social Behavior* how more complicated social structures could emerge in small groups.

Besides behavioral psychology I was familiar with microeconomics and often used in my propositions words like *cost* and *profit*. Accordingly some scholars came to look on "exchange theory" as a direct application of economic ideas to the analysis and explanation of behavior not generally considered economic. As is usual in science, a number of scholars hit upon the same notion at about the same time. In this case they were particularly apt to be political scientists. A good example is Buchanan and Tullock's, *The Calculus of Consent*,[6] a much more sophisticated treatment of the subject than mine. This approach, too, has become a major intellectual growth-industry, under the name of "rational choice" or "public choice" theory. I am strongly in its favor, so long as its adepts recognize—and most of them do not—that "rational choice" and indeed elementary economics can be derived from a more general behavioral psychology, and that the latter can explain a range of social behaviors which "rational choice" can not. Yet within limits "rational choice" can explain a great deal. Most sociologists have been reluctant to adopt either a "rational choice" or a behavioral theory. This is a pity, because both are superior in explanatory power to any other theories sociologists are willing to accept, and thus much intellectual territory sociology might have exploited has fallen into the hands of political scientists and economists.

In short, some of the papers in this volume were harbingers of later developments of much greater importance and sophistication. Yet they were still harbingers.

The two longest papers in this volume, "The Frisians in East Anglia" and "Marriage, Authority, and Final Causes," pose rather more esoteric issues. As for the first, it entertains me that such a small folk as the Frisians—if they were a folk at all—in the darkest period of the Dark Ages should raise such interesting general questions. The paper grew out of my book, *English Villagers of the Thirteenth Century*,[7] which I had meant to be a study of a society at a particular period of time, in the manner of a "functionalist" study of a primitive tribe, except that this particular tribe could be described only with the help of historical, largely local, records.

In the course of this study I learned, as at least a couple of others had learned before me, that lowland England in the Middle Ages fell into two, roughly divided, cultural areas, one made up mostly of the south-eastern counties of Kent and East Anglia (Norfolk and Suffolk) and another, the so-called "open field" country, stretching in a broad band westward of the other from the Channel coast to Yorkshire and Northumberland on the North Sea.

The question for me was why the two areas should differ culturally. True, though the differences were discernible, they were not greatly different. In many ways considered important by social scientists the two were alike. Geophysically the two were alike in that the same kinds of terrain and soils were found in both. After the Germanic invasions, the people in both areas spoke the same language, with minor dialectical differences. Their techniques of agriculture were the same. Yet they differed in the social organization by which the techniques were carried out. They differed also in customs of inheritance, in the names of social classes, in both the name and the nature of political units. Some social scientists have come close to holding that geophysical conditions and technology (the relations of production) uniquely determine the nature of the social structure. This might be true of some societies in extremely constraining conditions, like the Eskimo, but no such one-to-one correlation existed here. Why?

My answer to the question took the form of trying to show that groups of Germanic invaders, other than Angles and Saxons, and bearing slightly different cultural traditions, had invaded different parts of eastern England. This was already known of Kent, which according to the Venerable Bede had been invaded and settled by Jutes.[8] But what about East Anglia, which differed in custom from Anglo-Saxon (open field) England but did resemble Kent, particularly in the rules governing inheritance of land. Were the East Anglicans Jutish too and, if not, what other Germanic folk could I find that shared some characteristics with Jutes? I soon thought of the Frisians, who probably occupied a coastal strip, right across from East Anglia, along the southern coast of the North Sea, from the Scheldt over into what is now Germany. I knew that

Frisian, which is still a live language, was the Germanic language most closely related linguistically to English. The Frisians were an obvious candidate for the role I needed to fill.

Guided by a hint in Marc Bloch,[9] I tried to learn what I could—and it was not much—about early Frisian social organization and compared it with what I had learned about medieval East Anglia. Though in both cases the evidence was full of gaps, there was enough left to suggest astonishing similarities, and so I concluded that bearers of Frisian culture had invaded East Anglia and established that culture there. I shall not review the evidence, as it is given in the paper. But the similarities only begged another question. The documents that began to give us some knowledge of either Frisian or East Anglican society dated from no earlier than the twelfth century. How could the cultures have maintained themselves so far unchanged that after seven centuries their similarities were still recognizable? Naturally I believed that under Dark Age conditions they could.

What I did not consider in my paper were the shadowy references in Old English literature that seemed at least not to contradict some of my ideas, especially about the relationship between the Frisians and the Jutes. The Venerable Bede had naturally assumed that the Jutes of Kent had come from Jutland,[10] which already in his time was the name for the northern peninsula of Denmark. Jutland is at some distance from Friesland by land—but the coastal Germans were good seamen. And the Jutes who invaded Kent were bearers of a culture that closely resembled those of the Frisians and East Anglians. Could the Jutes and the Frisians be in some way brought together? The answer is that literature does bring them together. For *Beowulf* places a group of Jutes in Friesland, and the old word for Frisians is sometimes used interchangeably with that for Jutes.[11] We must never forget how much the early Germanic tribes moved about and how fluid their membership was, so that at times they hardly resemble real tribes or nations. Yet they certainly did have distinct names.

The paper aroused a good deal of controversy, especially on the part of those historians of the English medieval economy who apparently believe in the one-to-one correspondence between the geophysical characteristics and technological practice of an area, on the one hand, and its social organization, on the other.[12] My argument for the detailed similarities between East Anglian and Frisian cultures has certainly not been accepted, partly for good reasons, for scholars still do not fully understand either one. Neither has it been rejected, but no later investigators have taken up the problem. My argument has been left in limbo and is likely to remain there. What has been accepted is the more general proposition that a far greater number of Frisians invaded eastern England than earlier scholars had been willing to believe. And that is something.

May I add that of all my books and papers this is the one I most enjoyed working on, both in the research and in the writing. Perhaps I ought to have become an antiquarian rather than a theorist, as I now profess myself to be. An antiquarian somehow sounds less important, but on such investigators who deal with original sources, alive or dead, the soundness of the theorist's work finally depends.

The second long esoteric paper (originally a small book) in this volume is "Marriage, Authority, and Final Causes." Surely no more pompous a title was ever given to a study of a phenomenon of so little worldly importance, for unilateral cross-cousin marriage in either of its two forms is practiced by only a handful of societies, and these are weak and small in membership. Yet the phenomenon raises some interesting theoretical issues: psychological versus other forms of explanation in social science and efficient-cause versus final-cause explanations. We, for D. M. Schneider and I wrote the paper together, attacked the views about the phenomenon that had been advanced by Claude Lévi-Strauss in his book, *Les Structures élémentaires de la parenté*. We argued that Lévi-Strauss' explanations were of the final-cause (teleological) type, which are not to be accepted in science when others are available, and we proposed to substitute for them an efficient-cause type of explanation, which was also to be psychological.

About seven years after the publication of our little book, we were in turn attacked by Rodney Needham, now Professor of Anthropology at Oxford in another little book called *Structure and Sentiment*.[13] I do not propose to repeat our argument in detail. We claimed that Lévi-Strauss' explanation of the common incest taboo was of the final-cause type, for according to him the taboo is instituted *in order to* create an exchange of women between groups (lineages) in a society, with the further implication that such exchanges are useful to the society in the sense of furthering its integration. But Lévi-Strauss described no mechanism that would explain how this desirable result was brought about: the taboo simply "is instituted." In the same way he claimed that the patrilateral form of unilateral cross-cousin marriage occurs in fewer societies than does the matrilateral (which it does) *because* "the latter not only permits but favors a better integration of the group." But again Lévi-Strauss produced no mechanism that would lead particular societies to follow one rule rather than the other. He simply argued from the fact that a larger number of societies follow the matrilateral form.

Pointing to a useful end without suggesting how the end is reached is the mark of a final-cause explainer.

In the place of such explanations, Schneider and I, starting from the different normative patterns of sentiment arising in kin-groups that also differed in their rules of territorial continuity, linearity, and above all in the locus of jural authority over kin-folk, derived an hypothesis that described the relationship between such variables and the preferred form of unilateral cross-cousin marriage. Tested against a sample of ethnographically recorded societies, the hypothesis turned out to be statistically significant. Again I do not give the details, as they are contained in the paper. Our explanation was both of the efficient-cause and the psychological type.

In his attack on us Needham had interesting things to say, especially about societies we had not studied, and some silly things about statistics. But he never came to grips with the theoretical issues. He claimed that Lévi-Strauss' theory was not a final-cause theory but did advance efficient causes: "He does see the formation of institutions as the unconscious production of 'certain fundamental structures of the human mind.'"[14] Such efficient causes seem pretty vague, and in any case in their reference to the human mind they are certainly psychological, though Lévi-Strauss's psychology is not ours. To this Needham added his own explanation: "that arrangements with certain solidarity advantages stand a greater chance of persisting."[15] Or again, "Matrilateral alliance can be regarded as a simple and effective way of creating and maintaining counter-fissive relationships in a segmentary society."[16] But the problem of the preference for one form or another of unilateral cross-cousin marriage is not that of persistence but of its being adopted in the first place. Indeed if maintaining counter-fissive relationships in segmentary society is such an advantage, why do so few societies, even among segmentary ones, follow such rules?

What Needham certainly did not do—and this is the crux of the matter—was produce an hypothesis alternative to ours describing how one or the other of the two types are distributed among societies differing in other aspects of social organization. He admitted that "the association [Homans and Schneider] claim to have established is interesting."[17] But he apparently has not pursued this interest further, and our hypothesis, so far as I know, still stands.

At the very end he wrote: "The present case is yet another demonstration of Durkheim's contention: 'Whenever a social phenomenon is directly explained by a psychological phenomenon we may be sure it is false.'"[18] Yet the efficient cause Lévi-Strauss himself proposed, and which Needham was defending, was, as we have seen, itself psychological. Alas! more and more later thinking and research on social theory and the nature of explanation have undermined Durkheim's position. Perhaps I may cite a French sociologist, Raymond Boudon, of two generations later than his: "A fundamental principle of the sociologies of action is that social change ought to be analyzed as the resultant of an ensemble of individual actions."[19] And not change only, but social stability. This primacy of the actions of individuals at once entails psychology, for psychology is the science of such actions.

The tumult and the shouting die. I myself have not investigated unilateral cross-cousin marriage further, though I am sure that our hypothesis does not capture all the causes that determine the adoption of one form rather than the other. Yet I have become more and more interested in the most general issues our study raised: the nature of explanation itself and the use of psychological propositions in explanation in social science.[20]

I must end on a gayer note. "Giving a Dog a Bad Name" was originally a *jeu d'esprit* delivered over the radio for the British Broadcasting Corporation. After my talk had been taped, the young woman who had charge of me in the studio played it back to me. As usual I complained about how awful my voice sounded. "Oh No!" she replied, "What an interesting folk-accent!" The classic tones of a Boston Brahmin characterized as "an interesting folk-accent"! I must say that I never enjoyed a put-down more than I did this.

Notes

1. G. C. Homans, *Sentiments and Activities* (N.Y.: The Free Press, 1962).
2. G. C. Homans, *Coming to My Senses* (New Brunswick, N.J.: Transaction Books, 1984).
3. Aristotle, *Nichomachean Ethics*, Bk. V.
4. There were notable exceptions, for instance, R.K. Merton and Alice S. Kitt, "Contributions to the Theory of Reference Group Behavior" in R. K. Merton and P. Lazarsfeld, eds. *Continuities in Social Research: Studies in the Scope and Method of "The American Soldier"* (Glencoe, Ill.: The Free Press, 1950).
5. G. C. Homans, *Social Behavior: Its Elementary Forms* (N.Y.: Harcourt Brace & World, 1961: revised ed. 1974).
6. J.M. Buchanan and G. Tullock, *The Calculus of Consent* (Ann Arbor, Mich.: University of Michigan Press, 1962).
7. G. C. Homans, *English Villagers of the Thirteenth Century* (Cambridge, Mass.: Harvard University Press, 1941).
8. J.E.A. Jolliffe, *Pre-Feudal England: The Jutes* (Oxford: Oxford University Press, 1933).
9. M. Bloch, *La Société féodale* (Paris: Albin Michel, 1940) Vol. II, pp. 377-8.
10. Bede, *Ecclesiastical History of the English Nation*, Bk. I., ch. 15.

11. Fr. Klaeber, ed., *Beowulf and the Fight at Finnsburg*, 3rd. ed. (Boston: D.C. Heath, 1950) pp. 232-35. See also J.R.R. Tolkien, *Finn and Hengest: The Fragment and the Episode*, A. Bliss, ed. (Boston: Houghton Mifflin, 1983).
12. For my reply to such attacks, see "The Explanation of English Regional Differences" in G. C. Homans, *Certainties and Doubts* (New Brunswick, N.J.: Transaction Books, 1987) pp. 159-73.
13. R. Needham, *Structure and Sentiment: A Test Case in Social Anthropology* (Chicago, University of Chicago Press, 1962).
14. *Ibid.*, p. 27.
15. *Ibid.*, p. 27.
16. *Ibid.*, p. 97.
17. *Ibid.*, p. 125.
18. *Ibid.*, p. 126: E. Durkheim, *Les Régles de la méthode sociologique* (Paris: Alcan, 1901), p. 128.
19. R. Boudon, *La Place du désordre* (Paris: Presses Universitaires de France, 1984), p. 39.
20. For examples, see several of the papers in G. C. Homans, *Certainties and Doubts* (New Brunswick, N.J.: Transaction Books, 1987).

Sentiments & Activities

1

Autobiographical

Introduction

IN a volume of collected essays a reader will be looking for some unifying principle other than that they were all written by the same man—as if that were a unifying principle! He may know of volumes whose essays mark stages in a single line of investigation, pursued by the author year after year with cumulative success. At the least, he will expect some unity to be provided by the author's official discipline. I am a sociologist, but the reader who has sense enough to scan the table of contents of this book and see what he is letting himself in for may well wonder whether even sociology provides the unity here. Should he know the field, he will, to be sure, find some essays that will strike him as legitimately sociological. Industrial sociology is a recognized department of the field, and so is the study of small groups, though it is a department sociology shares with psychology. But when he comes to a long paper on unilateral cross-cousin marriage, the "cross-cousin" will surely tell him that he has crossed the boundary into primitive kinship, which belongs to anthropology. And as for "The Frisians in East Anglia"—what business has a sociologist with English history?

I have indeed scattered my shots, and the best thing I can do by way of introduction to these essays is to take advantage of this very deficiency by explaining it. Few of us social scientists have tried to write our intellectual autobiographies and to tell as best we could why we got interested in the subjects we have worked on and what influences have played upon us as we worked. Without trying to analyze the deeper and less conscious influences, I shall explain the scattering of my subjects by giving, as well as I can at this late date, the more obvious reasons why I took them up and why I pursued them as I did. The reasons were seldom what the picture of an ideal scientist says they should have been. Often they were opportunistic, designed to advance a career rather than a discipline; often intensely personal rather than dictated by a reasoned appraisal of what was best worth doing in the field; and often matters of chance, in the sense that the choice could not easily have been predicted ahead of time. I should be more ashamed of myself if I thought that many others had let themselves be dominated by the mere flux of circumstance less often than I have.

Whatever my nonintellectual reasons for embarking on my various subjects, I found, once fairly embarked, that they were running into intellectual problems of wider scope than the subjects themselves. This collection includes most of the papers, other than reviews, that I have published during my professional life. Some of them are occasional pieces or the by-products of other work, and I shall explain at the beginning of each essay what the occasion for it was. The others are different. Although they certainly deal with their subjects, they should also be looked on as points where a dialogue that has been going on in my mind for a long time thrust itself for a moment above the surface of consciousness, a dialogue between the data of social science and certain kinds of general ideas. These ideas are the final justification of this collection, and the second purpose of this introduction is to explain what they are.

The trouble with sociology is not a dearth of information but a glut: every human being has more than he can handle. The problem is how to get hold of such a vast and slippery body of data. As Robert K. Merton once pointed out, the approaches are many, the arrivals few.[1] What is our subject finally *about?* Is it about men, or is it about societies? And how shall we go about organizing the subject? No one has any doubt what it ought to look like when organized: it ought to look like a theory. But what *is* a theory? And the way a theory looks when organized may be very different from the way that organization was brought about. What is the strategy of reaching a theory that will explain the facts? The general ideas that came into my dialogue had to do with these questions.

[2]

Becoming a Sociologist

My very entrance into sociology was a matter of chance; or rather, I got into sociology because I had nothing better to do. I graduated from Harvard College in June, 1932, having concentrated academically in English literature and nonacademically in writing verse. In line with my literary interests I had decided to make myself a newspaperman. I was quite wrong; literary ability is the last thing a newspaperman needs to get ahead. But I was saved from the consequences of deliberate decision. Although I had gotten myself a job beginning in the fall with William Allen White of the Emporia, Kansas, *Gazette*, the Depression was still getting worse, and when the time came for me to go to Emporia, White wired me that the circulation of the *Gazette* had gone down so much that he would have to withdraw his offer of a job. This made me, like so many others at the time, unemployed.

In that same fall of 1932, Lawrence Joseph Henderson, Professor of Biological Chemistry at Harvard, was offering a seminar on the *Sociologie Générale* of the Italian economist Vilfredo Pareto;[2] the first such seminar given, I think, anywhere in the world and certainly the first in the United States. Henderson was by profession a physiologist, whose work on the chemical equilibrium of the blood was the foundation of later work on blood plasma. But Henderson was more than a physiologist. For years he had attended seminars in the Philosophy Department on problems connected especially with the philosophy of science, and he had given for years the first and only course at Harvard on the history of science. William Morton Wheeler, whose work on insect societies had led him to read all the sociology, human or animal, he could put his hands on, had suggested the *Sociologie Générale* to Henderson, and Henderson was at once taken with it. As a student of engineering, Pareto had written his thesis on the equilibrium of elastic solids, and Henderson thought the views expressed in the *Sociologie* on the nature of science were among the soundest he had ever encountered. There was an even better reason for his enthusiasm: with all its limitations the *Sociologie* is a great book.

Henderson used to say that some of the men he most disapproved of were among the most enthusiastic about his course on the history of science. Among those of whom he did not disapprove was the historian and essayist Bernard DeVoto, who had come back to Harvard as an instructor in English and who had renewed his friendship with Henderson. In my last three undergraduate years DeVoto was my tutor in my field of English literature, with whom I met once a week to discuss my reading. Henderson had urged the *Sociologie* on DeVoto, as he urged it on everyone; DeVoto in turn urged it on me, not because it was sociology but because it might clear a lot of nonsense from my mind. In my senior year I bought the book and read at least the first of the two big volumes in French.

I took to Pareto because he made clear to me what I was already prepared to believe. I do not know all the reasons why I was ready for him, but I can give one. Someone has said that much modern sociology is an effort to answer the arguments of the revolutionaries. As a Republican Bostonian who had not rejected his comparatively wealthy family, I felt during the thirties that I was under personal attack, above all from the Marxists. I was ready to believe Pareto because he provided me with a defense. His was an answer to Marx because an amplification of him. Marx had taught that the economic and political theories of the bourgeoisie—and I was clearly a bourgeois—were rationalizations of their interests. Pareto amplified Marx by showing that this was true of most theories of human behavior, Marx' included. In the *Sociologie* and *Les systèmes socialistes*,[3] Pareto was careful to point out that Marx was not *mere* rationalization, and that when he talked about class warfare he was talking about something real. But in showing that some of Marx, like the famous theory of surplus value, was certainly rationalization Pareto provided a kind of answer to him. At least the proletariat had no more intellectual justification in demanding my money or my life—and it looked as if they were demanding both, and my liberties to boot—than I had for defending myself. Emotional justification was something else again. As a beneficiary of inherited capital I was a good emotional target, and I was fond of quoting the lisping Bostonian who said: "Someday the pwoletariat is going to wise up and take away my pwopetty." But it was some comfort to realize that the proletariat did not have reason as well as emotion on its side. If we could only meet as honest men—or honest rationalizers—we might divide up the take without fighting. It was the intellectual guff talked by the alleged leaders of the proletariat that put one's back up and got in the way of a settlement. Whatever one did, one was not going to yield to men like that.

DeVoto did more than introduce me to Pareto: he introduced me to Henderson himself. And when, in the fall of 1932, Henderson was collecting recruits for his seminar on Pareto (he could not rely on volunteers, since he had a reputation for landing hard on men who disagreed with him) Henderson asked me to join. I knew something about Pareto, and I was known to be on the town. I had nothing better to do and accepted.

Henderson had recruited well. Besides DeVoto himself, Crane Brinton, and Joseph Schumpeter, among those who attended regularly was Charles P. Curtis, Jr., a lawyer and a Fellow of the Harvard corporation but also, which was unusual in either lawyers or Fellows, a man interested in any ideas that were going around the university. Curtis was a lifelong friend of my family's, and whether for that reason or, what is more likely, because he knew I was employable, he suggested in the course of the seminar that he and I should write a book introducing Pareto's sociology to the English-speaking public— it had then been translated only into French. I still had nothing better to do, and again I agreed. We wrote the book: *An Introduction to Pareto*.[4] It came out the next year, and it is the best brief introduction to what Pareto actually said. Since Pareto's book was about sociology, writing the *Introduction* made me a sociologist too, though his was the only sociology I had then read.

Circumstances then went to work to keep me a sociologist. Pareto was not the only enterprise Henderson had in hand. For several years he and Curtis, together with President Lowell of Harvard, Alfred North Whitehead, Professor of Philosophy, and John Livingston Lowes, Professor of English, had been holding informal discussions on graduate instruction in the arts and sciences. They were dissatisfied with the type of training that ended in the Ph.D. degree, believing that it gave the abler men too little freedom to pursue their own ideas wherever they might lead. The discussions finally resulted in a plan for a Society of Fellows.[5] A number of graduate students were to be chosen every year as Junior Fellows, paid a small scholarship, and allowed to work on anything they were interested in. They were to be subject to no restrictions except that they might not be candidates for the Ph.D. and that they were to dine once a week with their elders, the Senior Fellows, who were to choose the candidates and administer the funds of the Society. Unable to get foundation support, President Lowell finally founded the Society with his own money—the last thing he did before retiring as President—and its first academic year of operation was 1933–34, that is, the year after Henderson had given his first seminar on Pareto. The original Senior Fellows were Henderson, chairman, Lowell, Curtis, Whitehead, and Lowes.

Someone—perhaps Curtis—had put me forward as a candidate for Junior Fellow in the first year of the Society. I had run as a poet and had rightly been rejected. But the second year, 1934–35, was another matter. By that time I had demonstrated my Paretan faith; I was Henderson's man, and Henderson was chairman of the Society of Fellows. I had worked with, and become a great friend of, Curtis. As an undergraduate I had studied under both Whitehead and Lowes. If the Society was what I wanted, I was in with the right crowd. Moreover I was still unemployed, or at least unpaid, though I had not tried very hard to get employment. Accordingly, when Henderson suggested that I should run for the Society a second time, and this time as a sociologist, I again agreed at once. I had not been able to make anything of myself, but I had learned that, if I would only relax and say "Yes," other people would make something of me. What they made me was a sociologist, and I am grateful. I was a Junior Fellow from 1934 to 1939, and, as I shall try to show, most of my ideas come, even if only by way of reaction, from men the Society put me in touch with.

Although in 1933–34 Pareto's was the only sociology I knew, I was at least aware in a general way that the subject did not end with him; and so, to prepare for entering the Society, I asked Henderson, in effect: "Master, what shall I do to become a sociologist?" He knew no more about the matter than I did, and he certainly did not propose to ask any of the sociologists who were then at Harvard; but his answer was, as always, decided. Sociology must be a science. In the end, mathematics was the language of science. As a man who had done his undergraduate work in English literature, I was mathematically illiterate; I must learn the differential and integral calculus forthwith. German was still, for a scientist, the most important foreign language; I must also refurbish my German. Finally, I must learn historical method, for according to Henderson history was the only social science that had worked out a good method. Faithfully I did everything Henderson told me to do, with ambiguous results. The German at least allowed me to read Max Weber before he was translated. The calculus has enabled me to understand a great deal of classical physics and economics, though statistics, which Henderson did not suggest, would have served me better as a sociologist. As for historical method, I learned that there is no historical method other than the commonest of common sense, but in the course of learning that I got interested in history itself.

But Henderson was to do me a much more useful turn: he arranged for me to take a course of reading with Elton Mayo. Wallace Donham, Dean of the Harvard Graduate School of Business Administration, had gotten Henderson and Mayo to the school to study the behavior of industrial workers. Henderson, who had finished his work on the blood, was to head the Fatigue Laboratory and study the physiology of work. Mayo was to study its psychology, and at the time when I first knew him, he had already been engaged for some years, with T. North Whitehead, son of the philosopher, and Fritz Roethlisberger, on the famous researches at the Hawthorne Plant of the Western Electric Company.[6] Henderson and Mayo occupied adjoining offices in Morgan Hall and, though very different in character, had come to like and admire one another. Above all it was the superb clinician that Henderson, a laboratory scientist but an M.D. by training, admired in Mayo.

Mayo undertook to put a few of us through a course of reading in the authors he thought it most important for young social scientists to be familiar with. Although he was himself a psychologist and psychiatrist by training and practice, he started us off with social anthropology, specifically the new "functional" anthropologists, Radcliffe-Brown and Malinowski. Both of these men Mayo had met, either in London or in his native Australia. Radcliffe-Brown's disciple, W. Lloyd Warner had come to Harvard, fresh from studying a tribe of Australian blackfellows; he had given Mayo some good advice on the later stages of the Western Electric research, and with Mayo's encouragement he was trying to apply the ideas of functional anthropology to the study of a modern community, Newburyport, Massachusetts.[7] One of his assistants in this work was Conrad Arensberg, who had become a Junior Fellow in the same year I did.

Mayo was never much interested in the details of behavior in the Andaman or Trobriand Islands for their own sake. What he wanted us to get from our reading in social anthropology was a picture of societies in which human collaboration was supported by established ritual. This ritual, Mayo felt, modern society had lost, to the impairment of the human capacity for collaboration, and with the consequences in individual neurosis and collective conflict that in the 1930's he could see all around us. Some of his critics to the contrary, Mayo never argued

[7]

that the modern world should try to return to the primitive type of society—what he called the *established* society. His question was rather: How can the human capacity for collaboration be maintained in a society of a very different kind, one in process of continuous change? What are the conditions for an *adaptive* society?[8] It was only as background for attempts to answer that question that Mayo felt his students should be familiar with traditional forms of human collaboration. His eyes were always on the modern world. But if the master proposes, the pupil disposes. You can start a student reading, but you cannot be sure he will get out of it what you want him to. For reasons I shall try to give later, I forgot about the modern world and got interested in the details of primitive behavior.

The second group of books we read with Mayo followed naturally from the first. They centered in Durkheim's *Suicide* and lay in the field now called social pathology. Mayo was concerned to show how the breakdown of an established society—the condition Durkheim called *anomie*—led to disorders of individual behavior. But again, I did not get from Durkheim quite what, I think, Mayo wanted me to. It was not that I could not get interested in social pathology, but that I could get more interested in something else. In the course of an essentially literary education, I had absorbed one of the unstated assumptions of the Western intellectual tradition, the notion that the nature of individuals determined finally the nature of society. Reading *Suicide* led us to Durkheim's other books, especially *The Rules of Sociological Method* and *The Elementary Forms of the Religious Life*. Both the *Suicide* and the *Rules* implied that the unstated assumption should be turned around and—to put the matter as naively as I then saw it—that the nature of society might determine the nature of individuals. As for the *Elementary Forms*, which had been the inspiration of Radcliffe-Brown's *Andaman Islanders*, it suggested, as the latter did, that the purpose or function of human institutions was not—to put the matter naively again—the satisfaction of human needs but the maintenance of society. Unlike Pareto, who made clear, however admirably, only what I was already prepared to believe, Durkheim upset me. His was a revelation, but a revelation I never was quite comfortable with. Though at the time I did not see what was wrong, he started an itch that took me further and further away from Mayo's concern with social pathology.

Mayo finally turned to the disorders of individual behavior themselves, and led us through the main works of the psychiatrists he most admired: Pierre Janet and Sigmund Freud; accompanying his discussion of the text with cases, light-heartedly described, from his own wide clinical experience. Later, he arranged that we should get clinical experience of our own. At the Boston Dispensary and the Boston City Hospital we interviewed patients who complained of physical ills certified by the physicians to have no physical reason for existence. Although we were not supposed to attempt psychotherapy, our methods of nondirective counseling did sometimes result in the alleviation of the symptoms. I do not know that it is possible for youngsters who are not medical students to get this kind of experience today. It helped in the treatment of my own neuroses, and it prepared me for later interviewing in the field. Otherwise it made little difference to my thinking as a sociologist. The plain fact was that I could not long remain interested in individual psychopathology.

I do not know why this should have been so, but as a fact it fell into a pattern. Given the chance, I have always deserted anything that had contemporary practical importance or that might lead to reforms. I have deserted the twentieth century for the thirteenth, social pathology for primitive kinship, industrial sociology for the study of small groups. It may have been mere escapism: my nerves may have been too weak for the modern world. More likely I was reluctant to change a world that, on the whole, was behaving so well toward me. But I have found a description of the syndrome that is more flattering to me and that may well be true. I have come to think now—I did not see it then—that what never failed to interest me was not sociology as an agency of change or as a means of understanding my immediate environment but sociology as a generalizing science. What were the best possibilities for establishing generalizations? What were the main intellectual issues? What was the subject really about? By what handle should we lay hold on it? A science may naturally turn out to have practical applications, but it certainly does not grow just through its practical applications. The modern world offers plenty of material for generalizations about social behavior, but it is not the only world that does. Thus the briefest look at primitive kinship showed plenty of generalizations lying embedded in the matrix of fact and crying for formulation. So did industrial sociology if one forgot about reforming industry and thought only of the opportunities its captive groups provided for studying social behavior at first hand. If the emphasis was on science, what made a particular subject matter "important" was simply the chance of exploiting it intellectually. Did the vein lie near the surface?

Mayo was interested in training men who, through a clinical study of human behavior, should learn how to take the lead in fostering free human collaboration. Though certainly a scientist, he was finally a reformer. Unfortunately, in exposing me to science he deadened me to reform. My behavior froze at what may well have seemed to him an immature level. I failed him; I feel guilty but grateful. For though I did not get out of the books I read with him, or read during the years I was working with him, just what he wanted me to, it was still he who introduced me to them. I turn now not to the questions they should have raised for me, but to those they actually did raise.

History and Social Structure

The field that Mayo did least to encourage my interest in was English social history. According to Henderson one of the things I must do in order to become a sociologist was learn historical method; his suggestion was that I should do so by working with the ablest Harvard historian he knew, Charles H. McIlwain, who had taught for many years a famous course on English constitutional history; and he approached McIlwain on my behalf. I doubt that McIlwain had any better idea what Henderson meant by historical method than I did, but he was ready to do Henderson a favor and take me on as a research student, especially as I was reasonably well prepared for working in the English medieval field. I had had much school Latin, which is harder than medieval Latin, and as a candidate for honors in English literature, I had taken a course that taught me to read simple Anglo-Saxon texts. McIlwain put me to work on the coronation oaths of the English kings beginning with the earliest records. What point it was McIlwain was interested in establishing I have now forgotten; but I became reasonably expert in handling the original sources, and as time went on I got less and less interested in medieval constitutional theory and more and more interested in medieval behavior. One of the prerogatives, for instance, of medieval English kings was taking the profits from stranded wrecks. Although I became one of the few men who knows the difference between flotsam and jetsam, to me the law of wreck was only interesting for what it had to say about medieval seafaring.

In the course of my reading on medieval England I ran into Frederick Seebohm's *The English Village Community*, the first description of what is now called the open-field system of agricultural organization.[9] I was fascinated by a system in which every element seemed to interlock so neatly with every other, especially as the reading I was doing with Mayo on social anthropology taught me that this was just what the elements of a social system ought to do. I was coming up for election to the Society of Fellows, and I ought to have some plan or project to carry out if I were elected. It occurred to me that no one had studied a society of the past using the ideas of functional anthropology, and that I might as well study English rural society in the thirteenth century. Had I known then how much had already been written about the open-field system I might not have been so rash; but I laid the project before the Senior Fellows, and when I was elected to the Society I was stuck with it. Besides working with Mayo, I spent my time in the Society reading all the published material, documents and secondary works, about the society I had chosen, and then spending a long summer in England reading all the manuscripts I could lay my hands on quickly. The result was *English Villagers of the Thirteenth Century*,[10] together with two of the articles that are reprinted here.

I am sure there was another and deeper reason for my interest in medieval England. I was a New Englander and, as a New Englander, preoccupied with my ancestry. I was, moreover, in the language of New England, a Yankee, that is, a descendant of Englishmen who had come to America in colonial times; and we Yankees were being numerically and politically overwhelmed by what we were pleased to call the "newer races." Whether we liked it or not, they, "ethnic groups" themselves, were making *us* into just another ethnic group. They called in question what we English-Americans stood for, what we meant, what indeed we *were*. The answers might be sought in English history, not just its political history to which the United States owed its freedom, but in its underlying social and economic history, especially in the centuries before the Englishmen came to America, for it was obviously not the modern Englishmen who were our ancestors. The study of medieval English countrymen was a search for what the Nazis called *blut und boden*, though I was slow to recognize the similarity. And I still deny the implied prejudice: I was not looking for my superiority, to the Irish, for instance; I was looking for my own identity.

Nor was the medieval part of English history my final though unconscious objective. I studied the thirteenth century because it was the first from which enough documents survived to give us anything like an adequate picture of the social order, but given the documents I should have been happy to go back earlier. In my father's library there was a Victorian book for boys called *Popular Romances of the Middle Ages*.[11] In the best Victorian way it assumed a high standard of boys' interests. It was not written down or popularized in any manner, but consisted simply of excellent shortened forms of the main heroic stories of the Middle Ages from *Beowulf* to *Le Morte D'Arthur*. I read it sometime before I was thirteen years old. I never enjoyed the romances, like the Arthurian series, that came down to us through a Celtic and French tradition; they were too obviously romantic, magical, and fanciful, too utterly removed from anything that people could really have done. This was not true of the stories coming down to us directly from the Germanic heroic age—say, from the invasions to the battle of Hastings —*Beowulf*, the stories of the Volsungs, and especially the Icelandic sagas, of which *Popular Romances* included Njal and Grettir: even their trolls were more real than Arthur's knights.

And in their reality they were versions of myself. In literature, I suppose, one is always looking for something that tells him about himself and not just about mankind. Much as I loved Homer or Virgil, I could not see myself in Achilles and certainly not in Aeneas. They were no closer to me than the Irish: they were humans but not Homans. Or, as we should say now, they were products of a different culture. But in the men of the sagas, Grettir, Gunnar, Skarpheddin, even the powerful old schemers like Snorri the Priest, and later, best of all, Egil Skallagrimson, seaman and skald, I could see myself for good or ill. If I could see what I took for the same independence, I could also see the same impulsive aggression: I did not swing a war axe but I knew the moods that swung one. Not only were they myself but they were the earliest versions of myself: there was nothing before them. No need to explain to me the importance of the origin myth in primitive society.

Ever since I first opened *Popular Romances* I have kept up my reading in the literature and history of the Germanic heroic age. In studying the England of the thirteenth century I was getting as close to the heroic age as I could and still remain a sociologist. Later, in asking for the origins of the different types of English medieval society, I have gone back to the heroic age: "The Frisians in East Anglia" shows how far I have gone. And in going back I have been looking for myself: I was among the Frisians who crossed the North Sea at the news from Britain that the emperor had withdrawn the legions.

Let me add one minor reason for the pleasure I found in research on early medieval history. In some parts of the field the clues are so few that the investigator must make the most of every one, and so he has all the fun of being a detective without the risk of being shot at as he closes in on the murderer. I remember the anticipation with which I untied the red tape—for here alone it literally survives—around each new roll of parchment, hoping I should find in the document some single entry—some single entry, mind you—that might confirm a pet theory or throw a new beam on the darkness of medieval life. No one who works in modern sociology, where data are so plentiful they become mere statistics, can know the joy sheer, single facts can give of their own sweet selves.

Whatever the nonsociological reasons for undertaking a study of English villagers of the thirteenth century, the study itself immediately raised good sociological issues. To begin with, it raised the question of the relation between sociology and history. Some sociologists are still fond of implying that, with their training and theories, they could do a better job of writing history than the historians can. All I can say is: let them do it; let them put up or shut up. By and large they have not done it yet. They may cite Max Weber as a sociologist who has bettered the historians, but when he wrote Weber *was* a historian, and historians, including Weber himself, have had good reason for believing that Weber's famous discussion of the relation between radical Protestantism and the development of capitalism was one-sided. Before they can better the historians, the sociologists will have to do the work of the historians and learn some history. By and large they have been unwilling to do that kind of hard work.

To bring the matter closer to home, what did I, as a sociologist, have to add to the study of thirteenth-century society? What did I have that the historians did not have? Not specific hypotheses to be tested against the data, for as far as that century and most others are concerned, sociology had no such hypotheses then, nor does it have them now. Not special techniques of investigation: some simple statistical methods could have been used with the data, but I doubt that they would have come up with findings very different from those reached by less systematic methods. Most such methods are not, in fact, methods of discovery but methods of persuasion: they are designed to persuade the reader that

[13]

certain kinds of statements are probably true. The actual findings about thirteenth century society consisted of just the sort of statement that the statistician supports with standard deviations and chi-squares: they consisted of statements about central tendencies in the data, statements that such and such a practice was most frequent or most typical in particular circumstances. The historian's method of persuading people, notably other historians, of the truth of his statements of central tendency is simply to cite such evidence as he can. He expects other historians to come along and cite further evidence, contradicting or qualifying what he has said. If these new statements turn out to persuade other historians they stand for the moment as accepted historical doctrine. In theory a correlation coefficient should persuade a social scientist of the truth of a statement of central tendency more rapidly than a mere piling up of data. I am not sure that it does so in fact. I am far from sure that the sociologist's methods of showing relationships among his variables succeed in obtaining general consensus any more rapidly than the methods of persuasion used by historians.

If I could add neither hypotheses nor techniques, what did I have left? The whole question of what was worth studying. An earlier generation of medieval social historians in England had been lawyers by training, like Maitland and Vinogradoff, but the generation contemporary with my own was more apt to have an economic background. The problems they were interested in, they had investigated very well. A sociologist, for instance, had little to add to their account of the open-field system of agriculture, and what he did have, he added by methods just like their own. But they were little interested in phenomena that could not easily fit into their categories of technology and economics, especially as they felt these phenomena were secondary, the mere result of the others. In contrast, a sociologist fresh from a reading of functional anthropology was persuaded—even if the assumption had yet to be proved—that every custom, every institution, was related to everything else in a social system, and if everything was related to everything else, everything was worth studying.

Everything was a tall order. Scanning the data and what had been written about it, I soon came to the conclusion that the most neglected aspect of English rural life in the Middle Ages was the one an anthropologist would look at first and an economic historian last—the kinship system. In particular, the manorial court rolls contained a great deal of information about the villagers' customs of inheritance of land; and inheritance in an agricultural society was the heart of the relationship between kinship, economics, and technology. The first or legal generation of historians, naturally interested in family law, had recognized the importance of the court rolls but had only begun to work on them. The second or economic generation had given them up altogether, for they had little to say about either technology or prices. I put in my main research effort on the court rolls, and my main empirical contribution to the study of English rural society was the mapping out of the different rules of inheritance followed by the countrymen.

Earlier work had already established that, once the Celtic areas of the West were left out of consideration, there were two main kinds of agricultural organization in medieval England. Various forms of the classical open-field system dominated most of the North, the Midlands, and Wessex. Another system—perhaps not one system but a number of systems whose common bond was that they were *not* open-field—dominated the Southeast, notably East Anglia and Kent. My studies in inheritance now showed that the boundary between the two field-systems coincided roughly with the boundary between two customs of inheritance. Statistically speaking, though I used no formal statistics to establish the relationship, the open-field coincided with the area in which a villager's holding descended undivided to one of his sons and one only, whereas the Southeastern system coincided with the area in which a villager's holding either descended jointly to all his sons or was divided between them. It looked, moreover, as if the differences in customs of inheritance were only one aspect of wider differences in family organization. The rule of impartible inheritance implied what anthropologists called a stem-family, the rule of partible inheritance, what they called a joint-family.

This finding about the coincidence of boundaries was delightful. If one institution of a social system differed from the corresponding institution of another system, then, on the assumption that everything intermeshed with everything else within each system, the other institutions of the two systems should differ too, and it appeared they did. To a naive social scientist, functional anthropology seemed to make this assumption, and now he saw it borne out.

To observe the correlations of institutions was one thing, to find an explanation for the correlations was another. What was there, for instance, about the open-field system that gave it a predilection, in England at least, for impartible inheritance? I do not know that we have yet an answer to this question. But there was another problem of explanation that occupied me more deeply and that still occupies the English students in this field without ever becoming fully explicit. Why should there have been two systems at all?

The economic historians tended to be intellectual, though seldom political, Marxists, and held one form or another of the economic interpretation of history: the other institutions of society were determined by its means of production. In their way they were also good functional anthropologists in that they assumed a one-to-one relationship between a particular institution (in their case agricultural technology) and the other institutions of a society. To a single technology should correspond a single set of other institutions. Note that this argument is a very general one and has a bearing in much more important fields than English medieval sociology. It has been argued, for example, that since industrial technology and methods of factory organization are substantially identical in the Soviet Union and the United States, the other institutions of the two countries must become more and more alike.

Applied to the England of the thirteenth century, the economic interpretation led to two sorts of argument. If the differences between the social system of the open-field and that of the Southeast were real, then there must be some technological difference between the two areas. But if, on the other hand, the technologies of the two areas were the same, then the social systems must be the same too. Proponents of the first argument naturally looked hard for technological differences. If the institutions of East Anglia differed from those of the open-field, it was because of the special prevalence of sheep-farming in East Anglia.[12] Aside from the fact that it was hard to show what sheep-farming had to do with partible inheritance, the trouble with this argument was that the geographical differences between the two areas, like good pasture for sheep, were not really all that great—the geographical differences within each area were greater than the differences between them—and that therefore there can have been no reason for great technological differences.

Proponents of the second argument naturally looked hard for social similarities. They admitted that the two geographical environments were much the same, and that Englishmen of the thirteenth century knew one single agricultural technology, which the proponents tended to identify with the technology embodied in the open-field system. And if the technologies were the same, the other aspects of the social system must really have been the same too. They liked to believe that the agricultural systems of East Anglia and Kent must really after all have been open-field systems, and they were delighted when they could discover evidence that seemed to point in this direction.[13]

I was with the proponents of the first argument in believing that there were many social differences between the two areas, though it would be easy to argue further that the two systems had more in common with one another than they had with any really primitive society. At the same time I was with the proponents of the second argument in denying that there were technological differences between the two. Accordingly I was forced to deny the economic interpretation of history in its narrow form.

I could readily conceive of an environment so rigorous, and a technology for exploiting it so limited, as to leave little latitude in the ways men could organize themselves. The society of the Eskimo or of the Bedouin might be examples. But in most conditions was there not more play, more looseness, more room for variation in the relation between environment, technology, and other social institutions? I was not denying the force of the economic interpretation. I was not denying that the means of production bore some relation to the other institutions of a society in the sense that they set limits to what was possible outside the productive sphere; but they only set limits, within which considerable variation was possible. I was only arguing against the generality of a one-to-one relation between the two.

Medieval England knew only one agricultural technology. The type of plow, the animals, the grains, the rotation of crops were the same in the Southeast as they were in the open-field. But field systems were much more than a technology. Thus the same rotation of crops could be, and was, applied to a compact block of land in the hands of a single joint-family in the Southeast as was applied to the scattered strips of a single villager in the open-field. It was not just technology that determined the differences in family and village organization, for the same technology was compatible with either of the two systems.

It was easy to show that many of the features of a field system were not even technologically determined in any simple sense. For instance, a common feature of the open-field system was that villagers of the same class held equal areas of land, and this had been interpreted as a survival from a time when each villager who contributed a single ox or a single span of oxen to a joint plow-team was assigned, out of the land the plow had tilled, a share equal to that of other villagers who had contributed as much as he had. But it was not technology that determined the equality, not the indubitable technological fact that an ox cannot be subdivided without becoming beef. It was rather a notion of justice: people who contributed equally should be rewarded equally. People's behavior was determined by the relation between their values and the ways they had learned of satisfying their values, which we may call, if we like, their technology. Neither the values nor the technology was independent of the other. In the present example, the technology was being used to obtain justice, just as it was being used to obtain food.

Let me put more generally the problem I had encountered. Recent social anthropology seemed to imply that every institution, every customary way of behaving, in a social system was related to every other. The economic interpretation appeared to be a special case of this, the structural, assumption; special in the sense that it implied not just a relation but a one-way relation. A particular type of technological base would determine one and only one type of social superstructure. But what did the assumption mean? If it meant that a change in one institution, over the dimension of time or place, would be accompanied by a change in the others, some of the evidence from medieval England seemed to bear it out; but some did not. A change in field systems over the geographical dimension was empirically related to a change in customs of inheritance, but not to a change in technology. Or, to state the problem in terms of the economic interpretation, a single technology was associated with two somewhat different social superstructures. Perhaps the lesson was that the assumption was not to be accepted wholesale except as a guide to research. The assumption led one to look for the interrelations of institutions, but the interrelations that actually held good in a particular society remained to be empirically established.

In the meantime the problem of explanation was still nagging: if geography and technology did not determine the differences between the two forms of rural social organization in medieval England, the question remained, what did? An obvious hypothesis at once presented itself, again an hypothesis from social anthropology, but the cultural hypothesis rather than the structural one. The assemblage of the beliefs and practices of a society, which we called its culture, tended to persist over time, like its language, which was indeed a most important part of its culture. The culture was the more apt to persist the less it was subjected to external influences, such as a changed environment or contact with a culture of a very different sort. Though the culture tended to persist, it never remained quite the same, but changed slowly, again like its language. Accordingly the culture of one society tended to differ from that of another, but the closer was the historical relationship between them; the more recently they had formed a single society, the smaller the differences tended to be.

The society of England in the Middle Ages was the work of Germanic tribes who invaded the country from the other side of the North Sea in the period following the collapse of Roman rule in the fourth century. Could not the differences between the two types of agricultural organization, and their areas of distribution in the thirteenth century, be explained on the hypothesis that different Germanic tribes, having somewhat different cultures in the homeland, had invaded different parts of England? The doctrine of cultural persistence certainly applied to overseas invasions, especially when, as in the present case, the invaders did not encounter in the new country environmental conditions very different from those of the old. It was true that the hypothesis still did not explain the differences between the two cultures. It simply drove the problem back to Germany and back in time. But as far as England was concerned, it explained why there should have been two different cultures, if not why they differed in just the ways they did.

This hypothesis was not new with me: it was at least as venerable as the Venerable Bede, and in more recent times the great Chadwick was its exponent.[14] All a sociologist had to contribute was a fuller knowledge than Chadwick's of the social differences that had to be accounted for and of their geographical distribution. The hypothesis was also acceptable in principle to the archaeologists. They were quite ready to accept cultural continuity across the North Sea for their pots, pins, and burial customs. All a sociologist had to insist on was that social organization as well as artifacts ought to be taken into consideration. Indeed he suspected that social organization in the Dark Ages was even more apt to persist than the styles of pots and pins, and to provide even better evidence for cultural continuity.

Historical records would, of course, have settled the question at once, and the very few we possessed tended to support the hypothesis. The Anglo-Saxon Chronicle had the Saxons landing on the southern coast of the open-field area, while a tribe with a different name, the Jutes, landed in Kent, which was part of the Southeastern cultural area. (The Homans family had come from the island of Thanet in Kent, not ten miles from Ebbsfleet, where Hengist and Horsa beached their ships.)

[19]

But so far as records were concerned, the fifth century was the darkest in the whole of Western history since Herodotus. The Chronicle was written at a much later date, and there was no historical record whatever of the landings that must have been made on the east coast of England.

If the narrative record was practically a blank, and the archaeologists had not yet reached firm conclusions from their pots and pins, what could the study of social organization contribute? If it could be shown that recorded cultures on the other side of the North Sea differed from one another in the same ways as did the two cultures in England, it would go far toward proving the hypothesis. The conclusion would be hard to escape that bearers of the different cultures had invaded the corresponding areas in England. Unhappily no such demonstration could be fully carried out. Social organization hardly showed itself at all on the ground, in the kinds of things the archaeologists dug up; the evidence for it must mostly be written; and the written records, like charters, on which our knowledge of medieval social organization depended, usually began at an even later date than did narrative history. It was stretching the hypothesis of cultural continuity pretty far to base an argument about what happened in the fifth century on charters dating from the thirteenth. Moreover some of the cultures on the continental side of the North Sea, like the continental Angles and the Jutes of Jutland, appeared to have left no records at all.

And yet I felt that something could be done. There was one obvious place to look for continental parallels to English medieval social organization. Frisian was the language most closely related to English, and archaeology showed many similarities between the material culture of the earliest invaders and that of the Frisian islands. I determined to take a look at the social organization of medieval Friesland, especially as I knew that a book had been written about it, and that I should not have to do the original research myself.[15] Reading the book showed that, if its author were correct, the social organization of medieval Friesland bore an astonishing resemblance to that of the Southeastern area of England, especially its East Anglian version. This similarity did not necessarily mean that Frisians invaded England in the Dark Ages, though it was a good bet that they did. It certainly meant that the invaders came from some Germanic society closely related culturally to Friesland. The coastal Franks were one possibility, and so were the Jutes of Jutland, but we should probably never know anything about Jutish culture in its continental form.

[20]

Even if the similarity between the Southeastern culture and Friesland were fully demonstrated, which it was not, it would only support one half of the original hypothesis. Finding a continental parallel to the open-field culture of England would still be necessary. Certainly some of the continental Germanic cultures were based on open-field agriculture. The question is whether they lay near enough to the North Sea in the fifth century to have provided a possible source of invaders. If the bearers of the Southeastern culture were Friso-Jutes, it was tempting to identify the bearers of the open-field culture with the Angles and Saxons. We should probably never know enough about the continental Angles, but someone ought really to take a close look from this point of view at the surviving evidence for the social organization of the continental Saxons.

But I have carried the argument far enough, and what I must do now is show how the articles reprinted in this volume are related to it. The main results of my work on the open-field system in England were presented in my book, *English Villagers of the Thirteenth Century*. Practically contemporary with that book is the first of the present articles on the subject, "Men and the Land in the Middle Ages." It was written to take its place in a volume planned by The Medieval Academy of America but never published; a volume in which a number of scholars would write for the intelligent public on different aspects of medieval society. I tried, therefore, to make the article a broad and not technical description of the rural societies of northwestern Europe. The second article, "The Rural Sociology of Medieval England," was, in contrast, written for an audience of specialists. It raised the question of the two types of English rural society, their ethnic origins and their influence on later economic developments. Finally, the third article presents in full-blown form the hypothesis of the Frisian origin of East Anglian social organization.

The fourth article on England, "The Puritans and the Clothing Industry," falls outside the sequence. When I had finished *English Villagers of the Thirteenth Century*, I thought I would keep on with English social history, but shift to a later century and study the social origins of the Puritans. The Puritans were my ancestors, and many of them had come from East Anglia, whose medieval origins had been one of my great interests. But this did not disbar them as a subject for research in religious sociology. The converts to a religious movement were seldom distributed at random among the different elements of a society, but were more apt to come from some elements than from others. The English Puritans were especially apt to be middle-class people; they were also, as my paper showed, especially apt to come from the districts dominated by the largest English industry of the time—the cottage manufacture of woolen cloth. The fact was clear; why it should be the fact was nothing like so clear. Max Weber had argued that radical Protestantism, of which Puritanism was one form, encouraged the development of capitalism. My paper took up the other side of the Weber argument—a side Weber himself was perfectly well aware of. If Puritanism encouraged the growth of capitalism, did not capitalism, or at least certain forms of industry, encourage the growth of Puritanism? But World War II put an end to this piece of research and I never took it up again.

Pursued for its own sake, the study of English medieval social history is pure antiquarianism: it has nothing to teach the modern world. My reasons for taking it up were, moreover, largely personal and opportunistic. And yet the scholar who will take it up not just to establish facts but to ask for their explanation will find it leading him into some of the most characteristic general problems and issues of social science. But I doubt that it therefore deserves any special credit. For this purpose the study of any other time or place would have served just as well.

Anthropology and Function

The second main subject matter of these papers is anthropological. Mayo had started me reading anthropological monographs, and I was further stimulated by coming into contact with Conrad Arensberg. Arensberg had been working at Newburyport, and he was about to go to Ireland and make an anthropological study of a townland in County Clare.[16] His influence was somewhat different from Mayo's. Mayo, as I have said, wanted us to get from our reading in social anthropology a picture of societies in which human collaboration was supported by established ritual. He was largely indifferent to current anthropological theories except so far as they bore out this view. But Arensberg was interested in the theories; he was an accomplished proselytizer, and when his influence was added to Mayo's, I not only developed a taste for reading anthropological monographs, but also began to think about the general ideas.

[22]

This was the time when "functional" theories in anthropology were flowering. I was never happy with functionalism. I was suspicious of it from the beginning without knowing why. It has been a splinter under my skin that it has taken me a long time to get out. One thing was soon clear: anthropologists made at least three different kinds of statement in which the word *function* appeared. The first kind of statement said that one institution in a society was a function of another in the sense that the two were interrelated, as when a particular rule of exogamy was associated with a particular form of lineage organization. More generally, each of the institutions of a society was functionally related to each of the others to form a social structure. The great functional anthropologists of their time, Malinowski and Radcliffe-Brown, agreed in making this sort of statement, which also fitted in nicely with Henderson's insistence on the complex mutual dependence of the variables in a biochemical or social system.

I have shown what use I made of this kind of leading idea as a practical guide to research on medieval England, and I have never felt uncomfortable with it, unless it be pressed too far. The interrelatedness of some institutions is often easy to demonstrate empirically, but that each institution of a society is related to all the others so that a change in one produces a change in all the others is not something to be taken for granted but something to be investigated. Were the United States government to be replaced by a communist one, would the characteristic American type of family organization change? All I can say is that I am not sure ahead of time. I have argued that there is a good deal of play in any institutional structure: institutions do not mesh with others mechanically like the parts of a machine. Institutions *are* the behavior of men; their relations are mediated by the behavior of men. Nor is the nature of one institution in a particular social structure to be explained only by its unique relations with the other institutions within *that* structure, for if it were, we should not be able to explain why certain interrelations of institutions hold good for a number of societies, differing from one another in other institutional respects. Indeed, functional statements of the first class offer in themselves no explanation: given that a particular rule of exogamy is associated with a particular form of lineage organization, we must still ask why this should be so.

If Malinowski and Radcliffe-Brown agreed in making the first kind of functional statement, from there on they parted company. The second kind of functional statement said that an institution was functional for members of a society in the sense of meeting their needs. It was a favorite with Malinowski, who argued, for instance, that the performance of fishing magic in the Trobriand Islands had the function of alleviating the anxiety of fishermen who could not be sure of making a catch.[17] This kind of functional statement was very different from the first. The two terms that the statement linked together were not one institution and another, but an institution and the characteristics of individual members of the society; and the statement tacitly assumed that the members shared to some degree the characteristics of men everywhere. Although the detailed circumstances that created anxiety in the Trobriands no doubt differed from those that did so elsewhere, anxiety was still an emotional problem the Trobrianders shared with all men. The statement also differed from the first kind of functional statement in that it implied an explanation: not only did the performance of magic in fact relieve anxiety, but magic was performed *because* it relieved anxiety. More generally, institutions existed because they were functional for men, as men.

The third kind of functional statement said that an institution was functional for a society in the sense of helping to maintain the society as a going concern. When combined with functional statements of the first kind, this was a favorite statement of Radcliffe-Brown's: "The *function* of any recurrent activity, such as the punishment of a crime, or a funeral ceremony, is the part it plays in the social life as a whole and therefore the contribution it makes to the maintenance of the structural continuity."[18] This kind of functional statement differed from both the others in that the two terms were an institution and society, but it resembled the second in that it implied an explanation: the institution existed *because* it contributed to the maintenance of the structural continuity. It was always the third kind of statement that constituted my splinter.

Instead of using *function* in three different ways, we may call the first kind of statement *structural*, the second, *psychological*, and the third, *functional*.

Not only was Radcliffe-Brown fond of making the third kind of statement but in a little book called *Taboo*[19] he asserted that Malinowski was plain wrong in making his kind. Reading this book was the stimulus to my first published excursion into anthropology, "Anxiety and Ritual," reprinted here. It attempted to reconcile the views of the two great anthropologists by showing how the different effects each man had in mind needed to be taken into consideration in analyzing the concrete phenomena. But if it tried, it certainly failed to reconcile the two types of explanation, and since it failed, the problem still rankled in my mind.

In fact, several different things about it rankled in my mind, and if I take them up in order it does not mean that I disposed of them one at a time. My first difficulty was with the truth of the third kind of functional statement. It asserted a positive association between the existence of a particular institution and the "maintenance of the structural continuity" of a particular society. It therefore implied that if the institution changed or, worse, disappeared, the structural continuity would somehow be broken. To be sure, the institution was part of the social organization and, were it to disappear, the whole of which it was a part would necessarily be different. Although this sense of "the maintenance of the structural continuity" was vacuous, any stronger sense raised the problem of empirical demonstration; especially for an historian, whose business it was to trace structural continuities. If the Roman Empire, for instance, was an institution of Italian society in the fourth century, then its collapse should, if the proposition were true, have led to some break in the structural continuity of Italian society—other than the collapse of the Empire itself. To be sure, new governmental institutions replaced the old ones, but historically no other break occurred; the same sort of thing seemed to be true of the disappearance of institutions in other cases.

The problem was to find some criterion of "maintenance of the structural continuity" precise enough to allow a statement containing these words to be empirically tested. The solution adopted by some functionalists was to define the maintenance of a society as its survival. This strengthening of one term in the proposition was usually compensated by a weakening of the other, so as to make it refer not to a particular institution but to any institution that fulfilled a particular function, like "conflict-resolution." The latter change would take care of the fact that, though the Roman Empire disappeared, it was at least replaced by other *governmental* institutions. These scholars spoke of "the functional prerequisites of the survival of a society."[20] The difficulty they then faced was in finding a society that had *not* survived. Most societies were like Roman Italy: although in the past they might have been conquered or absorbed, there had been no other institutional discontinuity between them and some modern society. Yet there were a few cases of societies that had disappeared without leaving any institutional traces behind, peoples like the Ona of Tierra del Fuego or the Tasmanians. If they failed to survive, surely they must have lacked one of the functional prerequisites. Unfortunately the monographs—when we had any—on such extinct societies showed that they possessed institutions fulfilling *all* the functions on all of the usual lists of prerequisites. If they died it was not for lack of institutions but for lack of resistance to measles, or firewater, or gunfire, or something of the sort. Faced with these facts, the functionalists were always at liberty to add new functional prerequisites like "resistance to measles" to their lists, but then their statement tended to become: "The functional prerequisites for the survival of a society are the characteristics of modern Western societies." This statement had indeed looked at times as if it were going to be true, but it surely was not what the functionalists wanted to say. All the societies that had survived had met the usual functional prerequisites—but so had all that had not survived. Under these circumstances, the third kind of functional statement became undemonstrated if not undemonstrable.

None of this meant, of course, that institutions did not have consequences, even unintended consequences, even consequences that were bad (dysfunctional) rather than good (functional). The issue was not whether they had consequences but whether anything was added by saying that the consequences were functional or dysfunctional, not just for some of the members of a society but for the society itself. The absence of dysfunctional institutions was no more to be explained by the survival of a society than was the presence of functional ones. The method, for instance, of voting in the Polish parliament may have been one of the reasons that Poland lost her independence in the eighteenth century; when she regained it in the twentieth century, the institution was not revived. But if it were impossible to show that the loss of independence meant Poland's extinction as a society—and the fact of independence later regained showed it *was* impossible—or even that there was some sharp break in the continuity of Polish institutions outside the governmental sphere, then the statement (in this case) that institutions had consequences became a structural statement and nothing more: the method of voting was associated with the disappearance of the old Polish government.

Although it was impossible to show, on either the criterion of survival or that of continuity, that the consequences were good or bad, functional or dysfunctional, for the society, they certainly appeared to be bad for at least some of its members. Many Poles fiercely resented the

[26]

loss of Polish independence, struggled long and hard to regain it, and when they did so, took good care not to revive the old method of voting. But this reason for the absence of the bad old institution was not a functional statement of the third sort. It was one of the second, or psychological, sort—a statement about the relations between the experience of men, their motives, and their institutions. No doubt what was good for Poland was good for the Poles, but it was the good—as they saw it —of the Poles that made the difference.

Considerations like this brought up my second kind of difficulty with functionalism. Even in the unlikely case that functional statements of the third class could be empirically supported, how could they be explained? Suppose that a particular institution were good (functional) for a society. What process produced the fit between the institution and the good of the society? Two sorts of answer were offered to this question. The first was the Darwinian. It presupposed something like random variations in institutions and something like free competition between societies, from which the societies whose institutions had survival-value did in fact survive. We were back at survival again! But the competition between societies was something very different from the Darwinian struggle for existence. The weaker did not get eliminated but, in all but a few cases, absorbed. The victors were usually content to let the institutions of the weaker people alone so long as they themselves controlled the government and collected the taxes. It was impossible to demonstrate any general Darwinian mechanism that would eliminate dysfunctional institutions. Defeat in war might eliminate a governmental institution, but would it eliminate a rule of marriage? The functionalists were certainly not limiting themselves to governmental institutions. The Darwinian argument was based on the organic analogy, and the organic analogy failed all along the line: the institutions of society did not mesh as closely as did the organs of a body, nor did societies compete in the way animals were supposed to do.

The second kind of argument I shall call the rationalist. The members of a society were intelligent and could "see" what institutions were good not only for themselves but for their society, and they therefore proceeded to adopt the institutions. Of course there were examples of something that looked much like this: the adoption of the United States Constitution was perhaps an example. The trouble with this argument was not just that, if the mechanism in question operated generally and unfailingly, we had a right to expect the history of mankind to be happier than it appeared in fact to be. Instead what made the difficulty was, once more, the historian's knowledge. He knew that to explain events like the adoption of the United States Constitution he would have to explain why certain members and groups in the society found the proposed institution to their interests, why others did not, and how the former, in the context of the other institutions of society, managed to get the institution adopted in the teeth of the opposition. History was full of institutions that had been proposed for adoption and that looked at least by hindsight awfully "good," but that the members of society had still not adopted. Why? The historian knew that answers to these questions could only be given by functional statements of the first and second classes; statements about the relations between institutions and about the motives of men. Even at the extreme, a desire for the good of society was still a motive of men—some men. And if this was true of the examples, like the United States Constitution, that the historian did know about, was it not likely to be true of the others, like the institutions of primitive societies, that he did not know about because no history was available? Even if he accepted functional statements of the third sort to be demonstrable, he would still have to explain them by functional statements of the first and second sorts.

While for years a confused dialogue between Homans the sceptic and Homans the devil's advocate of the functionalists was going on in my mind, I was actually learning something about the details of primitive social organization. What turned out to interest me most were not the facts that Mayo drew attention to nor even those that Arensberg did, but facts that had a peculiar property. Whatever their intrinsic importance, they at least looked capable of being easily stated in a generalization—a generalization of the kind so dear, I believe, to the hearts of scientists—that revealed similarity within difference. These were the facts about stylized forms of interpersonal relations between kinsmen. Malinowski's books on the Trobriands had shown how in that society a man tended to be "close" to his father but "distant" from his mother's brother.[21] (Of course "close" and "distant" are inadequate as descriptions of actual behavior, but quite adequate to illustrate the ideas the descriptions suggested.) On the other hand, Raymond Firth's book on the Tikopia showed how in that society a man tended to be "distant" from his father and "close" to his mother's brother.[22] In at least these two relationships the Trobriands and Tikopia appeared to be mirror opposites of one another, yet when further differences between the two societies were examined, the opposition disappeared. For while in the Trobriands his mother's brother exercised jural authority over a man, in Tikopia his father did; and then a single generalization summed up the facts: of two men in the older generation that were closely related to ego, ego's relation to the one who had authority over him was "distant," to the one who did not have authority, "close." So far as I had then read the literature, this generalization seemed to hold good of other societies in which authority over ego was firmly localized, notably of the primitive Germans described in Tacitus' *Germania*, which I had run into in the course of my medieval studies. The facts about other kinds of interpersonal relations could, moreover, be summed up by generalizations of the same type.

The proposition was a functional proposition of the first, or structural, sort: it stated a relation between institutionalized authority and institutionalized interpersonal relations. Much more important than the proposition itself was the implication of any effort to explain it. The societies for which the proposition held good were so far separated in time and space—the Germans and Tikopia by eighteen centuries and half the circumference of the globe—that their institutional similarities could hardly be attributed to diffusion. They were, then, independently invented, which meant that the proposition could be explained only by assuming that the characteristics of the behavior of men, as men, were in some degree and under some circumstances, the same the world over. At least some men were the same in their reactions to authority. But assumptions about the behavior of men were, again, functional statements of the second, or psychological, sort, like Malinowski's statement about anxiety and magic. I came to the conclusion, though I could demonstrate it even to my own satisfaction in only a few cases, that the ultimate explanatory principles in anthropology and sociology, and for that matter in history, were neither structural nor functional but psychological: they were propositions about the behavior of men as men. I rejected as having no final truth, however much it might have liberated me when I first encountered it under Mayo, Durkheim's assertion that society was an entity *sui generis* and that sociology was not a corollary of psychology.[23] I now think the conclusion is obvious; I take no credit for it, and I mention it only because it appears not to be obvious to everyone.

Let me put the matter as tersely as possible: *structural* (Class 1) propositions were testable but had to be explained by other propositions;

psychological (Class 2) propositions were both testable and required for the explanation of Class 1; *functional* (Class 3) propositions were neither testable nor required for explanation. What I meant by explanation will appear later.

In the controversy between Malinowski and Radcliffe-Brown I had finally rejected the latter, at least so far as concerned his insisting, as a theorist, on societal functionalism. But Radcliffe-Brown was a great man, great enough not to let a theoretical position get in the way of good empirical work. It seemed to me amusing that, in papers like "The Mother's Brother in South Africa,"[24] he had done at least as much as Malinowski to work out those propositions about interpersonal relations that seemed to me, by implication, so destructive of his theoretical stand. The only time I met him—it was just before he died, but the old warrior was still full of intellectual fight—I taxed him with this, and, yes, he admitted he had been working toward what he called a "general psychology." If I needed to be reconciled with the illustrious dead, I needed no more than this.

The conclusion I had reached did not lack challenges in the intellectual environment. The period just before and just after World War II was dominated in American anthropology by the "culture and personality" school of thought, heavily influenced by psychoanalysis. Its advent is best marked by the publication in 1934 of Ruth Benedict's *Patterns of Culture*, and it was represented at Harvard by my friend Clyde Kluckhohn. The culturalists had many virtues, particularly in emphasizing the influence of childhood training—not just toilet training —on the later behavior of men. Education in its broadest sense does, of course, build a strong element of persistence over time into any social organization. But the actual, if not the intended, effect of their teaching was to play up the uniqueness of any culture and to play down what different cultures had in common. Indeed, they were apt to heap scorn on the old saw "human nature is the same the world over," and if they looked for "cultural universals" at all they were apt to find only things like *the* incest taboo, and not propositions like the ones about interpersonal behavior that I was interested in. But such propositions, which brought out similarities within differences, went far to reconcile the obvious and superficial differences with the underlying similarities in human behavior from society to society.

I felt, finally, that education by itself was an inadequate explanation of social institutions. If an anthropologist were asked why a man acted in a certain way toward his mother's brother, and he answered, "Because his elders taught him to behave that way as part of his manners," he at once begged the further question: "But why did they teach him *that* way rather than another?" The latter was the question I wanted answered. If any sort of culture could be maintained through generation after generation by education alone, there would be no room for social change, and no explanation of the propositions that held good cross-culturally about the relations between institutions.

My casual reading about the Andamans, the Trobriands, Tikopia, the ancient Germans, and, as the years went by, many other primitive groups, naturally led me to compare the institutions of different societies. In *The Human Group* I briefly compared interpersonal relations in Tikopia with those in the Trobriands.[25] But I had undertaken no systematic comparisons, in the sense, for instance, that I might have examined all, or a large sample, of the societies whose members were expected to be "close" to their mothers' brothers. I was too busy with other things, and both before and after World War II systematic comparison was a little in abeyance. Although Radcliffe-Brown had insisted on its importance, his English followers had not carried on the work. Both higher standards of field work and the functional doctrines themselves had contributed to this result. Each member of the rising generation, men like Evans-Pritchard, Fortes, and Gluckman, tended to concentrate on the intricate interrelations of institutions within his own primitive society. Indeed, he was apt to do his field work so well that the rest of his life was not long enough for writing up the results. In *English Villagers* I had concentrated on the same problem, and only the fact that I could not talk to my villagers had prevented my being overwhelmed, like the others, with data. The American culturalists, otherwise so different from the British structuralists, supported the same trend by emphasizing, in practice, the cultural uniqueness of every society. Not until George Peter Murdock's *Social Structure* appeared in 1949 were the eyes of anthropologists once more opened to the power of the cross-cultural method—the statistical testing against data from a sample of societies all over the world of propositions about relations between institutions.

Marriage, Authority, and Final Causes—surely the shortest book to have so impressive a title—represents my only excursion into systematic cross-cultural comparison. Once more it was stimulated by my quarrel with functionalism of the third type. In 1950 Clyde Kluckhohn had urged me to read Claude Lévi-Strauss's *Les structures élémentaires de la parenté*, a book about the rules of marriage in primitive societies.[26] Among other things, Lévi-Strauss argued that a preference for marriage with mother's brother's daughter occurred in more societies than did the alternative rule of marriage with father's sister's daughter because it led to a better organization of society—better for the *society*. I do not want to repeat his argument at length here, as it is given in the paper. Here was functionalism again, and I would have none of it. I knew that one of the societies practicing father's sister's daughter marriage was Malinowski's Trobriands. I knew that the Trobriands vested jural authority over ego in his mother's brother, and that, accordingly, ego was "close" to both father and father's sister. I suspected that marriage would follow the ties of sentiment, not only in this patrilateral case but also in the matrilateral one. I predicted, therefore, that, if they practiced unilateral cross-cousin marriage at all, societies vesting jural authority over ego in his mother's brother would prefer marriage with father's sister's daughter, and that societies vesting it in his father would prefer marriage with mother's brother's daughter. I further assumed that the former kind of society would be matrilineally organized and the latter, patrilineally. This assumption turned out to be inaccurate, but not so much so as to send the whole investigation astray from the very beginning.

I put these views forward in a critique of Lévi-Strauss's book that I presented in 1951 to the anthropological section of the American Association for the Advancement of Science. At that time I had done little in the way of examining the actual evidence, but Murdock was in the audience, and in the discussion of the paper he stated that his own unpublished cross-cultural researches bore out my proposition. Thus dramatically encouraged, I enlisted the help of my friend David Schneider, who was a real anthropologist, not an amateur as I was; we searched the literature for societies that practiced unilateral cross-cousin marriage; we found well over half the cases that we now, years later, believe exist, and we tested our proposition against the data for these societies. It turned out to have a high degree of statistical significance.

Lévi-Strauss had predicted that more societies would practice mother's brother's daughter marriage than would practice father's sister's daughter marriage, and he was right. But he was right, we felt sure, simply because more societies vested authority in father than vested it in mother's brother, and not because of any inherent functional virtue for a society in the matrilateral form. Or, if Lévi-Strauss could predict that *more* societies would practice one form than would the other, we could predict *which* societies would practice *which* form, and in this case Lévi-Strauss's proposition appeared to be unnecessary.

Ours was a tested structural proposition: it stated a relationship between two kinds of institution: the locus of jural authority and the form of unilateral cross-cousin marriage. What is more, our explanation why the relationship existed, though far from being thoroughly spelled out, appeared to be made up of psychological statements; statements about the behavior of men as men, as members of a species, specifically statements about the reactions of men to the behavior of others placed in authority over them. The statements made no reference to the "good" of society, measured by survival or in any other way. Of course we were far from completely explaining the phenomena. We could not explain why more societies vested jural authority in father than did in mother's brother, nor why a society should practice unilateral cross-cousin marriage at all. All we could do was explain, once the locus of jural authority and the practice of some form of unilateral cross-cousin marriage were given, why a particular society practiced one form rather than the other. It was conceivable that these givens could themselves be explained only by functional statements, that even if we did not need functionalism to explain the forms of unilateral cross-cousin marriage, we might still need it to explain other institutions. We might—but I doubted it. My conviction grew stronger that if we did not need it in one case we did not need it in any, and that, if ever we got explanations of these givens and others like them, they too would turn out to be psychological explanations—in terms of the behavior of men as members of a species. Since in most cases the explanations had not yet been formulated or tested, my conviction could only be a matter of faith, but it was a faith I could not help holding. I saw all its difficulties and still believed.

Of course I could see and feel for some of the human reasons why sociologists—some sociologists—found functionalism congenial. They wanted to preserve their intellectual identity. Theirs was a young science, young at least as an academic discipline; they wanted a type of theory that could be distinctly their own, and they thought they had found it in functionalism. There were even some to claim that functionalism of the second, or psychological, sort was distinctive.[27] But is was not. Any statement explaining an institution as being "functional" or "dysfunctional" for men could readily be translated with no loss of meaning into one that said it was "rewarding" or "punishing." Indeed, explanation in these terms was more general than the functional one, for men did many things that were "dysfunctional" for them, in the sense of being bad for them, but that they nevertheless found rewarding. And far from being "distinctive," "reward" and "punishment" were familiar terms in psychology.

The attempt to find a distinctive theory for sociology failed, as it had failed for history. People had looked for general historical laws in the wrong place. They had tried to find them in history itself and had found none. This did not mean in the least that history had no ultimate explanatory principles. History had principles, but they were so much a part of common sense, they were lying in such plain sight, that history could afford to take them for granted, as too boring to spell out. It had taken a Newton to discover the explanatory principles of mechanics. History had never needed a Newton: from the beginning it had known its principles, at least in their vulgar form as the characteristics of human nature. It had had to go through no struggle to discover them, and so perhaps set too little store by them, though they were Newtonian in scope. The result had been that the explanatory principles of history had become by default a matter of explicit attention, not for history itself but for another science—psychology.[28] Yet history did not therefore become irrelevant. Though it fudged ultimate explanation, it concentrated admirably on establishing the concrete circumstances that were to be explained and that were needed in turn for explanation. Indeed, the first line of explanation, even for sociology, traced psychological principles working within historically given circumstances.

There are a few societies that have something like adequate written histories; there are many that have not. If we wish, in the former, to explain the existence of particular institutions or the interrelations of institutions, we use the available history. We trace out the historical process in which the clash of men and groups pursuing more or less successfully their varied, and by no means always material, interests made these institutions what they are; and we trace out the interests that sustain these institutions today, in the context of other institutions. At any given time the interrelated institutions may form a structure, and the structure may condition the interests of men, in the sense that their readiness to overturn the government may be affected by the fact that they are fathers of families. But the structure is never sufficient to explain the behavior, if only because the nature of the structure itself always remains to be explained. If, moreover, the members of a society can never, as it appears, tear up all their institutions at once and start fresh, their present behavior is always conditioned by their particular past. But the past, again, is never sufficient to explain their behavior. Let some new event, like the discovery of America, impinge on their society and offer new possibilities for, say, gaining wealth, some of them will take advantage of the opportunity, not just because they learned the value of wealth at their mother's knee but because it is the nature of men, as men, to take advantage of opportunities for reward. And their opportunity-taking behavior is apt to change their institutions. In the case of the discovery of America we know it did. However great the variation in human institutions and in the historical processes that produced them, the institutions and the processes are all alike at least in being man-made. Institutions *are* human behavior and therefore they are to be explained by the characteristics of that behavior. The historical kind of explanation is long and arduous, but it is often convincing, and, when we have the history, it is the kind we must use if we are to avoid the traps of functionalism.

With the societies that have no history we must naturally use another method, and luckily these societies have two characteristics that go far to make up for their lack of written records: compared with the historical societies, they are rather large in number, so that cross-cultural propositions about the interrelations of institutions can be tested statistically; and they are primitive societies, which means in practice that the range of variation in their institutions is relatively small, largely limited to the themes of kinship and subsistence economy, and in their unknown histories they must have encountered many of the same limited number of institutional choices. Let us tease out of the anthropological monographs as many cross-cultural propositions as we can about these societies. The more we have, the more apt they are to suggest, as did my proposition, the psychological processes from which, under the given conditions, they may be derived. From these processes under different givens let us then deduce new propositions to be tested against the data. If we are successful we shall have explained a variety of empirical propositions about human institutions and their interrelations just as surely as if we had the full historical record. Again, I do not underestimate the difficulties; we shall probably never be able to explain everything, but this is the only method open to us.

The third of the main fields into which these essays fall lies across the border between sociology and psychology. It is the field that is usually called "the study of small groups," but that I now like to call "elementary social behavior." It has been my chief field of interest, and my work in it, more than in social history or social anthropology, has gotten me into general problems of investigation and explanation in social science. What is a theory? What are the strategies for arriving at a theory? What is the relation between a theory as constructed and the strategies by which it is reached?

My interest in small groups began again with Mayo. The years in which I was reading with him and interviewing under his supervision were the years in which the results of the Western Electric researches, carried out under his leadership, were being written up and discussed, and I naturally became steeped in them. At least two of the Western Electric researches were studies of small groups: the Relay Assembly Test Room and the Bank Wiring Observation Room. True, they were thought of as industrial studies: the notion of studying the small group for its own sake had hardly been conceived. And Mayo was more interested in the relation of the individual to the group than in the organization of the group itself. Small-group studies they were nevertheless, the most detailed that had yet been made, and their findings were available for analysis from a different point of view.

I went on to do strictly industrial research, under Ben Selekman of the Harvard Business School on a men's-suit factory[29] and under Mayo on technological unemployment in the tin-plate mills of New Castle, Pennsylvania. But the latter study was cut off abruptly when I was called into the Navy as a reserve officer in May 1941. And by the time I resumed industrial research after the war, I knew it was small groups rather than industry that I was interested in: the advantage of industry was simply that it provided a large number of captive small groups. The research was reported in "The Cash Posters," "Status among Clerical Workers," and "Status Congruence," reprinted here. The fact that my main interest lay elsewhere has not, however, prevented my sounding off about industry. See "The Sociologist's Contribution to Management" and "Bureaucracy as Big Brother."

Let me now turn to the other, or methodological, theme of the story.

In the 1930's Harvard was full of men who were concerned with what is vaguely called the philosophy of science, and most of them were connected with the Society of Fellows. There was Whitehead, benign logician and philosopher, whose *Science and the Modern World*[30] was one of our bibles. There was my patron Henderson, historian of science and formulator of the biochemical equilibrium of the blood, who led me to read widely from Bacon to Poincaré. There was Charlie Curtis, my collaborator, who kept me up on the contemporary authorities. All these were Senior Fellows, and among the Juniors was Willard Quine, who was introducing us to logical positivism.

But in the short run the greatest influence on me could be traced to a man who was not a member of the Society. We had all read *The Logic of Modern Physics*[31] by Percy Bridgman, Professor of Physics at Harvard. Bridgman had formulated the doctrine of operationalism: the meaning of any concept was given by the operations used to measure it, and if there were no such operations the concept was meaningless. Bridgman's influence was indirect: I reacted less to operationalism in itself, which seemed to make sense, than I did to the conclusions drawn from it by Conrad Arensberg, my anthropologist friend in the Society.

Arensberg and his friend Eliot Chapple had been members of W. Lloyd Warner's research team at Newburyport, and Chapple had taken on the task of formulating a general theory to be used in stating the findings. In the course of this work, Chapple and Arensberg had become dissatisfied with the way various big words came into current anthropological theory. Under the influence of Bridgman's book, they began to ask what operations, if any, defined words like "solidarity" or "authority."

This was a good question, but the answer they gave it seemed far too drastic. They concluded that the chief concepts of anthropology could be rigorously defined only by the operations of measuring the order, frequency, and duration of interactions between men, an interaction being an event in which an action of one man was the stimulus for an action of another, in abstraction from the content of the action, whether it was a pull on a saw or a chuck under the chin.[32] They argued, moreover (and this had nothing to do with Bridgman's teaching) that the measures of interaction were the independent variables in social behavior. To put the matter crudely, whether a man liked another or not depended on the timing of the interactions between them, but the interaction did not in turn depend upon the liking.

It should be clear by now that I have reacted against others' ideas more than I have produced ideas of my own. Friend though I was of them both, I felt that Chapple and Arensberg were in danger of getting hard-boiled too soon. I had no doubt that the measures of interaction were important variables, that they would have to enter any general propositions about social behavior, and that in emphasizing them Chapple and Arensberg had made an important contribution. But I did not like disregarding other kinds of observations simply because, as it appeared, they could not be measured as rigorously as interaction could. Lack of rigor need not mean lack of importance. And I thought the decision to treat interaction as the eternal independent variable was grounded in too little evidence. From then on my mind turned to the question: In anthropological and industrial research, what were the main classes of observations, besides interaction, that investigators had made? In classifying the observations I began the construction of what Henderson had taught me to call a conceptual scheme.

The answer I came up with was that, besides interaction, there were at least two main classes of observations: sentiment and activity, which had to be included in order to deal with the content of interaction. Sentiment was behavior expressive of a man's attitudes toward other men or women, like a chuck under the chin. Activity was other kinds of behavior, like pulling on a saw. I sketched out this scheme in the last chapter of *English Villagers of the Thirteenth Century*, where it was wholly out of place. I elaborated it further during the war in a paper I wrote for my own benefit, when my ship was laid up for repairs in Willemstad, Curaçao, and I had a little leisure. I added the notion that each of the classes of observations should be divided into two parts: the part determined by the environment external to the group or society in question, and the part determined by the relations between the classes within the group or society. But what were these relations? Both Henderson and Pareto had taught that they would in general be relations of mutual dependence, not of one-way causation such a Chapple and Arensberg had postulated. I had my conceptual scheme. Almost as an afterthought, I began to look for propositions stating relations of mutual dependence between its elements. I had no trouble finding them. Right after the war I wrote out the whole scheme a third time in my "Conceptual Scheme for the Study of Social Organization,"[33] which is not reprinted here because it is too far from my present views and because it is better embodied in my book *The Human Group*.[34]

Note that I was still talking about "social organization." My idea was to use the scheme in a book about social organization in general, not specifically about social organization in small groups. But once again chance took a hand in my affairs. In December of 1946 I went to Chicago to give a paper at the annual meeting of the American Sociological Society, and I met my friend Arensberg. I asked him what he was doing, and he said that he and Solon Kimball were writing a general book on social organization. The book was never written, but that unwritten book made me a "small group man." Arensberg knew a lot more about social organization than I did; I did not like to get into competition with him, and on the train going home I reluctantly decided to confine my book to the social organization of small groups.

Other considerations besides the risk of competing with Arensberg ended by reconciling me with the decision. The Western Electric researches, though conceived as industrial, were from another point of view studies of small groups, and I was thoroughly familiar with them. I was familiar also with William F. Whyte's *Street Corner Society*,[35] a wonderful study of a gang of corner-boys: Whyte was a contemporary in the Society of Fellows. Though I must not talk about social organization in general, I could bring in my studies of interpersonal relations in primitive society on the possibly specious excuse that kin groups were also small groups. I had also had some practical experience: the ships I commanded during the war were manned by small groups. (See "The Small Warship," reprinted here.) Finally I was used to an idea that had been going around Harvard—I do not know who started it. If we wanted to establish the reality of a social system as a complex of mutually dependent elements, why not begin by studying a system small enough so that we could, so to speak, see all the way around it, small enough so that all the relevant observations could be made in detail and at first hand? At any rate I embarked upon a book that would apply my conceptual scheme to a number of field studies of small groups and state the propositions, empirically holding good in these groups, about the relations between its elements. The result was *The Human Group* (1950).

For the last two years before the war I had been a member of the Department of Sociology at Harvard. When I got back from the Navy in 1946, I found the new Department of Social Relations in process of formation, and in it we sociologists were to be brigaded with clinical and social psychologists on the one hand, and with social anthropologists on the other. The new department did me nothing but good, if only because it brought me into contact with people like the social psychologists, whose methodological traditions were different from my own. What I was familiar with in anthropology, industrial sociology, even in history, was field work: the observation of a large number of aspects of groups in real life, unguided by explicit hypotheses other than the assumption that the aspects were somehow related, and unfettered by any attempt at experimental or statistical control of the propositions that did empirically appear to hold good. The social psychologists, including those that studied small groups, behaved very differently. They started with an explicit hypothesis, which they claimed to derive from a general theory, and tested it experimentally in a laboratory, controlling some of the variables through the design of the experiment itself and others by statistical methods. Their subjects were undergraduate volunteers, usually unrelated to one another before the experiment started. The social psychologists who studied real-life groups made up for their usual inability to use experimental controls by elaborating the statistical ones. This meant that they needed a large number of subjects, with the further result that they had to use survey methods and forego the detailed observation of the behavior of men.

I do not say that this is the whole story of the methods of social psychology, but only that this is the way I saw them then. In talking to the social psychologists, moreover, I got the impression that they thought little or nothing of the kind of work I was doing or most admired. It was not so much anything they actually said, and personally they could not have been kinder, as that I felt (and I may have been oversensitive) something patronizing in their references to field work: it produced "mere case studies" with *ex post facto* explanations. Yet I could not bring myself to believe that the methods used in the Western Electric researches and in the anthropological work I had been reading about had not produced findings just as valuable for social science as the methods of the social psychologists. I was therefore forced to defend my own tradition, to find a rationale for case studies, if that was what they were. What were the strengths and weaknesses of the two traditions? What could each do that the other could not do? Above all, how could case studies be better used? If a proposition that held good in one case study was not worth much, because the conditions in which it held good were not clear, was this true of propositions that held good in a number of case studies? After all, I had tried in *The Human Group* to show that a number of propositions held good in at least a few field studies of small groups, and Murdock had shown the same thing for a much larger number of propositions and a much larger number of primitive societies.[36]

As for *ex post facto* explanation, both Newton and Darwin were *ex post facto* explainers, so we were in good company. Of course one could not have much confidence in an explanation invented to account for the facts of a particular case after they had been gathered, but there was nothing that said you had to stop with one case. You went on to see whether the explanation that worked in one case worked in another. If it did, you were in just as strong a position, indeed in just the *same* position, as the psychologists with their doctrine of "hypothetico-deductive" methods. I was not sure that all science had not begun with *ex post facto* explanations, and in social science we were close to the beginning. If indeed good science had been done by some of the damnedest methods, we were free to come to grips with nature, no holds barred.

Some of these preoccupations are reflected in two papers reprinted here: "The Strategy of Small-Group Research" and "The Strategy of Industrial Sociology." Whatever its title, the latter is in fact a comparison of field work with the methods of the social psychologists.

One last thing bothered me about the social psychologists. Why had not methods apparently so rigorous produced more in the way of cumulative results? According to the rules the psychologists accepted for their game, each paper began with a statement of general theory, deduced at least one hypothesis from it, and then went on to describe a test of the hypothesis. If the hypothesis received significant confirmation, the psychologists were apparently supposed to accept the general theory too. But this is just what they did not do. Although they seldom questioned the actual results of an experiment or survey, they had seldom accepted the accompanying theory. Had they done so, there would by now be some generally accepted theory in social psychology, and there was none. Instead pretty nearly every psychologist had his own theory—at least he used his own words. Whatever the reason for the situation—perhaps the theories were not as precise nor the deductions from them as rigorous as they appeared—the practical conclusion seemed to me obvious: what was most solid about the work were the actual empirical findings themselves. And if this were the case, the findings had no different intellectual status from those of field work, which had not resulted from the testing of hypotheses but had emerged, by something much more like pure induction, from the effort to describe carefully the behavior of particular groups.

But what could be done with a great mass and variety of mere findings? One possible strategy was called in the early fifties *codification*.[37] Forget about the theories the investigators said their propositions were derived from, and look for the actual propositions, of the form *x* varies as *y*, for which their data provided support. Collect the propositions within a particular field, and examine in each the ways in which the various *x*'s and *y*'s had actually been measured: the actual variables not the "theoretically relevant" variables were the important ones. On the basis of this examination, reduce the number of the propositions. If two investigators measured similar variables and found similar relations between them, even though they called the corresponding variables by different names, recognize that they had stated only one proposition between them. Then try to shorten the list still further by asking which propositions were truly independent of the others. Examine the special circumstances of each piece of research. Of two apparently different propositions, could one be recognized as a corollary of the other, given the special circumstances? Only when the list of apparently independent propositions had been reduced as far as possible, ask what theory they themselves might be derivable from.

Codification might be a useful strategy, but it was hard on the codifier. It could never be carried out completely even within a pretty circumscribed field of research, and even at that it would take a lot of time. The codifier would have to give up his own independent research, and turn himself into a mere parasite on the work of other men. But a codifier in a small way I had been in writing *The Human Group*; I liked the work, as a louse likes his warm home in the rat's hair; I was prepared to be a parasite again, and I soon got the chance when Gardner Lindzey asked Henry Riecken and myself to write a chapter on "Psychological Aspects of Social Structure" for the new *Handbook of Social Psychology*.[38] To prepare the chapter I was forced to review a great deal of the experimental and survey work I was not then familiar with and to make at least a beginning of codification. I had to do a great deal more in teaching for several years a course called "An Introduction to the Study of Small Groups." The greatest

[42]

reward from lecturing was one's own learning, not the students'. They might not be motivated; the lecturer always was.

Reflection on the rationale of field work and experimental social psychology brought up the whole question of the relation between empirical findings and theory, between investigation and explanation. In this field what held me most transfixed was the Parsons problem. I had met Talcott Parsons before the war; after the war he had become the excellent first chairman of the new department; I had a high regard for him, but a regard not incompatible with strong intellectual disagreement. Before the war he had largely been busy with his critique of the theories of Durkheim, Weber, and Pareto. After the war he began to set out his own brand of theory.

Parsons could be an empirical investigator of the first rank. When, for instance, he was writing about something like the medical profession, which he had studied at first hand, he had things to say that seemed shrewd and true. But what he was in fact good at was not what he would be thought good at: he took his stand as a theorist, and it was as a theorist that he vexed me. The trouble was not that he was a particular sort of theorist: his functionalism, as time went on, became more and more perfunctory. What I quarreled with were his ideas about the characteristics of a theory of any sort and about the relations between theory and investigation. I quarreled both with what he said about theory and with the way he himself practiced theory-building. The fact that it was not always easy to discover what he did say only served to vex me the more.

From my reading in the history and philosophy of science, I felt sure that a theory was a set of propositions, each stating a relationship between properties of nature.[39] The named properties constituted a conceptual scheme, but the conceptual scheme by itself was not enough to constitute the theory, which also had to state the propositions. The propositions were contingent, in the sense that their truth did not follow automatically from postulates assumed *a priori*, as did the truth of the theorems of geometry. Nature, not logic, made a proposition what it was. A lower-order proposition in the theory represented an empirical finding. It could be deduced from higher-order ones under specified given conditions, and the deduction might make use of the rules of logic and mathematics. When the lower-order proposition was so deduced, it was said to be explained, so that a theory was also an explanation. From the higher-order propositions, under different givens, a number of other lower-order propositions could likewise be derived. This increasing scope was what we meant when we called them higher-order propositions. At the top of any theory stood one or more propositions of the highest order, in the sense that for the time being no proposition of still greater scope was known from which they could in turn be derived; but this condition was unlikely to last forever. No highest-order proposition could be derived from others at that level, for if it could, it would not meet the condition for remaining at that level. In other words, the highest-order propositions were logically independent of one another. If any lower-order proposition, derivable from the theory under specified givens, repeatedly failed to represent the observed facts, the theory was liable sooner or later to be modified; but scientists were apt to cling to a theory, even when it was known to be inadequate, until some more adequate formulation was invented—and even after that. Science was, among other things, a method of persuasion, and some scientists, since they were also men, were not easily persuaded, even by science.

If these were the characteristics of a theory, the official sociological theorists often seemed to be talking about something else. One sort of statement they were fond of making distressed me particularly. Parsons said: "A theoretical system in the present sense is a body of logically interdependent generalized concepts of empirical reference";[40] and Robert Merton echoed him by saying that "the term *sociological theory* refers to logically interconnected conceptions which are limited and modest in scope, rather than all-embracing and grandiose."[41] The two differed in degrees of modesty but agreed in the view of theory as "logically interdependent concepts." If they meant that lower-order propositions in a theory could be logically deduced, under specified given conditions, from higher-order ones, then all was well. But if they meant that the higher-order propositions could be deduced from one another, they were in trouble. The propositions at any one level could not be deduced from one another: they must be logically independent not interdependent. And if the theorists meant that any single proposition stated a logical relation between two or more terms (concepts), they were no better off. A theoretical proposition did not state a logical relation but a contingent one.

Perhaps even now I was giving the theorists too much credit. What right had I to mention propositions when they spoke only of concepts or to assume that "logically interdependent" meant "deducible"? From concepts alone nothing could be deduced; there was no deduction without propositions, and a conceptual scheme was not a theory. It was true that some forms of classification concealed propositions within them: to class whales among mammals was to imply the testable proposition that the next female whale one met would suckle her young. But the conceptual schemes of the sociological theorists did not appear to be classifications of this sort: their concepts were innocent of propositions. I began to wonder whether the theorists knew what a theory was. At least their theory looked different from mine.

I had to admit that Parsons practiced what he preached. He said a theory was a body of generalized concepts, and the theory he himself constructed was just that. Actually he constructed a number of theories, but they were all alike in consisting of sets of categories. At the highest level of analysis, for instance, a social system would be divided into four functional aspects, and at successively lower levels each subsystem would be divided into the same four.[42] If I failed to find contingent propositions about the relations between the categories, I had to admit again that Parsons was consistent: he had not said that a theory should contain such propositions and his own did not. True, he was human: he sometimes slipped and came out with a proposition. He even claimed that it could be deduced from the categories in his theory, which sounded for a moment as if he had abandoned his notion of theory for mine. But only for a moment. Since he never, as far as I could see, tried to show the steps in the deduction, no great harm was done. It was a pity he did not try: his might have been the first proposition to be deduced from something that was not itself a proposition. Under the circumstances his small departure from consistency could easily be forgiven.

In fairness to Parsons I also had to admit that his conceptualization often stimulated other investigators to do research in which real propositions were formulated and tested. That they were stimulated by his theory rather than derived from it did not prevent their being good propositions. Some graduate students, moreover, took great comfort from Parsons' scheme. Like a well-designed cupboard, it appeared to provide a place, where they could easily lay hands on it in the dark, for everything in the social world. I was not denying that Parsons' theory often had good effects in practice. If the comfort it provided was a doubtful advantage, the stimulus was all to the good. After all, it had stimulated me to discover where I stood. All I disputed was its claim to be a theory.

Parsons was consistent in another way too: he seemed to think that the way a theory looked when it was completed—though no theory is ever more than provisionally completed—corresponded to the way it was arrived at. A completed theory consisted of a set of highest-order propositions, from which under specified givens lower-order propositions could be logically derived, the process continuing until the empirical findings were reached. In short the reasoning worked downward from the general to the particular. But if I understood the practice of the great theorists—Newton, Gibbs, Clerk-Maxwell—the process of building the theory, the strategy of theory-construction rather than the theory itself, moved in the other direction: the theorist started with a careful examination of the empirical findings and then tried to invent the more general propositions from which they could be derived. Deductive theories were inductively arrived at! Of course there were exceptions. Einstein might be one, but Einstein's reasoning could start from a theory, supported by much empirical evidence, that was already in existence. In sociology we were in no such position; we had no theory to start from and had to make one. Under the circumstances the practice of the earlier theorists in the physical sciences was a better guide than that of the later ones.

Parsons seemed to think that both the process of reasoning in a completed theory and the process by which that theory was arrived at worked in the same downward direction. He started with very general considerations and hoped to work downward to the empirical findings. That he started from concepts and not propositions, and so could not work downward deductively, does not concern me now. Downward was the direction in which he thought the construction of a theory proceeded. He was always a little patronizing toward "mere empirical generalizations" and once complained that " a great deal of current research is producing facts in a form which cannot be utilized by any current generalized analytical scheme."[43] So much the worse, I was inclined to think, for the scheme. In keeping with my own idea that good science had been attained by some of the damnedest methods, I could not rule out the chance that Parsons' strategy might someday pay off. But if I had to make a bet, I would bet on the strategy that started with the empirical propositions and worked upward, the strategy well described by Willard Gibbs: "It is the office of theoretical investigation to give the form in which the results of experiment may be expressed."[44] The fact was that, in my efforts at codification in the field of small-group research,

I had already made the bet. My reflections on Parsons only served to reassure me that I had made a good one.

At first I thought that codification was enough, that I could collect the empirical generalizations, reduce their number as far as possible, and let it go at that. One of the first books I had read under Henderson's influence was Bacon's *Novum Organum*, and I always remembered his statement: "The most general principles in nature ought to be held merely positive, as they are discovered, and cannot with truth be referred to a cause."[45] After the war, Thomas Kuhn, another member of the Society of Fellows, had started me reading once more in the history of science, and in Ernst Mach's *Science of Mechanics* I had encountered the argument, which can be traced back to Buffon, that science consisted "in the careful and complete exposition of the mere facts," that it dropped the question "Why?" and looked only for the "How?" of phenomena.[46]

I still think this may be a good rule of scientific tactics: one may be in so much of a hurry to explain phenomena that one does not get the phenomena themselves straight. But it could not be a permanent rule of strategy. Men were not to be denied the right to ask the question "Why?"; to ask for explanations. To answer the question was to find, if possible, the higher-order propositions from which, under specified given conditions, the empirical findings could be derived. To answer the question was therefore to construct a theory. The trouble, finally, with Parsons' theory was that, since it contained no higher-order propositions, it could not explain; and I had to find another that did.

I did not have to invent a theory of my own: one was ready to hand. I finally came to the conclusion that the empirical findings of small-group research, social anthropology, and history could best be explained by the propositions of behavioral psychology. To call behavioral psychology "learning theory" was misleading because it also dealt with the determinants of behavior after it was learned. And of the behavioral psychologies, I found the formulations of B. F. Skinner most to my purpose.[47] In their main lines his propositions did not differ from those of the others, but they were stated with the fewest unnecessary assumptions.

I ought to have reached this conclusion much earlier. Fred Skinner, too, had been a contemporary of mine in the Society of Fellows; when I found him back at Harvard after the war, I revived my friendship with him, and I had long been familiar in a general way with his work.

But for an equally long time I could not see what use it might be to me. It took the long struggle with the findings about small groups and about primitive kinship, it took above all the struggle to explain them in some way other than that of the functionalists, to make me pick up what was lying all the time in plain sight.

Fred Skinner would have hated to hear his propositions called a theory, and if a theory meant, as it so often did, ideas unsupported by evidence, of course he was right. But a theory in my sense it certainly was. It consisted of contingent propositions and not just of categories. The propositions were ordinary causal statements, not teleological ones. They were of high order: whatever the future might hold, they could not at the moment be derived from more general propositions. They were of wide scope: they could be used to explain many findings other than those I was interested in. Sometimes, it is true, the derivations that constituted the explanation were a little sketchy, but at worst they were more rigorous than those of official sociological theory. Perhaps the propositions of behavioral psychology were better at explaining the findings of small-group research, findings about the face-to-face interactions of individuals, than they were at explaining the more complicated facets of personality or institutions. But even with institutions I did not lack hope. I had said that the cross-cultural findings about institutionalized relations among kinsmen could only be explained by the characteristics of men, as men. What I now meant was that they could be explained by the propositions of behavioral psychology. If a tribesman tended to be "distant" from a person set in authority over him, the reason was that persons in authority often had to use punishment or the threat of punishment in controlling their subordinates, and that men, as men, tended to avoid punishment and its source—which was a proposition of behavioral psychology. Of course behavioral psychology could not explain everything, but I became convinced that its failures could be accounted for by lack of data or by the difficulties in tracing out long and complex causal chains rather than by any inherent inapplicability of its propositions. Sociology *was*, Durkheim to the contrary, a corollary of psychology. I first stated these views in "Social Behavior as Exchange," reprinted here, and I developed them further in my book *Social Behavior: Its Elementary Forms.*[48]

And that is where I stand now. My views on the nature of theory, on the strategy of theory-building, on the difficulties of "functional" explanation, even on psychology as providing the explanation of sociological findings are not in the least new. Scientists in many different fields and at many different times have rediscovered them again and again. All I have done is record the particular experiences and preoccupations that led me to rediscover them.

Sociologists have, I think, a special need to bear them in mind, to think about them at least if not to believe in them. Sociology in my time has gone through wild oscillations between extremes: it needs some ballast. Fleeing the straw man of "mere data collection," we have almost ended in "general theory" without data. Reacting against broad generalizations that did not stand testing, we have almost ended in broad categorizations that cannot be tested at all. Anxious to find our identity in a kind of theory that was truly our own, truly sociological, we have almost ended in the trap of functionalism. Only the hard work of many steady men, often the very men who in other manifestations contributed to the vagaries of doctrine, have carried us through and have advanced our science.

I have, finally, no doubt that some of my reactions to sociological doctrines have been moral. The study of human behavior is the most complex to which the mind of man may be applied,[49] and therefore social scientists are peculiarly tempted toward facile solutions. Whatever else I thought about it, I thought functionalism was a facile solution to the real difficulties of explanation. Whatever else I thought about it, I thought that creating "logically interdependent generalized concepts" was facile: anyone could do it easily who could bring himself to do it at all. Since my puritan background taught me that nothing valuable could be obtained without hard work, the facile solutions came under moral suspicion. There was nothing in the code of the scientist that said he must be a puritan, nothing that said a theory was less valid for being easily arrived at. But I came to the conclusion that, practically, puritanism had something to be said for it: there were no easy ways out for sociology that were also good ways.

I do not want to overdo the puritanism. If we need more discipline on one side, we need more freedom on the other. We need both stricter ideas of what we are trying to get at—deductive explanations—and more toleration for the many different ways of getting there—our methods of investigation. We need fewer people to tell us, as they tried to tell me about "case studies" of small groups, that certain kinds of research are illegitimate. No method can go far wrong that puts human behavior under close scrutiny. And all we finally need be afraid of is that sociologists will come to do any mad thing in order to avoid being at the pains of studying men.

2

The Small

Warship

M y experience in World War II was different, I believe, from that of most social scientists who entered government service. For many years I had been an officer of the Naval Reserve, so that when the time came, instead of being assigned to some such field as public opinion analysis or military government, which were obviously related to sociology as an academic discipline, I was sent to sea as an ordinary line officer. And out of four and a half years on active duty, more than two were spent in command of small ships engaged in antisubmarine warfare and the escort of convoy operations. Looking back on it, I feel that I was extremely lucky to have had this kind of responsibility, but I am not indulging in reminiscence for its own sake. If, in the end, sociology does not teach students something they can actually use in handling men effectively, it is nothing. Eventually we must be able to do that, or we shall not be worth our salt. I wish we could say that we do it now. I myself learned much from sociology which made me a more effective sea captain than I should otherwise have been. The point I am making here is that I did not do a better job than the young man who was educated, intelligent, sensitive—who was, as we used to say, "a good joe"— but who had not been exposed to social science. We do not yet teach leadership. It must be taught, soon and well, if we are to train the men who will hold our industrial civilization together.

Reprinted from *American Sociological Review*, 11 (1946), 294–300, by permission of the American Sociological Association.

If the average sociologist, like myself, cannot do a better job of leadership than the average intelligent young man, he should at least be a better observer. I think I did learn, usually by making mistakes, some of the factors which make for good or bad morale on a small ship: a group, shall we say, of not more than two hundred men, differing from other groups of comparable size in being isolated and self-contained, sometimes for weeks at a time. Nothing that I learned was new,[1] except in its application to this particular *milieu*, and nothing complex. No doubt our intellectual elaboration in this field will keep pace with our ability to teach a skill. Note also that I say some of the factors in morale. I make no pretense of including all of them. For instance, there is formal discipline. Armies and navies have had hundreds of years of experience in formal discipline, and most of the remarks wise officers have made on that subject seem to me well taken. The factors I shall speak of are less often discussed in professional military circles, though often in fact well handled. They are: the problem of technical competence, the problem of balance, the problem of reciprocity, and the problem of communication.

The Problem of Technical Competence

All warships work with other warships, and comparisons are always being made between them. When a group of ships has been together for a long time, the character of each is well established and the subject of the most ribald comment. How quickly does U.S.S. "Blank" react to a submarine contact? How many hits does she get shooting at a towed sleeve? What kind of chow does she serve? What kind of guy is her skipper? All these things come up for discussion. Take a minor problem like coming alongside a pier. Almost always other ships are present in port, and men from these ships will be on the pier to handle the lines. If the captain misjudges his approach and scrapes off some of his paint, if the engine room force does not back the engines promptly when ordered, if the gang on the fantail allows the stern line to get fouled in the screw, the fact will be observed with delight and remembered. Now no seaman wishes to be one of the crew of a ship whose reputation is not good. The kind of smartness he asks for may not be the kind admired by many officers. He is a man of sense and loves sound seamanship and sound cooking more than a magnificent paint job. But there are certain practical, simple things about the mission of the ship which must be properly handled if his willingness to cooperate is to be kept at a high level. Morale is just a fancy name for willingness to cooperate.

These things are the responsibility of the captain. They demand all his skill in organization and training. We used to comment ruefully on the fact that if anything went wrong, at any time, anywhere on the ship, the Navy automatically blamed the commanding officer. It does seem unfair at times, but the instinct behind it is sound, since the crew itself, the men most concerned, blame him too. The excellent Army pamphlet on absence without leave emphasizes that the commanding officer is in fact responsible for every unauthorized absence which occurs in his unit. He must contrive that conditions favoring loyalty to the group are maintained everywhere in his command. And the first among these conditions is that the command shall be known as one which is doing an important job, has the means to do it, and does it well. Without this, nothing else in morale is possible, but all the factors are interdependent, and unless the others are adequately handled, technical competence itself will fail. Discontented men are not good seamen. They will "slow down" as surely as their brothers in industry.

The Problem of Balance

Like other societies, large and small, the crew of a ship does not consist of an undifferentiated mass of men, but is segmented, largely on the basis of rank and job. In the class structure, if we may call it that, there are three main levels: the commissioned officers, the chief petty officers, always called "chiefs," and the rest of the sailors, with a less important distinction among these others between the "rated" men and the "nonrated" men. In the grouping by jobs, there are two main units and several smaller ones. The deck force is represented by the gunner's mates, the boatswain's mates, and the nonrated seamen. Their work is mostly topside, and I must report that they are sometimes referred to as "deck apes." The engineering force is represented by the machinist's mates, the electricians, and the nonrated firemen. Their work is mostly below decks, and they are known as the "black gang" or the "snipes." (The origin of the latter word is still in dispute.) These are the big groups; there are several smaller ones. One is the bridge gang, made up of the signalmen and quartermasters who work in the immediate neighborhood of the bridge. Another is made up of the radiomen. Then there are a number of specialties, no one of which musters more than a handful of individuals on any one ship: cooks, steward's mates (Negroes), yeomen, pharmacist's mates, carpenters, and shipfitters. Some of these segments are marked by differences in uniform; almost all are set apart by subtle differences of behavior, which would not be immediately obvious to an outsider, and which even a Navy man would have a hard time describing, although he is acutely conscious of them. Even the angle at which a chief wears his hat is distinctive.

Since every ship has to meet the same fundamental demands and remain self-sufficient, every ship has on board at least a few members of each of these groups. This fact implies that the crew of a small ship is actually more differentiated than its numerical size might suggest. At the end of centuries of experience—and it can be argued that the western world has had a longer experience with ships than with any other form of elaborate working group—the organization of any warship is essentially that of every other ship of the fleet. This similarity, which enabled a newcomer aboard ship to find his way around socially with a minimum of bewilderment, was one of the factors which allowed the Navy to absorb the enormous numbers of transfers between ships which took place throughout the war. Furthermore, perhaps again as a result of the long tradition, it always seemed to me that the actual social groupings of men, seen in the friends who went around together when on liberty, corresponded fairly closely to the segments called for by the formal organization.

Here, then, are a number of small groups of men, their sharp differentiation by job being heavily reinforced by tradition. The problem is that one of these groups may set itself in opposition to another or to the ship's company as a whole. I recall one ship which received on commissioning a draft of young seamen who were fairly new to the Navy, but who had recently served together in the North Atlantic convoy routes. This was before Pearl Harbor, when the Navy as a whole had not taken part in a shooting war. Naturally enough, the members of this group were cocky, and a series of incidents occurred in which they were insubordinate to the chiefs, who were old hands at the Navy, but who had not yet received the accolade of action.

In this connection, I think more often of another incident. On a large vessel, the deck force, the engineering force, and the other groups that make up the ship's company are physically separated while at work to an extent unknown on a small ship. They may lose some sense of unity, but much friction is also avoided. Now it is a doctrine of the Navy that all men should be at work during "turn to" hours, whether or not they happen to have a watch. A ship I commanded was cruising in tropical waters. The engine room was small and hot, and the high-speed diesels were noisy. Under these conditions we threw doctrine overboard and did not require the engineers to work in the engine room throughout the day, though of course they had to stand their regular four-hour watches. The case of the deck force was different. These men worked topside, where there was plenty of breeze to temper the hot sun. Furthermore, their labors were urgently required. The battle against rust which is fought on a small ship is endless and without quarter. Unfortunately, the engineers used their leisure time sun-bathing and reading on deck in full view of the seamen who were sweating it out at paint-chipping. Let me add that I believe that the morale of the deck force on a long voyage where the chance of action is remote tends to be low in comparison with other groups. The deck force has the dirty jobs of maintenance: chipping, painting, slushing down, which do not bear immediate comparison in interest with, for instance, the work of the quartermasters on the navigating bridge or the work of the machinist's mates in the engine room. On this occasion it appeared to the officer in charge on deck that the efforts of his seamen were not being spurred on by the sight of the engineers taking it easy, and I gave the order that, so long as the deck force was at work, the engineers, while still not required to turn to, should spend their leisure time elsewhere than topside. I am sure that I made a mistake, for as soon as I gave the order the black gang let me know that it was being discriminated against, and the whole issue of balance was raised. As on so many other occasions, I should have done much better if I had done nothing, although there was a real difficulty which called for some solution.

The chance that the problem of balance may assert itself must always be in the skipper's mind, together with the recognition that there is no single, simple way of handling it. A ship's party, when all hands, officers and men, go ashore to play a game of baseball against another ship (the loser providing the beer), reinforces in the ship's company a sense of unity, but only if this unity exists to begin with. It must be created in the work of every day, not in special occasions. The skipper could not, even if he wished, break down the segments into which his crew is divided; and their corporate strength, enlisted in the common effort, will serve him well. What he must do is take care that no one segment sets itself apart from the rest and against them.

The Problem of Reciprocity

It is well recognized that a good leader should look after his men. It is not so well recognized that he should look after them in the matters they consider important and not simply in the matters the commanding officer and his superiors consider important. On a small ship some of the items were obvious, and the most obvious was pay. Many of the men had made allotments for the support of their dependents. It made all the difference to their enjoyment of liberty that the small amounts which still came to them for their personal expenses should arrive on time. In the early part of the war, before the Navy devised a plan for meeting just this problem, it was not simple to arrange. A small ship did not carry a disbursing officer; her accounts were held at a base, often a long distance from the area in which she was operating. Sometimes the sailors did not get paid on payday, though they were always paid eventually. Furthermore, the Navy has a complicated pay system. There is a good reason for each of the complications, but they did not always make it easy, in the absence of a disbursing officer, to satisfy the men that they had received the proper amounts. A commanding officer had to do everything possible to see that the men were getting what they rated, and, what is much more important, show that he was doing it, even if it meant carrying on guerrilla warfare with the rest of the Navy. It was unfortunate that sometimes a sharp remark from his own superior officer helped the skipper prove to his men that he was fighting for them.

The commanding officer had to see that the men were getting all that was coming to them in the matter of promotions and transfers. The Navy had an admirable set of service schools, up to and including the Navy College Training Program. Aside from the chance for advancement, almost all of these carried with them the most prized of rewards —"going back to the States." Further, the commanding officer was continually being called upon, in a Navy which was expanding like an explosion, to send a certain number of men back to the United States to man newly built ships, the choice of men being, within limits, left to him. He was always under the temptation to use these openings to send his worst and not his best men away. It seemed an easy means of getting rid of a man who was hard to handle, and it often looked as if the ship just could not get along without certain key technicians. It never paid to yield to the temptation. Rewarding a man for good and faithful service obviously strengthened the spirit of the ship, and, with this spirit, you always found that you could train, much more rapidly than you had believed possible, a new expert to take the place of the one lost.

The commanding officer had to see that his men were protected against unnecessary irritations, even when it meant protecting them against the Navy itself. Uniform, for instance, was sometimes a vexing matter. In the peacetime Navy, a sailor is required to wear the "uniform of the day" unless he is doing obviously dirty work, in the engine room or overside, when he is allowed to wear dungarees. In the West Indies in 1942–43 the rule was still in force. Unfortunately the uniform of the day was "whites," and the ship in question was operating out of the great oil port of San Nicholas, Aruba, where crude oil floated in rafts on the water and oozed from every bit of piling, and where every line hauled back aboard the ship spread the sticky muck over the decks. Under these circumstances, whites could be worn on liberty without too much trouble, but it was impossible to keep them clean for any length of time on board ship. Any work was, in effect, dirty work. The Navy rules about uniform had to be disregarded, and were disregarded. The crew wore dungarees at all times.

I should have a hard time implementing in detail the remarks that follow, but I set them down for what they may be worth. A number of officers who were familiar with the British Navy felt that, in comparison, our own navy was "hard on its men." Granting that the distant field is always greenest, these officers believed that the British Navy allowed its sailors to take it easy when there was no obvious reason for keeping them on their toes, and that this kind of relaxation was important in maintaining resilience. The British paid a price for what they did. At least an article in the American credo was: "Limey ships are filthy." The United States Navy, on the other hand, in its very desire to be clean, efficient, and well trained at all times, tended to put its men through a number of activities the necessity of which was not always clear to them. They tended to be overtrained, in the athlete's sense of the word. I think there is a national difference at work here and not simply a difference of naval policies. In any event, a sailor, as a member of a military organization, is subject to a vast number of orders and regulations which he must obey without question. For the maintenance of his personal integrity, he must be able to escape from the organization at times. He must have all the liberty that can conceivably be given him, and when he is on board ship the rules which govern his life with his fellows must be as clear and simple as possible. Far from being multiplied, they should be cut down to the point of anarchy.

Much of the action that a commanding officer takes to help his men he is required to take by the regulations of the Navy. And nothing he does is in any sense a favor. The relation between himself and the crew is never that of politician and clients. If he ever claimed something from his subordinates in return for the good deeds he had done on their behalf, he would get nothing more than some exceedingly irreverent remarks made behind his back. At the same time, nothing he does is taken wholly impersonally. Only if the skipper is doing his best for the men, and they know it, will they do their best for the ship. This is the meaning of reciprocity.

The Problem of Communication

Adequate communication is a two-way process, moving both upward and downward in the organization. Of the two, the latter, the job of explaining to the crew the action which the commanding officer and his immediate assistants believe should be taken, is the easier and the more obviously necessary, but it is by no means absolutely easy. Take the matter of conserving water. In the tropics the demand for water always exceeded the supply. Men drank much water, and they wanted to take showers as often as they could. Yet the evaporators were barely adequate at best; they were notoriously delicate, and the commanding officer had to bear in mind the necessity of maintaining a sufficient reserve in the tanks to enable the ship to reach port even if the evaporators failed completely. One might think that these rather simple considerations could have been explained to the intelligent young men who made up the crews of our ships as something which concerned, not the higher-ups only, but every member of the ship's company. I believe that many a commanding officer could relate incidents which showed that they had not been so explained. Perhaps the fact that most of the sailors had recently come from civil life, where water was one of the things there was always plenty of, had something to do with what happened. Perhaps the rules for the conservation of water were looked upon as just some more of the many restrictions imposed on the men from above. In some cases, the ship's company had not been together long enough. The Navy expanded violently throughout the war, and sometimes officers and men were only just beginning to understand one another when a good number of them were taken off the ship to man new construction. I do not know the answer, but the fact is that communication downward often failed.

If communication downward failed, how much more likely was it that communication upward, a kind which is, formally at least, not encouraged in military organizations and sometimes even discouraged, should fail also. I have said that the skipper must take care of the crew in those matters which they consider important and not simply in those which he, or the Navy, considers important. How can he tell what these matters are? How can he tell what pressures are building up that may threaten the balance of the organization? To put the matter more simply, I think that an honest commanding officer would be devastated by an effort to answer the question: "What do I know about the crew?" Without the score, he may play well by ear, but he cannot be sure he is doing a good job in building morale.

I do not think that the chaplain is the answer to the problem of upward communication. To say this is to imply no disparagement of the corps of chaplains. The job does not really belong to them. If a man has something on his mind which involves his family or his life away from the ship, it may be sensible for him to go to a chaplain who is trained to be a good listener. But many of his preoccupations will concern his life with his shipmates, both officers and men. Now it was generally recognized in the Navy that a man who took his troubles to the chaplain took them, in effect, outside the organization. If a man was irritated by something in his naval experience, is was a common joke to offer him the chaplain's address, with the understanding that he would have a good chance to blow off steam but that no other change in the circumstances would ever, by any possible coincidence, be made. Many of the matters about which men were told to talk to the chaplain carried important implications for morale. With the chaplain they stayed. As far as I know, the chaplain was not commonly consulted by the commanding officer. In any case, he could not have violated the specific confidences he had received, and he was usually too far removed from the daily work of the ship to interpret the general implications of the confidences. Yet I assume that any matter whatever which in fact concerns morale should ultimately be transmitted to the man who is responsible for morale, that is, the commanding officer. And I do not consider insoluble the problem of transmitting this kind of information in such a way that no individual will be injured and that the ship will not seethe with gossip.

Small ships did not have chaplains, yet there was usually at least one man on every small ship who was a good listener and to whom sailors would talk freely as they would to no one else. Though such men were invaluable, they were incapable by themselves of encouraging communication throughout the organization. I am thinking of a pharmacist's mate on one of my ships and the executive officer on another. The latter had been a member of the relief organization of a southern state and was a good natural interviewer. Many of the men got into the habit of talking to him. He was always available and always interested. Now immediately below the executive officer in the ship's organization was a chief boatswain's mate with more than twenty years of splendid service in the Navy. He had come to our little escort vessel from an important job on a much larger ship in which the prewar Navy traditions were still dominant. Rightly or wrongly, he interpreted his transfer as a come-down, and though he never said so, I am afraid that at the time in question, which was early in the war, he considered some of us naval reserve officers absolutely crazy. I still do not know whether his high blood pressure was the cause or the effect of his experiences with us. Extremely competent as a seaman, he still had some difficulty fitting into the organization, until he began to know us all better, when we became good friends. At any rate he was in immediate charge of many of the men who were in the habit of talking to the executive officer whenever they felt the need of getting something off their chests. As the chief saw it, they were going over his head, and he protested to me. It is true that the executive officer had never disclosed anything he had heard, or taken any action on it, and outside of being interested in what they had to say, was not treating the men as his intimates. Yet the chief's view of the matter, that the men were jumping a link in the chain of command, had some cogency.

The incident is significant. It is not enough that the captain should announce that "his door is always open." The prestige that surrounds "the old man" will prevent most sailors from crossing the threshold. It is not enough that there should be some one person who can be counted on to listen sympathetically to anything a sailor wants to talk about, especially if the person in question is to some extent outside the group. It is essential that at every level of the organization men should be trained to listen with interest and attention, and without interrupting, to everything their subordinates are trying to say, trained also to fit what they hear into some relevant picture which they in turn can communicate. I do not know whether anything of this sort can be built up. I do feel that something of the sort is required if the commanding officer is not simply to play by ear in the matter of morale.

At the end, as always, I return to the commanding officer. In the ship's roster of officers, morale is listed as one of his special charges. By ancient tradition, he is the last to leave the ship if she goes down. He is held responsible by the Navy for anything that goes wrong, and it is right that he should be, for I believe that he is, in fact, responsible and is so considered by the men under him. To help him bear this burden, he is, in theory, made dictator aboard his ship, but, as he stands on the bridge and gives his orders, no one is more aware that he is helpless without the willing cooperation of the crew. And he is the man above all others who may, at any moment, put that willingness in jeopardy. He is subject to strains unlike those met by an executive in civil life. He is on call at all times; his judgment may be warped by lack of sleep. He is still more dangerous when he is angry. Much of the work of a warship is of an emergency nature. If a mistake is made at a crisis, it is only human for him to be furious; his fury will be in proportion to his desire to do a good technical job, and it will take the form of an overwhelming urge to bawl somebody out. It is then that he must watch himself. I suppose that if one is going to give a reprimand, there is some virtue in giving it on the spot, immediately after the mistake has been made. This is the theory we follow with a pet: we "rub his nose in it." And I suppose, too, that in military organizations there is a general recognition of the strains put on officers and a greater readiness to put up with a bawling-out than is usual in civil life. But the risk is not worth taking; there is too much danger that a humiliation in front of his fellows will turn a man into a rebel. The skipper must keep his mouth shut, if he can, and then the time may come when he wonders whether he is learning more about the crew than about himself. This is not the least of the rewards of command.

3

Status

among Clerical

Workers

STUDENTS of industrial organization have long been interested in the connection between the relative status of workers on different jobs and the characteristics of these jobs, especially differences in pay. But surprisingly few studies of this connection have been reported in any detail.[1] In this paper, I shall describe how a group of workers complained because the high status conferred on them by some features of their job was not reflected in other features. By the *status* of a job I mean the rank assigned to the job by the workers, insofar as it is better or worse than other jobs, and according to the degree they feel it realizes certain values or norms.[2]

I encountered this "status problem" in the course of a series of studies I made of clerical workers in a certain company. All the reader needs to know about the company is that it had a large number of customers to whom it sent out monthly bills. From December 1949 through April

Reprinted from *Human Organization*, 12 (1953), 5–10, by permission of the Editor. This is the first of two articles, "The Cash Posters" being the other, in which I describe research in a company I call, incorrectly, "The Eastern Utilities Co." The present article is reprinted unchanged, except that certain paragraphs have been left out to avoid later repetition, and certain fictitious names have been changed to reconcile them with those used in "The Cash Posters."

1950, I made a study of one division of this company, consisting of sixty workers and supervisors, men and women, who carried out various operations in accounting for the payment of these bills.

Method of Study

The study went through several phases. I obtained the approval of the management and the union executive committee for making the study. The union was then an independent one, which, while not a "company union," was limited in membership to the workers of the company in question. The workers have since voted to join a CIO union, whose officers have approved various later studies in the company. I explained the purposes and methods of the study to the supervisors of every echelon who were responsible for the division in which I planned to work. Then I made the same explanation to the supervisors and workers of the division itself, assuring them that I should make no private report of my findings either to the management or to the union, and that if I published any report—as I am doing here—I should not quote anything any person said to me in such a way that it could be traced back to him to his detriment.

Immediately after this explanation, I moved to a small table at the back of the large room in which the division worked, so placed that it commanded a substantially clear view of the whole room. With this as a base of operation, I spent about a month introducing myself to each of the workers individually, learning the various clerical procedures, some of them quite complicated, that the division carried on, and getting a general impression of behavior in the room. The period of social constraint due to the presence of a stranger seemed to end after I attended the workers' Christmas office party. From then on, I could get no evidence from the supervisors, the union representative, or the office boy in the room that the workers' behavior was any different from what it had been before I came in; but output, in those operations whose output was measured, showed a tendency to go up, and the industrial relations department was inclined to give me undeserved credit for an improvement in morale.

The second phase of the study, which took two weeks, was systematic observation of interaction in the room, specifically of which persons talked to which other persons, and how often.

With sixty persons in the room, I could obviously not keep a continuous interaction record, so I adopted a sampling procedure. Every fifteen minutes, I scanned the room and made a note of which persons were talking together at that time.[3] In theory, talking except on business was discouraged. In practice, it was tolerated, and there was a great deal of strictly social chit-chat, especially among the younger girls. Naturally I was not interested in checking up on the workers, but in getting a quantitative record of interpersonal contacts. Yet I must report, incidentally, that contrary to official ideas, but not to the unofficial ideas of some of the supervisors, there turned out to be no inverse relation between talking and output. In fact, some of the girls who talked most also produced most.

The third and longest phase of the study consisted of individual interviews with the supervisors and workers, conducted on company time in a private room away from the office floor. Before the interview, I asked each worker individually whether she was willing to talk to me; they all agreed, except one whom I did not press further. The interviews, which lasted from one to two hours, were nondirective except in two respects. After explaining again the purpose of the study, I always began the main body of the interview with the question: "How do you like your job?" That is, the focus of the interview, at least in the beginning, was on attitudes toward the job. Then, at some appropriate time in the course of the interview, I asked the sociometric question: "Who are your close friends here?" I wanted to get further evidence on informal social organization. I recorded each interview as I remembered it as soon as possible after it finished.

During the interviewing period, I kept in touch with the division office every day, to make arrangements for the next interviews, etc. When the interviews were over, I returned to my table in the office for two weeks to check my first impressions and to make further interaction records. The whole study took four and one-half months. Let me say here that I very much enjoyed my association with a fine body of American men and women. In fact I had a wonderful time.

The Jobs

The "status problem" was not my only focus in the study of the division, and to describe it I need consider, besides the supervision, only the two largest of the job-groups within the division—the cash posters and the ledger clerks. The workers of the division were mostly women, all of whom were at least high school graduates. The cash posters were ten young women, from about seventeen to twenty-five years of age, who had from less than one to about four years' service in the company; the ledger clerks were twenty women, from about twenty-one to over sixty years of age, with from three to thirty years' service. Thus, the two groups differed greatly in average age and length of service; the reasons for this difference were as follows.

The usual channel of advancement in the division started with a job of Pay Grade I, then went to Cash Poster (Grade II), and then to Ledger Clerk (Grade II). Turnover was high among the younger girls, who were much interested in getting married. A company rule stated that when a girl married she had to leave its employ. The result was that promotion to cash poster might come after three or four months' service in the division, and promotion to ledger clerk hardly more than two years later, but promotion from ledger clerk to a Grade III job might take decades. Promotion was largely by seniority; turnover among the older ledger clerks was slow, as those who were going to marry and leave had already done so, and the others stuck to their jobs because of the company's well-deserved reputation for providing job security. ("Nobody ever gets fired around here.") Thus many of the ledger clerks were older women with high seniority in the division and in the company.

The management had tried to make amends for the very slow advancement in the ledger clerk's job by giving Grade III pay to four of the most senior of the ledger clerks, as well as the title of "group leader." These were not in fact supervisory jobs. The group leader continued to do her regular job as ledger clerk, but held herself ready to answer the questions of the less-experienced clerks.

Though the transfer from cash poster to ledger clerk was officially considered a promotion, the two jobs were in the same pay grade with equal pay for a forty-hour week of five eight-hour days. It was common knowledge that three of the girls in the division had refused a "promotion" to ledger clerk when it was offered to them. The reasons the two jobs paid equally were at least in part historical. In the not-too-distant past, cash posting had been done at night by men and, therefore, had commanded relatively high wages, which were not changed when it was transferred to the daytime and to women.

[64]

The titles "cash posters" and "ledger clerks" came from the processes of old-fashioned double-entry bookkkeeping, though more modern methods had long ago replaced the ledger book and the written entry. The "ledgers" now consisted of ten blocks of files, each holding the accounts of one main section of the company's customers. In these files were trays of cards representing the sums of money each customer had been billed during the month, that is, the "arrears." Not all the customers were billed on the first of the month; instead, to avoid enormous peak loads, a certain number of customers were billed on each working day of the month.

Two ledger clerks were assigned as partners to each of the ten ledgers, dividing the work between them as they saw fit. They sat at desks between the ledger files and within easy talking distance of one another. Their supervisor changed the assignment to partner and to ledger in the last hour of the last working day of every year, to the accompaniment of a good deal of excitement. Of the ledger clerks' job, it is enough to say that they did everything necessary to keep customers' accounts up to date, except cash posting: transfers of address, breakdowns of over- and underpayments, etc. One of the two desks at each ledger was equipped with a phone, and the clerks answered questions regarding the state of the accounts from customers themselves and from other employees of the company. Whereas the cash posters had, in the main, to do one single repetitive job on a production basis, requiring little thought but plenty of physical mobility, the ledger clerks had to do a number of nonrepetitive clerical jobs on a nonproduction basis, requiring some thought but little physical mobility.

I must mention one other vital fact. The supervisors thought of the ledger clerks, the largest group in the room, as the chief reservoir from which woman-power could be drawn when other jobs in the room were shorthanded. They also regarded cash posting not as the most important job of the division, but as the one they could least afford to get behindhand with: it had to be cleaned up every day. It was therefore standard daily procedure for their supervisor to take some of the ledger clerks (but not the group leaders) off their stations in rotation and send them to fill in on other jobs, usually cash posting. This happened far less often to other groups in the room. Since many of the ledger clerks had been "promoted" from cash posting, they were thoroughly familiar with the work.

I do not need to describe in detail the informal social organization of the division, except for some points in the relation between cash posters and ledger clerks. In spite of the fact that both groups worked at the same ledgers, only one of the ledger clerks (O'Brien) interacted more with posters than with other ledger clerks. She was also the only ledger clerk chosen as friend by more cash posters than ledger clerks. She had, in fact, only recently been "promoted" to ledger work. Only one of the cash posters (Burke) interacted more with ledger clerks than with cash posters. She also was the only cash poster chosen as friend by more ledger clerks and others than by cash posters. She was the oldest of the cash posters. Burke and O'Brien were themselves mutual friends. In short, cash posters and ledger clerks, in relation to one another, tended to form distinct social as well as job groups. So far as any informal leadership was exercised in the room, O'Brien and Brooks, two of the younger ledger clerks, tended to exercise it. Of all the ledger clerks, Brooks was first in sociometric choices given to her, and tied for first with O'Brien in number of persons contacted, that is, in range rather than frequency of interaction. O'Brien talked more often than any other ledger clerk and more than all but one of the cash posters. (All names are changed from the originals.)

Attitudes toward Jobs

The above information about the two jobs is objective in the sense that I could have gotten most of it without talking to the women themselves. The "status problem" was not discovered in the same way: it led to no outbreak in overt action that I observed, but emerged instead from the attitudes expressed in interviews. Since it was a "problem" chiefly for the ledger clerks, I shall concentrate on their attitudes. In my experience in holding nondirective interviews with persons who interact frequently with one another, I have found that many of them express the same opinions in almost the same words, often without realizing that they are doing so, and giving instead every impression that they think their views are original. I do not know why I once found this surprising, but I did. The workers of the division were no exception to

[66]

this rule. Although the accidents of an interview may prevent any one person from expressing all the opinions he holds, I assume that, given enough interviews and the freedom of the nondirective situation, the frequency with which particular attitudes are expressed is an index of their relative importance in the group as a whole.

I interviewed 19 of the 20 ledger clerks—one refused. Each interview began with the question: "How do you like your job?" and 13 out of the 19 said they liked it, none that they positively disliked it. (Of course a person is always under pressure to say she likes her job, for to say she does not is to confess herself a fool for not trying to get out of it. In the case of the ledger clerks, the very low rate of leaving the job except for promotion and marriage is some evidence that they *did* like it.) More important are the reasons given for liking the job. In this connection, ten of the ledger clerks spoke of the general friendliness of the division, and six said they liked their bosses; these of course were not conditions specific to the ledger job itself. Of the more specific conditions, eleven women mentioned the pay, and six the job security as being good. Ten said that what they liked about the job was its responsibility, eight its variety, eight the chances for contact with customers by telephone, and four the pleasure of "straightening things out." In the minds of the ledger clerks, as in those of most of us, a job is "responsible" to the degree you can do harm if you make an error. The pleasure the clerks found in contact with the customers (which I myself found somewhat surprising) seemed to derive both from the wider social contacts so made, and from contacting the persons to whose needs it was the ultimate purpose of the company to minister. The clerks felt an admirable responsibility to the consumer. "Straightening things out" meant bringing order out of chaos in a customer's account. Clearly the women were appraising their jobs favorably in terms of the values of pleasant social atmosphere, good bosses, pay, security, responsibility, variety, outside contact, and what we may call "problem-solving."

Though attitudes toward the ledger job were generally favorable, the women held that the job had two specific drawbacks. The first, mentioned by 11 of the 19, was that it offered little or no chance for advancement: ability received little recognition and promotions by seniority were slow in coming. This opinion was fully justified by the facts. The second drawback, related to the first, was the "status problem" on which this paper is focused. But here I had better begin by quoting directly from an interview with one not untypical clerk:

[67]

I like the work. There's only one thing I don't like about it. Everybody talks around here as if cash posting was the only job that counted. They take us off stations (ledgers) to work on cash, and they think that the stations can just take care of themselves. The work piles up and you get behind. Of course we've got to get the cash out, but I think the station work is just as important. And it's much more responsible. Cash posting, most of it, is just mechanical, but station work is a responsible job. You have to deal with the customers and with the stores, and if you don't do something right, someone is going to suffer. Of course that's true of cash posting, too, but there are a lot more things that a station clerk has to do. It's a more responsible job, and yet the station clerks get just the same pay as the cash posters. It seems that they ought to get just a few dollars more to show that the job is more important.

This states the chief recurring theme of the "status problem," and with this background let me return to crude statistics. Fourteen of the 19 ledger clerks interviewed said that the ledger clerks ought to get more pay than the cash posters, usually adding, like the clerk I have quoted, that they ought to get "just a couple of dollars a week more, to show that our job is more important." (The only ledger clerk who specifically disagreed with this view was O'Brien, whose peculiar social position has been described above.) Note that they were pretty well satisfied with their general pay level, at least in the sense that they felt they could not do better in another company. What they wanted was a pay differential between themselves and the cash posters.

Thirteen ledger clerks complained that they were "taken off their own jobs" to fill in on cash posting and other jobs, and 13 further complained that when this happened "they got behind in their own work." This calls for further comment. The ledger clerks did indeed get taken away from the ledgers. I could not determine independently whether their own work suffered, but I am quite ready to believe them when they say it did. Eight of the ledger clerks said they liked cash posting when they did it; it was not the cash posting itself that hurt, but being taken away from their "own" job. What is more, the bosses made no objection when they fell behind on the ledger work as a result of filling in on other jobs. They suffered not through criticism from the bosses but through damage to their own sense of closure—of "straightening things out." In fact, when they complained, the bosses seem to have taken the line: "You get paid to stay in here for eight hours a day. What odds does it make to you what kind of work you do? We don't bawl you out if you get behind"—a good example of the conflict between the "logic of management" and the "logic of the worker," especially identification with one's "own job." The ledger clerks summed the situation up by saying they got "pushed around."

Ten of the ledger clerks also claimed that "our boss won't stand up for us." Let us see what this means. When the supervisor or one of the other work groups in the division felt he needed extra help, he would go to the supervisor of the ledger clerks and ask for a certain number of women. The ledger boss seems always to have acceded to such requests and to have picked out the women whose turn it was to go off their own jobs. When they said their boss did not stand up for them, the clerks meant that he should not automatically have agreed but, rather, should have refused to release them if their own work might thereby suffer, especially as the women felt it was wrong for them to be taken off their own jobs at all. He allowed others, theoretically his equals, to originate action for him. It is hard to see how the ledger supervisor could have done otherwise, as it was standing policy in the division that the ledger clerks should serve as the main pool of floating labor. The members of a job group have an almost pathetic expectation that their boss should represent their interests and help them behave according to their own norms as against everybody else's norms, including management's. When he cannot or will not, the workers will try to find some other agent who can and will. This need for someone to exercise the "representative function," and not in matters of pay alone, is one of the strongest reasons for the formation and behavior of unions. Some of the ledger clerks had in fact complained to their union representative but, as they said, "nothing happened." All the union had done was to help get the group-leader job set up. The feeling that in this as in other cases the union had been inactive was probably one of the reasons why the workers voted to abandon the independent union for the CIO.

The fact that the ledger clerks were taken off their own jobs to fill in on others, especially on cash posting, while the cash posters did not fill in on the ledgers, led to the further comment, made by seven of the clerks, that "we can do what the others do, but they can't do what we do," which carried the inference that it was therefore wrong that both should get paid the same amount. Finally, eight of the ledger clerks mentioned the fact that some of the cash posters had refused "promotion" to the ledgers, the inference here being that if ledger-clerking were given the recognition it deserved, this would not have happened.

To round out the picture let me give a few of the attitudes of the cash posters bearing on the "status problem." Nine out of the ten cash posters said they liked their job, and six mentioned the friendly atmosphere. Of the specific job characteristics, four mentioned the pay as good, but only three thought the job was varied or interesting, and none talked about its responsibility. Four simply made the comment, "It's a job," that is, better than no job at all. As for their attitudes toward the ledger-clerk job, four said they did not like it or would not blame a girl for not taking it, and four (two of them the same as the first four) mentioned the fact that the pay was the same. Burke's comment was characteristic:

I wouldn't mind going on stations. . . . I probably will go on stations pretty soon. Cal is engaged and I will probably take her place. Jessie is senior but she will probably be married pretty soon, so unless they bring someone in from outside, I will probably get the job. I wouldn't turn it down. It's got more variety than cash posting. Some of them have turned it down. . . . I don't blame them for not taking station clerk. After all you don't get paid any more. But I wouldn't turn it down.

As a matter of fact, she did turn it down a little later. I asked her why, and she said, "It's too much trouble."

So far as I can speak of a general opinion among the cash posters, it was that the ledger-clerk job offered more variety and responsibility than cash posting—though less chance for moving around, which appealed greatly to some of the younger girls. But, as usual, the better job was the more demanding job, and unless the rewards, in this case the pay, were appropriate, no girl was to be blamed for not taking it.

The Status Problem

The problem described in this case was not an acute one. The ledger clerks felt aggrieved; some of them had complained to the supervisors and the union; nothing had been changed, but there was no further revolt. My impression was that the general morale in the division remained good. Nevertheless, I think the case illustrates some of the features that will be found in more serious cases of status conflict.

Why do I call this a status problem at all? I do so because the ledger clerks felt—and the cash posters somewhat grudgingly conceded—that they had the *better* job, that is, the higher rank or status. They felt their job had more variety—and on any definition of variety, it certainly had. They felt it had more responsibility—and according to their definition of responsibility, which is much like yours or mine, it certainly had. They felt it demanded more skill—they could do their own job and the cash posters' too. The transfer from cash poster to ledger clerk was held to be a promotion, and certainly in service to the company the ledger clerks were senior, sometimes by decades, to the cash posters. By all these standards the ledger clerk's job was of higher status than the cash poster's. The problem arose because by some other standards the ledger clerk's job was no better and even worse than the cash poster's. In particular, it brought no higher pay—and by emotional logic if one job is better than another, it ought to get better pay although not necessarily a great deal higher. And in some ways it had even less autonomy—for the ledger clerks were taken off their own jobs and put on others far more often than the cash posters, and without their having any say in the matter. As they said, they felt "pushed around." To add insult to injury, when they were taken off their own jobs, they were often put "down" on the cash posting job. The better job was not being recognized as such by the management or by some of the workers themselves, for a few of the cash posters had refused promotion to ledger clerk.

Let us now put the matter in somewhat more general terms. The status or rank of a job, in comparison with that of other jobs, is determined by the degree to which it realizes certain values. (More generally, the rank of a member or subgroup within a group is determined by the degree to which the member's or the subgroup's activities realize certain values.) Values, I hardly need to say, are *ideas*, ideas of what is *desirable*, even if not always what is in fact *desired*—what you ought to want, even if at heart you do not really want them. And values are many. There are probably few cases where rank is measured by a single value. In this particular division, these values were such things as pay, security, seniority, responsibility, knowledge and skill, opportunity for outside contact, and autonomy (not being "pushed around"). The values were not always called by these names, but they were present, none the less. A basis for an established *ranking* of jobs (or of the activities of persons or subgroups)—that is, agreement that Job *A* is better than Job *B* and worse than Job *C*—exists to the extent that the facts about the jobs are admitted, and the values are shared by the persons concerned. This sharing depends on the interaction between the persons and on the background of ideas (culture) they bring to the company from society at large. The interviews in the division showed that the facts about the different jobs were certainly common knowledge and that the values were very largely shared, that is, the members of each job group, in evaluating their own job or other jobs, mentioned the same values. It is true that a minority of the values were *not* shared. For one thing the younger girls, for obvious reasons, set more store by the chance to move around on the job than did the older women, whose feet got tired. Certainly there was very general agreement on the ranking of the different jobs. Even the cash posters were inclined to admit that the ledger job was, or should be, better than their own.

The fact that the values by which jobs are ranked are many has an important consequence. To the extent that one job is better than another job by *all* the important values of a group, to that extent its rank in relation to the other job is *established*. The job may present human problems but they will not be status problems. This condition was realized by some of the highest-status jobs of the division—jobs I have not described. No complaints were made involving comparison of these jobs with others. This condition was also realized by the lowest-status job, that of filing clerk. It was highly repetitive, physically tiring, low paid, closely supervised (little autonomy), and allowed little social contact or mobility. But since it was held by the girls newest to the division, all the status factors were "in line," and there was no status problem. While the filing clerks did not like their job, they felt, in effect, it was just and right they should have it.

But if one job is better than another by many of the values of a group but not by all, then there are apt to be status complaints and efforts to bring all the status factors "into line," that is, an effort on the part of the generally higher-ranking group to make their job better than the next lower on all counts. This was the situation of the ledger clerks in relation to the cash posters. Their demand that they should get paid a little more than the cash posters, and that they should not get "pushed around," can be interpreted as an effort to bring all the status factors in line in their favor.[4]

I can now raise some hypothetical questions. Suppose there are two work groups, each of which ranks higher than the other on about half the important values. Will the situation be stable, such that they rank as equals? Or will there be some form of jockeying for position? Not enough research has been done to answer this problem. (I sometimes feel that the laws of sociology are the laws of snobbery.)

And what if the ledger clerks had gotten a little more pay than the cash posters, but were still taken off their own jobs and put on posting? Would they be more satisfied or even madder? That is, what are the conditions of greatest status dissatisfaction? Again we do not know.

Let me mention one other obvious point. Some of the characteristics of a job are apt to be only dubiously rewarding. Take "responsibility." To the extent that a responsible job is a high-status job it is rewarding, but we all know that responsibility can also be a burden. One of the ledger clerks said:

I have done both cash posting and ledger work. There's a lot to cash posting, but when you've done your posting you're all through. At the end of the day there's not one thing you have to think of. But on the ledger you go home at the end of the day and you wonder whether you have done everything right. . . . And you think of what you have to do when you come in the next morning. It's really a more responsible job.

Other characteristics of a job are much less ambiguously rewarding: pay is an example, hence in part its great importance. When many of the characteristics of a job are ambiguous from the reward point of view, its unambiguous rewards must be increased if people are to be motivated to take it.

Some Implications for Administration

A case like this always has implications for administrative practice. I shall mention only two. It suggests, first, that in setting up wage differentials through job evaluation, a company and a union will minimize dissatisfaction if the relative pay assigned to different jobs reflects the relative evaluation of these jobs by the workers themselves. I believe that this is what successful job evaluation always accomplishes, though often under a smoke screen of "scientific" procedures. In practice, of course, this rule is hard to follow in detail. It might lead to the multiplication of small wage differentials, and thus to the creation of a wage structure difficult to administer; especially when company and union must consider not one small division but a multitude of jobs in the company as a whole, and when the workers in one division know pretty well what is going on in the rest of the company. A certain amount of jockeying for position is probably unavoidable.

The case suggests, second, that when arrangements must be made, as they often must, for workers to fill in on jobs other than their "own," there will be less dissatisfaction where holders of lower-status jobs fill in on higher-status ones than where, as in the division I have described, the opposite takes place. This rule, of course, comes into conflict with the strong union feeling that if a worker can do a certain job, even if only temporarily, he should have the pay of the job and seniority on the job; and it is true that the rule could easily be abused by management. Nevertheless I feel that these rules represent the human ideal and that wise administrators will seek to approach them as closely as circumstances will allow.

4

The Cash

Posters

SINCE the Western Electric researches,[1] few studies of single groups of workers have been reported, and even fewer that combined the measurement of individual effectiveness with the systematic observation of social behavior and the interviewing of all the group members. I shall briefly describe here a study that did combine these features. It is a study of the ten girl "cash posters" in an accounting division of a certain company, and it formed part of a study of the division as a whole, which I carried on from December, 1949, through April, 1950. Since it deals with only one group and that group had only ten members, it can hardly hope to establish general hypotheses about small group behavior. Several such studies, made with comparable methods, might hope to do so, and they would provide the indispensable background to more macroscopic studies of worker behavior, made by questionnaires. But by itself the present one can only be called a case study of the relations between repetitive work, individual behavior, and social organization in a clerical group.

Reprinted from *American Sociological Review*, 19 (1954), 724–733, by permission of the American Sociological Association. Certain paragraphs have been left out because they repeated information reported in the preceding article, "Status among Clerical Workers."

The division contained sixty persons, doing several different clerical jobs. I am concerned here with only ten of the workers and only one of the jobs—the ten girls that did the "cash posting."

The cash-posting job was next to the bottom of the grades that made up the usual channel of advancement in the division. At the time of the study, a poster made $42.23 for a forty-hour, five-day week. The posters were all high school graduates, young in age, and relatively new to the company, as promotion to cash poster from lower grades came fairly rapidly. The reason for this was that the company required girls to leave the company when they married, and most marrying takes place at the ages represented by the cash posters. So vacancies on the job were frequent, but promotion to higher grades took place much more slowly. None of the girls looked forward to cash posting or to work in the company as a permanent job.

The day before a girl left the company to get married, the others, in the afternoon "relief" period, decorated her desk and covered it with candy and presents. Since none of the supervisors felt he should take it on, the girls assigned me the job of handing out the presents and, far more unnerving, of pinning a corsage on the girl who was leaving. In this way I came to be of some use in division society.

One supervisor, who also had special clerical work to do, was in charge of cash posters, and he reported to the division head.

All the reader needs to know about the company is that it had a large number of customers to whom it sent out monthly bills. It was the business of the division to account for the payment of these bills. Because there were so many of them, they were not all sent out on the first of the month but some on every working day. The bills were printed by machine from punch-cards, whereupon the cards were brought to the division and placed in files, ten in number, which ran in four rows up and down the floor. Although old-fashioned bookkeeping had long disappeared from the company, its language was still preserved, and so the files were called "ledgers," and the cards, since they represented unpaid bills, were called the "arrears."

As customers paid their bills, their cash and checks, together with the bill stubs, went to the cashier's office, not on the floor. There the receipts were added, and from there bundles of stubs, each wrapped in an adding-machine tape showing the total of each bundle, came to the desk occupied by the posters' supervisor, which was close in front of my own. He arranged them on the desk in order of size. A cash poster took the first bundle in order, went to the appropriate ledger and, flipping through the arrears cards, pulled out the cards whose printed numbers corresponded to those on the stubs in her "tape." This was called "pulling cash" or more formally "cash posting"—another survival of the language of ledger books. The removal of a card from the arrears meant that a customer would not be billed again for that amount next month.

When she had pulled all the cards corresponding to stubs in her bundle ("tape"), the cash poster brought cards, stubs, and tape back to the supervisor's desk, took the first new tape, and repeated the process. The pulled cards and tape were sent down to the machine room, where the cards were mechanically counted and added. This addition revealed any failure of cards and tape to balance and thus any mistakes—wrong cards pulled—that the poster had made. Since each poster kept a record of which tapes she had worked on, it was easy to calculate how many cards she pulled and how many errors she made per hour of work. These output and accuracy records were written up daily and placed in a drawer of the supervisor's desk for the posters to see. The cash posters did look at them, and in summary form they were made available to me.

Ninety per cent of all bills were paid in the exact amount shown on the stub. In the case of over- or underpayments, the posters had to perform certain operations on the cards besides simply pulling them, but for the sake of brevity these will not be described. The number of such payments in a tape, the number of stubs in a tape, and the degree to which the cards corresponding to the stubs were concentrated in a single ledger affected the speed at which the tape could be completed. But the order in which the tapes were picked up equalized these variations, in the long run, among the cash posters.

Besides cash posting, the girls spent some time every afternoon working on "collection stubs." This was a job of determining, before the company put pressure on delinquent customers, whether long-overdue bills had been recently paid. No output records could be kept of this work. When they finished it, the girls returned to pulling what they illogically called "next day's cash."

Cash posting was the only "production" job in the division—the only one it had to stay caught up with every day. And no girl was accepted as a cash poster unless, by the end of her training period, she could pull, on the average, 300 cards an hour. This was called the "quota," and it served as a standard of minimum output. The records show that all the girls did, on the average, make the quota; most of them did not find this hard to do, and some of them made a great deal more. In theory, the supervisor "bawled out" a girl if she failed for two days in a row to make the quota. In fact, he rarely had to, and when he did the bawling out was gentle. But neither did he praise a girl when she made a high record, and there was no incentive payment. The public output records themselves seemed to suffice to keep output up. One of my field notes reads as follows: "Murphy, LoPresti,[2] and others gathered around their boss's desk looking at the output records with cries of 'I made it!'" The fact is that cash posting looked to an outsider like a hard and dull job. A number of girls who were offered it had turned it down. The supervisors wisely felt that they would have a still harder time getting recruits and getting out production if they tried to bear down on a group of young girls like this one.

The girls liked their immediate boss. He never tried to use "human relations skills." He was frank and outspoken when they broke the rules, but they felt they knew where they stood with him and said—which is the highest of all praise from workers—"He's fair." Or even, "He's a *man!*" For his part he said, "I have a good bunch of girls working for me. I really don't think you could get a better one anywhere. Of course, some of them carry the others. They're not all equally fast. But they do a good job, even the slowest of them. Some of them are so good they really ought to have something better than they have now."

The cash posters were on their feet most of the day, moving, "tapes" in hand, from ledger to ledger. This gave them many chances for social contact, both with members of their own job group and with other workers, many of whom also worked at the ledgers. They made the most of their opportunities, especially as they were convinced they could do their work without concentrating on it—they could work and talk at the same time. In theory, talking was discouraged. In practice, the supervisors made little effort to stop it, except when it got so loud they thought it disturbed some of the older workers. In part, they felt that they could not stop it; in part, that talking did not always get in the way of work. As one of them said, "If you get them on the carpet for talking or making mistakes, you usually find that the girl who talks most or has made the mistake is one of your best girls."

The cash posters spent most of their time on their feet, but they were also assigned small tables, four in one place and six in another, where they could work on collection stubs or where, if they had to pull many cards in a single ledger, they could bring the card tray to work on it seated. Assignment to neighboring tables was an important factor in the formation of friendships. In the last half-hour of the last working day of the year, all tables were reassigned in accordance with the supervisor's plan, secret until then. The girls took their new seats to the accompaniment of squealing and giggling. This move was supposed, among other things, to break up cliques that might get in the way of work.

The characteristics of the cash-posting job should by now be clear. It was an exceedingly routine and repetitive clerical job, which could be done with little concentration by girls whose main interests were not in the job itself and who were not deeply concerned with promotion in the company. In view of the fact that it required no previous outside training, such as stenography, it paid well. It required no cooperation among the girls but allowed much social interaction. Little pressure was put on the girls to work fast, and morale was generally good.

Attitudes toward the Job

I opened the interviews with the question, "How do you like your job?" And nine out of the ten cash posters said they liked it, the next comment usually being, "It's a job," i.e., better than no job at all. Since the interviews were nondirective, I got no further systematic information on the reasons why they liked the job, but I suspect that the frequency with which they spontaneously mentioned some of its features is a pretty good index of their importance to the posters. Only one feature of the job was mentioned favorably by more than half (6) of the girls, and that was the general friendliness of the group and the "niceness" of the people in the division. The only other attitude expressed by more than half (6) may be summed up as: "I do my work and get my quota and that's all."

A characteristic comment was Elizabeth Rourke's:

Then there was an opening on cash posting. I learned the job in three weeks. Most of them take four. I got so I could do 297, so they qualified me and forgot about the last three. After all, a job's a job. It really isn't hard to get the quota. Of course, you have to keep working, but if you do, you don't have any trouble getting over 300. That's all I worry about. As long as I get over 300 I don't care. Sometimes they bawl you out, if you don't make 300 two days in a row. But half the time I think Al Johnson (former boss of the cash posters) is kidding. He says, "Aren't you ever going to stop talking?" I have to talk, and I think that a lot of the time it helps you to talk. You speed up a little afterwards so's to be sure to make your quota. It makes you feel better. Half the time you can do your work with your eyes and talk at the same time. The other day I wasn't thinking of what I was doing—I guess I was thinking of something else—and I made 400. I don't usually do that, but Dotty Murphy does it all the time. It's just as easy for her to get 400 as it is for me to get 300. But if you do make 400 no one says anything. You don't get anything for it. You don't get any more pay, so what good does it do you to get 400? Then they might expect you to get 400 all the time.

This last remark is characteristic of situations where restriction of output exists. And other remarks of the same kind were made, for instance: "If you pull a lot of cards, you spoil the job for the other girls. They're expected to pull that many too." In point of fact, no one in the room remembered a time when the quota had been anything but 300; it had never been raised. It served as a floor under output, but a glance at the output records later in this paper will show that output varied greatly above the quota. No group norm put a ceiling on output. A couple of years before, when relations between the posters and a former division head were strained, there may have been some restriction. And when Lillian Granara became the first cash poster in recent history to pull over 400 cards an hour, she said she was criticized for doing so. But such behavior seemed to have disappeared by the time of my study. When Murphy began to match Granara's performance, she escaped attack. Only the two posters, Asnault and Burke, who had been on the job in the old days expressed, in interviews, disapproval of the speed at which others were working; and on the floor no girl brought effective pressure on any other to keep her output down.

The attitudes characteristic of restriction of output were present in the group; the thing itself was not, certainly not as an organized group practice. But neither did the girls feel under any pressure to work particularly fast. Indeed the lack of pressure may have been the very thing that helped some of them to work, in fact, very fast indeed.

Social Organization

Besides forming a job-group, the cash posters formed a distinct social group, in the following sense. The interaction count showed that only one cash poster (Burke) interacted more often with members of other job groups than with her own. The so-called ledger clerks formed the largest job-group in the division and the one next above the posters in the ladder of promotion, though their pay was the same. Only one of the ledger clerks interacted more often with the cash posters than with members of her own group. This was O'Brien, the youngest of the ledger clerks and the one who had been most recently a cash poster. This tendency of the cash posters to interact with one another took place in spite of the fact that nothing in the work itself or in the layout of the room prevented their interacting more often with members of other job-groups.

Within this over-all unity of the posters, subgroups could be mapped out both by sociometric choice and by interaction. The sociogram result-ing from answers to the interview question: "Who are your close friends in here?" is shown in Figure 1. It reveals two main trios: Donovan, LoPresti, and Murphy on one side and Asnault, Coughlin, and Granara on the other, with Rourke a link between the two. The second trio was linked by Coughlin to O'Brien, the newest of the ledger clerks. Burke,

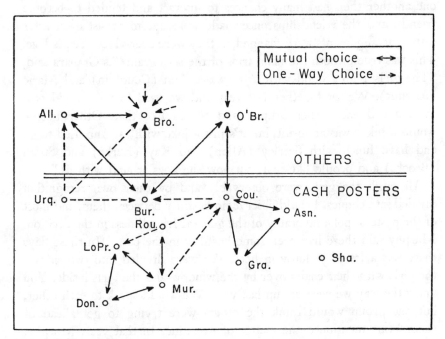

Figure 1.   Cash posters: sociogram.

though generally popular and friendly, did not express close friendship with any cash poster but was attached to a ledger-clerk clique centering around Brooks. Urquhart, the newest cash poster, chose three of this clique but was chosen by none. And Shaugnessy, a true isolate, neither chose nor was chosen.

That these choices represented real social groupings is best shown by data of another sort. Once in the morning and once in the afternoon, the girls left the floor for ten minutes to take their "relief" periods. At these times the same girls regularly gathered at the same places. O'Brien, Coughlin, Asnault, Granara, and Rourke regularly went "downstairs," and Shaugnessy attached herself to them. Murphy, LoPresti, and Donovan went to the "washroom." Burke went to the "vault" with the group that included Allen and Brooks, and more and more often, as time went on, Urquhart attached herself to this group. Not surprisingly, friendship choice and interaction off the floor were closely related.

The most important determinant of clique formation was the position of a poster's table during her first year on the job. Girls who sat near one another then had many chances to interact and tended to become friends, and the friendships once made were apt to persist even after seating arrangements were changed, as they were every New Year's Eve. This was true of both the main trios of the sociogram. As Granara said, "The girls I go around with in here are Ann (Coughlin) and Marie (Asnault). We sat together last year and we used to talk. We'd pass by and call each other 'stupid' and things like that. Other people would think it was an insult, but it's just a joke with us. Ann used to go and have lunch with Shirley (Allen) and Kay (Burke) and Susan (Brooks) and people like that, but now she goes around with us."

Although the girls were observably and by their own recognition divided into cliques, I could observe no hostility between them, and most of the posters spoke favorably of the general friendliness in the division. Murphy said there had been some hostility in the past: "In those days there was a lot of jealousy in here. We were divided into two sides— the girls with their chairs over by the window and the girls inside. You know the way we were set up last year. We would speak to each other, but one group would think the others were trying to get ahead of them." She mentioned the matter of overtime. In that year, Murphy, Donovan, LoPresti, and Urquhart sat together "inside," the others "by the window." While I was in the room, the posters got no overtime work.

Just as I could observe no hostility between the posters' cliques, so I could observe no systematic differences between them in off-the-job activities. But there were some differences between the two groups— they might almost be called moieties—that provided the larger social structure of the division. The older women were not much interested in organized social activities, and leadership in them fell to the younger ledger clerks, notably Brooks and O'Brien. When the office gave a party, these two were elected cochairmen. Two bowling teams from the office occasionally played against one another, and Brooks and O'Brien were captains of the teams. A tall and beautiful girl and a good bowler, Brooks received more friendship choices than any other person in the division, and was fourth in total interactions. O'Brien interacted more than anyone save Murphy, whom I shall speak of later. The sociogram shows that each headed a different circle of friends, though there were important links of friendship, notably that of Burke with O'Brien, between the two groups.

Compared to the O'Brien group, the Brooks group contained a higher proportion of girls that lived in the suburbs of the city—particularly the "better" suburbs—and they engaged in what were, in their view, somewhat more sophisticated activities, for instance, a skiing week-end. O'Brien, Coughlin, Asnault, and Granara were asked on this party but did not go. As one of the Brooks group (Allen) said: "I used to think that city girls were sophisticated, but when I came in here I found that the country girls knew twice as much as the city girls. By country girls I mean people like Susan Brooks, Kay Burke and myself. Kay likes classical music. The city girls haven't been anywhere, and all they are interested in is getting married when they are eighteen, sitting at home, and going out to the movies once a week. When I talk about music, they just say, 'Don't say those names to me.'" It is easy to exaggerate these differences and in any event they were not very important to the cash posters, as only two of their number were members of the Brooks group: Burke centrally and Urquhart peripherally.

All I need say in summary of this brief section on social organization is that certain familiar relationships between the distributions of interaction, interpersonal sentiment, and differences in off-the-job activity have turned up here as they turn up in many observational studies of working groups.[3] Friendship choice was associated with interaction off the job. Cliques, defined by frequent interaction and friendship choice between members, tended to display mutual hostility and different styles of off-the-job activity, though the tendencies were slight. Note also the influence of "external" factors, such as differences in social background and assignments to seats and job, in setting initial values of interaction and activity variables.

Individual Effectiveness

I turn now to the behavior of individual cash posters, especially in relation to effectiveness on the job. Table 1 summarizes the quantitative data I obtained in the study. The "Time on job" column gives in years

Table 1. Cash Posters

	Age	Time on job	Late- ness	Cards per hour	Errors per hour	Interaction January 9–26				Sociometric choices		
						IN	OUT	TOTAL	RANGE	IN	OUT	TOTAL
Asnault	22	3–5	6	363	0.57	38	8	46	13	2	0	2
Burke	26	2–5	3	306	0.66	11	53	64	24	2	3	5
Coughlin	20	2–0	4	342	0.40	38	20	58	17	4	1	5
Donovan	20	1–9	7	308	0.79	20	10	32	14	2	0	2
Granara	21	1–3	6	438	0.65	27	10	40	16	2	0	2
LoPresti	25	–11	8	317	0.03	40	8	56	14	3	0	3
Murphy	19	–7	0	439	0.62	52	34	92	22	3	0	3
Rourke	17	–4	3	323	0.82	33	27	60	16	1	0	1
Shaugnessy	23	–2	16	333	0.44	13	2	16	9	0	0	0
Urquhart	18	–2	11	361	0.49	21	9	32	13	0	0	0

and months the length of time each girl had been cash posting at the time I began the study. The "Lateness" column gives the total number of times each girl was late in the five months of the study. Absences are not included, because they seemed, far more than latenesses, to be determined by forces beyond the girls' control. The "Cards per hour" column gives the five-months' average of output. The output of only one of the girls, Urquhart, showed the characteristics of a learning curve by being higher every successive month. "Errors per hour" is the same kind of figure as "Cards per hour." The "Interaction" columns show the number of times a girl was seen talking to another girl during the period in which I counted interactions by the method described above. The figures show the times she talked to another cash poster ("In") and the times she talked to some other worker ("Out"). These are raw scores. The "Total" figures are corrected to make up for the absences of certain of the girls. "Range" is the number of *different* persons a girl talked to. "Sociometric choices" are those *received* by a girl, either from other cash posters ("In") or from other workers in the division ("Out"). The way choices were *given* is shown in the sociogram (Figure 1).

Ten cases is a small number on which to base statistical relationships. Yet there is at least one significant correlation among these figures: frequency of interaction is significantly related to sociometric choices received.[4] Popular girls talked, and were talked to, a great deal. This finding may seem to run counter to one of Bales and his associates. Tabulating the data from twelve meetings of five-man discussion groups, these investigators appear to have found an over-all relationship between interactions *initiated* and "liking" choices received. But the *top* men in interaction initiated were not highly chosen on a "liking" question. Indeed they were only third, on the average, in likes, and received *most* dislikes. Unlike my finding, high interactors were not popular. What can account for the difference in the findings?

The members of the Bales groups were working on problems, common to all the members, which they were to solve by discussion. In moving towards a solution, the most frequent interactors seem to have taken control of their groups. At least they were the most highly chosen on the question, "Who gave the most guidance?" And as Bales writes, "The more 'directive' and 'constricting' the quality of activity, the more likely it is to arouse negative reactions."[5] Or as I should put it, the authority, recognized or unrecognized, of one person over another will tend to cut down the other's liking for the person in authority.[6]

Unlike the Bales groups, the cash posters were working on individual jobs. Their interactions were largely "social"; not directed to common tasks. The person in authority over them was their boss; no one of them had much occasion to exercise control over the others. These differences in the conditions under which the groups were brought together go far to account for differences in the findings. Let us remember Claude Bernard's dictum: "The experimenter will be convinced that phenomena can never be contradictory if they are observed under the same conditions, and he will know that, if they show variations, this necessarily results from the intervention or interference of other conditions, which mask or modify these phenomena."[7]

To return to the data on the cash posters, one relationship that would be important if it did exist is in fact absent. Contrary to the theory that talking interfered with work, the figures show no correlation—for this kind of work and this kind of workers—between output and frequency of interaction. Indeed the lowest producer and the highest were the two most frequent talkers.

Inspection of the table shows that a girl whose score was extreme on one of the measures was also extreme on some of the others. The number of individuals is too small to establish as general hypotheses the relationships thus suggested. Instead I shall briefly describe a few of the posters as each exhibiting a distinct constellation of traits, in the hope that other researchers will discover similar constellations.

The Isolate

Mildred Shaugnessy was late more often than the others. She interacted far less than they. She named no one, and was named by no one, as a close friend. Her low interaction was not just the result of her having been in the division a short time. Urquhart had been a cash poster just as briefly, interacted quite a lot, named three girls as friends, and was gaining acceptance. Shaugnessy was the only girl the others expressed any hostility toward, usually giving the reason that she made personal remarks she thought were funny but they did not. She came from a "poor" section of the city, and appeared to this observer less well dressed than the others. She was not married, but it was believed in the division that she was not living at home, that she had had some kind of quarrel with her family. In her interview, she expressed more attitudes that differed from the modal ones in her group than did any of the others. In particular, she expressed general approval of all the bosses, in spite of the fact that they often "called" her for being late—the other girls were much more selective in their approval—and she said that talking got in the way of posting. She had to concentrate; the other girls were more apt to feel that talking helped work. How far this was a rationalization of the circumstance that people did not in fact talk to her I cannot tell. As a job she would like to have, she mentioned a telephone switchboard of her own in a small hotel, that is, an isolated job. Other studies have found a relationship between absenteeism and failure to be accepted as a member of an organized group at work.[8] In this case I believe lateness to be more closely linked to acceptance. If one is not liked at work, one will be that much less eager to go to work—though Shaugnessy did not make this connection. She has since left the employ of the company to get another job.

The Low Producer

Catherine Burke was a tall, heavy girl, but I doubt that her physical slowness had much to do with the fact that her output was lower than that of any other cash poster. She had been a cash poster longer than any other girl but one; she expressed no liking for the job, but she had several times refused "promotion" to ledger clerk, saying "It's too much trouble." (The job did not carry any more pay.) Her choice and interaction pattern reflected the facts that she was popular and that many of her friendships were with girls who had moved out of cash posting. Only one poster talked more than she did, but unlike all the others, Burke talked far more with other members of the division than with posters. She tied with Coughlin on sociometric choices, but again, and unlike Coughlin, her choices came more from the others than from the posters. She talked to more *different* people not only than any other poster but than any other person in the whole division. She was also the only cash poster who had any higher education—two years at a Catholic junior college. She got a job in the company because her father had worked in it for many years. The family had done well, lived in a "good" suburb, and her brother had an excellent job in public relations. By reputation she had the most active social life outside the office; she belonged to more outside organizations and spoke of herself as "the traveler of the division": "In the summer I'm always coming in on Friday with a bag and coming in with it again on Monday morning." Popular though she was, she believed in keeping her social life at the office and her social life outside separate. "I don't believe in having your friends come from the office. Most of my close friends are not in here. They are the girls I went to college with. When I talk to them, I find out that I am getting a lot more pay than they are. I tell them that cash posting is something pretty wonderful. I don't let them in on the truth." Perhaps the best way to sum up this fine and able girl is to say that she was bored with the work of the division and wasted on it. Even more than the others, her deepest interests were outside cash posting and indeed the company—just as her interactions were.

She was also a survivor of days when relations with the bosses were much less good than they were in my time. As she said, "Some of the girls that have come in recently think that we (Asnault and herself) are silly. They try to get four or five hundred and walk their legs off. I tell them they don't know how we had to fight to get things the way they are now." She has since left the company to enter a Catholic religious order.

The Accurate Worker

Helen LoPresti's record was remarkable for her extraordinarily small number of mistakes. This cannot be related to her social position; her interaction and sociometric scores were in no way extreme. She herself explained her accuracy by an experience in her past. During the war she had worked for a firm, famous for its efficiency and high-pressure methods, that runs a chain of department stores. As she said, "I worked for a man who was a buyer in jewelry, and kept his figures for him. If I didn't have them right, he would be out hundreds of dollars. He couldn't do the work himself. He had to trust me. So when I work here, I try to be accurate . . . and of course that slows me down on production." Intelligent and conscientious, she won rapid promotion in the firm and became supervisor of a small number of other girls. She went on to say: "The girls were inexperienced, and it got so that I was doing all the work. I tried to do it all myself. I was too efficient for my own good. I would do the work after hours and take it home with me. Finally it got to be too much for me. I'm sensitive. I was worrying about everything and I couldn't stand it, so I quit." A girl who wants everything done just right may have trouble delegating work to others. Certainly she is under specially heavy strain in a firm like the one LoPresti worked for. Not only does the firm put her under pressure, but she puts it on herself. Cash posting allowed LoPresti to do everything right without being under pressure, and she liked it: "You have nothing to worry about. You do your work and that's that. I worry about a lot of things. Am I normal, you must be asking yourself? Well, *am* I normal?"—Interviewer: "Don't be silly." (Giggle from both.)—LoPresti: "I don't want to get into a spot like I was in at ———." (Note the interviewer's nondirective technique.) LoPresti has since been promoted in the company.

The High Producer

I could never develop any subtle social or psychological theory to account for the behavior of Dorothy Murphy. For me, she simply had a high activity rate: she had the highest output among the posters, and she also talked more than anyone else in the room. Her interview was the longest; I had to stop it so that she could take her "relief" period. She was never late. A stocky girl, she never, unlike her nearest rival, gave the slightest appearance of making an effort to work fast, and she herself felt that if she concentrated she did not do so well. It may be significant that she reported a very energetic mother, active in association work, and a father who probably, as production manager of a factory, had a better job than the fathers of the other cash posters. She was easily intelligent enough to go to college. Both her brothers had gone, and her family could have afforded it, but she did not want to. And yet she cannot have been without ambition. Although she liked her present job, she was the only poster who had formally applied for transfer to some other division. She has since transferred to a division where the chances for advancement were greater than they were in ours, and as a result this very effective girl has moved higher in the company than any of the former cash posters.

The Popular Girl

Ann Coughlin received most sociometric choices from other cash posters and tied with Burke in total choices received. In other respects her record was not remarkable. She talked often but not very often; her output was neither low nor high—and this fact itself may be significant. Unlike Murphy, she had wanted to go to college, but her family could not afford it. She can best be described as a sweetheart— strong in all the less sophisticated and more familial virtues. She stands in sharp contrast to the social isolate, and she was the only girl who said, "I *love* my job." She has since left the company to get married.

I have tried to describe a small group of working girls—a study clinical in intent, but employing some systematic observations of work effectiveness and social organization. I have described the attitudes of the girls toward a job that was highly repetitive, done without restriction of output or pressure for production from supervision. The analysis of social organization brought out again some familiar generalizations. Finally, I have tried to describe certain constellations of traits in individual behavior, related to work effectiveness, to social position in the group and outside, and to the worker's past history, that may prove suggestive to other researchers. In conclusion, let me express the hope that the kind of research described here will not be wholly abandoned in favor of more macroscopic investigations.

5

Status

Congruence

I<small>N</small> this paper I shall try to present an idea by which various different forms of human behavior may be usefully brought into relation with one another. This idea has been called *status congruence.*

I shall begin by describing the situation in which I first found myself obliged to think in terms of status congruence. I had seen many situations that might have brought the idea to my mind earlier, but the fact was that they did not do so. Interested in the behavior of workers in the new semimechanized clerical processes—a subject at that time little studied—I made in 1950 an observational and interviewing investigation of a single department, the Customers' Accounting Department, of a company I shall call the Eastern Utilities Co. It consisted of sixty workers engaged in keeping accounts of the payments made by the 450,000 customers who received electric power from the company.

I became particularly interested in the relations between two of the groups in the department: the cash posters and the ledger clerks. The former took bundles of "stubs" representing paid bills, went to files (the "ledgers") containing punch-cards from which the bills had originally been printed by machine, ran through the cards and removed

Given as a talk to Professor Georges Friedmann's seminar at the École Pratique des Hautes Études, Paris, in April 1956, and published in French translation as "La Congruence du Status," *Journal de Psychologie*, 54 (1957), 22–34. Reprinted, with minor changes, by permission of the Editors.

those whose numbers were the same as those printed on the "stubs." This removal prevented the customers being billed again for amounts they had paid; and the removed cards, when added by machine, accounted for the company's receipts. I need not go into technical details. The cash-posting job was highly specialized and repetitive, requiring only a simple coordination of eye and hand. But it allowed much moving about and presented many opportunities for conversation with others while the work was going on. The young girls who did the job enjoyed these features of it and took full advantage of them.

The ledger clerks did everything, other than what the cash posters did, necessary to keep the customers' accounts in order. For instance, they kept addresses up to date; they recorded changes in the type of service the customers received; they dealt with overpayments and underpayments of bills. Over the telephone they answered customers' questions about their accounts. The ledger clerks' job was more varied than the cash posters'; in their words it was more "responsible," by which they meant that a mistake could do more damage; and the ledger clerks were older and had greater seniority in the company than the cash posters. In fact to be transferred from poster to ledger clerk was considered a promotion. And yet the ledger clerks received the same weekly wage as the posters, and from time to time they were, as they said, "taken off their own work and put down on posting." The company felt that the current posting had to be completed every day if the work of the department was not to fall badly in arrears; and the ledger clerks provided the pool of additional labor by which this could be accomplished.

In their interviews with me, both cash posters and ledger clerks said they liked their jobs, the job security the company offered, and the absolute amount of their wages. In these respects, they felt they could not have done better in another company. But within this general satisfaction, the ledger clerks—not the posters—had two specific complaints to make. They felt it was wrong that they should be taken off their own jobs and put on posting (note the proprietary feeling about the jobs), and they felt that their pay should be just a little higher than the posters': "We ought to get just a couple of dollars (a week) more to show that our job is more important."

This sounds like a familiar problem in wage differentials; and so it is, but I want to put it in a more general framework that will allow us to see that problems of the same species arise over matters other than wages. Workers evaluate every aspect of a job in terms of the degree to which its characteristics, or what I shall call its *status factors*, realize values brought to the workplace from the culture of the society at large. These values are many. In the Customers Accounting Division, some of the values were variety, responsibility, seniority, pay, and what I shall call autonomy: the degree to which a worker is left alone to do what he considers his own job. The workers feel that one job is "better" or has higher status than another, if its characteristics realize these values to a higher degree than the other. More than this, they feel that if one job is better than another in most of its characteristics, it ought to be better in all of them. If it is not, the workers will complain and try to see that action is taken to render the job better than the other on all counts. The ledger-clerk job was "better" than cash posting by the values of variety, responsibility, and seniority, but equal in pay and worse in autonomy: unlike the cash posters, the ledger clerks were taken off their own jobs. Their complaints were addressed to bringing all the status factors of their job "in line" with one another: to making their pay and autonomy better than those of the cash posters, just as the other characteristics of their jobs were better.

There were two job-groups in the department which made no complaints of this kind. The cycle-balance clerks had to strike, once a month, the balance for the whole clerical operation; and if the accounts failed to balance they had to discover and correct the error. These clerks were paid more than any of the others; they were most senior in service, and they possessed the greatest knowledge and skill. All the status factors of their job were "in line." The file clerks had to keep up to date a special address file. Their work was inherently repetitive and dull; it allowed little movement, and being physically isolated, little social contact. But it got less pay than the other jobs, and the youngest and least senior girls held it. They did not like the job, but they never said it was unfair that it should have the characteristics it did, or that they should hold it. Again, all the status factors of this job were "in line." I infer that complaints about the relative standing of jobs are made only when their status factors are "out of line," and that workers feel "in-line-ness" to be the condition of relative and distributive justice (not necessarily of absolute justice).

The human tendency I am describing here has long been recognized. Speaking of the parties of oligarchy and democracy in the Greece of his time, Aristotle said: "For the one party, if they are unequal in one respect, for example wealth, consider themselves to be unequal in all; and the other party, if they are equal in one respect, for example free birth, consider themselves to be equal in all."[1] More recently Bertrand de Jouvenel has written: "What men find just is to preserve between themselves, as regards whatever is in question, the same relations that exist between them as regards something else."[2] I am certainly not arguing that the theory I am putting forward is new, but only that (like other theories) modern social science has rediscovered it; and that when it is made explicit, it is a great help in understanding certain kinds of behavior in American industry and elsewhere.

Indeed it has been rediscovered several different times by modern social science. Just before the last war, the social psychologist Benoit-Smullyan posited a tendency toward what he called *status equilibration*: a tendency in persons and groups to bring those characteristics of their activities that are "worse" by cultural standards up to the level of those that are "better."[3] He posited an effort to equilibrate by bringing "up" what is "down" rather than by bringing "down" what is "up"—and this is just what the ledger clerks tried to do. But in that case, the "down" factors were in the minority. If they had been in the majority, we do not know what the direction of effort would have been. For myself, before I ever had read Benoit-Smullyan's paper, I had called status equilibration *status in-line-ness*, which is graphic and corresponds to everyday American speech, but is otherwise cumbersome. In a paper I shall speak of later, Lenski calls it *status crystallization*.[4] Perhaps a better, because shorter, term has been suggested by Stuart Adams in still another report of research. He calls status equilibration *status congruence*.[5] Or better, he would say that the status of the cycle-balance clerks in the Eastern Utilities Co. was *more* congruent than that of the ledger clerks. But whatever the names they use, these men are all talking about the same phenomenon.

Now let me bring up some forms of behavior on which, it seems to me, our very simple theory of status congruence throws some light. Or rather, because in one way we already understand these things, forms of behavior which our theory helps bring into relation with one another. One of them is what has been called *status anxiety*. In the course of moving a clerical department in the Hawthorne Plant of the Western Electric Co. from one room to another, one of the men workers was assigned a desk across the aisle from the rest of the department, his only companions being three women. The reason for his being placed there was simply that someone had to sit across the aisle, and he was known to be friendly with the women. But he knew, himself, that the women were in a lower pay grade than his own and were about to be transferred to a shop department. At the same time, he discovered that his name had been omitted from the company telephone directory, in which all office workers with jobs of his own rank or above were normally listed. The omission of his name was wholly an accident. But the conclusion he drew from all these signs was that he was about to be demoted and assigned to the shop, the latter being also a social demotion. His anxiety became so great that he was unable to work.[6]

Now let us put the matter in somewhat more abstract terms. The new characteristics of his job—his association with the women, the omission of his name from the telephone directory—were signs pointing downward. He assumed that the other characteristics of his job, social and financial, would also go downward soon. That is, he was himself thinking in terms of a theory of status congruence. If a group of workers on a particular job feel that the status factors of the job ought to be made congruent, and get angry if they are not made so, an individual worker may assume that the status factors of his job will be made congruent, and may get anxious if this implies a demotion. In their different ways, both have adopted the belief that in social affairs status congruence is both the way things are and the way things ought to be. You may say that the behavior of the man placed across the aisle with the women illustrates the theory of social symbols as applied to industrial workers. All I am saying is that the theory of social symbols *is* a theory of congruence.

I am not at all suggesting that the usual reaction to status incongruence is anxiety. More often, I suspect, it is the one illustrated in a weak way by the ledger clerks: a demand for change and reform. There is evidence for this outside the field of industry. As I have said, Gerhard Lenski gives the name of status crystallization to the thing we have agreed to call status congruence, and he succeeds in relating the political opinions of persons in the United States to degrees of status crystallization. The status factors he takes into account are four: income, occupation, education, and ethnicity. Let me explain the last. The United States is not organized in social classes in the European sense. Instead, a large number of ways exist of assigning people rather finely differentiated degrees of social status. And one of the ways, though one only, depends on a person's ultimate ethnic origin, even though (or partly because) the origin now lies as much as three hundred years in the past. Thus a person of English Protestant ancestry ranks rather better, so far as ethnicity is concerned, than, for instance, a person of Catholic French-Canadian origin. Of course on other criteria the latter may rank higher than the former, which raises precisely the question of status congruence. At any rate, Lenski shows statistically that people with high status congruence tend to vote for the Republican Party—that is, for what is the nearest thing to a conservative party in the United States—and people with low status congruence for the Democratic Party.[7] (Note: not low status but low status congruence.) No doubt differences of income are the best predictors of party alignment, but for finer degrees of prediction status congruence must be added to it. That is, both rich men of English Protestant origin and poor farmers or poor French-Canadians (status congruents) would be apt to vote Republican. And rich Jews or well-educated Puerto Ricans (status incongruents) would be apt to vote Democratic. I think this point has long been appreciated by students of political behavior. I am not trying to say anything new but to bring a number of bits of old knowledge together in a single scheme.

But let us leave politics and the larger society and return to the smaller society of the plant. When a supervisor or a social scientist notices a group or an individual that is incongruent in status, he may expect or predict some kind of "trouble": complaints, anxiety, or something else. The next question is: What kind of trouble? For a long time I have held, though I do not propose to demonstrate it here, that some of the most general propositions of sociology will turn out to be similar in kind to those of economics, though applicable to somewhat different data. At any rate, let us make a quasi-economic classification of the status factors that are in fact important in American industrial jobs. The first kind of status factors I shall call *investments*. These include such things as age, sex, seniority, skill, ethnicity. These are things that the worker brings to the job, some through the accidents of birth (age, sex, ethnicity), others through working long and hard at a particular trade or in a particular plant (skill, seniority). At any rate, they are things that he can at the moment do little or nothing to change, and he thinks of them as long-term investments. ("I have *put in* a lot of time at this plant.") The second kind of status factor I shall call current rewards or *income:* pay, the interest of the job, the respect of other workers. They are, so to speak, current returns on

[96]

investment. A third kind I shall call current *costs:* fatigue and limitations on free time are examples. And there is a final kind whose nature is ambiguous. Responsibility is an example. A responsible job is in one sense burdensome, and in another sense and for many people intensely rewarding.

Now let me restate the theory of status congruence. The equilibrium condition or, roughly speaking, the condition of "no trouble" exists when income in the broadest sense is roughly proportional to investments, for instance, when an older, senior, skilled worker has a well-paid, interesting job. We can then distinguish at least two other cases:

1. When income is felt to be proportionately less than investment, for instance, when an older, senior, and (in the neighborhood of Boston, Massachusetts) Irish worker has a low-paid, dull job. What will his reactions be? We may expect complaints, anger at the company, and, quite likely, a tendency to reduce the amount of work he does for the company, or, as we say in the United States, a tendency to "goof off," in order, as he might view it, to bring what he gives to the company in line with what he feels to be a low return on investment. At any rate, I am altogether persuaded that workers think, not only of material goods but also of others, in terms—inarticulate for the most part—of a generalized economics.

2. But how about the case, perhaps rarer, of the worker whose income is felt to be proportionately greater than investment, whose investments are, so to speak, bringing in more than "five percent"? The example might be, again in the neighborhood of Boston, a worker of low seniority and Armenian ethnic background who has managed to get a highly-paid and responsible job, when older Irishmen have jobs less good. What will be his reactions? Perhaps a feeling of guilt and a willingness to take on extra burdens in helping others out, in order to make up for his speculative success.

I think these are good questions to raise. We do not know the answers, but we are trying to get them. Last year Fritz Roethlisberger, myself, and two others at the Harvard Business School began a small research in predicting workers' behavior—not predicting the results of change, but predicting from limited information about a working group what certain other information (which we did not have) would turn out to be upon later investigation. Among other things, we collected complete personnel information about the working group: age, sex, ethnicity, pay rates, job assignment, etc.; from them we predicted some of the other kinds of behavior, loosely lumped under the term social organization, that we should expect to discover in the group when we went—as we later did—to the workroom, observed the behavior of the workers, and interviewed them. In order to make our predictions, we constructed from the personnel data indices of the investments, costs, and rewards of each worker. This enabled us to specify those workers whose rewards seemed roughly proportional to investments, those whose rewards were less than investments, and those whose rewards were greater than investments, and to predict that we should discover different kinds of behavior exhibited by workers of each kind. The data we got when we went to the workroom are still in process of analysis. All we can say at the moment is that our predictions were not as badly wrong as might have been expected.[8] But the point I am making is that an adequate theory of status congruence ought to be able to predict not only the association of some kind of trouble with incongruence, but what the nature of that trouble will be in different circumstances.

I have spoken so far of the reaction of persons to their own status incongruence. I now raise the question of the reactions of others to them, the question, that is, of incongruent relationships between persons. So far, also, I have spoken of status incongruence as a problem of distributive justice. I now wish to speak of it as a problem of social uncertainty. If I am a worker in a Boston, Massachusetts, plant, and I am talking with a highly skilled, well-paid, senior Irishman, I know where I stand with him. On all counts his social position in the plant is both good and established. There is nothing about him that sets up a conflict in my behavior. But what if I am talking with a well-paid, highly skilled worker who is also of low seniority, a woman, and of Armenian origin? Not only are her status factors out of line, but in being out of line one set of factors—her pay and her skill—teach me to take one kind of attitude toward her, while another—her low seniority, her sex, and her Armenian background—teach me to take quite another attitude or series of others. What is going to be the effect of this ambiguity on my behavior, especially if my own status factors are incongruent, so that my position looks ambiguous to her as well?

Here, as elsewhere, we can get help from the social anthropologists. They study societies that may be relatively stable, and that certainly are made up of groups resembling one another more than do most groups in our modern urban societies. And the anthropologists pay particular attention to kinship relationships, which are especially apt to persist over time and to repeat themselves from group to group. Because they have these characteristics, the kinship relationships get enshrined in the norms of a tribe; they become, so to speak, highly visible; their determinants are to that extent more easily discovered. At any rate, the social anthropologists have described forms of behavior that they call avoidance relationships and joking relationships.[9] The former are particularly apt to occur in affinal ties (ties formed by marriage) and their great exemplar is the avoidance practiced in many primitive societies, and indeed to a lesser and less stylized degree in our own, between a man and his mother-in-law. Before the marriage, the woman may have stood in some kind of kin relationship with the man; at any rate she may have known him, and he may have known her, as a member of the same village or neighborhood. It is not that no relationship existed before, but that the relationship they now enter into is new and more intimate. Particularly the man, as husband, is now vested with jural authority over a woman who was formerly, as daughter, the subordinate of the mother-in-law, with all the danger of conflicts of authority that this implies. Under these circumstances, the tendency to behave in a certain way toward one another, represented by the original relationship, is at war with the tense and ill-defined tendencies represented by the new relationship. The man and his mother-in-law are, over against one another, in a state of social ambiguity or uncertainty. They express their feelings in words that we should translate as *shyness* or *embarrassment*, and they feel more at ease if they avoid having contact with one another. All the evidence is that in the absence of other serious conflicts they get used to their new position, and with time the avoidance becomes somewhat relaxed.

Anthropologists may be referring to one or another of two quite different things when they speak of a joking relationship. They may be referring to a relationship between two persons that is so easy, so relaxed, so equal, that they can say anything they like to one another. The anthropologists may also be referring to a relationship of social ambiguity where the chances for conflict are less high, and the replacement of one form of behavior by another less rapid, than it is in the case of the avoidance relationship. This kind of joking relationship is not an easy, relaxed, and equal one, but neither is it particularly tense, and in this case the ambiguity in the relationship between individuals or groups is resolved by a rather stylized form of joking, including "practical" jokes. We know occasions in our own society when a slight embarrassment is passed off with a witticism. In some primitive societies the embarrassment is built into certain kinship relationships, and the joking appears whenever their ambiguity is brought into relief.

An example is the way in which, in some patrilineal societies, a man teases his mother's brother. The latter is an older man, and should be respected as such; at the same time, since the organization is patrilineal, the man is not under the authority of the mother's brother, and his attitude toward the latter is colored by the warmth he feels toward his mother. Stylized joking resolves, or exploits if you like, the mild tensions of this condition of social ambiguity. Note also that, unlike the case of the mother-in-law, there is no question here of a sudden change in the relationship between two persons. The ambiguity, if mild, is also permanent.

Assuming that human nature is the same the world over, in the sense that men have the same kinds of reactions to the same kinds of circumstances (an assumption that leaves plenty of room for concrete variations), we should expect to find some of the same kinds of behavior appearing, less fully stylized, in conditions of social ambiguity in modern industry. And it begins to look as if indeed we did find them. I have already described briefly the investigation that Roethlisberger, myself, and various members of the Harvard Business School conducted last year. You will remember that we constructed from personnel data, indices of the status congruence of all members of the group we were to study. In the present context, a person who has a high degree of incongruence is a person whose relationship to others is ambiguous. When our investigators made their direct observations in the department, they found one group of five persons who associated with one another a great deal, and who were all rated fairly low on social congruence. This meant concretely that they were men with pretty good jobs whose ethnic origins were different from those of most of the other people in the room. The investigators counted for a period of two weeks the interactions of persons in the department. They found that the members of this particular group, which we came to call the "ambiguous," were particularly high on the initiation of interaction: going to others and starting conversations. They were particularly low in the receipt of interaction: others coming to them. And much of their interaction took the form of practical jokes and horseplay.[10] Can it be that the reaction to the ambiguous of persons themselves nonambiguous is avoidance, and the reaction of the ambiguous themselves is joking? At any rate, I feel confident that a closer study of social ambiguities will help us understand a good deal more about the rich detail of actual behavior in industry. But note that in investigations like this we are not studying specifically industrial problems. We are not, for instance, studying reactions to monotonous, repetitive work. We are instead using industrial situations as convenient places in which to study certain features of human behavior which have, no doubt, their industrial manifestations, but which have also many others.

Finally I mention a study that relates status congruence to two matters I have not mentioned so far. A few years ago Stuart Adams made a study of fifty-two bomber crews in the United States Air Force, each crew made up of eleven men.[11] He developed measures of the status congruence of individual members and of each crew as a whole, taking into consideration the following status factors: age, rank, length of service, amount of flying time, amount of time in combat, education, reputed ability, popularity, and the importance of the job held. He also developed measures, first, of the technical performance of the crews based on optical and radar target bombing scores, and second, of social performance, based on the degree to which members of a crew expressed friendship for and confidence in one another. Adams found that social performance varied directly as status congruence. The more congruent the members of a crew, the easier they found it to like and trust one another. But the relationship of congruence with technical performance was curvilinear. Plotting the congruence of crews against their target bombing scores, he found that medium scores were associated with low congruence; that, following the curve, bombing scores improved as congruence did and were at their highest for medium congruence, but that very high congruence was associated with very low bombing scores.

What do these results means? How do very good human relations between the members of a group get in the way of the technical performance of the group? That they do so in fact is something that we in America should not like to believe. We want both friendship and effectiveness. It is perhaps less hard to understand how the absence of social ambiguity promotes friendship and confidence. On the other hand, the persons whose status is congruent are those who have something like established social positions. But do we, in a democracy, approve of established social positions even in bomber crews?

At any rate I have tried to take a rather obvious idea, but one not often used in the past in social science, the idea of status congruence, and to show its connections, in the same sense either of distributive justice or of social certitude, with a wide variety of forms of social behavior—the demand for wage differentials, the predictions people make about their own industrial future, liberal attitudes in politics, avoidance and joking relationships, and finally, friendship, confidence, and group effectiveness.

6

The Sociologist's

Contribution

to Management

in the Future

SOCIOLOGY is the profession of studying and teaching about what happens when at least two persons are in a position to influence one another. I emphasize the profession because all of us, as men, study the subject, though not all professionally. As a profession, sociology is quite old: Auguste Comte gave it its name more than a hundred years ago. It is also a profession that is trying to become a science, but in this regard— the degree of its progress toward scientific status—it is still quite young. Fifty years ago the great French mathematician Henri Poincaré called it the science with most methods and fewest results. If, quite properly, one means by the results of a science general statements that hold true in a first approximation in a variety of circumstances, Poincaré would still be right today. There are still no general statements about social behavior that most sociologists agree are true. Of this fact no sociologist talking about the contribution his profession may make to management can remind you too strongly. There are sociologists

A talk prepared for the National Conference of the British Institute of Management, 1955, and published in *The Manager*, 23 (1955), 1033–1036, 1085. Reprinted by permission of the Editor.

who will tell you, wholly sincerely, that they command an established science, capable (if given, of course, quite a little more money) of curing the ills of a troubled world. They are utterly wrong, and in my view the future of sociology can only suffer from such overselling. Even if we had the established knowledge, which we do not, the problem of applying it would remain. Atoms cannot read physics, but men, perhaps to their advantage, can read sociology, judge what the sociologists plan to get them to do, and make their arrangements accordingly. Thus the polls' prediction of voters' behavior is always, in some measure, defeated by the voters' ability to read the polls.

If what I have said is true of sociology in general, it is all the more true of the study of social behavior in business and industry. As a matter of deliberate professional research it dates from the First World War, and its first great effort was the Western Electric researches, begun under the leadership of Elton Mayo in 1925. Elton Mayo was my own first teacher in the field.

If industrial or business sociology has no established results in the shape of general statements—or propositions or principles if you like—what does it have to offer you? The usual answer to the question "What use is a young science?" is not an answer at all, but an appeal to faith. In the words of Mark Spade in *Business for Pleasure*:

Resist the temptation to ask the Research Department what the blazes is the use of anything it is doing. There are at least six very crushing replies which research people keep for those who ask this question: "Sir," as Faraday said to Mr. Gladstone, "can you tell me the use of a newborn child?"[1]

For the physical sciences this reply is crushing only because, as a matter of experience, the children have grown up and proved giants. Faith has some evidence to go on, and is to that extent less faithful. In the social sciences, we can bring forward such evidence only in economics, and so I forbear from making the appeal to faith on behalf of sociology. Though I myself have faith in our future, I see no reason why you should share it. I propose to make a case for the usefulness of sociology to management here and now, or in the immediate, not the distant, future. But to make the case I must first examine wherein the usefulness of a science consists.

Science is a process, not a completed thing. It is the effort, in the words of a great president of my own university, to reduce the area of empiricism in understanding and action, to reduce the area of intuitive knowledge, the area in which action is taken as a matter of judgment based on hard-won experience, and to substitute a growing area of explicit intellectual recognition and understanding. Science makes this effort not because intuition and experience are bad in themselves— far from it, they provide the growing edge of any science—but because their results are slowly gotten and not easily communicated, that is, taught. The practical value of any science, and this holds good of algebra as of sociology, is that by making experience subject to explicit intellectual control it speeds up the learning process and so sets intuition and judgment free to work on new ground rather than old. The practical value is always at first educational.

The process of science, of reducing the area of empiricism, takes, moreover, several stages. No doubt the historians of science would not agree on what the stages are, and whatever they are, no doubt they must be mixed, in different proportions in different sciences. But this does not bother me, as I put forward my stages only to help me build my argument. First comes the painstaking observation and description of situations; second, the recognition and naming of what I shall call factors, of kinds of things that seem to recur in situations and be important; and third, the statement of recurring relations among the factors. The presence of some degree of the later stage always informs, though it does not wholly determine, the one preceding. Thus you cannot observe wholly satisfactorily without knowing the kind of thing you are looking for. But I shall not pursue these complications, which do not help us now.

The appeal to faith makes extravagant claims for what a science will do when it reaches the third stage. No one asks if it may not help by earlier application to practice. No misunderstanding had I rather clear up than this one. My claim is that some sciences, and I number industrial sociology among them, can make a contribution to practice, not at the last stage only, the stage at which in Poincaré's terms it has results, but at all three stages. Indeed sociology's claim must rest on the first two, as it has not reached the third. Moreover, the earlier the stage, the more purely educational the contribution. But let me go into details.

A few sociologists—and, very important to remember, anthropologists—are at this moment excellently well equipped, with your cooperation, to go into a department of a firm, to establish the kind of relations with the people, including yourselves, that will allow them to study it without changing it beyond recognition in the process, and to describe accurately and dispassionately what they see. And since, whatever else they may be, sociologists are academics, they are equipped to present their descriptions to students.

To what students? If I am to be banal, let me do a good job of it and remind you that on business and industry depends the extraordinary standard of living enjoyed by the Western world. It may be that there, too, the angers and anxieties of the Western world have their birth. And yet there is no subject of which the university student is more ignorant. Of my own university, one wise industrialist said that a man could easily graduate knowing nothing of American industry, save that it suffered from monopolistic competition. Can you say that the same is not true of British universities? The reason for this ignorance lies in the alliance of aristocratic values with academic ones, of the view that trade is not the thing for a gentleman with the view that a university only studies human behavior dead. The old traditions are in fact breached: gentlemen will go into business, and economics will busy itself with the discount rate. But the defence yields only slowly. Of course I am being unfair, for there is a serious case against including sociology in the academic curriculum. It is that the subject has as yet no purely intellectual content: a body of doctrine from which one can by reason and analysis draw conclusions to be tested against observation to the reformulation of theory. But the same charge can be made and proved against history. In this respect it is in the same case as sociology, and yet history is a most respectable academic subject. "Ah," you will say, "it is respectable as a humanity." That is just it. Academically, sociology is not respectable because it is neither *able* to establish general laws, like physics, nor unwilling to *try*, like history.

If, for all that, history is still the school of the statesman, sociology may be the school of the businessman, and for the same reasons. To be more specific, let me take the case of the young engineer. In my country, when he leaves his engineering school, he is apt to think of himself as a professional, with all that that implies. He holds high status; he commands a body of technical knowledge that others do not; he has firm ideas on what makes good practice in his field. His assumption is akin to the doctor's: you do not have to engage his services, but if you do you must take his advice. With his articulate intellectual discipline he has absorbed these inarticulate major premises. Holding them, he is, when he is hired by a firm, almost bound to get frustrated and the frustration will get in his way. For he is not in the assumed position at all. He will be useful only if he is able to listen to and in turn persuade of the importance of his views men in production and finance, older than himself, unimpressed by his professional standing, inclined to look on him as a long-hair, and, far more than the patient facing the doctor, possessed of knowledge and experience bearing on the practical problem. If he has any sense, he will get over his frustration and be the better man for it. But cannot we speed the process up?

Industrial sociologists have now made and are able to present several realistic studies of what we call in America line-and-staff problems, of which one variety is the problem of the young engineer. I am persuaded that the mere presentation of such studies to an engineer in training will make him better able to cope with his frustration. Of course they will not be exactly like the problems he will encounter, though they will bear a family resemblance. No doubt they will not tell him just what to do, but they can be useful without achieving anything like that. They will give him the courage that comes from realizing that, intellectually, he has been here before, that he is not alone with his experience. He will take the first step in mental control that follows the shock of recognition. He will be less apt to find the reason for his difficulties in some private witch, more apt to look on them with a measure of detachment. That is, he will be in a position to assimilate his experience more rapidly.

I believe these things because I have seen them happen. I have made the observations, written the descriptions, presented them to the young, and heard them tell me how they helped them later in business. They have even said they were helped to make money. This kind of description the industrial sociologist is equipped to make, this kind of teaching he is equipped to do—now. This is the first and indispensable stage in the development of a science, but it is also the first stage in that science's useful application. The collaboration of theory and practice begins at the beginning.

The question is not one of producing better managers than there are today. Many managers today are excellently well able to turn out and sell high-quality goods at a profit in an expanding firm, and in the process maintain an admirable willingness to cooperate on the part of employees. The question is rather one of producing more good managers sooner in circumstances where I take for granted that more of them are needed. Nor is it a question of sociologists' teaching students more than a good manager now knows. For that matter, a successful social climber knows almost all there is to know about sociology in the sense that he must work on valid assumptions. I am sure that there were good mechanics before mechanics became a science. The difference is in the nature of the knowledge. It is acquired by trial and error, and it tends to be inarticulate. On both counts it cannot be taught. It is not often recognized how costly is learning by direct experience, and how great an economy for society even a little science and its teaching means. They save learning by experience for the one place where it is indispensable—at the growing edge of understanding. This kind of contribution sociology can begin to make here and now.

I have used as my illustration the young engineer, but the argument applies to any young man that aspires to management. I think it also applies, though this is not our main concern here, to any man who wants to call himself educated. Public opinion is badly informed on what goes on within industry. I have the impression, for instance, that the public looks on the origins of some strikes as utterly mysterious. They are baleful creatures that dart out from a thicket, seize their prey, and are lost again. Slowly the mystery dissipates. Through painful experience, like your railway strike, people are beginning to learn something about such matters as wage differentials. But could not the learning process be usefully speeded up?

Mere exposure to realistic descriptions of industrial behavior will do much for the young manager. But this is not all that sociology can give him. The second stage in the development of a science is that of recognizing and giving names to recurrent factors in the situations observed and described. Indeed the observation itself will grow in detail with the recognition of the kinds of thing to be looked for. As he describes industrial situations, the sociologist will begin to point out to his students the factors that often make their presence felt. And I argue that the possession of such a simple set of concepts—of things to be looked for—is of the greatest use to the young manager.

Let me illustrate. Suppose two departments are to be merged—I speak of a situation I was once familiar with—and the first consists in large part of fairly senior men, the second of junior women. The first group formerly worked in the main office of the company downtown, and the second in a somewhat outlying building, which will be the location of the merged departments. The new head of the department will be the former head of the second group and will keep the title of assistant superintendent, though the other department heads are superintendents. No doubt an experienced manager in this situation will foresee trouble: in the relations between the two groups, in their different attitudes toward the "boss" and the company, in the effectiveness with which the joint job is carried on, and not least in the manager's own feelings.

I am not interested in him, but in speeding up the learning process of an inexperienced manager caught in such a squeeze. If he has been exposed to realistic descriptions of industrial behavior, and if his teacher has gone just a little further, set apart certain kinds of observations, called them observations of *status*, and illustrated them with a range of problems called status problems, he will be in a better position to expect trouble, recognize its nature, and avoid the blind reactions of bewilderment and anger. Mind you, the ordinary sensible man, without training, may expect trouble, too—if he stops to think.

The whole point about training is that it may make the inexperienced manager just a little more apt to stop and think. The sociologist will give him little to help him predict just what form the trouble will take or just what he is to do about it, for the sociologist, while recognizing some of the factors, has not much to say about their relations: he has not reached the third stage of science. But I hold it an advantage to know that something is apt to swing around and hit you in the back of the neck, even if you do not know just how. Sociologists have begun to develop a sort of checklist of important factors in industrial behavior. And a checklist is a great step forward in intellectual control: it tells you some of the things you can neglect only at your peril.

The sociologist can do more if, in presenting his realistic descriptions of cases, he encourages the young man to discuss them and suggest what range of actions might usefully have been taken in them to accomplish a given end. The sociologist will not be able to tell the young man that he is right or wrong, but he will at least help him to make his assumptions explicit and thus subject to his own critical appraisal. Discussion will also help him to appreciate, if vicariously, what his own feelings in similar situations are apt to be, and thus help him control them. To be sure, a case system of teaching will not speed up the assimilation of experience much if it eschews, as a matter of doctrine, the development of an intellectual scheme of analysis, but it is not my purpose here to linger over teaching methods at the Harvard Business School.

Once again, then, a subject like sociology need not wait till it is a science—until it has reached the third stage—before it is useful. It can be put to work right away. In something as important as management, anything that even begins to get us free of empiricism, or better to set empiricism free for new advances in understanding, makes a contribution. But the contribution will be indirect and educational, not direct and applied. Still, I must say something about the third stage, which means I must say something about the sociologist, not as a teacher of young managers, but as a direct advisor to, or consultant for, management, in the role that the specialized engineer so often plays today.

You can usefully go to a social scientist if you want certain kinds of specific procedure applied, for social science is at least strong in methods. If you want to know what sort of man will be good at what sort of job, you can go to the psychologists and they will be able to give you a lot of help on selection procedures. Of course, you had better bear in mind that a good man on this job here and now may not be one that will keep on being good at it. Sometimes the better he is now, the worse he will be in the long run, for good men are unduly apt to get bored. Much depends on his motivation, and psychologists are much less well able to assess that than they are manual coordination. If you wish a survey of plant opinion on certain subjects, a sociologist will be able to make it for you, and even explain the precautions you should take in interpreting the results. But the survey will be more representative if it is known that you are not going to take action on it than if it is suspected you are—and in this case you may not think it of much use to you.

But I question if at the moment, and for a long time to come, you will be able to go to a social scientist and say to him: "Look here, I have this human problem. What is the solution?" and expect to get one that is worth the money you have paid for it. I do not mean that the solution will be bad. Like anyone else, the sociologist may have a good hunch. But it will probably not be enough better, just because he knows sociology, than what one of your own good managers could provide, to justify the extra cost. After all, you engage an engineering consultant because you are pretty sure he can give you better advice than your own men can. This is not now the case with sociologists. The reason lies in the difficulties and costs of prediction in sociology. Though the sociologist may know some of the important factors, he is far from possessing tested propositions about their interrelations. Even if he had the propositions, the number of variables and the complexities of their mutual dependence are often greater than that which makes successful prediction possible in engineering. And the cost of getting the necessary information is probably higher. For these reasons I believe money is better spent indirectly, using sociologists to help train managers, than directly, using them as consultants. I say this as strongly as I can, for I want support of sociology to be based on realities and not on illusions that may turn into disillusions.

If, of course, you feel like saying to the sociologist: "Let us try your solution to the problem, with you on hand to observe and record the results," I am strongly in favor of your doing so. This is the beginning of an experimental approach, and it is exceedingly important to the future of sociology. All I ask is that you entertain no conviction that the solution itself, in its direct results, is bound to be good. You will be spending money for sociological research and not necessarily for the better management of your company.

Let me be personal. I have never done a piece of research in industry for the purpose of devising a solution to a particular problem. I have never been a consultant. I have simply wanted the chance to observe characteristic situations. After some trepidation, management usually takes the following line toward me, though they put it more tactfully: "We are satisfied to have you study Department X, provided that in your writings you hide the fact that it is Department X and our company; but we don't want any advice from you." Working under this arrangement, a perfectly satisfactory one to me, I have of course encountered human problems. By this time I have built up close enough ties with some members of management so that I can talk over the problems with them. And I must confess that informally I have made suggestions as to what might be done. They have never been adopted, and my belief is that the solutions, if any, finally reached were better than mine. At the same time, I am persuaded that my influence was useful practically. In discussion I helped bring out into the open some things that managers knew intuitively but, for lack of words for them, might not have made part of their deliberate thinking. What you cannot talk about, you cannot think about; you can only hunch. Then, with their far wider knowledge than mine of the company and what could be done in it, they were able to think up better solutions than mine. The cost of teaching me all they knew would be worth paying only if I were going to become a member of management myself. After all, a consultant is valuable to the extent that he does not have to know all that the president does. Note again that my influence was indirect and educational, not direct and advisory.

Any claim that sociology will contribute to management in the future must be either an appeal to faith or a projection of what it can already do. I eschew the appeal to faith. Sociologists are good observers and teachers, now, today, and they are beginning to be a little more. Expect them to contribute in what they are good at now, not in what they may be good at someday. Their science grows in phases, but need not wait till it is of age before it can be put to work. Observation and classification themselves, when presented to the young, will speed up their assimilation of experience by bringing it under a degree of intellectual control and to that degree set trial-and-error free to gain new ground instead of forever recapturing the old. Observation and classification are also necessary steps to the establishment of general principles from which specific applications may be deduced. But for sociologists to claim or for you to believe that the principles are here now (or will be soon) will boomerang, put the preliminary work itself in danger, and prevent your getting out of it what you reasonably might. It is not necessarily true that the newborn child is of no use, or that it is bound to be useful grown up. But it will certainly be spoiled if you force its growth.

Finally, let me reverse the question with which I started and ask what management can contribute to sociology. If what sociologists do best at the moment is observe, and if observation is the foundation of a more developed science, give us a chance to make the observations. Let us into your factories and offices. In America, at least, getting in is the hardest part of the industrial sociologist's job. He gets in, if at all, at the top; top management must first agree to his presence in the organization, and I have always found that suspicion of him is greatest there and steadily decreases as he goes down. Why this law, which is one of the few great generalizations of industrial sociology, should be true you will have to tell me. Of course management is never rude enough to say, "I distrust you." The usual line is, "Of course, it's all right with me, but down on the floor no one will talk to you." I have never, never found them right. For a sociologist is not such a disturbing influence in the plant as you suppose. We can really train him not to be. And you will find that you get surprising, indirect benefits from his presence, besides the purer satisfaction of having contributed, without thought of gain, to the advancement of science.

7

Giving

a Dog

a Bad Name

I T feels clear to me that sociology has a bad name
in Britain, but just what sort of a bad name and
why is not so obvious. At least my friends in
Cambridge are apt to say to me: "You used to be a historian. What did
you get into *that* for?" But when I ask: "Why, what's the matter with sociology?" the replies tend to trail off: "Well, you know, old boy, it isn't
quite . . . Well . . ."; and heads shake. One feels the lack of a phrase,
at once comprehensive and precise, like the one sometimes overheard
at American cocktail parties: "She isn't quite our class, dear."

Inarticulate Reasons for Articulate Attitudes

It is one of the duties of a sociologist to find the inarticulate reasons
for articulate attitudes, and accordingly I have tried in Britain to discover the bases for the attitude toward sociology. I cannot tell how far

For three academic years, 1953–54, 1954–55, and 1955–56,
Cambridge University tried the experiment of appointing a
visiting Professor of Social Theory to lecture on sociology. I was
the last holder of this chair, and so was much interested in the
position of sociology in Great Britain. This talk was given on
the Third Program of the British Broadcasting Corporation
and printed in *The Listener*, 56 (August 16, 1956) 232–233.
It is reprinted with thanks to the Editor.

[113]

my researches have been conclusive. Nor, since it is the further duty of a sociologist to analyze human behavior without evaluating it, shall I try to judge whether a look at sociology justifies the attitudes of the British, or the attitudes of the British justify a look at sociology.

Sociology has a bad name because it has a bad *name*. The word is a barbarous mixture of Latin and Greek roots, intolerable in a society where a classical education is the mark of a gentleman. That, I suppose, is why the temporary chair I hold at Cambridge is not called the Professorship of Sociology but that of Social Theory, for verbal miscegenation occurs only when two roots actually become one word. But this is only one way in which sociology sadly lacks style. If a gentleman's education is classical, his prose must be English. Yet some of the most eminent sociologists write sentences that take fifteen minutes to pass any given point, pregnant with undeliverable meaning, bulging with a jargon by Harvard out of Heidelberg, delightful in a German because it confirms one's opinion of him, but unnerving in an American, some of whose words appear to be in one's own language. How are Englishmen to be attracted to sociology if its current literature is not even in German? But how is its literature to become English if Englishmen are not attracted to it? All that a sociologist can say is that these self-reinforcing circular processes are common, and provide whatever stability a social order possesses. Thus, drain pipes remain on the outside of British houses so that they can easily be got at if they freeze.

To explain the next reason for the British attitude to sociology I must go back a little, for the question "What did you get into *that* for?" is only the second I am asked. The first is: "What is sociology (not that I really want to know)?" Sociology, in my view, is the study of what happens when two or more creatures are in a position to influence one another. And induction from observation suggests that Britons object to sociology—indeed, for them sociology *is* sociology—only if the creatures in question are alive, human, and British. I insist on all three criteria. For the British are enthusiastic students of the social behavior of dead Britons. How, otherwise, account for the popularity of Professor Trevelyan's great book?[1] But that is social history—not sociology. Again, the study of the customs of native tribes flourishes in Britain as it does in no other country. It is held to be useful for the administration of the Commonwealth, so long as all is going well there. Note that, as an academic subject, it was first introduced at Oxford and Cambridge, where it remains respectable in spite of its adoption by London and "redbrick." Its body of theory is indistinguishable from that of sociology. Indeed, its practitioners say that they *are* sociologists. That is, they say so to one another. But since it deals with alive non-British, it dare not in fact *be* sociology. It is social anthropology, and it is O.K.

My final and crucial test is that of the nonhuman Britons: the bird and the dog. Shamelessly, the British observe their social behavior, not only in the field but in the home. What country has more bird watchers per square mile? Where was Lorenz a best-seller?[2] And now there is David Lack's admirable and popular Penguin, *The Life of the Robin,* a study made by methods regularly used by sociologists: the direct observation of social behavior followed by statistical analysis of the data. I am told that his work earned him a Fellowship of the Royal Society. (Note: a scientific academy.) But this is not sociology: it is the branch of zoology called ethology, and it is decidedly O.K.

The Creatures Who Can Talk Back

Faced with these facts, elementary scientific method suggests that one should ask what characteristics the medieval villein, the native, and the robin possess in common. I have been able to discover only one: they cannot read sociology, or, what amounts to the same thing, they cannot talk back—or not much. Only the study of the social behavior of creatures who can talk back—who are, that is, alive, human, and conceivably British—is sociology and vaguely disapproved. Why should this criterion—talking back—be so decisive? One explanation, itself sociological, is the "Don't Give the Show Away" theory. It runs as follows. Any society rests on a set of unstated assumptions, British society more than most: that is, indeed, its strength. The examination of these assumptions and their statement to people who can read will, therefore, tend to undermine the social order, that of Britain, in the nature of the case, more than the rest. Subconsciously the British recognize this, for their intuitive sociology is so far advanced that they need no other, and therefore they must disapprove of sociology as a science; but disapprove vaguely, for to make the reasons explicit would itself give the show away. Or, better, let the serious discussion of British sociology escape in one of the characteristic British safety valves, like the pages of *Encounter,* the Hyde Park of the intellectual world.

The "Don't Give the Show Away" theory itself makes an assumption about the British; that they are at once highly suspicious of explicit verbal statements and highly vulnerable to them; suspicious *because* they are vulnerable, Freud would have said. Unfortunately this theory, which will account for many of the facts, will not account for all of them, and so I must reluctantly reject it. For take the British Constitution, an unwritten constitution more written about than any other. Has it been undermined by having its hidden principles brought to light? Not if I can believe Professor Devons' recent discussion of political myth.[3] No, if the British want to preserve their social order they will do well to let the sociologists study it, like the anthropologist friend of mine to whom the natives finally came and said: "You know our customs. Tell us whom we are allowed to marry."

There is a better theory to account for the objection to sociology as the study of people who can talk back. Sociologists are seen as people who try to get others to discuss themselves, their families, their neighbors, their jobs. They are rightly so seen, for if these things are denied them, they have little subject matter left. But their behavior makes them busybodies, violating two principles of the British Constitution: an Englishman's home, and *a fortiori* his job, is his castle; and, a gentleman never talks about himself. It makes no difference that sociologists, apparently unprincipled in other respects, do have their code: that what is told them shall be held confidential so long as it can embarrass identifiable individuals. Nor does it make any difference that a sociologist cannot get people to talk about these things unless they want to. They should not want to; and a sociologist who asks them to do so incurs the sin of leading others into temptation. Not only should Britons not talk about these things, but apparently they just do not. Englishmen have proudly and confidently said to me: "You can get Americans to answer questions like that, but never an Englishman, and that's why there can be no sociology in Britain."

Evidence for "Delighted Abandon"

Unfortunately all the evidence, and it has been accumulating rapidly in recent years, is that the ordinary Englishman will talk to the sociologist with just as much delighted abandon as will the most extrovert American. The members of what has been called the Establishment (and it is they that hold most of the attitudes I have described) must become reconciled to the fact that the British working class, middle class —how far up dare I go?—are more like Americans than they have any right to be.

Above all, it makes no difference that the things sociologists study seem to be important, and even interesting, to Britons. If I read your press right, you are much interested in industrial production, juvenile delinquency, the new housing in the new towns, and the problems of the elderly in an aging society. Young Englishmen have even said to me: "We of this generation are anxious about social class as the generation of the 'twenties was anxious about sex." The trouble with sociologists is that they will not be satisfied with impressions on these questions and others, or even with statistics, dear as these are to their hearts. They will go out and talk, face to face, with the people concerned, in a systematic and plonking way. Don't they know that serious subjects should be treated lightly?

At a wholly different moral level is the objection to the very goal that sociology shares with the other social sciences—the discovery of natural laws, as distinguished from moral laws, of human behavior. This objection tends to come from deeply religious men. Far from laughing at the pretensions of sociology to be a science at all, they take them more seriously than do most sociologists themselves. Their objection implies a fear that there may indeed be such laws, and that some men might apply them to control the behavior of others. But to control their behavior, even for their own good, would be to cheat them of their birthright. Was not man created "sufficient to have stood, but free to fall"? And if he is not left free to fall, where is his humanity?

Success in the sociologists' aim might lead, in T. S. Eliot's phrase, to "systems so perfect that no one would need to be good." This view forgets that men long ago committed themselves to the endeavor to control their own collective behavior, not only in the ways sanctioned by the churches but in others, by making it to men's interest to do good. And they have increasingly based the endeavor on an understanding of natural laws of human behavior, those of economics, for example. So that the question is not: Shall this kind of control be undertaken? but: Where shall it stop? A sociologist might also argue that his religious critics have more faith in him than in their own doctrine, the doctrine that man is infinitely tough and resourceful and is not easily cheated of his freedom to sin. What God has given no man can take away, certainly no sociologist. More seriously, he might argue that the social sciences are not in train to eliminate morality but to make greater demands of it. A sociology that shows us unsuspected or not hitherto understood ways in which men are bound up with one another invites more refined answers to the question: "Am I my brother's keeper?"

"At Great Pains to Find the Object in Plain Sight"

Then, again, one hears it said that sociology not only ventures on subjects better left alone, but we know all about these subjects anyhow. I am far from holding that the British objections to sociology do not exist in the United States, and it was an American novelist who defined a sociologist as someone who spent $40,000 to find a brothel. This view, that a sociologist is at great pains to find the object in plain sight, takes a special form in academic circles. When the question of founding the department to which I now belong came up in a meeting of the faculty of Harvard University, we proposed to call it the Department of Human Relations. At once there were protests, from the economists, the political scientists, the psychologists, the historians, and the philosophers. Human relations were what *they* studied. Only because a clearly second-best word was available did we manage to avoid disaster and get founded under the title of Social Relations. We might be social, so long as they were human.

If sociology is as I have defined it, it is clear that many other academic subjects are already in the field. Why then, people argue, should this upstart be allowed in, especially an upstart who claims the whole field as his own and—still worse—who claims to be a science? Have not history and philosophy got on very well without being sciences? The only trouble with this objection is that it is bound to be swept aside by the majestic course of British social history. The different social studies can have only one possible intellectual goal—a general theory of social behavior. They are engaged in a race for this pole, except perhaps for history, which has come along to admire the stupendous scenery. And it is in the geometry of polar exploration that the territories covered by the expeditions become more alike the closer they get to the goal. But they may well start from different bases and use different techniques. One feature of the British weakness for the exploration game, as for other games, is that they have never been willing for long to keep anyone out who wanted to play. And if players have long since been allowed to meet gentlemen at cricket, it is only a question of time before sociologists meet them in the academic arena.

Left Hand and Right Hand

But will sociologists use the same entrance to the clubhouse? In spite of all objections, a great and increasing amount of sociology is being done in Britain. But it tends to be done in research institutions, not as part of a regular university program; or, if in universities, then in London and the provinces, not in Oxford or Cambridge; or, if in Oxford and Cambridge, not under the name of sociology. There is a Professorship of Race Relations at Oxford and one of Industrial Relations at Cambridge, possibly on the theory that if one accepts part of a subject one escapes the rest, plus the name of the whole. That is, the British will do sociology, but will withhold, in a carefully graded fashion, like negative knighthoods, recognition that they are doing it. As the British Commonwealth grew great on the principle, at once moral and practical, "let not thy left hand know what thy right hand doeth," this may do no harm, except to the sociologists themselves, for it is a Lucky Jim that does not need to be loved. Some sociologists say that every attitude has its function in maintaining society. If this is the case, the function of the British objection to sociology is to produce sociologists who can be objected to. But that brings us back to the drain pipes.

8

Bureaucracy

as Big Brother

WHEN the American business man has downed his chicken à la King at the Chamber of Commerce dinner, pushed away his apple pie à la mode, and settled down to the oratory—that is, when he settles down to talk about himself—he still makes noises like an independent entrepreneur, preferably a small one, best still a newsboy with his own paper route. He has gotten where he is by honesty, by working hard at letting no one tell him how to run his own business, by saving his money but meeting his payroll, by using his horse sense even if it means flying by the seat of his pants, by taking risks that are never gambles. If he succeeds his success is both personal and moral; equally, if he fails his failure is also personal and moral. In short, he talks as if he still followed the Protestant Ethic, a rugged individualist out of *Poor Richard's Almanack.*

Hard Work in a Different Setting

There are still such business men in the United States, though they are having a hard time competing with the chain stores. Certainly the honesty, hard work, and common sense are still much alive—but in a

Given as a review of William H. Whyte, Jr., *The Organization Man* (New York: Simon & Schuster, 1956) on the British Broadcasting Corporation's Third Program and printed in *The Listener*, 58 (November 7, 1957), 731–732. It is reprinted with thanks to the Editor.

different setting. Since about 1900 the characteristic American business man has been changing from an independent entrepreneur to a junior executive in a large corporation. He has not come up from his own paper route but from a university, though he has not been well educated there, for he has usually studied business and commerce even as an undergraduate. He has not even had to look for a job but has been recruited straight from the university by the executive development staff of a corporation, which is apt to send him to its own school for further indoctrination. He does not want to start out for himself: the bigger the organization he can join the better, because the safer, he feels, for him. He expects to stay with the corporation for a long time, though in fact the men that change firms most are apt to go farthest. He expects to move from post to post, as the corporation changes his assignments. Accordingly he will not get himself mixed up for long in the affairs of a particular city. He will not hope to become a prominent citizen of Indianapolis but of the Standard Oil Co. of Indiana. With each change of post he will be meeting colleagues whom he knew elsewhere.

He will expect to be seeing them, on and off, all his life, and so what he is like off the job, how he fits in socially, even the kind of girl he marries make an increasing difference to his business career. For several ranks he will be promoted by seniority; even if he does not go much farther, he will expect the company to keep a place for him, do his saving for him, and retire him with a pension. Ill-educated to begin with, he tends to lead a rather sheltered existence as a specialized manager. He may well know less about the political and financial facts of life than did his father who ran his own hardware store on Main Street. Yet if he does well he may spend the last years of his career in positions of great power, where questions of public policy are his main concern. Far more than the old entrepreneur, he resembles, without the aristocratic tradition, the career officer in the army or navy in the days when armies and navies were the only really big organizations. Or rather he has become a bureaucrat, though bureaucrat is the worst word in his dictionary.

The Organization Man, by William H. Whyte, Jr., is about this new business man. The book has been a best-seller in the United States, not altogether because what it says is new, for many of us have had some sense of the things it talks about and found them vaguely disturbing, but because it makes clear to us just what our experience has been, how widespread are the facts on which it is based, and why we found them disturbing.

Whyte is less concerned with the official business of the organization man than with the other things about him: his origin, his education, his wife and children, his parties, his reading, his religion. Whyte gives us, for example, a splendid account of his life with his fellows in the great cantonments of the new suburbia. But above all Whyte is concerned, as I shall be concerned here, with his ideas of good and evil, with the major premises that have been replacing the Protestant Ethic as working guides to behavior. These Whyte calls the Social Ethic, by which he means "that contemporary body of thought which makes morally legitimate the pressures of society against the individual. Its major propositions are three: a belief in the group as the source of creativity; a belief in 'belongingness' as the ultimate need of the individual; and a belief in the application of science to achieve that belongingness."

The American postgraduate business schools are in some ways more businesslike than business itself, and I shall suggest the shape of the new ethic, admittedly in a debased form, by giving you the advice that I have for years given unscrupulous undergraduates who nevertheless wanted to get into business school. "The decisive moment," I say, "is your interview with their admissions people. If you have good academic grades, never mention them. They know all about your shortcomings anyhow, and will give you no credit for cheap candor. Indeed, if you can manage it, avoid having any *A*'s on your record. A physician connected with the school once said of a certain student: 'He has four *A*'s —he must be a very sick man.' *B*, though, is an O.K. grade. Instead of going in for marks at the university, go in for extracurricular activities, for they will make you an all-round man, so long as you bear in mind that you get to be an all-round man by not getting around too much. Stay away from the arts and the literary magazine. You might just get by with the glee club, and the college newspaper is all right. In these activities, be sure not to get the top job. If you did, the school might suspect you of ambition, which would prevent your becoming a good team-man. Vice-president is an O.K. job to have. Above all, when they ask you why you want to go into business, never say it's because you want to make a pile of money. Say you like people and want to work with them, for, as you will remember, business *is* people."

Men who have taken this advice have invariably gotten into business school, and business has acquired, in spite of itself, a very few of the kind of men it needs—men of cool head and detached intelligence.

Readers of Whyte's book will find even more valuable the advice he gives on a similar problem: how to cheat on personality tests.

Fitting into the Team

You probably will not find the ethic that my advice plays up to anything very new. It much resembles the working ethic that a boy may have picked up at a second-class British public school preparing him for the Civil Service—no doubt fifty years ago. Not being too intellectual, too ambitious, too different—or at least not letting it show—and, above all, fitting smoothly into the team keep a man out of trouble in bureaucracy, or so some practical people have come to think; and it is not surprising that institutions feeding men into bureaucracy should teach them, in fact if not officially, what is believed to work there.

But it is one thing to learn under the table what is believed to work, another to accept it openly as a moral good. The new business bureaucracy is comparatively benevolent. It does not send its servant to an isolated district on a jungle frontier and forget about him until he is actually eaten by cannibals. It sees its executive personnel as a valuable asset, which has cost much to develop. It is forever moving its men so that they can get wider experience, forever calling them in for further training—though the experience and training may still be limited to company specialties. It looks out for its men and is felt by them to do so. The old Civil Service bureaucracy was a rather chilly place, and its creed was negative: it kept you out of trouble. The new bureaucracy is Big Brother, and the ideas of anyone so kindly may easily come to be seen as positive virtues.

Not that the organization imposes its creed on organization man, even through kindness. He is already prepared to believe it. Even before the rise of the trusts, Americans were peculiarly ambivalent in their attitude toward the intellectual qualities. In the Calvinist tradition of maintaining a learned ministry they founded more universities than did most other peoples. Perhaps for that reason they were convinced that booklearning had little to do with secular life. And long ago De Tocqueville warned Americans against that facile cooperativeness, that gregariousness, which, on the one hand, allows them sufficient confidence in one another to get big enterprises going and, on the other, gives them leave to look on the man who will not "go along" as a mere crank. The or-

[123]

ganization man turns out to be an old American. He may turn out to be a future Englishman, for Britain has the organizations too, and their influence may be strong enough to upset the Englishman's happy conviction that he has all the American virtues in less than American excess.

Social Ethic Backed by Science

The ideas of the Social Ethic may be old in bureaucracy and in America. What is new about it is that these ideas are now supposed to be backed by science. Because American business is vaguely anti-intellectual without thinking much about it, American business men are permeable to ideas, for it takes an intellectual to intercept and if necessary reject the ideas coming his way; and some of the ideas of social science have been absorbed by business to strengthen tendencies that were strong enough already.

For instance, the whole psychological tradition beginning with Freud has pointed up the ambiguity of the intellectual processes: how often thinking is obsession sticking above the surface, how often difficulty in getting on with oneself is revealed in difficulty in getting on with other people. These things may be true, but it does not follow that "smooth adjustment to the group" is the modern outward and visible sign of an inward and spiritual grace. Yet this seems to be the conclusion that many of us are delighted to reach. Long before Freud we distrusted the "temperamental long-hair"; now we can do so and feel psychiatry patting us on the back. One of the ironies of recent social thought is that the most radical ideas have confirmed us in our prejudices, and the great innovators have played into the hands of the conformers.

I speak with feeling and to purge myself of guilt. Since the war a flourishing branch of American psychology and sociology has been the study of the behavior of men in small groups. It is true that some of us implied that so-called group dynamics, if only backed with enough cash, was in train to conquer most of the known miseries of social intercourse. But some of us—and I was one—were more sceptical of salvation. We were interested in small groups simply because we could make the detailed observations of social behavior, on which we might hope to base the generalizations of a future science, only if the number of persons we observed was small. If, to take a trivial example, we found that a man is better liked by his fellow members the more closely he conforms to the standards of his group, there was no implication that conformity is an ethical good regardless of what the standards are, no implication that work done in a group is ethically or even practically superior to work done alone. If there was an ethical implication, it was that the rewards of conformity, like those of whisky, are so great that a group may easily abuse them. But what has been done with our work? The study of small groups has provided moral support for that very "groupiness" of Americans against which De Tocqueville warned us. The American of the Social Ethic turns out again to be an old American, sanctified by psychology.

One company, for instance, deliberately set "harmonious group thinking" as the goal of its research staff, and sacked a brilliant man who was not able to group-think. And a documentary film made for the Monsanto Chemical Company in order to inspire young men to go into chemistry ends by taking us to the Monsanto laboratories, where three young men in white coats are seen talking over a problem. The voice on the sound track rings out: "No geniuses here—just a bunch of average Americans working together."

This does not add up to an attack on social science, which is making progress though more slowly than it thinks. But it should be supported for the right reason and not made to confirm us in our bad habits. Nor does it amount to an attack on the corporations. They are our essential instruments. Capitalism and socialism fight only over what name they shall be called by. The danger is less that they will oppress their working men than that they will kill their officers with kindness, and their officers is what more and more of us are getting to be. Cooperation for its own sake and a distrust of individual thinking are things that bureaucracy has seldom found trouble in fostering. They have gotten effective, though unintended, moral support from social science, in a culture that sets a high value on science.

On top of all this, the organization takes such good care of its men that they may come to look on its ways not as habits to be put up with if they want to keep out of trouble but as virtues to be loved for themselves alone. In America, we were ready to love them anyway. Americans were never quite the rugged individualists they professed themselves to be. Rather, their easy associativeness was both their glory and their danger. When all three forces—American culture, corporate bureaucracy, and social science—work in line, the pressure may squash out qualities that give the life to men and nations. *The Organization*

Man ends with an old plea in a new form, a plea that we render to the organization only what is the organization's—our service, not our souls.

With this I heartily agree. The individualist is a pretty tough man. In the loosely knit societies of the past, there were plenty of places where he could hole up and glare out at us. And we could trust him to do it. Today the holes are getting fewer. We may need to take some thought how to make the world safe for him, for the world's sake as well as his own.

9

Men

and the Land

in the

Middle Ages

I

To find out what any ancient society was like, students must look at landscapes, for the peoples who know the plow and the cultivation of cereals leave their characteristic marks upon the land they occupy, and these may well be their most enduring memorial, just as the stone walls they built are likely to be the most enduring memorial of the invasion of New England by the English. Long after the bloodlines of a society have died out or the society itself has changed its ways, by the surface of fields, their shape, and the distribution of the old house sites may be

---

Designed for a book, never published, that was to have included essays by various persons on various aspects of the Middle Ages, this essay appeared in *Speculum*, 11 (1936), 338–351, and is reprinted by permission of the Editors. Toward the end of the essay I make a distinction between "logical" and "nonlogical" behavior that I took from Vilfredo Pareto, *Traité de Sociologie Générale* (Paris, 1917) and that I no longer find useful. In the present reprinting I might have revised the distinction out of existence, were it not absurd to pretend that in 1936 I believed something different from what in fact I did believe.

read the traditional arrangements by which the society made its living: the agricultural techniques people had at their command and the ways in which they grouped themselves and worked together in using these techniques. Furthermore, these traditional ways of making a living are in a relation of mutual dependence with the other customs of the society, so that the study of landscapes that are not natural but made by men is more than the study of different farming practices. It is the study of societies insofar as they are determined by and determine their use of the land.

The people of Europe in the Middle Ages were busy, almost wholly, with tilling the soil; therefore a study of medieval landscape is a good beginning for the study of medieval society. And it is no more nonsense to talk about medieval landscape than it is to talk about medieval art, for in many parts of Europe we can still look at medieval landscapes just as we can still look at cathedrals. Indeed, the landscapes are older than the cathedrals, for they are the engravings of societies that were in their prime when written history begins. Four hundred years ago, when people first began to take an interest in such matters, the lines were even clearer, and at that time observers made a distinction between two main kinds of English countryside, which they called *champion* and *wood-land*. *Champion* country—the word comes from the French *champagne* —was the country of great open stretches of arable fields broken only, here and there, by stands of trees and by the buildings of the villages clustered around the spire of the parish church. *Woodland* country did not always mean what we mean by woodland, that is, forest. Rather, *woodland* was country in which the fields were small and were surrounded by ditches, and walls made of the earth thrown up in digging the ditches. And often hedges or trees were grown in these walls, to give this kind of countryside the look of being wooded, in contrast to the open fields of the champion land.

What is more, to these two different landscapes corresponded two different kinds of human habitation. William Harrison, an Elizabethan Englishman, described them thus:

It is so, that our soile being diuided into champaine ground and woodland, the houses of the first lie uniformelie builded in euerie towne together, with streets and lanes; whereas in the woodland counties (except here and there in great market townes) they stand scattered abroad, each one dwelling in the midst of his own occupieng.[1]

In short, in the champion country were found compact villages, in the woodland was found some kind of dispersed settlement.

The boundaries of landscape are international, and the same contrasts were recognized on the southern shore of the English Channel as were recognized on the northern. Nowhere were the two kinds of landscape set apart by a sharp line like a surveyed frontier, but in a long-range view the provinces of each are plain. The country of the big villages—what is called the open-field country—stretched in a long band across England from the North Sea coast to the Channel. Crossing the Channel, it reappeared in northeastern France and went on across the Rhine into the lands of old held or conquered by the Germans, and into Denmark and Sweden. In the peninsulas and islands of the Western Ocean ruled the land of small, walled fields and scattered settlement, in Brittany and western Normandy in France, in Cornwall and Devon in England, in Wales and the northwestern English shires bordering on Wales, in Ireland, and at least so far as scattered settlements are concerned, in Scotland. Finally, to the east as well as to the west of the open fields, in the southeastern corner of England, especially Kent, and in Flanders, is a country of old enclosures and scattered settlement. No one knows much about the traditional field systems of these countries, and to make matters more interesting, Kent was the district overrun by the first Germanic invaders of England, invaders less like the Angles or the Saxons than either of these two were like each other—the Jutes.

II

The influences that determine the character of landscapes are of three kinds: geographical, technical, and social. The geographical factors include the terrain, the soils, and the climate. The technical factors include the ways in which the people who live on the land in question make a living from it: what tame animals they keep and how they care for them, what grains they know, what implements they use and how they use them, and so forth. These first two kinds of factors are economic factors. The third kind of factors, the social factors, include the customs according to which particular groups of people work together in making a living and in carrying on the other businesses of a society. Something must be said about each of these in talking about the difference between champion and woodland country. But no one of the three kinds of factors is independent of the other two. For instance, grain cannot be grown in a swamp.

The sort of thing geographers have to say about the way men settle on the land can be illustrated in the matter of soils. In France, they point out, the land of scattered settlements, both in Flanders and in the west, is by and large the land of the soils that hold the water. The big villages, on the other hand, lie on the soils that allow rain to soak through them quickly. For, in the first kind of country, surface water is abundant and habitation can be dispersed, whereas in the other kind of country springs are rare and wells must be sunk deep; accordingly people come together in numbers by the sources of drink for their cattle and themselves.

Unhappily, the coincidence of soils with kinds of human settlement is only a rough one. The weakness of arguments that trace the differences between woodland and champion landscape to one or another geographical influence is that woodland is often found where champion country should by rights have been, champion country where woodland should have been. People of the present day have become attached to the economic interpretation of history. And they have become used to hearing about manufacturers in fact changing their methods in order to obtain greater efficiency. Accordingly, they always overrate the importance of economic motives in the behavior of men. Of these supposed motives, the desire of men to make the most of their geographical environment is one. To be sure, the economic motives underlie all others, for most men have always been determined to get enough to eat and to keep themselves warm. But once they have worked out techniques which satisfy these needs reasonably well, they are slow to make them more efficient. They do not adopt such of the methods other people use as are better than their own, because they do not hear of them. And they do not conceive of the possibility of themselves reflecting upon their methods so as to invent better ones or to adapt the old ones more accurately to the requirements of the economic environment. They neither adopt nor adapt. This is especially true of times when useful information spread slowly and the feeling that it was wrong to change established custom was stronger than it is now. In those days a farmer would do his work in the same way as his neighbors did it and as his father taught him, and would not dream that another was possible. And when he moved into a new country he would try to adapt the country to his customs rather than his customs to the country.

A proof of this is at hand. The old world contrast between villages and scattered settlement repeated itself in the new world. The first colonists in Massachusetts settled in big villages and tried to establish open, common fields like those they had known in the east of England. In time the "commons" had to be abandoned, save in the form of parks, but the big village remained and became the New England town. But the first Frenchmen in Quebec came from woodland country in Brittany and Normandy, and settled, as at home, not in villages but in scattered farms. Villages grew up later, but only when churches were built, and the houses of shopkeepers and tradesmen clustered around these general meeting places. The colonists, then, made little attempt to adapt themselves, at least in the beginning, to specifically American conditions. They lived as they were used to living in the old country.

What was true of the French and English in America was perhaps true of their distant forefathers who made the woodland and champion landscapes of Europe: that they were moved less by the geographical features of the countries in which they settled than by the customs which had been handed down to them from previous generations. This brings up the question of race, for the fact which overshadows all others about the distribution of the woodland landscape in the western rim of Europe is that it coincides with the country in which large numbers of the peoples we vaguely call Celtic lived throughout the Middle Ages and in modern times, and it has been claimed not only that the woodland landscape is part of the traditional culture of the Celts but also that the contrasted champion landscape is the work of the Germanic races. But what the history of races has been, or even what the word *race* means is debatable, whereas the customs by which men have lived can be found out with some certainty. It is these which must be considered if anything interesting or important is to be said about contrasts in landscape.

The most interesting features of the woodland countryside were the small groups of people by which it was inhabited. The settlements were dispersed, but they were not isolated farms, each the home of a man with his wife, children, and hired men, like those of most of the rural parts of the United States. Not, at least, in early times. To be sure, isolated farms existed in land that was being cleared of forest, but in the older arable land this was not so. The woodland settlements were somewhere between a farm and a big village in size. They seem seldom to have been made up of more than twenty families, and there are signs that a hamlet of this sort was the natural group of homesteads of people using in common a single plow and having their cattle in a single herd.[2]

Whatever the economic bond, the social bond that held the dwellers in the woodland hamlets together may in the old days have been kinship, kinship in the extended family of descendants of a near and common ancestor. Certainly in out of the way parts of Ireland today the sentiments and ceremonies associated with the kin are more elaborate than they ever were in the country of the open-field villages. But the villagers made up for falling short in feelings of kinship by their neighborliness in the larger community. And after centuries of living in hamlets or villages, many of the attitudes characteristic of each, impressed by the older generations on their children, must still be vigorous even in peoples who have abandoned their old homes.

It is a mistake, then, to look on landscapes as the result of isolated activities of men, economic or social, for such activities are in fact seldom isolated, but are found in a state of mutual dependence with many other activities. What is more, these activities are mutually dependent not only directly but also indirectly, in that they all take part in the functioning of the organic wholes or systems which are called societies, and these wholes are greater than and unlike the sums of their parts. Landscapes must be conceived of as the physical shell of such organic social wholes, each perpetuating through the centuries its particular organization.

III

The techniques people use in making a living are one of the influences determining what sort of landscape they form, just as they are one of the influences determining many of the features of a society. Before the villages of the Middle Ages are described it is well to talk about some of these methods. We of the present day are inclined to think of ourselves as the first people who have used elaborate techniques. But the older traditional techniques were in some ways as elaborate as our own, if not as mechanical, and they required a vast amount of skill and experience. Practically speaking, a man cannot become a farmer unless he is brought up as one. The necessary training takes years to acquire. If this is true today, when farmers can buy most of the articles they need, how much more is it true of a time not so long ago when farmers had to clothe themselves and make their own tools as well as raise their own food? A village of the Middle Ages usually supported a smith, who made the plow-irons and the horseshoes, but nearly everything else a villager had to do for himself. He had to be master of a number of rather elaborate skills.

Of course no society is quite without a division of labor, and one of its early forms is the distinction drawn between men's work and women's work. In the Middle Ages it was largely the men who raised the food and the women who made the clothing in so far as the clothing was of cloth and not of skins. At least we know that people are likely to reflect in their myths the actual facts of their society. And when in medieval pictures Adam is shown holding a spade and Eve a distaff, and in medieval literature it is Adam who delves and Eve who spins, there is reason to believe that what was supposed to be true of the father and mother of mankind was really true of most medieval fathers and mothers.

Most of these techniques were handed down from fathers to sons, from mothers to daughters, substantially unchanged. Each little district was likely to develop its own varieties of the standard tools or cloths and maintain their individuality from generation to generation. When any of these goods were especially well made, demand for them grew among outsiders, and the district in which the skill was developed might become a center of manufacturing and trade. Our own age is clearly not the only one which has made inventions, and in the Dark Ages, from the discovery of the use of fire on, clever men have worked out new devices, and these by force of their usefulness have been imitated over immense distances and have made older methods obsolete. Such once must have been the flail and the winnowing-fan, and though we now look on them as crude implements, we should be lucky to remember how to make them if by any chance we should lose our modern threshing machines. For they save time, like any modern piece of machinery, and in their day their invention must have seemed just as marvellous. But there is another thing to remember about inventions. That is that they do not often and can seldom come singly. There is little point in learning how to cultivate cereals if at the same time you do not know a way of separating the grain from the straw and the wheat from the chaff.

One particular invention had much to do with the form of the open-fields of the champion villages. That was the plow, the most important implement of agriculture. And it was a true invention, for the plow, with its heavy frame, iron share and colter, and moldboard, seems to have displaced the crooked stick drawn through the sod with a pair of oxen, which is and was used by many primitive peoples, European and other. This displacement in some countries was still going on in recent times. The advantages of the plow are that it breaks up the ground to a greater depth than the crooked stick, and with its moldboard, always on the right-hand side, turns over the furrow. This second feature allows the plow to become an instrument for drainage. In the Middle Ages it was the custom to plow land in narrow strips. The plow would begin at the centerline of the strip and go round and round the strip, from the inside out, always turning the earth toward the middle of the strip. After a few plowings of this sort, the earth would be taken from the two outer edges of the strip and heaped up in the middle in a ridge. In wet weather the ridges would stay dry, while the water collected in the troughs between the ridges. Where people chiefly lived in England in ancient times and most likely through the Roman occupation was on the high downs. Perhaps the conquest of the valleys was possible only after the introduction of the heavy plow with the moldboard, accompanied by the technique of ridge-plowing, had enabled people to drain the low-lying arable land.[3]

IV

In the *champagne* of northwestern Europe in the Middle Ages, the village was the farming unit. The village was a unit in that its houses, each set in a close,[4] were all near together, in rows on either side of a long street or more planlessly clustered around the parish church. The village was a unit in that the fields which spread out in a ring around the houses and closes were village fields, cultivated according to a rotation of crops that was customary and binding on every villager. The commonest practice was to divide the village fields into three great sectors—the fields properly so-called. Each year one of these sectors would lie fallow; one would be seeded to winter grain (wheat or rye), and one to spring grain, where, as the folk song says,

Oats, peas, beans, and barley grows.

In the next year, the fallow field would become the winter wheat field, the winter wheat field, the spring wheat field, and so on in succession through the centuries. The village was also a unit in that the cattle of the village, under the tending of village herdsmen, ranged in one herd over the stubble of the fallow field and other village pastures.

Finally, the woods and wastes within its borders were kept for the common use of the villagers. That the village was a unit means simply that the sentiments of people, according to which they worked together as a village in raising their food, dominated those according to which they might have worked as separate families. Unquestionably this was true in early times, but the physical framework and arrangements of the village remained long after the sentiments which had determined them had disappeared.

The village, then, was what it was because the villagers worked together, and if a man works face to face with his neighbors day after day, year after year, perhaps the feeling is encouraged that he should share equally with them in the fruit of their common labor. But whatever the reason for it, the arrangement of the big villages was such that every villager shared with his neighbors in the wealth of the village, which was mostly land. His stake in the village consisted of a house and close in the village proper, a share in the use of the village woods, wastes, and pastures, and a number of acres in the village fields, so divided that an equal amount lay in each field. By this means the villager was assured of a steady supply of grain year by year, no matter which field lay fallow. Moreover, in no field did the holding of a villager lie as a compact block of land, but as a series of narrow strips, consisting of a number of the parallel and adjacent ridges made in plowing, scattered all over the village fields, and divided from the strips of his neighbors by lines of turf left unplowed, or simply by the furrows between ridges. By this means, the villager was assured that he shared proportionately with his fellows in the bad and good soils, in the favorable and unfavorable locations in the village fields. But also, since his lands lay scattered in small strips, and the fields were submitted to an unvarying rotation of crops and fallow pasture, the villager was forced to cultivate the same grains as his fellow villagers and at the same times. All these provisions put out of the question a villager's setting up permanent walls or hedges around his land or building his house in the fields outside the village proper. This is why the country of the medieval villages is open-field country.

The holdings of the villagers were not only scattered in the same proportions over the bad and good lands of the village, they were also in fact, for any given class of villagers, equal in size. But as far back as the records go, the medieval village was never a classless society. Two main classes of villagers were set well enough apart to be called by special names, and the equality of holdings held good only within these classes or their subdivisions. Even more clearly than most class structures, that of the village was related to the division of labor. Oxen were the most important single requirement in tillage, for many of them were needed to drag the crude and heavy plow through the ground—eight made the commonest plow team of the Middle Ages— and the class that a man belonged to depended on whether he owned and used plow-oxen or worked with his hands. The upper class were the villagers proper, who possessed plow-oxen, yoked them with those of their fellows in plowing, and held a substantial number of acres in the village fields. The lower class were the so-called cotters, who possessed no plow-oxen and, as their name implies, a cottage and a close, but only a few acres, if any, in the fields. The cotters furnished the villagers properly so-called with the necessary supply of spare hands.

Last of all, however standardized, traditional, and unvarying this open-field village plan may seem to be, it could not work unless it could be adjusted to conditions which vary from year to year. Farmers, for one thing, have never been able to take the weather for granted. Villagers cooperated in plowing; therefore they had to agree among themselves every season as to when plowing should begin. They had to choose herdsmen, make regulations about pasturage, meadows, harvest, and harvest laborers. Not least, the open-field system left many chances for clashes between villagers. Such matters seemed to have been settled in village meetings, held separately or together with the court of the feudal lord. Not only in England, but all over Europe, there has always been a large measure of local self-government.

V

No one feature of a society can for long be usefully considered apart from the other features of the society. This is as much true of the society of the Middle Ages as it is of any other. Outside of the Church, the two most important institutions of that society were the towns and the feudal-manorial system, and there is something to be said about the relation of the village to each of these. Towns were set apart from the country in the Middle Ages in more ways than by walls. Foreign and long-distance trade centered in the towns, and they were mostly free of feudal and manorial arrangements. More important, perhaps, towns were the chief means by which able people from the lower rose into the upper classes, probably something that must go on in any society if it is to be kept healthy. Even now, and much more so in old times, a man has to get out of the community he was brought up in if he is to rise in the world. The towns took care of this. Ambitious plow-boys moved to the towns to escape the bonds of village life. If they prospered, their daughters might marry into the landed gentry.

Though town and village were separate worlds, they were worlds that were similarly organized. Many of the towns began as farming villages, and some of them, especially the smaller ones, always kept their common fields. The countrymen who deserted their villages to contribute to the great growth of boroughs which began in the tenth century clearly did not wholly get rid of the habits their mothers and fathers had taught them. People today talk much about town-planning and succeed in doing very little about it. But the open-field villages were arranged according to a plan which was standard and customary over much of Europe, and the people who made the towns of the Middle Ages imitated it as far as the difference in occupations allowed. At least in the early stages of borough history, the tenements of the burgesses were equal, like those of open-field villagers. Every burgess was supposed to share equally with every other burgess in whatever bargain any one of them made. The townsfolk, too, governed themselves, by means of an elected council. These arrangements, similar in town and country, are important means of reckoning what were the fundamental sentiments of the common people of the Middle Ages.

The ruling and warring classes of the Middle Ages were supported by tillers of the soil who paid them labor, food, and money rents. There has been much controversy whether or not the villages of Europe were originally independent communities upon whom lords later thrust themselves. Talk about origins that are not recorded and cannot be observed is usually inexpedient, but there is this to be said. The so-called manorial system, with its great estates and its labor services, was in full force only in the parts of Europe where the large villages and open-field system existed, and it is possible that the heavy services of plowing and other agricultural labor which the villagers of the Middle Ages, in cooperation, were bound to render toward the cultivation of the demesne of the lord of the manor could have been exacted only where the villagers were in the habit of working together in the same way in cultivating their own lands. Perhaps it is significant that in later times a job of plowing or other work which villagers as a body did to help out a needy neighbor was called a boon-day, the name once given to such work when rendered to the lord.[5] The men of Kent and Flanders were freemen by 1300, that is, were bound to do few labor services for their lords, or none at all; although there were many unfree in the lands around them. The reason may have been that neither the open-field system nor its concomitant, the typical manor, existed in these two countries.

VI

The first thing to be said in general about the open-field village system is that, in economic terms, it worked. Ridge-plowing is a way of draining land; a bare fallow is a way of restoring land exhausted by crops. Even if better ways of doing these things have since been invented, it must not be forgotten that the old ways did do the job. However much people suffered from famine and other hardships, open-field agriculture supported an increasing population for at least a thousand years. The system even gave some classes a security which they lost when the system was abandoned. A poor man in England in the old days was sure of a few acres of croft and could send a cow to graze on the commons of the village. Afterwards, such a man was wholly dependent on his wages as a farm laborer.

The open-field system worked in that it kept a large number of people alive. But even when the crudities of the farming techniques are left out of account, it is clear that the system was not efficient. For its arrangements were dictated by custom as well as by the economic situation. A plowman plowed in a day, not as much land as he could, but as much as was recognized by custom as a fair day's job of plowing. He plowed with eight oxen, not because eight oxen were just enough to draw his plow through the soil, for the soils varied in heaviness, but because it was the custom to plow with eight oxen. And it is likely that he began to plow, not on the days each year when the weather was the very best for beginning to plow, but on the days each year when it was customary to begin to plow, and these were tied to the religious calendar.

When the first scientific farmers, like Arthur Young, ran up against this sort of behavior at the end of the eighteenth century, they of course cursed it as folly. It was folly to plow with eight oxen, when two horses could do the work. It was folly to cleave to the old three-field rotation when turnips and the grasses could be introduced. The ways of the scientific farmers won out, but they forgot, just as those who today talk about "America's capacity to produce" forget, that capacity to produce depends on two factors, not one. It depends on techniques and implements of production. It depends also on the feelings of the men who carry out these techniques. The theorists talk as if the second factor could be taken for granted. It cannot.

The open-field system seems a strangely formalized one to people of the present day, especially if they are intellectuals and are not used to working for their living from dawn to dusk in close contact with their fellow men. They do not appreciate that in any such situation a set of customs are built up which prescribe what the conduct of every member of the group which is working together shall be toward every other member of the group. These customs tend to fall into a fixed and definite pattern. Behind them is the force of sentiment, not the logic of the economic situation. Indeed, they often run counter to the demands of the economic situation, and in many modern factories make their presence manifest in restriction of output by the workers. Conforming to this set of customs, a member of the group is able, without taking conscious thought, to work with the other members of the group as fellow human beings. Successful cooperation is impossible without such a set of customs.

Whenever men are working together to make their living, and of course in many other social situations, such a set of customs exists. In some modern factories, blueprints show what the technicians believe the personnel organization ought to be for maximum efficiency. But investigation often reveals the nonlogical customs of cooperation. They are not those called for in the blueprints, and indeed, among the customs, there are some according to which the workers act to nullify any attempt to make their behavior accord with the blueprints. Such a set of customs, then, is not officially recognized, but must in fact be taken into consideration.[6]

Whereas in such modern factories the nonlogical customs of behavior are not recognized, but can actually be found by looking for them, the reverse is true of open-field villages. The villagers are long since dead; we cannot directly observe the ways in which they worked with one another. Seldom, in literature or in surviving rolls of village courts, did they leave direct expressions of their sentiments. On the other hand, the open-field system was old and deeply rooted. Its nonlogical customs of cooperation, unlike those of the factories, had time to become recognized in its dispositions and institutions.

An example is the notion of the fair and customary day's job of work. Such a feeling exists among the workers in many modern factories. Often the specific output felt to be proper for a day's work bears no relation to the actual time it takes to turn it out. Of course, the management, which usually would like the workers to produce as much as possible, does not recognize such customary standards and will not tolerate them if discovered. In like manner, in the Middle Ages the amount of land to be tilled in a day or fraction thereof was fixed by local custom. But such standards were sufficiently well recognized and accepted to become official measures of area, such as the *journal* of France or the *morgen* of Germany.

Such arrangements as the day's work of plowing, the eight-ox team, the scattering of village holdings in small strips, and the compulsory rotation of crops, clearly did not run utterly counter to the demands of the economic situation, and could not, if the village was to survive. At the same time, they were not perfectly adapted to the economic situation. There is a gap, because two considerations, not one, determine the dispositions made by any group of people working together to make their living: the techniques they use, and the customs according to which they cooperate in using these techniques in a manner satisfactory to them as human beings. These customs are the important thing about any society and they are the important thing about medieval villages, for the villages were simply the units of land and of people within which they were in force.

VII

Polybius and Machiavelli—one after personal observation and the other after a study of history—have expressed their opinion that the Roman religion was valuable in giving rise to well-regulated conduct. But many other religions which have existed and still exist are more like the Roman religion than they are like a set of camp meetings, and it is probable that they have had in a greater or lesser degree a like good effect on the behavior of men. In particular it is probable that the religious practices of the Middle Ages were among the forces maintaining the elaborate customs which then governed farming life.

The old Roman religion was what may be called a religion of ritual. That is, it consisted of a set of acts, to be carried out in a particular way on particular occasions, and little attempt was made to explain in a theology why these acts were performed. Of the religious practices of the Middle Ages, those that conformed most closely to this model were the ceremonies of the folklore year. People maintained them through many centuries, and do not seem to have offered any reason for doing so other than custom. More important, though not from the present point of view more religious than the folklore practices, were the ceremonies of the Christian year. Catholic worship in the Middle Ages was made up of many elements; but it consisted at least, like the Roman religion and the folklore rites, of sets of acts to be carried out in particular ways on particular occasions. True, unlike the other two cults, there was an elaborate theology which explained the meaning of the liturgy; only the few educated men, however, were familiar with this. The common people, townsfolk and villagers, venerated the mass and the other ceremonies of the Church to a large extent as magic, especially since they were conducted in an unknown language.

In any age, farming has been a profession full of anxieties. Chief among these is the weather. Its tyranny forces the farmer to get certain pieces of work done on time if he is to survive. Fall plowing must be finished before the ground freezes. Hay must be harvested with dispatch, for fear of rain. But beyond a certain point the farmer is at the mercy of forces beyond his control, and if he worried steadily about all the things that might happen to his crops he would become a nervous wreck. The seasons and their occupations, each with its anxieties and, if all has gone well, its joys, bind the sentiments of farmers to the cycle of the year much more than the sentiments of men who do not till the soil.

A religion must adapt itself to these needs and sentiments. Therefore its calendar is vital to any religion of ritual; and in spite of the variety of its sources, the cycle of ceremonies of the Catholic church became geared to the farming year of medieval Europe. This took place only at a price. There were feasts that were more important in the eyes of a plowman than they were in the eyes of a member of a cathedral chapter. And many pagan customs were tolerated, since they could be neither assimilated nor destroyed. But on the whole the adaptation was successful, as will be seen.

A religion of ritual gives rise to well-regulated conduct because the spectacle of acts carried out in prescribed ways at prescribed times in one department of life must affect, as it is affected by, the way acts are carried out in other departments of life. More directly, one of the functions of a religious calendar is to help people get things done at the proper times. It is common in village customs of the Middle Ages to find various kinds of work associated with the neighborhood of definite Christian feasts or saints' days. Thus the slaughtering and salting of such cattle as were not to be fed through the winter was supposed to take place on or near St. Martin's Day. Arrangements like this accomplish two things. They make it perfectly plain to a man and to his neighbors when he is late with his work, and give the neighbors an excuse for laughing at him for it. They also allow a man to get through the routines of the year to some extent without taking thought, simply by doing the customary things at the customary times. Of course, since the weather varies somewhat from year to year, such dates fixed in the religious calendar may never be perfectly adapted to economic conditions. But they are well enough adapted, and at least the work gets done.

There is another way in which a ritual religion gives rise to well-regulated conduct. When a farmer has done the best he knows how to see that his fields are properly tilled and his cattle properly tended, he is still not safe. Bad weather or a murrain may overwhelm him. When a man is not sure he can accomplish something he wants by practical and logical actions alone, he worries and is likely to take out his worry in nonpractical and nonlogical actions. Perhaps it is better to say that he would worry, and his worry might hamper his work, if there were not some regular way, preferably in company with his fellows, by which he might accomplish these nonlogical actions. In the Middle Ages, the Catholic church took care of this for the farmer, in rites like that of blessing the fields in springtime. The fact that he had a recognized method of manifesting in actions of this sort his sentiments of uncertainty may have been one ingredient in the well-known fatalism of the tiller of soil. "The fact is that when the peasant has been working steadily, and has fulfilled the religious and magical ceremonies which tradition requires, he 'leaves the rest to God,' and waits for the ultimate results to come; the question of more or less skill and efficiency of work has very little importance."[7]

Finally, nothing is more common than that people should associate particular festivities and ceremonies with the turning points of the year. The feasts of the Church, as well as the surviving pagan feasts, tended to fall at these turning points, and the villagers of the Middle Ages celebrated them in village gatherings. Christmas, for one, came at the time when the plowing and sowing of the winter grain field had been finished, that of the spring grain field not yet begun, and when the ground was either frozen or sodden, so that little outdoor work could be done. A religion of ritual, then, like that of the Catholic church, gives rise to well-regulated conduct in at least two ways. It helps insure that the routines of life are carried on in the usual manner, since these routines are tied to the religious calendar. And it gives men's feelings of helplessness and those linked with the changing seasons adequate and orderly social expression.

Some attention must be paid to these considerations when it comes to deciding whether or not people were "happy" in the Middle Ages. On the whole, people pass two sorts of judgments on the life of those times. Some look on it as a wretched state of misery and violence. To others it is a kind of Gothic idyll. These judgments of the past are likely to be linked with judgments of the present. If one looks on the present as an age of progress, one takes the first attitude toward the Middle Ages. If one looks on the present as an age of social disintegration, one takes the second attitude. Both attitudes are right, but are concerned with different things. Certainly the physical side of a peasant's life was hard. But the well-being of most men depends as much on the social as on the physical side of their lives. And the compact, socially well-organized villages of the Middle Ages seem to have arranged the relationships of fellow human beings better than do most institutions we have today. It is only fair to say that these relationships were then less complicated.

Two main kinds of landscape survived from antiquity in northwestern Europe. Any description of the differences between them must take into account geographical, technical, and social factors. It must have something to say about soils, about plows, about two different traditional human groups, the hamlet and the village. Most has been said here about the last. Customs by which men live and work together, accepted not because people appreciate that there must be such customs but because their forefathers taught them to behave in certain ways, are indispensable to any society we now know, were indispensable to any dead society we can reconstruct, and they must be taken into consideration by any sensible person who predicts what sorts of society are likely to exist in the future.

10

The Rural Sociology of Medieval England

I

As a sociologist who has worked with material traditionally called historical, I may be excused for beginning this essay with some ideas on the relations between sociology and history in general, before going on to suggest the contributions a sociological point of view may make to the study of English society in the Middle Ages.

The classical historians from Herodotus to Gibbon did not find specialization a problem. Their main emphasis was political, but they had no inhibitions about entering any field of social behavior. With the appearance in the nineteenth century of professional historians, history has tended to develop into a set of historical specialties. Of these political history was the earliest, as being closer to the classical tradition, but it was soon joined by constitutional, legal, religious, and economic histories. Social history was the last to enter this company, and it naturally took as its province whatever the others had left untouched.

Based on a lecture given at the University of Cambridge, March 6, 1953, and published in *Past and Present*, No. 4 (1953), 32–43. Reprinted by permission of the Editorial Board.

[145]

Its field was residual—such things as cultural history and the history of social classes. When I first attended lectures on social history, I even heard the history of the two-pants suit. Such was the American school of the "New History"—now several decades old.

Although social history as a new and residual historical specialization has a rich vein to work, this is not what I have chiefly in mind when I speak of the contribution sociology can make to history. Whatever its specialization, history is the study of changes in human behavior over time. In the period when professional history was developing, another method of studying social behavior made its appearance; this was called sociology or social anthropology and, by and large, did not concern itself with changes over time. Sociology was concerned with contemporary literate communities, and found the study of their past already pre-empted by historians. Social anthropology was concerned with contemporary nonliterate communities, which by that fact did not possess a recorded history, and when the discipline attempted historical reconstruction, it found the results less illuminating than others it could more easily obtain.

Forced out of the time dimension, sociology did its work in another dimension, that of the contemporary interrelations of institutions. Politics, law, economics, kinship, religion were not, for sociology, specialties to be pursued by different professionals, but institutions whose contemporary relationships in a community—usually a small one—were to be examined by one professional. The guiding theoretical idea of sociology is that of the social system, in which all the institutions of a society are assumed to be interrelated until proved otherwise. A change in one institution will, on this theory, be accompanied by changes in other institutions, but in practice these changes are not followed over the time dimension but rather over space—by comparison of different societies.

In order to make a distinction at all, I make it too sharp. But here it is: there are now two main methods of studying social behavior, one specializing, upon the whole, on particular types of institution, concerned with time series, and mainly noncomparative; another specializing on the contemporary, concerned with the interrelations of institutions, and often comparative in its emphasis. The former is history, the latter, sociology. We can at once think of studies that fall easily into neither class. Where does Toynbee fit? Yet the distinction seems to me to reflect differences in behavior between many historians and many sociologists.

So defined, the two disciplines are so obviously complementary that I believe we may look forward to their fusion in studies of society as a system of interrelated institutions changing as a whole through time. Then indeed we shall be close to the systematic scientific history some of us, though not perhaps those who cling to history as an art, have looked forward to for so long. I do not believe in the least that the two are natural enemies.

II

I shall now try to illustrate the kind of contribution a sociologist may make to the common task I have just set for us. I shall give a sociologist's view of two main types of English social organization in the Middle Ages and their historical consequences, the two being the social organization of East Anglia and Kent, on the one side, and, on the other, that of central or open-field England. I shall leave out of account both the Celtic world of the West and the debatable land of Essex, Middlesex, and Surrey. In this work, I shall take both the roles I have already sketched out: that of the social historian who occupies himself with kinds of history which other historians eschew—in my case, the history of family organization—and that of the sociologist who occupies himself with the interrelations of institutions.

The facts of English ethnography in the Middle Ages are simple enough in their main lines. I speak of what are in effect statistical differences, differences between the commonest, not the only, forms of social organization in two distinct areas. Central England is marked by large, compact villages, whose fields are managed according to customary rules binding on all villagers—one or another variety of the so-called open-field system or champion husbandry. In these fields, a villager's holding lies in strips scattered all over the fields, with approximately equal acreage in each one. The holdings tend to be equal, class by class: there may be yardlands and half-yardlands, but each yardland is normally equal to every other one. A holding in villeinage or socage is commonly held by one man and descends to one of his sons. And many of the holdings are villein holdings, subject to heavy labor-services for he lord of the manor.

Arrangements in Kent and much of East Anglia differ at almost every point from those just described.[1] Let me take Kent first. Kent is marked by settlements smaller than the open-field villages, settlements I shall call hamlets. The holding does not originally consist of scattered strips. The earlier the date, the more often it appears instead as a compact body of land, the hamlet apparently lying close to the land. The holding is managed as an independent farming unit, not subject to many communal rules, though often following in fact a traditional rotation of crops. The holdings may once have been equal in size, but by the end of the thirteenth century such equality has degenerated, and irregularity is the rule rather than the exception.

A husbandman's holding tends to be in the hands of a group of men often called *participes*, sometimes called *heredes*, and it is often clear that these men are patrilineal kinsmen. The custom of inheritance in Kent is called gavelkind, and recognized by the lawyers as being different from most of the rest of England. Land descends to a number of heirs jointly, as when in Lewisham in 1301, Walter, Robert, Richard, and John take seisin of a holding as "the sons and one heir of Gerard Ate Pirie."[2] It looks as if we had to do with joint-family communities like those Le Play described as still existing in the Auvergne in the nineteenth century: groups of men claiming descent from a common patrilineal ancestor, living in one house or a small group of houses, and managing in common a compact body of land, under the leadership of the oldest or ablest male of each successive senior generation. But the custom of Kent also allows an action for the physical partition of a holding among heirs, and hence, we must presume, for dissolution of the joint-family community. Already in the thirteenth century lawyers are claiming that this is resulting in what the French were later to call *morcellement*: division carried so far that holdings are too small to get a living from.[3]

Again unlike open-field England, Kent by the end of the thirteenth century holds few villeins. Week-work for the lord of the manor is the badge of villeinage, and week-work is uncommon in Kent.

The customs of East Anglia, including the villages on the southern shore of the Wash, are mixed, but in many places identical with those of Kent. The fact of gavelkind inheritance is certainly common, though not the name. Holdings seem at one time to have been fairly compact, but they have become much broken up by partible inheritance. The proportion of free socage to villein tenures is higher than in central England, though lower than in Kent. East Anglia differs from Kent chiefly in the fact that settlement seems to be in big villages rather than hamlets, but even here the two districts are alike in lacking strict two- or three-field systems of husbandry.

There is some evidence that these contrasts repeat themselves on the southern shore of the Channel, notably between the Old Saxon area of Germany and the Frankish-Frisian area.[4] We have on the one hand a strong village community linked with what Le Play called in *Les ouvriers européens* a stem-family, and on the other hand a weak or nonexistent village community linked with a joint-family. Big village, small family or small village, big family—the contrast is oversimple but not fantastically so.

III

As far as tenements and field systems are concerned, the facts just cited have long been known to, and attentively studied by, economic historians. But aside from the old family solicitor and an occasional great man like Maitland, it takes a social historian, a snapper-up of trifles unconsidered by other historians, to show any interest in the history of inheritance, and especially a social anthropologist, whose first task in the field is usually to grapple with a society's kinship system.

The facts are further interesting in that no historical account of their origin has ever been given. Here are two parts of England, Kent and East Anglia, which in the thirteenth century resemble one another in custom and differ sharply from the rest of England. Moreover, the differences are, in 1300, already old. They certainly go back to the twelfth century,[5] and statistical contrasts, revealed in Domesday Book, between southeastern England and the rest of the country suggest that they were present at the time of the Conquest.[6] I shall speak of the statistics later. From the Conquest back to the invasions is a long jump, but the presence of parallel differences in custom among the continental Germans of later centuries is at least one point in favor of the view that the Anglo-Saxons brought at least two different types of social organization to England with them. We know that, in the absence of technical change, custom tends to persist, and that emigrants take their social organization across the sea with them, as when the English of the seventeenth century took English institutions, including the open-field system, across the Atlantic to New England.

Of course it is no explanation of the particular character of custom, but I should be happy if we were at least able to attach these differences in custom to differences in the names and places of settlement of invading tribes, as the anthropologist attaches such differences to tribal names like Hopi and Navaho, but this we are able to do only in part. We may take some comfort from Kent, as Bede tells us it was settled not by Angles or Saxons but by Jutes, whose custom, Jolliffe suggests, most resembled that of the Franks, right across the Channel.[7] But nobody has hinted that the Jutes, whoever they may have been, also settled East Anglia. If, in fact, the latter name is really an old folk name—and I myself should lay more weight on the very distinctive county names—the settlers must have been Angles, and yet their custom, if my hypothesis of antiquity is correct, differed sharply from that of the Middle Angles to the westward. Or if we assume that East Anglia was heavily resettled by Danes, we must still account for differences in custom between East Anglian Danes and those of the rest of the Danelaw. Perhaps these problems are insoluble for lack of evidence, yet I do think it a pity that historians of the Germanic invasions, like Myres, do not consider the similarity of the customs of East Anglia and Kent to one another worthy of notice.[8] For myself, I believe that the distribution of custom, even if first recorded at much later times, is just as good a basis for historical reconstruction as the distribution of brooches and burials, and that England was invaded by two sorts of Germans—Anglo-Saxons and Friso-Jutes—whose areas of settlement were not quite those assigned to them at present. In short, East Anglia and Kent were invaded by the same kind of people.

IV

But I am not just suggesting that the distribution of field systems, types of holding, and customs of inheritance is interesting in itself and cries for some account of its origin. If the social historian picks up the scraps, like inheritance, that have fallen from the table of more respectable scholars, the sociologist is something more—a student of the interrelations of institutions in a social system. His cardinal assumption is that, if one or more institutions in a society are of a given kind, the variations in the other institutions are not random but rather to some degree determined. That is, the society has a structure. Or, to put it still more simply, different institutions have different consequences.

From his point of view, the concomitant variation of field systems, types of holding, and customs of inheritance over the same geographical boundaries in medieval England is a fact of the most significant kind, for it suggests to him that he is dealing with types of social organization that differ as structural wholes. These differences must have consequences for the other characteristics of social organization. I shall speak of three fields in which organizational differences between Kent and East Anglia, on the one hand, and open-field England on the other, may have had different historical consequences. These fields are: population, commercial interests in land, and manorial development. Here I am again in the area of speculation, though I have some facts to go on.

In his admirable papers on the Domesday villeins and sokemen,[9] Reginald Lennard shows that in Lincolnshire (I should be interested in knowing *what parts* of the county), Norfolk, Suffolk, Essex, and Kent the Domesday figures reveal a higher proportion of villeins and sokemen holding small numbers of plow oxen and small pieces of land than in other parts of England. I am aware of the booby traps that an attempt to translate such figures into population estimates may encounter, but Lennard himself believes that population was actually denser in the southeast. At any rate, the results are obviously compatible with the customs of inheritance in Kent and East Anglia. Not only should partible inheritance lead, under reasonably favorable economic and sanitary conditions, to a rise in population, but descent of land to one son should lead to relative stability of population. In the latter case, the sons who do not inherit have no land to support families; in some places custom explicitly forbids their marrying, and the son who is to inherit does not marry until his father transfers the holding to him.[10] As a breeder, he starts behind the man who marries early. He may catch up, but has his work cut out for him, and in any event his is only one breeding-unit on a holding that might, under different custom, have contained several.

We know that in other situations rules of inheritance may have an important influence on population. A good example is the recent history of the population of Ireland. Before the famine of 1846, land among Irish countrymen, like other Celts, was partible among the sons of the last holder. Observers spoke of the early age of marriage, and population in relation to resources was obviously high. As a result of the famine, laws were enacted that had the effect of restricting the inheritance of land to one son. As custom developed, this son did not marry until his father was ready to transfer management of the farm to him. Today in Ireland the average age of marriage is the latest in the world, and population has been cut in half in a century.[11] It is no use telling me that this was the result of emigration. The rule of inheritance provided the human material for emigration. (By the way, there is little illegitimacy in Ireland, in spite of the large number of unmarried adults.)

Nor is it any use telling me that the population figures for medieval East Anglia can be accounted for by the fact that the standard tenement was somewhat smaller than the midland yardland. This only begs the question why it should be smaller. In any event, many countrymen in southeastern England had, by the end of the thirteenth century and as a result of the subdivision of holdings, dangerously little land to live on. As I have pointed out, contemporary observers recognized this, at least in Kent. Poor farmers may look for other means of support. Is this a partial explanation for the early rise of a clothing industry in East Anglia? Or even for the Peasants' Revolt?

On the subject of a commercial market in land, I am on less sure ground because I cannot cite statistics. Some years ago, as I ranged through the custumals and court rolls of the thirteenth century, I certainly got the impression that the buying, selling, and exchanging of small parcels of land were more characteristic of southeastern England than of the open-field country. And I wondered why this should be. It is easy to point out that the Southeast was the country nearest to London and the big commercial cities of Flanders and thus peculiarly subject to commercial influences—whatever actual behavior we may subsume under that phrase. But granting the presence of these influences, I wondered if the social systems of the Southeast might not have been peculiarly vulnerable to their action.

We do not know what motives impelled men to dissolve the joint-family farms of Kent and East Anglia, but we do know that by the end of the thirteenth century partition had produced a large number of countrymen holding very small acreages indeed. If a man holds too little land to support him in any event, he may well feel few qualms at getting rid of some more of it, especially when other opportunities for making a living, such as weaving, may be open to him. Such conditions create the willing seller. As for the willing buyer, he certainly expressed in later centuries a desire to get land that he could manage more or less as he wished, without regard for rules of tillage binding

[152]

on the whole community. Such, by and large, were the lands of Kent and East Anglia, in comparison with those of the open-field.

A person's rank or status is, moreover, closely related to the standard of living he can maintain and thus, in peasant societies, to the size of his holding. When inheritance is partible, and some men have more male heirs than others (as they naturally will), the amount of land held by any line of single families is apt to change, generation by generation. That is, the status system is going to be relatively fluid. A family with many heirs is, by selling land, only hastening a process that will take place in any event, while a family with few may be able to reverse the process or hold its own by buying.

In the open-field villages, on the other hand, the tenements are normally equal in size, class by class, with sharp differences between classes: yardlands, half-yardlands, cotsetles. That the rank of these classes is important can be seen in their association with different manorial and village offices, which differ in responsibility. The reeve comes from the yardlanders, the hayward from the half-yardlanders, and the lord's plowman from the cotters.[12] The rule of inheritance by one son implies that, if all goes well, the rank of family-lines within the village, instead of being fluid, remains constant generation by generation. Under these conditions, the sale of land from a tenement threatens irreparable damage to the relative rank of a lineage: its equality with its peers. Sale does not merely add fluidity to a situation already fluid, but makes a fundamental breach in the status system. Hence we may argue that a responsible tenant will be reluctant to sell, and that an irresponsible one will be restrained by rules against alienation. We may also argue that the partible Southeast is more vulnerable, the impartible open-field less vulnerable, to commercial influences, so long as the sale of land is easiest where it does least social damage.

Commercial dealing in land, with its concomitant, the opportunity to consolidate holdings, together with freedom from overriding village custom in the use of land, may lead to the formation of new holdings managed by methods resembling modern ones. That is, these conditions may lead to enclosure. By the time of the Agricultural Revolution, the Southeast had become one of the old-enclosed parts of England. And gavelkind inheritance seems to have become a rule applied only in case of intestacy—which opens up a whole new field of inquiry.

As for the influence of different forms of peasant custom on different forms of manorial development, I have argued that the customs of countrymen, from field-systems to customs of inheritance, are primary and early, probably as old as the Anglo-Saxon invasions. But it has also been argued that at least the customs of inheritance are the mere creation of lords of manors pursuing their economic interest. Where their tenants pay them rents for the most part, they are willing to allow partible inheritance, since rents are easily divisible, but where heavy labor-services are attached to villein holdings, the lords insist on impartibility, since responsibility for services is not so easily divided. We do not have to accept the argument, as there are plenty of cases in East Anglia in which the holders of parts of a tenement combine, by arrangements unknown to us, to carry out the labor-services due from the tenement as a whole. The argument assumes, moreover, that a lord could always, in fact as well as in law, do what he would with his villeins, that he was an omnipotent village tyrant—an unrealistic assumption to which I shall later return. But even if we do accept the argument, it still leaves unanswered the question why some manors had heavy labor-services and some did not, that is, why the lords' alleged interests arose at all, and why heavy labor-services should have been associated with open-field agriculture.

For it is a fact, as I have pointed out, that a higher proportion of tenants in free socage to tenants in villeinage obtained in Kent and East Anglia than in central England. (I am leaving out of consideration the northern Danelaw.) This was true at the time of Domesday, and by the end of the thirteenth century very little villeinage remained in Kent. And the most characteristic stigma of villeinage is heavy labor-services for the lord of the manor. Nor was the phenomenon limited to England. One of the greatest of social historians, Marc Bloch, claimed that the full-blown *seigneurie* appeared in France "north of the Loire and on the Burgundian plain," that is, in the open-field part of the country.[13] He argued that the feudal system itself developed its classic form only under these conditions. Is this phenomenon a matter of chance, or is it, as a sociologist would assume as his first working hypothesis, related to other aspects of the social system?

For purposes of argument alone, let us assume that a man of war, sometime in the Dark Ages, wanted to secure from a body of husbandmen material sustenance for himself and his retainers. In those days, he might well be able to get work more easily out of them than money, and if work was what he wanted, how much more easy to mobilize the labor of a village community, its members living in one center and tilling their fields in cooperation, than that of a looser society, like Kent and its continental kin, where joint-family residence was scattered and interfamilial cooperation less fully developed. Since human material can be beaten into shape by force only at great expense, and is in any event not infinitely malleable, how much more easy to work with an organization ready at hand than to create one *de novo*—even if one knew what one wanted to create. Although humanitarian ideas weighed less heavily with them than with most invaders, the *conquistadores* of New Spain, when they tried to turn the Carib hunters and fishers into estate laborers, merely succeeded in killing them off. It was not until they discovered the settled agricultural populations of Mexico and Peru that they were able to establish themselves as country gentlemen. They had to work with the existing social organization. "So," said Marc Bloch, "it would be a grave error to assume any necessary opposition between the bonds of the village community and those of the *seigneurie*."[14] I should go farther and say that the manor could be strong only where the village community was strong.

But we are not bound to think of the original lords of manors as *conquistadores*, men of war from abroad coming in to impose their will on the natives. Manorial development must have been much more gradual than this, though no less closely linked to underlying social organization. As Bloch again pointed out, we have only to think of the lord of the manor as the successor to a village chief.[15] Here the sociologist finds his comparative perspective useful: he knows of classic studies of the chief in such primitive societies as Tikopia and the Trobriand Islands.[16] There the chief is titular owner of the land of the community, but he can exercise his rights only with due regard for the varied rights of his men, who make him gifts of food, which he distributes again in support of workers carrying out tasks (such as canoe-building) useful to the community as a whole, but beyond the capacity of any single family. He is the lord of the land, but also the mobilizer of large-scale cooperation.

What I have elsewhere called the ambiguous position of the lord as revealed in the thirteenth century custumals is quite compatible with continuous development from chieftainship of this sort. The lord is the titular owner of the wood and waste, but the community uses both. He provides whatever complex machinery is needed, such as the mill, but the community uses it, and pays him multure. His steward presides in the hallmote and takes its fees, but verdict is given by a jury of the villagers, finding their custom. The services on his demesne are supervised by the reeve, who is not an overseer of slaves but one of the villagers, often elected by them. At seedtime and harvest, they give him boon-plowings and boon-reapings, *benes* such as they would give to any needy villager. These are said to be done as a favor to the lord, though precedent has come in time to make no distinction between what is customary and what is, in fact, exactable. At Christmas the villagers give him hens, which he distributes again, cooked, at the feast he holds in the hall for his tenants. Of course he gets, through his exchanges with his tenants, a larger income than any one of them—otherwise he would not be the lord—but his role, in Bloch's words, is less that of a modern landlord than that of first citizen of the commune—*le premier habitant*.[17]

All that was needed to turn an original village chieftainship into a medieval lordship of the manor was some overturn among the chiefs and their replacement, as in conquest, by outsiders less close, ethnically, to the natives, together with a little legal interpretation by clerks less familiar with the real situation than with concepts suitable to the Roman *fundus*. Remember what happened much later when the rights of a Highland chief over clan territory were assimilated to those of an English landlord over his estates. Once the manor becomes the legal framework of landholding, all estates can be cast, as they are in Domesday Book, into the manorial form, but even then, outside of the open-field areas, manorial revenue tends to take the form of rents in money and kind, whose collection depends far less on the existence of a strong community organization than does week-work on the demesne.

V

Thus a sociologist, looking at the interrelations of institutions in a social system, sees a *slowly* growing population, a weak commercial market in land, and a strong manorial organization with heavy labor-services as more compatible with impartible inheritance, an open-field village community, and an original village chieftainship than with partible inheritance, joint-families settled in scattered hamlets, and a more remote, territorial chieftainship, if indeed any chieftainship at all. Whether or not this interpretation is more adequate than another, it will serve at least as an example of the kind of attack a sociologist might make on the problems of social history. Anyone, of course, might interpret the evidence thus, but a sociologist is more apt to do so.

One last word to the economic historians, in order to make explicit an assumption so far implicit, though no doubt evident enough, in what I have said. I am not asserting the primacy of so-called "social" factors over factors of economic or technical self-interest. That would lead to the worst kind of false dichotomy: the two—if they are two—are mutually dependent. I am not turning the usual economic argument upside down and saying that week-work produced the lord's interest rather than that the lord's interest produced week-work. But neither am I admitting that economic or technical interests are pursued in a vacuum—an assumption underlying the theory once put forward (tentatively, to be sure)— that the differences between medieval East Anglia and central England follow directly from the prevalence of sheep-farming in the former. At any given time, the interests of lord or tenant, like those of their descendants today, are partly determined by, and always pursued within, an institutional framework: what I have called social structure or organization. It makes a difference to the outcome of economic endeavor what sort of social organization it started in. It even makes a difference in the kinds of new institutions economic endeavor creates in place of the old.

11

The Frisians

in East

Anglia

I

THAT the institutions of medieval East Anglia differed sharply from those of Wessex and Mercia has long been recognized. It has been the fashion to account for these differences by the settlement in East Anglia in 879 of the Danes in Guthrum's army. Recently R. H. C. Davis has shown that the settlement cannot have been thick enough to justify the assumption that East Anglia was reorganized along Danish lines.[1] Except in the Norfolk Broadland, Danish place-names are not common, certainly not nearly as common as in the northern Danelaw. There are by no means as many Danish personal names in the early records as Anglo-Saxon ones. It is hard to demonstrate much Danish settlement in Suffolk, and yet the institutions of Suffolk are identical with those of Norfolk. Above all, the social organization of East Anglia

Reprinted from *Economic History Review*, Second Series, 10 (1957), 189–206, by permission of the Editors. The latter part of the article has been rewritten to clarify the argument and eliminate what now appear to be a couple of errors of interpretation. For the benefit of readers who are not medievalists, a small number of notes have been inserted to describe institutions they are unlikely to have heard of; and the chief quotations from Latin have been translated.

does not much resemble that of the northern Danelaw, where we know that large numbers of Danes settled, but does resemble that of Kent. Davis concludes that the peculiarities of East Anglian society must be traced back to a time before the Danish invasion. He does not try to answer the questions: Traced to what? To whom? The present paper offers answers. It will argue that the social organization of medieval East Anglia displays such close similarities with that of medieval Friesland that people of Frisian origin, or at least closely related to the Frisians in culture, must have invaded East Anglia in the fifth century.

To put the Frisians among the Germanic invaders is like finding an object in plain sight. Frisian, after all, not Low German, Danish, or Norse, is the language most closely related to English. Almost two centuries before Bede said that England was invaded by Angles, Saxons, and Jutes, Procopius wrote in Constantinople that Angles and Frisians were then living in England.[2] The Danish author of *Knutsdrapa* used "Frisians" as a synonym for "English."[3] And archaeology has shown the close relation between the culture of the Frisian *terpen* and that of the early Germanic invaders.[4] If Frisians did not cross the North Sea, they certainly ought to have done so.

II

The East Anglian cultural area includes not only Norfolk and Suffolk but also those parts of other counties that lie around the Wash on the northern side of the Fens. Long ago H. L. Gray showed that various forms of the open-field system prevailed to the west of this area, and we may accept his demonstration, provided we remember that, though other arrangements were significantly more prevalent in East Anglia, there may well have been some open-field there too; that the differences between the two areas are statistical, not absolute; and that the boundary between the two was no doubt a shaded border, not a sharp line.

It was Gray too who first provided a general picture of the different arrangements in East Anglia.[5] Settlement in East Anglia was by villages, not necessarily big villages, but certainly not always by isolated homesteads (*einzelhofen*). Attached to these villages were "fields" in which the holdings lay. The largest named tenement-unit was the 120-acre

[159]

carucate or *caruca*, also called in Walpole in the Norfolk Marshland by the interesting name of *tenmanloth*. By the thirteenth century the carucate is rarely in the hands of one man. Its subdivisions are called by a variety of terms: *fullonds* (*plenae terrae*), *eruings, quarteria, tenementa,* etc., which are not the same as those used in the open-field area.[6] Bovates and virgates are mentioned rarely in the documents and look like late importations. These smaller tenement units may well be equal in size within a given village, but there is little evidence of uniformity from village to village. Indeed the commonest way of specifying the amount of land a man holds is simply to state the number of acres. Analysis of the acreages recorded as in dispute in the earliest fines shows that the most frequent holdings were 30 acres and 12 acres, that is, one-quarter and one-tenth of a carucate.[7]

In the early charters and fines there is also evidence that a holding was often a compact area of land lying in one part of the village fields. In this, East Anglia resembles Kent. But in time the land became much broken up by division and alienation, so that the holding of a villager may lie in separate parcels. Even so, the parcels tend to lie in one part of the village fields, or unequally in a small number of parts, and not, as in the open-field, equally distributed over the fields. The inference is still that the original tenement to which the main body of parcels had belonged was a compact area of land.

There is little or no evidence of a regular rotation of crops binding on the fields of a village as a whole, and this is consistent with the tenemental arrangements, for if a holding lay in one part of the village fields, and if open-field arrangements had been in force, then once, say, in every three years the holding would have yielded no crop. But there is evidence that villagers intercommoned their beasts on the waste and marsh belonging to a village, and for the sixteenth century Gray found evidence for fold-courses each of which covered only a part of the village fields. A fold-course is the right to keep sheep in a fold on a particular area of land. The inference is not necessarily that the fold-courses determined the concentration of tenements in given areas. It is as likely that the latter determined the location of the fold-courses. We do not know the details of the East Anglian arrangements, but it is clear that in their main lines they differed from those of the open-field.

The second main distinguishing feature of the society of East Anglia was its custom of inheritance of land, which resembled Kentish gavelkind but differed from that prevalent, at least by the thirteenth century, in Wessex, Mercia, and probably the northern Danelaw.[8] In the latter areas, the general rule revealed in the manorial court rolls is that the tenement of a countryman descended to one of his sons and one only. Only in default of sons was the tenement divided among the daughters, and not always then. With this main rule a number of other arrangements were associated.

The geographical border between this rule of impartible inheritance and the East Anglian rule coincided with the border between the two types of field-systems. The test is the East Anglian panhandle around the Wash, which no more knew impartible inheritance than it did openfield agriculture. As in the case of the field-systems, one rule was prevalent but not universal on one side of the line, another rule on the other. Again the differences are statistical and not absolute.

Elsewhere I have provided much of the evidence for the East Anglian rule. Land held in socage, and for that matter in villeinage, was usually partible among the sons of the last holder, and in default of sons among his daughters. Sometimes a lord in granting land might change the custom of inheritance applicable to it, but the very terms in which he made the exception prove that partibility was the rule. Thus Abbot Samson of Bury St. Edmunds in a charter of date c. 1200–1211 granted lands in Rougham, Norfolk, to Roger son of Martin:

to be held by him and after his death by that one of his sons whom he shall wish to have inherit [them], so that he himself and his heir after him may hold the aforesaid lands with their appurtenances as a whole, without any division being made among brothers or sisters or any others.[9]

Had impartibility been the rule, the charter need not have protested so much.

Since brothers had ultimate rights of inheritance in undivided land, we find them in several East Anglian charters granting land as a group.[10]

Now let us go into details. If a man holding a divided share of his father's tenement died without issue, his land accrued, in the legal phrase, to his brothers as a group. But East Anglian custom, like Kentish, was more liberal to women than was the Salic Law, and if one of the brothers died leaving at least one daughter, she inherited his share. Accordingly, in a court roll of Westwood, Suffolk, in 1326, it is recorded that a messuage and arable had once been in the hands of Richard Hereward:

[161]

And from the same Richard the right descended and ought to have descended to Henry, William, and Thomas as the sons and the one heir. And from the same Henry the right descended for his part to Alice, the daughter and heir of the same Henry, who now petitions together with the aforesaid William and Thomas.[11]

This sounds as if Alice's part were not a physically divided piece of land but an ideal share or right of inheritance. If Alice married and had sons, her share presumably descended to them. At any rate, such an assumption would explain why divided shares of East Anglian tenements were often held by men bearing family names different from that of the first holder recorded in the documents.

But there is another reason for this last feature. Not only might land in East Anglia be divided among heirs, but at least if the land were socage, the divided parts might be quite freely alienated, and by the end of the thirteenth century East Anglia knew an active market in small pieces of land. Indeed partibility may have contributed to alienation: an heir might be left with too little land to make a living from and thus have good reason to sell out. Where one man had reason to sell, another had a chance to buy.[12]

If the land were physically divided among heirs, how was it done? Sometimes, we know, each quality of land was separately divided,[13] and if this practice was at all common in the cases of which we have no record, it would explain why the land of an individual holder often took the form of a number of parcels, but still lying in one part of the village fields. Indeed there is a little evidence that if a man held some land in socage and some in villeinage, his heirs shared proportionately in each.[14]

But let us not overemphasize physical partition. The word for the inheritance custom is *partible:* a tenement might be physically divided among heirs, but it was not necessarily divided. In East Anglia as in Kent, the heirs often continued to hold and work it in common and undivided, forming what anthropologists call a joint-family or minimal lineage. Thus we hear of groups of brothers, of uncles and nephews, and of first cousins holding land jointly. We hear of even more general terms for landholding groups: not only of *fratres* and *heredes* but of *socii, parcenarii,* and *participes.* Indeed, this is a very common feature of East Anglian extents and custumals.

Besides holding land in common, did a group of heirs ever keep on living together in one big family house, forming a house-community like those described in the sagas? All we have here are some curious East Anglian references to named "houses" (*domus*), references that seem unlike any found in the records of other parts of England. A list of the encroachments made in 1101–1107 by Roget Bigot and his men on the land of St. Benet of Holme in Norfolk contains entries like this:

And at Southstead the house of Elfgar with a plowland of land. . . . And at Oby the same S. took away the house of Leofchild and half its holding.[15]

At the end of this century, the *Kalendar* of Abbot Samson speaks of "houses" such as *domus Einulfi* in Hopton, Suffolk, and a little above this entry we read of *Gilbertus filius Einolf et socii*, as if the partners made up the "house." Finally, eighty years or so later still, there are entries in the Hundred Rolls for Norfolk specifying suit to hundred and leet as due from named "houses."[16] Such is the following entry for Fourhowe hundred:

Also William at the Church, John his brother, Richard at the Green, the house of Aylward [and] the house of Frauceys in Runhall withdrew themselves from the leet of Runhall pertaining to the hundred through the liberty of Costessey, by what warrant they [the jurors] know not.

It would be pressing these entries too far to argue that they provided adequate evidence for a house-community. They do suggest some special significance of the house, as a building and as a body of men, in land-holding and in the payment of rents and services.

If a group of heirs held land in common and undivided, under whose leadership did they act? Comparative anthropology would suggest the senior man. Even if a tenement were physically divided, the *participes* might still be held jointly responsible for the rents and services due from the tenement to the lord or the king. In this case we do find that the eldest bore a special responsibility. In an extent of Wykes in Bardwell, Suffolk, a freeholder, John Precius, is recorded as holding one-third of a messuage, one-third of the meadow, and three and a half acres of the tenement of John the chaplain, to which is added:

And because he holds the eldest-born's part (*eyniciam partem*) of the tenement of John the chaplain, he shall do suit at all the lord's courts for himself and his parceners.[17]

Eynicia is from the French *aisne*. It appears not to imply that the eldest got a larger share than the brothers, but only that when an inheritance was divided into parcels, the eldest had the right of first choice. Again, in the Hundred Rolls the jurors of North Erpingham hundred, Norfolk, find as follows:

They say also that Henry of Ingworth and Robert of the Stone of Aylsham, bailiffs of this hundred, unjustly distrain all the parceners of one inheritance (*hereditas*), from which only one suit is owed, to make many and heavy suits. And although the eldest-born's part (*eynecya*) of that inheritance ought to make the suit that is due, nevertheless they heavily amerce all the parceners for the defaults, to the heavy damage of all the suitors of this hundred.[18]

Note the use of *hereditas* for a holding of land.

A third difference between East Anglian institutions and those of most other parts of England lay in the way tenements were grouped together to form larger fiscal, judicial, and even economic units. Especially important here is the mysterious leet (Middle English *lete*, Latin *leta*), which, at least under that name, seems originally to have been limited to East Anglia. For these arrangements our best evidence comes, first, from the *Kalendar* of Abbot Samson of Bury St. Edmunds, of date 1186–1191, which contains a description of the Suffolk hundreds then in the hands of the abbey,[19] and, second, from the Norfolk and Suffolk Hundred Rolls of 1274–1275.

In East Anglia, the basic assessment unit was, as we know, the carucate of 120 *ware*, or assessed, acres, These carucates lay in vills, and the vills appear on the average to have been small. In the East Anglian Domesday, each vill is responsible for paying a certain number of pence to the geld. Such of these vills as appear in the *Kalendar* are grouped together to form leets, less often called *ferdings* or *ferderings* and, in Latin, *villae integrae*. Sometimes a large town, like Sudbury, is divided into several leets; sometimes a vill forms a leet by itself, but much more often two, three, or four contiguous vills make a leet jointly. In this case, the *Kalendar* says that each vill forms a definite fraction of the leet. Of three vills, for instance, that together make up a leet, one may be said to form half the leet, the other two one-quarter each. The proportions that these fractions bear to one another are usually the same as those borne by the number of pence that the vills paid to the Domesday geld. And every leet within a hundred contributes roughly the same, and often exactly the same, amount to the total geld for the hundred.[20]

The leet shows signs, then, of being a standard fiscal unit. D. C. Douglas argued that a leet was also a primitive "hundred." He edited an eleventh-century survey in Anglo-Saxon of lands belonging to Bury St.

Edmunds, which speaks of "hundreds," divided into "manslots," in the Norfolk Marshland, where we find at a later date the *tenmanloth* and leets rather than "hundreds."[21] These Marshland "hundreds" are different from, and much smaller than, the official Domesday hundreds. We may well ask what unit they made a hundred *of*.

Douglas also argued that the "small hundred" originally consisted of 12 carucates and, as such, could constitute a body of men with joint economic responsibilities. Twelve-carucate hundreds were known in parts of the northern Danelaw, but they were known in East Anglia too. A convention dating from the early part of the reign of Henry III records an agreement between the men of the "two hundreds" of Fleet, Holbeach, and Whaplode, on the one part, and the men of the "two hundreds" of Gedney, Sutton, Lutton, and Tydd, on the other, regarding the partition of marshland between them.[22] These "hundreds" are, again, not the official or royal hundreds. Indeed the first group of vills makes just 24 carucates in Domesday, as does the second, so that the 12-carucate hundred is certainly in existence here. It is, moreover, acting as a corporate body of men. Finally, the vills in question are not part of the "Danish" Danelaw, but lie next to the Norfolk Marshland in the East Anglian panhandle that stretches around the end of the Wash. They lie outside the open-field area, and Sutton, for one, had a rule of partible inheritance.[23] Douglas also cites an agreement of the early thirteenth century concerning the use of marshland between the Abbot of Bury St. Edmunds and many parceners, on the one part, and the Bishop of Ely, the Prior of Lewes, and *participes qui sunt de leta integra de Merslond*, on the other.[24] Here a leet is behaving in just the way a "hundred" did a little to the west. But is a *leta integra* more than an ordinary leet, as a *villa integra* is more than an ordinary vill?

We must now turn to the leet as a court. In the fourteenth and later centuries, under the name of court leet, it became a special session of a manorial court, summoned twice a year to hold the view of frankpledge and to put to the capital pledges the same questions, the "articles of the view," that the sheriff asked on his tourn. As the name for such a special session, the leet spread outwards from East Anglia, its original home.[25]

Consider now the earlier history of the leet. The word itself (*leta*) as the name for a district and a geld-paying unit is used twice in the Norfolk Domesday. Not twenty years later it is used as the name for a court for freemen and villeins. In the foundation charter of Wymondham

Abbey (pre-1107), William of Albini granted Wymondham to the prior and convent with

> ... his own court in the same town and all amercements of his men, as well freemen as landsetts, in my leet, in market and in court, and in whatever manner they may be amerced.[26]

In the *Kalendar* under Troston, Suffolk, there is another—apparent—reference to the leet as a local court.[27] And in 1295 the Bishop of Ely, the Abbot of Ramsey, and the Prior of Lewes (we have heard of them before) hold a *leta* jointly in Walsoken, and it is not identical with the manorial court of Walsoken.[28] Here the leet looks as if it had been able to preserve its identity as a district and a court in the face of the division of its territory among three lords.

But the most numerous references to the leet appear in the East Anglian Hundred Rolls. Here it is assumed that the leet belongs to the king; it "pertains" to the hundred; it meets with the bailiff of the hundred, but at its own meeting-place separate from the hundred court. The king may alienate the leet, as he may the hundred; if, indeed, he alienates the hundred, he seems to alienate *ipso facto* its component leets, but no one may presume to hold a leet without warrant of royal charter. In short, the leet, like the hundred, is assumed to be a royal or folk court, and not a feudal or manorial one. A meeting of the leet certainly includes the view of frankpledge, or *bortreming* as it is called in Suffolk; the capital pledges make presentments on the Articles of the View, and violations of the minor or police *regalia*, such as the Assizes of Bread and Ale, may be amerced on the spot.

Though the leet is presumed, in the absence of warrant for alienation, to be a royal court, a large number of entries in the Hundred Rolls show that by 1275 the lords of manors have been assuming the right to hold their own leets and drawing their men away from the royal leets. Consider, for example, one of the more elaborate entries for West Flegg hundred, Norfolk.

> They [the jurors] say that the Abbot of St. Benet of Holme drew to himself a certain suit in Ashby, Thurne, and Repps from his homages, which [suit] the lord King was for a long time wont to hold through his bailiff at the church of Ashby on the appointed day, to wit, the day of the beheading of St. John the Baptist, and to receive there all royal rights for the use of the lord King, to wit, sometimes more and sometimes less. Now the said abbot has that leet held by his own bailiff to the prejudice of the lord King, and receives all the yields therefrom to his own use, to the lord King's yearly damage of one mark; and this he has done for the past ten years.[29]

Apparently the lords made good their encroachments, and in the fourteenth century the leet becomes a special session of a manorial court, no longer meeting as a separate royal court.

Let me sum up the argument so far. Originally a leet is a district smaller than a hundred but larger than a vill. A vill forms a definite fraction of a leet, and the leets of a hundred pay equal amounts to the geld due from the hundred. A leet is sometimes called a "hundred," but as such it is clearly much smaller than the official or royal hundreds of East Anglia, and of the order of 12 carucates in size. The men of such a "hundred" or leet may make agreements concerning their collective use of marshland. A leet is also a court, in origin a royal or folk court below the hundred, but in the thirteenth century the landlords are trying to turn it into a special session of a manorial court.

Now let us move on to the relation between the leet or small hundred and still larger territorial units. Arguing from the geld assessments, Douglas claimed not only that 12 carucates originally made a leet, but that 12 leets made an official or royal hundred. No such regularity obtains in East Anglia in the thirteenth century, and yet suspicious single examples still stick out. Thingoe hundred, Suffolk, contains just 12 leets. If, moreover, there is one place where we should look for the survival of pre-manorial, or at least nonmanorial, institutions, it is in the boroughs. And it happens that records, beginning in 1288, have survived of the leet organization of Norwich.[30] At that time Norwich is a hundred in itself. It is divided into four Great Leets and into 11 (later 12) lesser units, also called leets in the fourteenth century. Three of the lesser leets ordinarily make up each of the greater ones. The Great Leets all meet in the Tolbooth, each leet on a different day, under the presidency of four bailiffs as representatives of the king. That is, the leet court in Norwich retains its royal or folk character. The leets may be held in Lent, which is "a proof of their antiquity; for if the privilege had been granted subsequently to Magna Carta, they would have to be held after Easter."[31] As we shall see, the arrangements may long have antedated Magna Carta and may never have been "granted" at all. The leet is a police court of broad jurisdiction including, as we should expect, the view of frankpledge. The capital pledges of the tithings present offences, and there are at least 12, and usually exactly 12, capital pledges for every lesser leet. Thus each lesser leet is made up of 12 tithings. Note that in the Marshland 12 carucates made up a small hundred or leet, which raises the possibility of some equivalence between the tithing, as a number of men, and the carucate, as an area. At any rate the Norwich leet records provide evidence for the following equations as a pattern or ideal: 12 tithings make one lesser leet; three lesser leets make a Great Leet; four Great Leets make an official or royal hundred. It was this arrangement in Norwich and perhaps elsewhere that led Sir Francis Palgrave to write:

In East Anglia there existed a duodenary division, the Hundred being distributed into 12 Leets or Tribes; that is to say, into four head Leets, each containing three subordinate Leets.[32]

Let us remember this "duodenary division," for we shall come back to it.

With the Norwich arrangements in mind, we are in a position to consider the *ferding* or *ferdering*.[33] The word must mean a "fourth" or "quarter," and then the question is what it was a quarter *of?* In Abbot Samson's *Kalendar*, Babergh double-hundred is said to be divided into ferdings *quas in aliis hundredis vocamus letas;* they are in fact of the same kind and order of magnitude as the other leets of Bury St. Edmunds, and as such they cannot be quarters of an official hundred, for there were 15 ferdings in the double-hundred, if—and here the ambiguity begins—we include the *parochia* of Stokes, which is described as *quarta pars hundredi*. The ferding is an old institution, for Domesday Book speaks of St. Edmund's ferding of Aldham. From the *Kalendar* we know that the latter was also called a leet, including Great and Little Aldham and Great and Little Elmsett, and that it was certainly not a quarter of a hundred but one-eighth of Cosford half-hundred.

On the other hand, Domesday also speaks of the Bishop of Thetford's *ferting* of Elmham, Norfolk, and this definitely was a quarter of Wangford hundred. Finally the documents describe certain districts as *quarta pars hundredi* without equating them with leets or suggesting that the Latin phrase is a translation of *ferding*. Stokes has already been mentioned. Wisbech was a quarter of a hundred. Thingoe hundred, we know, contained 12 leets; three of them made up Sudbury, which is called *quarta pars hundredi*. This arrangement is just like Norwich, where three of the lesser leets made a great leet or quarter of a hundred. We may perhaps accept the identification of ferding with leet and argue that the same confusion reigned over both words: a ferding (lesser leet) might mean something of the order of a twelfth of a hundred; a ferding (great leet) might also mean a quarter of a hundred.

To complete the confusion, we hear in East Anglia not only of a ferding but of a *thredling* (third). There once was a Thredling hundred in Suffolk, which was itself a third of Claydon hundred: *hundr' de thredling que est tercia pars hundredi de Cleydon.*[34] Note at least how often East Anglian districts are divided into thirds or fourths, and how occasionally, as in Thingoe and Norwich, a full-fledged $3 \times 4 = 12$ duodenary system makes its presence felt.

The final characteristic of East Anglia that sets it off at least from Wessex and Mercia is its weak, or perhaps late, manorialization. We have seen something of this in the transformation of the leet into a manorial court, and earlier students of medieval East Anglian society have observed that the manors themselves were still being carved out at the time of Domesday Book, carved with some difficulty, for the social order did not fit easily into classic manorialism. Specifically, weak manorialism meant a large number of free tenants. "The free peasantry of East Anglia—that is to say of the two counties of Norfolk and Suffolk alone—formed approximately one half of the total number of freemen and sokemen recorded for the whole of Domesday England."[35] The number should be increased by the free peasantry in the Lincolnshire end of the East Anglian panhandle.

Many of the East Anglian hundreds were in ecclesiastical hands, and the nature of the socage dues is revealed most clearly in such records as those of Bury St. Edmunds. The numerous sokemen rendered their services to the hundred, not to the local manor, and these services were not limited to suit of court but included hidage, carrying-services, fodder-corn, mowing, and the payment of reliefs and gersum. Indeed the services may have been older than the hundreds, for several vills received socage dues in 1086 and later that were not capitals of hundreds, and the dues came from sokemen whose lands lay scattered over a wide area and even outside the hundred in which the vill in question lay.[36] As R. H. C. Davis points out, such a vill with its dependent sokemen resembles nothing so much as the Kentish lathe, where royal dues, not only *gafol* but also light labor-services, were paid by freemen from all over the outland of the lathe to its capital, the *villa regis.* But if lathes or their like ever existed in East Anglia, their boundaries cannot now be determined. The crucial points to note are the amount of East Anglian socage and its prefeudal, nonmanorial nature.

To say that in 1086 there were many freemen and sokemen in East Anglia is not, of course, to say that there were no villeins, then or later.

In fact there were many, and in the Ramsey cartulary and elsewhere we find them called by a curious name. Villeins are *lancetti* or *landsetti* (note: not land*settles* but land*setts*); villeinage is *lancettagium* and so is a villein holding.[37] In this special sense the word seems to be a peculiarity of East Anglia. Let us bear it in mind for future reference.

Though we have long given up the notion that the "typical" manor coincided with a village, the subdivision of villages into manors went particularly far in East Anglia. In Domesday many of the lesser freemen were said to hold manors of their own, and these manors were small:

It is . . . the prevalence of small manors, *maneriola*, that especially characterizes Suffolk among English counties. Out of a total of 659 manors, 294, or nearly 45 per cent, are under one carucate in size, and about the same proportion range from one to five carucates.

And again:

The little manors of the Suffolk freemen and sokemen were often enough estates of 60 or 30 acres with no apparent division between demesne and tenant land, cultivated by one team or half a team, and by the labour of a bordar or two, or even, it may be, in some cases, by the "lord of the manor" himself and his household.[38]

Is it possible that the manors were small because the group of countrymen actually collaborating in tillage was small in number and had its holdings concentrated in one part of the village fields?

Such, in their main lines, were the characteristics of East Anglian society: the absence of the classic open-field system, peasant holdings that tended to be concentrated in one part of the village fields, partible inheritance as the outward sign of joint-family organization, the leet as a fiscal unit, an economic corporation, and a folk court between the vill and the hundred in size, hints of a duodenary system in the relations between carucate (and tithing), leet, and hundred, a large number of freeholders and sokemen, often holding small manors, dependent on and providing light rents and services to, what looks like a *villa regis*. Some of these features resemble those of parts of the northern Danelaw: the large number of freeholders, for instance. But the similarity need not bespeak a Danish origin, especially as the East Anglian institutions resemble those of Kent, where few Danes settled, far more than they do those of the Danelaw. The inference is that they were pre-Danish in origin. And if so, who were these East Angles, whose society differed so sharply from that of the Middle Angles across the Fens?

III

Although many of the facts are familiar, I have had to review the social institutions of East Anglia in order to establish a basis for comparison with medieval Friesland. By Friesland I shall mean the seven *seelande* of medieval Frisia, forming a coastal strip from the Scheldt to the Weser, and disregard the extension of Frisian culture east of the Weser, which seems to have occurred at some time after the invasions. Although the *Lex Frisionum* is an eighth-century document, anything like adequate evidence for Frisian institutions, as for East Anglian ones, dates only from the later Middle Ages. For my chief authority on these institutions I shall use B. E. Siebs' summary and synthesis of earlier work: *Grundlagen und Aufbau der altfriesischen Verfassung.*[39] The significance of the picture Siebs presents seems to have escaped English scholars.

Like the other Germanic lands, Friesland knows a basic tenement and assessment unit, which German scholars call the *hufe*. It is of the same order of magnitude as the East Anglian carucate, though it varies somewhat in size from one part of Friesland to another. Its name also varies. In South Friesland it is, among other things, a *ploeg* or *ploeggang* (*aratrum* in Latin), a *teen* or *teenland;* elsewhere it is *egge, rott,* or simply *land.*[40] For convenience I shall usually call it a *ploeg,* but what I shall say of the *ploeg* applies also to the basic tenement unit under other names.

Let us look first at these names, especially the South Frisian ones. Note, first, that whatever else the basic tenement is called, it is not called a *hide.* But it is called a "plow," which means that in looking for an ethnic origin for the East Anglian carucate we are not limited to the Danes. Note next the terms *teen* or *teenland.* The word may refer to the hedging-in of land, in which case it is related to *zaun* and *town,* but it may also be a form of the word *ten,* which should make us think at once of the Walpole *tenmanlots* and of the 12-acre holdings, one-tenth of a carucate, which are so common in East Anglia. For whatever the origin of the word, Siebs believes that the *teen* or *ploeg* was in early times the unit bound to furnish ten men for the *heer,* the army. There might be more than ten men living from the land, kinsmen or tenants of the holder, but of these at least ten were liable for military service.

In this case the hundred would be the unit providing 100 men, or 120 by the long hundred.[41]

Second, the *teen* or *ploeg* was a unit whose members were held collectively responsible for carrying out the legal duties of any one of their number. In this, of course, it resembles the English tithing, which is also in theory a group of ten.[42]

Third, and this is much more important for my argument, the *ploeg* is a compact area of land (*geschlossene Lage*); so is the East Frisian *rott* (*geschlossene Ortsteil*), and Siebs provides maps of villages showing the *rotten* lying as compact areas.[43] No doubt the land of the *ploeg* is internally divided into strips, but it is not scattered in strips, at least so far as the arable is concerned. Indeed the open-field system is definitely not a Frisian institution. Sometimes a *ploeg* or *rott* constituted a single vill (*thorp*); more often a vill would be divided into several *rotten*.[44] As new land was brought under cultivation, the *ploeg* might grow in size, or new ones might be created.

Siebs, moreover, equates the standard holding, the *ploeg*, with the land originally in the hands of a lineage (*geschlecht*).[45] In fact *egge*, one of the names of the standard holding, which means "part," may also be translated as "lineage." It is in this sense that the *ploeg*, like the hide, is *terra unius familiae*, the *familia* not being the small family of today but a joint-family: a group of men tracing their descent from a common ancestor and acting together in agriculture and elsewhere. Siebs believes, for instance, that originally the men of the *ploeg* went to war under the leadership of the head of the lineage (*geschlechtsälteste*). Whether the headship passed from one member of the lineage to another by male primogeniture, or passed from older male to younger male, and so forth, in the oldest living generation before going to the oldest of the next generation is not clear, but note that succession to the Anglo-Saxon kingdoms shows signs of following the latter rule. Certainly names referring to lineages are common in medieval Friesland as elsewhere in the Germanic world, especially the *-ing* names (*Benninga, Henninghmen*), and lineage names are often given to tenement units or parts of them.[46]

But we must not dwell too much on the *ploeg* being kept together as a joint-family holding, for Friesland has a rule of partible inheritance identical with that of East Anglia and Kent. The holding might be, and often was, left undivided among the heirs and worked by them jointly as a *hausgemeinschaft*. In this case, "the oldest brother shall protect his youngest brother and sister with their father's sword, that is, with their father's landright, so long as they will stay together on undivided property." This sounds like the East Anglian *eynicia*. On the other hand, the heirs might decide to divide the land, in which case brothers shared equally, and if one of these brothers, in his turn, left no male heirs but only a daughter, she had the right to his land. If the heirs decided to divide, special protection was sometimes given to the youngest son: the eldest dividing the land into shares, the youngest choosing first.[47] There is also a hint that the land was not divided into compact parcels, but rather that each part of the land was separately divided: "Then they must go afield and divide the land, the farthest (from the house) first and the nearest last."[48] In the course of time, in Friesland as in East Anglia, the holdings got much broken up by division and alienation, until the *ploeg* became hardly recognizable, at best a union of neighbors instead of a union of kinsmen.

Even if the heirs did not go on living together in the same house, as a *hausgemeinschaft*, but built houses of their own nearby, they might still continue to work the land of the holding together.[49] Then the head of the lineage, or the heir of the senior part of the holding, would remain in the house of his forefathers (the *stammhaus*). In Friesland this was often strongly built and fortified; it was called a *burg*, and it became the strong point of the lineage in time of trouble. Siebs produces maps of several Frisian villages, showing the boundaries of the *rotten* and, in the midst of each *rott*, the traces lasting to modern times of a *burg*, a specially large and strong house.[50] We are reminded of the tantalizing East Anglian references to "houses"—of *domus Elfgari* with a carucate attached to it, of *domus Aylward* and *domus Fraunceys* which withdrew themselves from the leet of Runhall.

Some of the subdivisions of the *ploeg*, notably halves and quarters, were recognized by name, but in the long run the size of actual holdings depended on the accidents of inheritance, on the number of heirs on hand to divide the land. Only in West Friesland are there signs that the arable of the *teen* might be divided into just ten shares. There is much more evidence that the meadow pertaining to the *teen* might be divided into ten lots, and that the *teen* might be responsible for providing ten or twelve men to work on the dikes.[51]

Of the names given to divisions of the *ploeg*, one is especially interesting. In Friesland we hear of holdings called by some form of the word *erf*, *erve*, or *erwe*, meaning "inheritance" or even simply "land."

We hear, for instance, of a *vullarve,* a "full inheritance."[52] I believe that the word variously spelled *eruing, erving, aruing,* and *aeruing* (but not *eriung*), which appears in Norfolk documents—and only in Norfolk documents—of the thirteenth century contains the same root and likewise means an "inheritance."[53] Similarly *vullarve* reminds us of the *fullonds* that appear in the Ely extents.

The study of the holding and its partible inheritance leads at once to the sorts and conditions of men. The earliest Frisian records name four social classes: the *ethelings (nobiles),* the *frilings,* the *laten* or *liten,* and the slaves. The first two classes made up the "free Frisians." They were the regular suitors at the folk courts; they paid geld to the Carolingian successors of the old Frisian kings: *huslotha, huslaga,* or *huisgeld.*[54] The *laten* were none of these things. Instead they were men who, unlike the "free Frisians," held no land in their own right but were settled as tenants on part of the holdings of the "free Frisians," paying rent and labor to the holders. They were bound to the holding—"Die laten standen in einem Hörigkeitsverhaltnis zu ihrer Gutsherrschaft"—but they might buy their freedom if they had the means.[55] We ought not speak of them as villeins, for that would be to apply the definitions of feudalism to a society that was hardly feudal at all, but we can see how the *laten* might be mistaken for villeins. As for the slaves, they disappeared early in the Middle Ages, joining the class of *laten.*[56] Let us see if we can find East Anglian equivalents to the *ethelings, frilings,* and *laten* of Friesland.

Let us suppose, which is not asking much, that a man's social status bore some relation to the size of his holding of land. If the holding went undivided to one heir, the later would have no trouble maintaining his father's estate. And if the land were held in common by the joint-family, the family head would represent the family estate. But holdings in Friesland did not remain forever undivided, and so the question arose: What is the lower limit of the amount of land held that lets a man qualify as a member of a given class? Siebs believes than an etheling's holding was originally a full *ploeg,* and that the holding of an ordinary freeman would be a half-*ploeg.* But with partibility it was hard to keep up such high standards. Later, the smallest amount of land that would qualify a man for the estate of etheling was set at a quarter-*ploeg,* and the friling's share proportionately lower.[57] We translate the word *etheling* as "noble" or even as "prince." But the prefeudal Germanic world must have been in some ways less aristocratic than it came to be later. Certainly "noble" is not a good word for a Frisian etheling holding as little as thirty acres of land. "Head of an important family" is much better.

Of course there were ethelings in Anglo-Saxon England, though "thane" and "earl" took the place of the word in the ordinary sense of "nobleman." If we can trust the place-name Athelington in Suffolk, there were ethelings in East Anglia. But there is no evidence of the status being associated with a definite amount of land—except for one charter of date 1189–1198 in which the Prior of Binham grants land in Edgefield, Norfolk, *que terra appellatur Adhelingesdele*.[58] In accordance with his general tendency, Douglas tries to give this word a Danish origin, "both *ing* and *adel* being common in the formation of Danish place-names."[59] But is it not easier to give the word the straightforward interpretation "etheling's share or part"? We cannot lay great weight on a single reference, but it may be just possible that, before the Conquest, there were in East Anglia as in Friesland ethelings who, to maintain their estate, had to hold a certain minimum amount of land. If this minimum had been in East Anglia, as in Friesland, a quarter of a carucate, the "etheling's share" would have been 30 acres—which is in fact in the East Anglian Domesday and fines a socage holding of very frequent occurrence. There is, moreover, just a hint that the possession of 30 acres or more made a difference in a man's legal responsibilities. Of sokemen in Fersfield the Norfolk Domesday says that, if they hold 30 acres or more, they owe soke to the hundred, but if they hold less than that, they owe soke to the manor. The words are:

In the time of King Edward [the Confessor] the soke and sake lies in Fersfield from all who have less than 30 acres. From those who have 30 acres the soke and sake lies in the hundred.[60]

As for the *frilings*, the middle class in Frisian society, they certainly do not appear under that name in East Anglia, but they may appear under another. In Friesland the hundred, about which there will be more to say later, was above all a folk court. It met under the presidency of a *bonnere* or *schelta*. Suit at court was owed by all the "free Frisians," that is, by the *ethelings* and *frilings*. These suitors were spoken of as the *lioda* or *liuda*, that is, as "the people" *par excellence*, but sometimes a distinction was made between two kinds of suitors. The West Frisian *Skeltana Riucht* speaks of *heran and liuda*, perhaps best translated as "lords and commons," being present in the court.

[175]

If the *heran* were the *ethelings*, the *liuda* must have been the *frilings*. The judgments of the court were handed down by what the English might have called a jury of 12 doomsmen, in theory one from each of the 12 *ploegs* of which the hundred was composed.[61] We are reminded that the Norwich leets were each divided into 12 tithings, and that the 12 capital pledges made presentment of offences. In Friesland these doomsmen were called collectively the *liodwita* or the *liudamonna*. When we encounter these words we must also remember the *leudes*, men who served a prince in war, of the Frankish neighbors of the Frisians.[62] All of them have the same root as the modern German *leute*, "people."

Now there are East Anglian words that look a little like *liudamonna*. A writ of Henry II confirming the manor of Potter Heigham and Ludham, Norfolk, to the abbot of St. Benet of Holme says:

And let him have and hold in his hand and in his demesne all the lands of his landsetts and the *lueicia* lands and his sokemen in the same towns.

Later the abbot grants at Ludham *terram luiciam quam Edricus Noteles tenuit*. The word was certainly also spelled *luitia*.[63] Again, the Ely extent of Pulham, Norfolk, made in 1222, refers to a class of men, then apparently servile, called *leudimen*.[64] It is further interesting that Pulham was divided into four sections, each called a *lete*, though this can hardly have been the leet in the sense of "small hundred." Can this *lueitia* land be the last trace in East Anglia of the land in the hands of the *liuda*, the ancient "folk" and can the *leudimen* be the institutional descendants of the *liudamonna*, the freemen of middle class?

In medieval Latin the form *lueitia* is surely identical with the word spelled *leuid*, *leude*, and *leud* in Middle English, which meant "lay," "unlearned," "layman," as distinguished from "clerical" or "clerk," and which has come down to us, debased, as *lewd*. Since there is no agreement among the learned on the derivation of *lewd*, a layman, that is, a lewd person, is free to speculate. Can the original meaning of *lewd* have been "popular" or "of the folk"?

As for the *laten*, the lower class in Frisian society, they do not appear under that name in East Anglia, though they certainly do appear in the earliest laws of East Anglia's close relation, Kent.[65] But like the *frilings* they may appear under another name. We shall remember that the *laten* were semifree tenants on the lands of the "free Frisians." Now in West Friesland in the eleventh century such a tenant was called a *landseta*,[66] and we have already encountered landsetts at Wymondham and Ludham, Norfolk. The fact is that the terms *landsetti* and *landsettagium* were used in East Anglia—and there alone—for a kind of villein and a villein tenure. Indeed it is tempting to identify the sokemen of places like Potter Heigham and Ludham with the *ethelings*, the leudimen with the *frilings*, and the landsetts with the *laten*.

Suppose, as I have been arguing right along, that East Anglia once had a Frisian social system. Then the post-Conquest freemen and sokemen would be the descendants of "free Frisians," members of a "house," holding shares in the plowgang, and the *landsetts* would be the descendants of their tenants. Indeed the plowgang, or one of its larger subdivisions, with its center in the big house and with its non-"free" tenants, the *landsetts*, might be the original ancestor of the small manor, *maneriolum*, often less than a carucate in size, worked by a freeholder, his kinsmen, and a couple of bordars, so characteristic of Domesday East Anglia. If a social system of Frisian type should ever have come to be described in the language of manorialism, this is just the sort of "manor" we might expect to find.

With the *ploeg* and its custom of inheritance we are on firm ground, but we must turn now to that far more obscure subject, the organization of the larger units into which the *ploegs* were grouped. In the Frisian constitution the next unit larger than the *ploeg* is the *burar* (*bauerschaft*). This might consist of a single *ploeg*, but also of more than one, and the actual number varied a good deal. Siebs believes that ideally three *ploegs* made a *burar*, which coincided with a village (*thorp*), but it was possible for a big village to be divided into several *bauerschaften*. As a body of men, the *burar* was originally the corporation that controlled the use of the pasture, but not the tillage, in which its constituent *ploegs* intercommoned. Later in the Middle Ages the *burar* came to set the rules for the use of the arable, in the manner of the English *byrlaw*, besides being responsible for the upkeep of dikes, ditches, paths, and roads.[67] This unit is of the right order of magnitude, and it is not hard to see in it the equivalent of the small East Anglian village.

More interesting is the next larger unit, the Frisian hundred. The hundred as a number was the long hundred, 120, and as a district the hundred was bound to provide 120 men for the *heer*, so that if each *ploeg* or *teen* provided ten men, the hundred consisted of 12 *ploegs*. And if the three *ploegs* made the ideal *bauerschaft*, four *bauerschaften*

[177]

made a hundred.[68] Here we have a 3 × 4 = 12 duodenary system. No doubt the accidents to which human affairs are subject would prevent so abstract a system being set up everywhere with utter regularity or, if so set up, would erode the regularity in time. Neverthless there is evidence that the Frisians had in their minds a duodenary system as an ideal pattern. We are not done with it.

Now this Frisian hundred is clearly smaller than the official East Anglian hundreds, but it is of just the order of magnitude of the small hundred of the Marshland panhandle. The Frisian hundred is 12 *ploegs;* the Marshland hundred is 12 carucates. If we must look for an ethnic origin for this institution, we are, again, not confined to the Danes. Moreover, the small hundred of the Marshland is of the same order of magnitude as the district called elsewhere a leet. As a territory, the leet is between the vill and the official hundred in size; as a body of men, it has fiscal, legal, and sometimes economic responsibilities. Leets divided into just four vills are found in East Anglia, but not regularly, any more than the regular division of the hundred into just four *bauerschaften* is found in Friesland. Three is the most frequent number of vills per leet in the *Kalendar.* On the other hand, Risby, Suffolk, counts as a leet by itself; the entry goes on to say: *Notandum est quod villa ista quadripartita est,* and names the four *terrae* that make up the vill. And there are other quadripartite vills in East Anglia.[69] I cannot point to a regular 3 × 4 = 12 duodenary system in the relation between carucate, vill, and leet, but I must emphasize again that the orders of magnitude of the units are the same in East Anglia as in Friesland, and in both places the vill is considered to be a definite fraction of the leet or small hundred.

Not only their orders of magnitude but also the functions of the two institutions were the same, for, as we have seen, the Frisian hundred like the East Anglian leet was a court—a folk court, moreover, and not a seigniorial one.

But if the leet was a hundred, how did it come to be called a *leet?* The fact is that *leet* (*lete* in Middle English, *leta* in Latin documents) is a mysterious word, and the etymologists are not agreed about its derivation. It does not appear to have a cognate in the Frisian language, so far as that is recorded in documents of the early Middle Ages. But outside Frisian there are two contemporary words to which it is akin. One is the Old Norse *leith,* which was used in Iceland for a local court and its district, as well as for one of the courts of the Allthing. Lest we jump too quickly to the conclusion that *leet* has a Scandinavian origin, the other is *lathe*, the name given to the districts into which Kent was divided.[70] Again and again Kent shows its cultural kinship to East Anglia.

The unit above the Frisian hundred was the *land* or *go* (*gau*), and ideally four hundreds made a *go*. In reference to this proportion, the hundred was sometimes called a "quarter"—*fiardandel*.[71] Remember that the East Anglian leets were sometimes called *ferdings*. Siebs believes that the traces of a Frisian "thousand" can also be recognized, each consisting of 12 hundreds, that is, of three *goen*. In short, the Frisians had, at least as an ideal, a duodenary system, not only in the proportions between *ploeg*, *burar*, and hundred, but also in the proportions between hundred, *go*, and thousand.[72] Just as the Frisian hundred met as a folk court, so did the *go* and, less often, the thousand.

A thousand made up of 12 hundreds would be of the right order of magnitude to match some of the official or "large" East Anglian hundreds. Two of the latter consisted of just 12 leets: Norwich itself and Thingoe hundred. (Remember, by the way, that both *thing* and *howe* are Frisian words.)[73] It is true that the arrangements in Norwich and Thingoe, together with the units called *quarta pars hundredi*, suggest a $3 \times 4 = 12$ system instead of a $4 \times 3 = 12$ system, which was, at this level, the Frisian ideal. Only the *ferding* in the sense of "lesser leet" and the single *thredling*, or third of a hundred, are strictly in accord with Frisian arrangements. But we must not ask too much.

It should now be clear why the word *hundred* has two meanings. The "small" hundred is a unit of a hundred (120) *men*. The Frisian thousand is a unit of 12 times this number of *men*. The official Anglo-Saxon hundred is originally a hundred *standard assessment units*, the unit presumably being the West Saxon *hide*. A hundred reckoned in *men* would be much smaller than one reckoned in *hides*. Indeed it is likely that the East Anglian hundreds, officially so-called, as distinguished from the small hundreds or leets, were set up under the influence of the West Saxon administrative tradition after the re-conquest, by 917, of East Anglia from the Danes. This putative reorganization may still have allowed the confused debris of an older duodenary system and a few older "thousand" units to survive.

I turn finally to a less specific similarity between East Anglia and Friesland. As compared at least with Wessex and Mercia, East Anglia and Kent appear to be lands of relatively late or weak manorialization.

In the thirteenth century the Kentish gavelkinders are recognized as freemen. We can watch East Anglia still under the process of manorialization in the eleventh century, when it still abounds in freemen and sokeman. This resistance of the social order to manorialization is even more characteristic of Friesland. The Carolingians laid Friesland under the rule of *grewan,* a word better translated as "governors" than as "counts," for they never became overlords in the feudal sense, and even the rule of the *grewan* broke down in time. Friesland never knew a *seigneurie* nor a manor, unless a *ploeg* on which *landsetts* were established might count as a small manor, like the *maneriolum* of East Anglia. Facts like these led Marc Bloch to postulate a relationship between feudalism and manorialism, on the one hand, and, on the other, the nature of the social order that lay under them. The infrastructure determines to some degree the characteristics of the superstructure. In France, Bloch pointed out, vassallage and the *seigneurie* appear fully developed only in the big-village, open-field country between the Loire and the borders of Flanders.[74] If a man of war in the Dark Ages wished to get support for himself and his followers in the form of heavy work-services on demesne land, how much more easy to exploit the big open-field village, whose members were already accustomed to large-scale cooperation in communal agriculture, than the small, independent, loosely-organized plowlands of East Anglia, Kent, and Friesland. Indeed we need not postulate any man of war at all. Wessex and Mercia may have known for ages, in England and in the German homeland, a rural social order that more nearly resembled what later came to be thought of as typical of a manor than did ever the society of East Anglia, Kent, and Friesland.

IV

The main task of this paper has been to point out the institutional similarities between medieval East Anglia and medieval Friesland. In the absence of the open-field system, in the concentration of the holding in one part of the village fields, in the customs of inheritance of land, and in the structure of the joint-family—the two are, it is not too strong a word, identical. Less precise, but none the less strong, are the similarities in structure and function of the larger social units above the holding, especially the small hundred or leet as a folk court and as a group of plowlands and vills. There are even traces in East Anglia of a double duodenary arrangement of territorial units from the plowland up Still less clear, but still present, are hints of survival of the Frisian social classes: the *landsetts* definitely, the *ethelings* possibly, and the *liude* as the name for the "folk" of middle rank. Even some of the words that are specific in their special senses to medieval East Anglia find their identities or parallels in Friesland: the *adhelingesdele*, the *eruing*, the *ferding*, the *landseta*, the *leudiman*, the *tenmanloth*. Finally, East Anglia and Friesland share a more general characteristic, which may have been a resultant of the others: a high proportion of free tenures, a resistance to manorialization except in the form of the *maneriolum*. East Anglia, indeed, is culturally more closely related to Friesland than it is even to its nearest English relative, Kent.

A few of these features: the word *carucate*, the small hundred, and the high degree of freedom, have their parallels in parts of the northern Danelaw, but the overwhelming majority do not, and for those that do, a Frisian origin is as much possible as a Danish one. This does not mean that, contrary to the historical record, no Danes settled in East Anglia. It must mean that the Danes were few enough in number to be assimilated by the earlier society instead of reorganizing it.

In the absence of evidence to the contrary, we assume that invaders bring their institutions with them, and that the more closely the language and culture of one people resemble those of another, the more recently the two peoples were one. As Frisian is the language most closely related to English, so Frisian institutions are the institutions most closely related to East Anglian ones. The conclusion must be that Frisians invaded East Anglia in the fifth century. The similarity of institutions, in spite of the fact that something like adequate written records about them begin to appear only in the eleventh century, at least six hundred years after the new Frisians must have separated from the old, seems to me to strengthen this conclusion rather than weaken it. How much more eloquently do the institutions speak for a common origin when they had so much time, opportunity, and reason to diverge.

12

The Puritans

and the Clothing

Industry

in England

R ICHARD BAXTER, writing in his autobiography, included in *Reliquiae Baxterianae*, about the different classes of Englishmen which at the opening of the Civil War adhered to the King and to the Parliament, says of the latter:

On the Parliaments side were (besides themselves) the smaller part (as some thought) of the Gentry in most of the Counties, and the greatest part of the Tradesmen, and Free-holders, and the middle sort of Men; especially in those Corporations and Countries which depend on Cloathing and such Manufactures.[1]

Since Baxter, as a Puritan preacher who exercised his ministry for many years in a clothing town—Kidderminster in Worcestershire—was

Reprinted from *New England Quarterly*, 13 (1940), 519–529, by permission of the Managing Editor. Whether or not it is true, as Max Weber argued, that radical Protestantism, especially Calvinism, encouraged capitalistic development in industry and elsewhere, it is certainly true that industrial development sometimes encouraged radical Protestantism. This article is addressed to the second thesis. It can also be seen as a further study of the social history of East Anglia, with which, at a much earlier time, the immediately preceding article was concerned.

in an excellent position to know what he was talking about, his classification is entitled to much weight. Of particular interest, however, is
the last part of his assertion—that dealing with the cloth-makers' adher-
ence to the Parliamentary side. By customary assumption, the men
who supported Parliament were also, very largely, Puritans in their
religious leanings. Is it, then, further justifiable to assume an equally
close connection between English Puritanism and the clothing industry?

What men of the seventeenth century meant by "cloathing" was the
manufacture of woolen cloth. In the early Middle Ages England did
not weave any large amount of cloth but exported her raw wool for
use by the looms of Flanders and Italy. In the course of the fifteenth
century, however, she developed an important native cloth industry,
and in the next two centuries she became, and has ever since remained,
the maker of woolen cloth for most of Europe and the world. Before
the Industrial Revolution the business was organized on what has been
called the "putting-out" system. It was a cottage industry, controlled
by the clothiers, a class of men who bought the wool, "put out" the work
in its different stages to the craftsmen: spinners, weavers, fullers, shear-
men, and the rest, and finally sold the finished product. The craftsmen
worked in their own homes and supplied their own tools.

In order to discover whether the England of the clothing industry
tended to be the England of the Puritans, we must know what parts
of England were strongly Puritan in the years before the outbreak of
the Civil War. Unfortunately there is little definite evidence on this
point, beyond such estimates as that of Baxter. We know something
about the distribution of Puritan clergymen, but almost nothing about
that of Puritan laymen, especially those of the middle and lower
classes. The best evidence, and that which will be particularly examined
here, comes from one great event of these years—the Puritan emigration
to the colonies of New England. A man who went to New England had
to make a definite break with his English home, he had to make a long
ocean voyage, and once he had reached the New World he became
an object of interest to his descendants—circumstances of the kind that
give rise to record and history. As a matter of fact, the New England
Puritans have been far more thoroughly studied than the English ones.

Among other things, studies have been made of their English places
of origin, the best of which is probably that of Colonel Banks. He says
of his investigation:

The statements which I make here are based on the records of 2,158 emigrants who arrived in New England prior to 1650, whose English origin is positively or, in some cases, probably known. It comprises emigrants to the six colonies of New England now constituting the six states of this section of the country.[2]

The total number of settlers that had come to New England before 1650 is estimated as being fewer than 25,000. Banks begins by classifying his emigrants according to their English counties of origin, and he finds—of course his results are here abridged—that the twelve counties which sent most emigrants were, in order, Suffolk, London and Middlesex, Essex, Norfolk, Devon, Kent, Somerset, Dorset, Hertford, Wiltshire, Gloucester, and York. Suffolk is known to have sent two hundred emigrants and Yorkshire fifty-eight. Banks next goes on to divide his emigrants by groups of counties, of which two, East Anglia (Norfolk, Suffolk, and Essex) and the West Country (Cornwall, Devon, Somerset, Dorset, Gloucester, and Wiltshire), with 537 and 504 emigrants, respectively, were the two most heavily represented. In fact, the West Country and East Anglia between them accounted for 49 per cent of the entire population of emigrants whose origin is known. The Midlands, between these two sections, and the North Country, supplied far fewer emigrants for New England.

To some extent, Banks's conclusions can be confirmed by independent evidence—for instance, the Massachusetts towns named before 1690. A large number of these took their names from English towns from which settlers are known to have come. Of the English counties, Suffolk has ten such Massachusetts namesakes, Essex seven, Wiltshire five, Gloucester and York four each, Devon, Norfolk, Kent, Lancaster, and Dorset three, and Bedford, Berkshire, Hampshire, and Somerset two. The distribution of English origins here indicated obviously differs very little from Banks's findings.

Although the manufacture of cloth was carried on to some extent in all parts of England, the industry, under the early Stuarts and for at least a century before, was concentrated chiefly in certain districts, just as industries are today.[3] For instance, Thomas Fuller, in his *Church History*, names in a list of the counties of England which were outstanding for their clothing, Berkshire, Devon, Essex, Gloucester, Hampshire, Kent, Lancashire, Norfolk, Somerset, Suffolk, Sussex, Worcester, Westmoreland, and York.[4] There is any amount of evidence to confirm what he says. The clothing industry was in fact concentrated in three main districts. The first and most important was on the southeastern coast, opposite the markets of Holland and the rest of the continent: Norfolk with its worsteds; Suffolk and Essex with their "new draperies": bays, says, and serges; London, the industrial and commercial capital of England; and Kent. The second was the West Country, where the hills and streams supplied the water power for fulling mills: Gloucester, Wiltshire, and Somerset, with the neighboring counties from Devon to Berkshire. The third was in the North: Yorkshire—that is, the clothing district of the West Riding and the country lying next to the West Riding: the districts around Manchester in Lancashire and Kendal in Westmoreland. The northern clothing district tended to specialize in cotton, but what was called cotton in those days was in reality a form of woolen cloth of the nature of frieze. Of other parts of England, Fuller said: "Observe we here, that mid-England, Northamptonshire, Lincolnshire, and Cambridge, having most of wool, have least of clothing therein."

Of the three great clothing districts, two contributed heavily to the Puritan emigration to New England. East Anglia, together with London and Kent, was of course pre-eminent. New England might properly have been called New East Anglia. But the clothing counties of the West—Devon, Gloucester, and Wiltshire—are high in any list of contributors. Dorset was perhaps more prominent as a source of emigration than it was as a place of manufactures, though much cloth was made there, especially about Sherborne and Dorchester, and Dorset spinners spun yarn for the rest of the West.[5] Only the North, among the clothing districts, failed to send a mass of emigrants, but those it did send were important, for the first native cloth manufacture in the new colony was set up by Yorkshire men. Master Ezekiel Rogers, who had preached at Rowley in Yorkshire, led a band of colonists to New England from Bradford Vale and elsewhere in the West Riding,[6] who in 1638 founded the town of Rowley, Massachusetts. Edward Johnson, in his *Wonder-Working Providence*, says of the men of Rowley:

These people being very industrious every way, soone built many houses, to the number of about threescore families, and were the first people that set upon making of Cloth in this Western World; for which end they built a fulling mill, and caused their little-ones to be very diligent in spinning cotten wooll, many of them having been clothiers in England, till their zeal to promote the Gospel of Christ caused them to wander. . . .[7]

[185]

An interesting incidental detail is the large number of early towns in New England that were named after important clothing towns in the old country. Ipswich, Sudbury, and Hadleigh in Suffolk; Dedham and Braintree in Essex; Bridgwater and Taunton in Somerset; Andover, Bradford, Marlborough, Newbury, and Sherborne in other counties, all important clothing towns, gave their names to settlements in Massachusetts. These are only a few of the towns that might be mentioned.

Thus Richard Baxter's observation, that among the people who supported Parliament at the opening of the Civil War were many from "those Corporations and Countries which depend on Cloathing and such Manufactures," has confirmation in the parallel evidence of the English origins of the New England Puritans. It is also confirmed, though in a less statistical way, by what we know of the historical prominence of East Anglia as the most important clothing district and at the same time the most important source of Puritan sentiment and leadership. Less important, but more striking as an example, was southeastern Lancashire, the country around Manchester. Like East Anglia, it was both a clothing district and a Puritan and Parliamentary stronghold. Yet the rest of Lancashire, the northern and western part of the county, maintained its traditional and agricultural society, untouched by industry, and not only was not Puritan but, as if in reaction against Manchester, was the most strongly Roman Catholic part of England.[8]

Another question now comes up. If the emigration to New England drew heavily on the cloth-manufacturing districts, the state of the clothing industry in the early days of the seventeenth century is evidently something to be studied. As a matter of fact, the industry seems to have been involved in a series of depressions. Trouble began in 1614. England had always exported a large amount of "grey cloth"—raw cloth which had not been dressed and dyed—to be finished in the Low Countries. English statesmen had long felt that native workmen should get the advantage of this finishing trade. Accordingly, in 1614, by the terms of a project promoted by Alderman Cockayne of London, the export of undyed and undressed cloths was prohibited; the charter of the company of Merchant Adventurers, which had exported the cloth in the past, was revoked; and a new company was formed under the leadership of Cockayne, to which was given a patent for dyeing cloth. The result was what might have been expected. The Dutch took up the challenge of a trade war, prohibiting the importation of dyed and dressed cloth from England. The cloth finished by Cockayne's company was found to be worse and dearer than that finished in Holland. Trade went to pieces, so that in 1617 the scheme had to be abandoned and the former arrangements restored.[9]

The troubles of the cloth trade, however, were not over. It could not recover at once from its shock. In May, 1620, the first reports of a severe depression reached the Privy Council,[10] but the crisis did not come until two years later. In the early months of 1622, complaints of the decay of trade were sent from Essex, Suffolk, Somerset, Gloucester, Wiltshire, and other clothing districts.[11] A letter of February 16 in that year asserted: "Money is very scarce; in the clothing counties, the poor have assembled in troops of forty and fifty, and gone to the houses of the rich and demanded meat and money, which has been given through fear; they have also taken provisions in the markets."[12] On April 22 the Council sent letters to the high sheriffs and justices of the peace in several counties, ordering them to send two clothiers from each county to London by May 2, to confer on the state of the cloth trade with the Merchant Adventurers and others.[13] The committee met and on June 22 reported to the Council, finding several chief causes for the decay of trade, including the opening of war in Germany—the Thirty Years War.[14] Recommendations were made, but no important action was taken, and the industry seems to have recovered in some measure.

But not for long. Beginning in the spring of 1629 and continuing well into 1631, another storm of complaints reached the Council from the clothing districts: Essex, Suffolk, Berkshire, Gloucester, Hampshire, Wiltshire, and Somerset.[15] For instance, on April 19, 1631, the Justices of the Peace of Essex, sitting at Chelmsford, wrote to the Council as follows:

The poor suffer much in respect of the high prices of corn, yet they are in far greater misery in the most populous parts of the country, by reason that the clothiers forbear to set the weavers on work, alleging that they have already disbursed more than they are able, and that their cloths lie upon their hands, which has occasioned many complaints of the poor weavers, and a more than ordinary resort of them unto the Justices at their present Sessions.[16]

As late as May 4, 1637, certain baymakers of Coggeshall, Bocking, and Braintree, in Essex, petitioned the Council, complaining of the multitude of poor and of the decay of trading, which had compelled many former workmasters to become workmen.[17]

Large numbers of the emigrants to New England came from the clothing counties. And there were depressions in the clothing trade during some of the years, at least, during which the emigration was taking place. It is clear that on these facts a historian might found a special form of James Truslow Adams's economic interpretation of the emigration.[18] He might argue that the colonists were driven out of England by a trade depression. In this connection there are further facts to be considered. Robert Reyce, a clergyman of Suffolk, wrote about 1618 a *Breviary* which is in effect a description of Suffolk—of one of the counties, that is, which furnished most men for New England. Reyce commented:

It is by common experience tried, upon what reason I know nott, that in those parts of this shire, where the clothiers doe dwell or have dwelled, there are found the greatest number of the poor, and in other parts where the meaner sort doe practise spinning of thred linnen and other such like womens imployments are nothing so many poor.[19]

In short, a common belief in Suffolk at the beginning of the seventeenth century was that the clothing districts were also districts full of poor. Again, John White, the famous Puritan minister of Dorchester in Dorset, and one of the men who did most to further the colonization of New England, published in 1630 his pamphlet called *John White's Planters' Plea*, in which he powerfully advocated the founding of new settlements. In this pamphlet White observed: "Many among us live without employment, either wholly, or in the greatest part (especially if there happen any interruption of trade, as of late was manifested not onely in *Essex*, but in most parts of the Land. . . ."[20] White, who must have been thinking of the depression that began in 1629, went on to use the fact of unemployment as an argument for emigration. Finally, we actually hear of English clothiers leaving for New England. On March 17, 1638, William, Lord Maynard, wrote to Archbishop Laud from Ashdon in Essex, saying that a certain Mr. Nevill had told him of "the intention of divers clothiers of great trading to go suddenly into New England," and that he heard daily "of incredible numbers of persons of very good abilities who had sold their lands and were upon their departure thence."[21]

In this connection a further point may be of interest. Anyone who studies the *Winthrop Papers* from the point of view of a social historian will be struck by the closeness of the connection of this Suffolk family with Suffolk's great industry. Adam Winthrop, the grandfather of the future Governor of Massachusetts Bay, was master of the Clothworkers Company of London. His son Adam took as his second wife a clothier's daughter, and she was John Winthrop's mother. In his diary there are many references to clothiers and clothworkers. John's sister Jane married a clothier. In short the Winthrops were typical members of the industrial aristocracy.[22]

In spite of all these facts, the theory that the emigrants were driven to the New World by a trade depression in the Old is probably too great a simplification. This statement does not mean that economic factors can be disregarded in describing the founding of the Puritan colonies. It means only that a number of other factors must be considered at the same time. Many weavers and clothiers are known to have settled in New England, but there were many settlers of other crafts and professions.[23] The English counties that sent considerable bodies of men to New England sent something like a cross section of their population. Of course this fact does not by itself rule out the economic interpretation. If there was a depression in the clothing districts, other classes of the population besides the cloth-workers would be affected. The question is: Did people come to New England from the clothing districts because the clothing districts were poor or because the clothing districts were Puritan? And the observation which can be made at once is that the clothing districts tended to be centers of Puritanism long before the depressions in the clothing trade and remained so long after the depressions were over. Indeed, they were zealous in the cause of religious reform long before the word Puritan itself had any meaning. Two of these districts, East Anglia and the West Country, were just the districts in which Lollardry made most headway at the end of the fourteenth and in the fifteenth century.[24] In those days East Anglia and the West Country were already centers of the expanding clothing industry.

The direct influence of economic disturbances, depression, and unemployment may have had some importance in determining the emigration to the colonies of New England. It did not determine why certain districts of Old England were inclined toward Puritanism and other movements for reform in religion. Here, on the other hand, the indirect influence of economic conditions must have been of the first importance— the effect of manufactures in giving a particular character to the social order as a whole, which made that social order particularly liable to new religious movements. The question of this influence is the question that remains. Why should a certain kind of society, a society of small villages and towns, half-industrial, half-agricultural, a society of cottage manufactures organized on the putting-out system, a society of clothiers and cloth-workers, capitalists and craftsmen—why should such a society have been more liable to infection with a new religious movement than the more purely agricultural society that remained in many parts of England? Perhaps it is better to ask the question in another form: Why should such a society have been more liable to abandon its ancient religion? Perhaps, instead of putting the question in terms of the society itself, it is better to put it in terms of the relation of the society to the larger society of which it was a part: What was there in the relation between this society and the society of England in general which made the former liable to abandon the established English religion?

At the beginning of the seventeenth century, the clothing industry was the greatest industry of England. But why was industrial England Puritan England? We may cite Unwin's statement in his history of the industries of Suffolk:

The industrial history of Suffolk falls into three well-defined periods. . . . In the first period, which may be reckoned as lasting from about the beginning of the fourteenth century to about the middle of the seventeenth, the counties of the south-east coast became the chief manufacturing district of England. . . . It was not by mere accident that the social discontent which found expression in the rising of 1381 should have blazed most fiercely in the eastern counties. From that time to the Civil War those counties held that kind of political hegemony based on pre-eminence which is now enjoyed by the cities of the Midlands and the North. The pre-eminence was, of course, a purely relative one. The actual number engaged in Suffolk was almost certainly not higher than at the present day. Even the proportion of the population fully engaged in industry as compared with that engaged in agriculture was probably never much greater than it is now. It was that proportion, as contrasted with the proportion obtaining in other counties of contemporary England, which gave a special character to the East Anglia of the fifteenth and sixteenth centuries. From that point of view we may consider the manufacture of woollen cloth as the dominating feature of this period of the economic history of Suffolk, though the industry never established itself outside the south-western part of the country.[25]

Such a statement has much to suggest. We can find many further hints in Max Weber's *The Protestant Ethic and the Spirit of Capitalism* and in R. H. Tawney's *Religion and the Rise of Capitalism*. But the problem of why an industrial society is a society prone to the adoption of certain novelties in religion is nowhere near to being solved. Certainly it appears early in history. It is not peculiar to the age of the Reformation and the Wars of Religion. Haskins says that the existence of heresy in the industrial centers of northern France and Flanders can be traced back at least as far as the eleventh century. The chief form of heresy was the Manichean, and "so popular did the dualistic doctrines become among the weavers that the name *textor* became a synonym for heretic. . . ."[26] Of course religious movements appear in many kinds of social conditions besides those of industry. The problem stated here is only part of a larger one.

13

Anxiety

and

Ritual

THE THEORIES
OF MALINOWSKI
AND RADCLIFFE-BROWN

I<small>N</small> his Frazer Lecture for the year 1939, published as a pamphlet under the title *Taboo*, Professor A. R. Radcliffe-Brown restates certain of his views on magic and religion.[1] At the same time, he makes certain critcisms of Professor Malinowski's theories on the subject. The appearance of *Taboo*, therefore, offers the anthropologist an occasion for examining the present status of the theory of ritual by means of a study of a controversy between what are perhaps its two most important experts. Incidentally, the reader will find illustrated a type of behavior common in disputes in the world of science.

Reprinted with minor corrections from *American Anthropologist*, 43 (1941), 164–172, by permission of the Editor. This article has also been reprinted in W. A. Lessa and E. Z. Vogt (eds.), *Reader in Comparative Religion* (Evanston, Ill.: Row-Peterson, 1958), 112–118.

Malinowski's theory of magic is well known and has been widely accepted.[2] He holds that any primitive people has a body of empirical knowledge, comparable to modern scientific knowledge, as to the behavior of nature and the means of controlling it to meet man's needs. This knowledge the primitives apply in a thoroughly practical manner to get the results they desire—a crop of tubers, a catch of fish, and so forth. But their techniques are seldom so powerful that the accomplishment of these results is a matter of certainty. When the tiller of the soil has done the best he can to see that his fields are properly planted and tended, a drought or a blight may overwhelm him. Under these circumstances the primitives feel a sentiment which we call anxiety[3] and they perform magical rites which they say will insure good luck. These rites give them the confidence which allows them to attack their practical work with energy and determination.

Malinowski clinches his argument with an observation made in the course of his field work:

An interesting and crucial test is provided by fishing in the Trobriand Islands and its magic. While in the villages on the inner Lagoon fishing is done in an easy and absolutely reliable manner by the method of poisoning, yielding abundant results without danger and uncertainty, there are on the shores of the open sea dangerous modes of fishing and also certain types in which the yield varies greatly according to whether shoals of fish appear beforehand or not. It is most significant that in the Lagoon fishing, where man can rely completely upon his knowledge and skill, magic does not exist, while in the open-sea fishing, full of danger and uncertainty, there is extensive magical ritual to secure safety and good results.[4]

On this understanding of magic, Malinowski bases a distinction between magical and religious ritual. A magical rite, he says, "has a definite practical purpose which is known to all who practice it and can be easily elicited from any native informant." This is not true of a religious rite.

While in the magical act the underlying idea and aim is always clear, straightforward, and definite, in the religious ceremony there is no purpose directed towards a subsequent event. It is only possible for the sociologist to establish the function, the sociological *raison d'être* of the act. The native can always state the end of the magical rite, but he will say of a religious ceremony that it is done because such is the usage, or he will narrate an explanatory myth.[5]

This argument is the first with which Professor Radcliffe-Brown takes issue, and his criticism seemes to the writer justified. He points out that the difficulty in applying this distinction between magic and religion lies in uncertainty as to what is meant by "definite, practical purpose." What is, in fact, the definite, practical purpose of a magical rite? To an anthropologist from western civilization, a magical rite and a religious rite are equally devoid of definite, practical results, in the usual sense of the phrase. The distinction between them must be based on other grounds. A scrutiny of the methods we actually use to determine the purpose of a magical rite reveals that what we take to be the purpose of the rite is the purpose as stated by a native informant. The native performs one rite and says that it has a definite, practical purpose. He performs another rite and says that it is performed as a matter of custom. If we call the first rite magic and the second religion, we are basing our distinction on a difference between the verbal statements a native makes about the rites. For some purposes the distinction may be a useful one, but one of the truisms of the social sciences is that we shall do well to look with extreme care at the statements men make about what they do before we take the statements at their face value. Or, to use Radcliffe-Brown's own words: "The reasons given by the members of a community for the customs they observe are important data for the anthropologist. But it is to fall into grievous error to suppose that they give a valid explanation of the custom."[6]

Without doubt there are many factors involved in the performance of magic, but the least number which must be taken into consideration are apparently the following. A sentiment that we call anxiety arises when men feel certain desires and do not possess the techniques that make them sure of satisfying the desires. This sentiment of anxiety then manifests itself in ritual behavior. The situation is familiar in American folklore: a man and his wife are held up in a taxi in New York traffic and in danger of missing their liner to Europe. There is nothing that either one of them can do that would be of any use, but the wife screams to her husband: "But do something, can't you?" Furthermore, the action taken under such circumstances, however useless it may be, does do something to relieve the anxiety. In the usual phrase, it "works it off."

A better statement, from the point of view of psychology, is the following:

From clinical, physiological, and psychological data, it has been shown that throwing into conflict powerful excitations toward and against motor reaction regularly results in disorganization of behavior, subjective distress, and persistent drive toward relief. This syndrome has been called variously "affect," "tension," "anxiety," and "neurosis." . . . The drive toward relief tends to set into operation implicit or explicit forms of behavior, the principal characteristic of which is their abbreviated or condensed or symbolic character and their relative indifference and impermeability (because of the necessity of attaining relief as quickly as possible) to the ordinary checks, delays, and inhibitions imposed by objective reality; thus they are objectively non-adaptive, but are subjectively adaptive to the extent that the relief aimed at is actually effected.[7]

In magic in a primitive society there is a further factor which must be taken into consideration. The primitives feel anxiety and perform ritual actions which have some effect in relieving the anxiety, but they also produce a statement. They say that magical action does in fact produce a "definite, practical result." This statement is to be taken simply as a rationalization, similar in character to other rationalizations. If the rationalization is to be used as a means of distinguishing magic from religion, it should at least be recognized for what it is.

The writer doubts whether the distinction between magic and religion, as formulated by Malinowski, is a useful one. In an effort to get away from the rationalizations, magic might be defined as the ritual which is closely associated with practical activities: hunting, fishing, husbandry. Then religion would be the ritual which is not associated with practical activities, in the sense that, for instance, the Mass of the Catholic church is not so associated. But could a distinction be made in many societies between magic and religion as so defined? Anthropologists will be aware that in many primitive societies native informants say of the most fundamental and sacred rituals, i.e., those ordinarily called religious, that if they are not performed the food supply will fail. Are these rituals closely associated with practical activities? The food supply is certainly a practical concern. Once more we are involved in the native rationalizations. In a sense these rituals are both magical and religious.

Nevertheless, Malinowski's general theory of magic seems sound, and it may be well to cite one of his statements as a summary:

We have seen that all the instincts and emotions, all practical activities, lead man into impasses where gaps in his knowledge and the limitations of his early power of observation and reason betray him at a crucial moment. The human organism reacts to this in spontaneous outbursts, in which rudimentary modes of behavior and rudimentary beliefs in their efficiency are engendered.

Magic fixes upon these beliefs and rudimentary rites and standardizes them into permanent traditional forms.[8]

One word of explanation is needed here. The present paper is concerned with ritual so far as it arises out of the sentiment we call anxiety. But there is no implication that other sentiments besides anxiety do not give rise to ritual behavior.

There are other and more important criticisms which Radcliffe-Brown makes of Malinowski's theory of ritual. He wisely bases them upon a consideration of an actual case, the ritual of birth in the Andaman Islands. In order to follow his discussion, his material should first be cited:

In the Andaman Islands when a woman is expecting a baby a name is given to it while it is still in the womb. From that time until some weeks after the baby is born nobody is allowed to use the personal name of either the father or the mother; they can be referred to only by teknonymy, i.e., in terms of their relation to the child. During this period both the parents are required to abstain from eating certain foods which they may freely eat at other times.[9]

To be sure, this is an example of negative ritual—avoidance of behavior that under other circumstances might be proper—rather than of positive ritual, but the same problems arise in either case.

Radcliffe-Brown admits that Malinowski's theory might seem to be applicable as an interpretation of this body of ritual. For a woman, childbirth is always a dangerous process, in which tragedy may suddenly appear for inexplicable reasons. It is dangerous today; it was supremely dangerous under primitive conditions. Under these circumstances, the woman may feel great anxiety, and the husband is naturally interested in the fate of his wife. But the husband and the wife perform certain rites and say that they are efficacious in warding off the dangers of childbirth. Therefore their fears are, to a certain extent, lulled.

Without explicitly rejecting Malinowski's interpretation, Radcliffe-Brown offers an alternative. He writes:

The alternative hypothesis which I am presenting for consideration is as follows. In a given community it is appropriate that an expectant father should feel concern or at least make an appearance of doing so. Some suitable symbolic expression of his concern is found in terms of the general ritual or symbolic idiom of the society, and it is felt generally that a man in that situation ought to carry out the symbolic or ritual actions or abstentions.[10]

Radcliffe-Brown presents this interpretation as an alternative to Malinowski's. The point to be made here is that the question is not one of either-or. The hypothesis is not an alternative but a supplement: both hypotheses must be taken into consideration.

In fact the problem that is raised is the ancient one of the individual and his society. Malinowski is looking at the individual, Radcliffe-Brown at society. Malinowski is saying that the individual tends to feel anxiety on certain occasions; Radcliffe-Brown is saying that society expects the individual to feel anxiety on certain occasions. But there is every reason to believe that both statements are true. They are not mutually exclusive. Indeed the writer has difficulty in believing that it should have ever come about that "in a given community it is appropriate that an expectant father should feel concern" if individual fathers had not in fact showed such concern. Of course, once the tradition had been established, variations in two directions would naturally be produced. There would be, on the one hand, fathers who felt no concern but thought that the expedient thing to do was to put on a show of concern, and on the other hand, fathers who felt concern but did not express it in the manner appropriate in the given society. But on the whole these persons would be few. The average citizen would feel concern at the birth of his child but also would express his concern in the traditional manner. The custom of the society would provide the appropriate channel of his sentiments. In short, a theory adequate to the facts would combine the hypotheses of Malinowski and Radcliffe-Brown.

A statement made by Malinowski in another connection is appropriately quoted here:

The tendency represented largely by the sociological school of Durkheim, and clearly expressed in Professor Radcliffe-Brown's approach to primitive law and other phenomena, the tendency to ignore completely the individual and to eliminate the biological element from the functional analysis of culture, must in my opinion be overcome. It is really the only point of theoretical dissension between Professor Radcliffe-Brown and myself, and the only respect in which the Durkheimian conception of primitive society has to be supplemented in order to be really serviceable in fieldwork, in theoretical studies, and in the practical application of sociology.[11]

Radcliffe-Brown makes a second and more important objection in applying Malinowski's theory to the ritual of childbirth in the Andamans. While a woman is expecting a child, and for some weeks after the birth of the child, both parents are required to abstain from eating certain foods that they may properly eat under ordinary circumstances, these foods apparently being dugong, pork, and turtle meat. Furthermore:

If the Andaman Islanders are asked what would happen if the father or mother broke this taboo, the usual answer is that he or she would be ill, though one or two of my informants thought it might perhaps also affect the child. This is simply one instance of a standard formula which applies to a number of ritual prohibitions.[12]

On the basis of this observation, Radcliffe-Brown goes on to make the following attack on Malinowski's anxiety theory:

I think that for certain rites it would be easy to maintain with equal plausibility an exactly contrary theory, namely, that if it were not for the existence of the rite and the beliefs associated with it the individual would feel no anxiety, and that the psychological effect of the rite is to create in him a sense of insecurity or danger. It seems very unlikely that an Andaman Islander would think that it is dangerous to eat dugong or pork or turtle meat if it were not for the existence of a specific body of ritual the ostensible purpose of which is to protect him from those dangers. Many hundreds of similar instances could be mentioned from all over the world.[13]

This attack on Malinowski's theory appears at first glance to be devastating. But let us examine it a little more closely. Put in simpler language, what Radcliffe-Brown is saying is that the Andaman mother and father do not apparently feel anxiety at the fact of approaching childbirth. They feel anxiety only when the ritual of childbirth is not properly performed. There is no doubt that similar observations could be made of backward peoples all over the world. It is true that their techniques do not allow them to control completely the natural forces on which their lives depend. Nevertheless when they have done their practical work as well as they know how and have performed the proper rituals, they display little overt anxiety. If anxiety is present, it remains latent. They are, as we say, fatalists. What Thomas and Znaniecki have observed of the Polish peasant seems to be true of most primitive peoples. They write:

The fact is that when the peasant has been working steadily, and has fulfilled the religious and magical ceremonies which tradition requires, he "leaves the rest to God," and waits for the ultimate results to come; the question of more or less skill and efficiency of work has very little importance.[14]

When the primitive or the peasant has done his practical work as well as he knows how, and has "fulfilled the religious and magical ceremonies which tradition requires," he displays little overt anxiety. But he does feel anxiety if the ceremonies have not been properly performed. In fact he generalizes beyond this point and feels that unless all the moralities of his society are observed, nature will not yield her fruits. Incest or murder in the camp will lead to a failure of the crops just as surely as will a breach of ritual. In the shape of famine, pestilence, or war, God will visit their sins upon the people. Accordingly when, in a village of medieval Europe, the peasants, led by the parish priest, went in procession about the boundaries of the village in the Rogation Days in order to bless the growing crops, they offered up prayers at the same time for the forgiveness of sins. This association of ideas is characteristic: nature and morality are mutually dependent.

As a matter of fact, the above observations are implicit in Malinowski's theory, and he was undoubtedly aware of them. He points to the initial anxiety situation, but he also states that ritual dispels the anxiety, at least in part, and gives men confidence. He implies, then, that anxiety remains latent so long as ritual is properly performed. Radcliffe-Brown's criticism does not demolish Malinowski's theory but takes the necessary further step. Once again, it is not an alternative but a supplement. Using the ritual of childbirth in the Andamans as an example, he asks what happens, or rather what would happen, if the ritual is not performed. And he shows that this occasion is the one in which the natives feel anxiety. The anxiety has, so to speak, been displaced from the original situation. But even granted that it has been displaced, Malinowski's general theory is confirmed by the existence of a secondary ritual which has the function of dispelling the secondary anxiety which arises from a breach of ritual and tradition. We call this the ritual of purification, of expiation.

In his description of the Australian Murngin, W. L. Warner sums up admirably what the writer has been trying to say. He writes:

The Murngin in their logic of controlling nature assume that there is a direct connection between social units and different aspects of nature, and that the control of nature lies in the proper control and treatment of social organization. Properly to control the social organization, the rituals must also be held which rid society of its uncleanliness. The society is disciplined by threat of what will happen to nature, the provider, if the members of the group misbehave.[15]

In summary, it appears from the discussion of the theories of Malinowski and Radcliffe-Brown that at least seven elements must be taken into consideration in any study of the rituals we are accustomed to call magic. Of course, there are other elements that are not considered here. The seven are the following:

1. *Primary Anxiety*. Whenever a man desires the accomplishment of certain results and does not possess the techniques which will make him certain to secure these results, he feels a sentiment which we call anxiety.

2. *Primary Ritual*. Under these circumstances, he tends to perform actions which have no practical result and which we call ritual. But he is not simply an individual. He is a member of a society with definite traditions, and among other things society determines the form of the ritual and expects him to perform the ritual on the appropriate occasions. There is, however, evidence from our own society that when ritual tradition is weak, men will invent ritual when they feel anxiety.

3. *Secondary Anxiety*. When a man has followed the technical procedures at his command and performed the traditional rituals, his primary anxiety remains latent. We say that the rites give him confidence. Under these circumstances, he will feel anxiety only when the rites themselves are not properly performed. In fact this attitude becomes generalized, and anxiety is felt whenever any one of the traditions of society is not observed. This anxiety may be called secondary or displaced anxiety.

4. *Secondary Ritual*. This is the ritual of purification and expiation which has the function of dispelling secondary anxiety. Its form and performance, like those of primary ritual, may or may not be socially determined.

5. *Rationalization*. This element includes the statements which are associated with ritual. They may be very simple: such statements as that the performance of a certain magic does insure the catching of fish, or that if an Andaman mother and father do not observe the food taboos they will be sick. The statements may be very elaborate. Such are the statements which accompany the fundamental rituals of any society: the equivalents of the Mass of the Catholic church.

6. *Symbolization*. Since the form of ritual action is not determined by the nature of a practical result to be accomplished, it can be determined by other factors. We say that it is symbolic, and each society has its own vocabulary of symbols. Some of the symbolism is relatively simple: for example, the symbolism of sympathies and antipathies. Some is complicated. In particular, certain of the rituals of a society, and those the most important, make symbolic reference to the fundamental myths of the

society. The ceremonies of the Murngin make reference to the fundamental myths of that society just as surely as the Mass makes reference to Christ's sacrifice on Calvary.

7. *Function*. Ritual actions do not produce a practical result on the external world—that is one reason why we call them ritual. But to make this statement is not to say that ritual has no function. Its function is not related to the world external to the society but to the internal constitution of the society. It gives the members of the society confidence; it dispels their anxieties; it disciplines the social organization. But the functions of ritual have been discussed elsewhere, and in any case they raise questions which are beyond the scope of the present paper.

Finally, a study of the theories of Malinowski and Radcliffe-Brown illustrates a common feature of scientific controversies: two distinguished persons talking past one another rather than trying to find a common ground for discussion, presenting their theories as alternatives when in fact they are complements. Such a study suggests also that the theory necessary for an adequate description of any phenomenon is often more complicated than the theories of the phenomenon that exist at any given time.

14

Marriage,

Authority,

and Final Causes-

A STUDY
OF UNILATERAL
CROSS-COUSIN MARRIAGE

THIS is a study of a rare phenomenon that provides a crucial test of theory. Preferential marriage is the familiar fact that in many societies ego, besides being forbidden to marry certain women, is expected to marry one or more of a class of women standing in certain kin relationships to him. Among the forms of preferential marriage, unilateral cross-cousin marriage exists when, as between his two female cross-cousins, ego male is expected to marry one but not the other: his mother's brother's daughter but not his father's sister's daughter or vice versa. Only a handful of societies follow such a rule: it is much less common than most of the other rules of preferential marriage. Uni-

Originally published as a small book: George C. Homans and David M. Schneider, *Marriage, Authority, and Final Causes* (New York: The Free Press, 1955). Mr. Schneider has very kindly consented to the inclusion of this paper here.

lateral cross-cousin marriage gets its interest from the fact that, perhaps just because it occurs only under special conditions, a study of what determines the adoption by a society of one rather than the other of its forms allows us to compare the usefulness of a final-cause theory with that of an efficient-cause theory of social behavior. We give the theories these names for want of better ones. The final-cause theory is in fact the one presented by Claude Lévi-Strauss in his book *Les structures élémentaires de la parenté.*[1] Whatever its title may imply, this is not a study of kinship behavior in general but of preferential marriage. The efficient-cause theory derives ultimately from A. R. Radcliffe-Brown's classic paper, "The Mother's Brother in South Africa."[2]

Introduction to Lévi-Strauss's Argument

Lévi-Strauss examines several forms of preferential marriage besides the unilateral cross-cousin one, and to bring out the nature of his theory we must begin with what he has to say about these other forms.[3] He starts from the assumption that marrying and giving in marriage are processes of exchanging perhaps the most highly valued of scarce goods, to wit: women. If my group gives its sisters and daughters to the men of another group, it must have some means of recouping its losses: it must get women back. Indeed he links the incest prohibition itself to preferential mating: "The prohibition of the sexual usage of the daughter or the sister requires that the daughter or sister be given to some other man, and at the same time it creates a right over the daughter or sister of the other man."[4] He goes even further, and this is the first hint of his final-cause interpretation of marriage rules, saying that the incest taboo is set up *in order that* an exchange may take place. His words are: "The content of the [incest] prohibition is not exhausted by the fact of the prohibition; the latter is instituted only to found and guarantee, directly or indirectly, immediately or mediately, an exchange."[5] Note this well: he is not saying that the incest taboo and other marriage rules in fact produce exchanges of women between groups of men, but that rules exist *because* they produce the exchanges. We shall see later why he thinks the exchanges so important.

In societies where membership in groups is defined by descent, a rule prescribing marriage with a parallel cousin like father's brother's daughter hardly creates any exchange of women between groups. You are giving your women to, and getting them from, members of your own lineage. Such a rule is very rare:[6] Lévi-Strauss would say because it failed to produce exchange. The division of a tribe into unilineally-defined moieties, with the rule that ego must marry a woman of the moiety other than his own, automatically turns a parallel cousin into a prohibited spouse and creates the exchange of women between groups. At this point Lévi-Strauss undertakes the study of the various forms of cross-cousin marriage, beginning with the classic Australian systems: Kariera, Aranda, Murngin, etc. His book makes clear (as few others do) how these rules work, and his exposition is often magnificent. This is one of the great ethnographic summaries. In differing from Lévi-Strauss at certain points, we shall never deny that his book is a most distinguished one—partly because its argument is clear enough to *make* us disagree.

Restricted and Generalized Exchange

Among the Kariera, ego is expected to marry mother's brother's daughter *or* father's sister's daughter. That is, the rules for a man and for a woman are the same: each may marry either cross-cousin. This is a form of *bilateral* cross-cousin marriage. The ideal is that a brother and sister should marry a sister and brother and that, in the next generation, ego should marry mother's brother's daughter who is at the same time father's sister's daughter. In any event, kin groups (usually called *sections*) in the society are paired, and they swap women. For this reason Lévi-Strauss calls the system *restricted exchange*. The Kariera have four sections. In other systems, such as the Aranda, the number of sections may increase by powers of two, and ego may marry, not his immediate cross-cousin, but some more distant one. Yet the characteristic of restricted exchange—pairs of sections that swap women—is preserved. Without this characteristic, it is doubtful that Lévi-Strauss would give the name *restricted exchange* to a rule simply allowing marriage with either cross-cousin.

As distinguished from bilateral cross-cousin marriage, the unilateral form exists when, as between the two kinds of female cross-cousin—mother's brother's daughter and father's sister's daughter—the members of the society say that they prefer or expect ego to marry one of the two, but disapprove or at best tolerate his marriage with the other. That is, the rule for a man is different from that for a woman: if a man marries his mother's brother's daughter, a woman marries her father's sister's son. This kind of rule Lévi-Strauss reaches with the Murngin, who want ego to marry mother's brother's daughter but *not* father's sister's daughter. And he spends most of the rest of his book on this, the *matrilateral* form of unilateral cross-cousin marriage, which realizes what he calls *generalized exchange* and admires as a step forward in human marriage arrangements. Preferred marriage with father's sister's daughter but *not* mother's brother's daughter is the *patrilateral* form of unilateral cross-cousin marriage. Because Lévi-Strauss himself lays so much weight on these rules we make them the focus of our criticism of his theory.

Lévi-Strauss is always interested in the formal properties of the social structure associated with a marriage norm. Thus he must neglect the degree to which natives depart from the norm in practice, and depart from it they must. If, among the Kariera, for instance, the number of marriageable, true, female cross-cousins does not equal the number of marriageable, true, male cross-cousins—and this must almost always be the case—the ideal system cannot be carried out, and the men will marry classificatory cross-cousins. Although this will be true to some degree of all marriage rules, Lévi-Strauss always deals with the ideal system, and for purposes of argument we shall follow him.

Let us now look at the structural properties of matrilateral cross-cousin marriage, strictly carried out. Lévi-Strauss can easily show (Figure 2) that, given mother's brother's daughter marriage and either patrilineal or matrilineal descent groups (lineages), the groups in question must be at least three in number; that is, a simple moiety organization cannot exist. For under the stipulated conditions the men of lineage A marry the women of lineage B, but the men of B do not reciprocate by marrying the women of A, or the system would become one of Kariera type in which marriage with either cross-cousin is allowed. The conditions require instead three lineages, in which the men of A lineage marry B women, the B men marry C's, and the C men marry A's, in a ring. Indeed the ring can be extended to any number of lineages, and for this reason Lévi-Strauss calls the system one of *generalized exchange:* the B's give women to the A's; they do not get women back from the A's— that would be restricted exchange—but they do get women back in a roundabout way from a lineage on the other side of them in the ring. It might be argued that in extending the idea of exchange in this way,

Lévi-Strauss has thinned the meaning out of it. Of course some of the tribes following this rule say they exchange women for *goods*, but when Lévi-Strauss talks about marriage exchange he always means the exchange of women for *women*, whether recognized as an exchange or not.

Leaving Australia behind him, Lévi-Strauss goes on to show that, with some variations, the system of generalized exchange, with preferred marriage between ego and mother's brother's daughter, exists or existed in the past in a number of societies extending in a crescent from India through China to eastern Siberia. We know, of course, that this type of marriage occurs in other parts of the world, but Lévi-Strauss chooses to make eastern Asia his area of demonstration, and again his sheer exposition of the marriage rules in this ethnographic area seems excellent.

Harmonic and Dysharmonic Societies

We now bring up a problem that we should like to avoid but cannot, because it will turn out to have incidental, though only incidental, importance for our argument. Lévi-Strauss makes a further distinction between the bilateral and the unilateral form of cross-cousin marriage. He says the former is associated with *dysharmonic* regimes and the latter with *harmonic* ones.[7] To understand what he means by this we must consider for the first time the rules governing the constitution of the kin-groups that, directly or indirectly, exchange women. Lévi-Strauss says: "We shall call a regime harmonic when the rule of residence is the same as the rule of filiation, dysharmonic when they are different."[8] Thus a patrilocal (residence), patrilineal (filiation) society is harmonic, a patrilocal, matrilineal one dysharmonic. Contrary to usual practice in anthropology, words like *patrilocal* do not refer here to the place of residence of a couple after marriage but to the place of residence of ego in relation to the place of residence of the member of the older generation from whom ego inherits lineage membership. Thus if descent is patrilineal, and ego resides in the same local group as his father, the regime, according to Lévi-Strauss, is harmonic.

Consider now an harmonic society of the patrilineal-patrilocal sort. If the marriage rule is bilateral and the society is dichotomized once, so that every person, male or female, has to marry into a moiety other than his own, the moieties being defined either by descent or by residence but not by both, no trouble arises. But if the society is dichotomized twice, so that there are two residence moieties and two descent moieties, and if a person belongs to the same residence moiety and the same descent moiety as his father (that is, the regime is harmonic), and if, finally, he must marry outside both his moieties, the following situation arises:[9]

If a man:	marries a woman:	the children will be:
A1	B2	A1
B2	A1	B2
A2	B1	A2
B1	A2	B1

That is, the society divides into two pairs of sections, in this example A1-B2 and A2-B1. The two members of each pair are linked to one another by marriage, but the pairs themselves are linked neither by marriage nor by descent. The society splits wholly in two.

But if, the other rules remaining the same, ego belongs to the same residence moiety as his father but to a different descent moiety, that is, if the regime becomes, in Lévi-Strauss's terms, matrilineal-patrilocal and thus dysharmonic, then the following situation results:

$$\updownarrow \begin{matrix} A1 = B2 \\ A2 = B1 \end{matrix} \updownarrow \qquad \text{descent} \leftrightarrow \\ \text{marriage} =$$

That is, the sections are all linked, two pairs by marriage and two, cross-cutting pairs by descent. This is the Kariera system, which Lévi-Strauss argues is matrilineal, patrilocal. In fact it makes no odds whether we call it that or a system of patrilineal moieties intersected by matrilineal ones or a system of patrilineal moieties further subdivided by alternating generations—the only required condition is that, in a doubly dichotomized society, a person should belong to one of his father's moieties but not the other.

Accordingly Lévi-Strauss argues that dysharmonic societies can go on dichotomizing themselves indefinitely into four, eight, sixteen, etc., sections, still preserving restricted exchange and some form of bilateral marriage rule and still linking all the sections together by marriage or descent as shown above. But harmonic societies cannot dichotomize themselves more than once and accomplish all the rest too. The question then arises: What form of marriage rule can an harmonic society adopt that will automatically link more than two common-residence-and-descent groups (lineages) together? Lévi-Strauss says it can only abandon a bilateral rule and adopt a unilateral one. Then any number of lineages can be linked together in a ring by marriage, as we have already shown for the matrilateral case and will show for the patrilateral one. For these reasons, Lévi-Strauss says, bilateral cross-cousin marriage, at least of the various Australian forms, will be associated with dysharmonic regimes, unilateral cross-cousin marriage with harmonic ones.

Marriage Rules and Organic Solidarity

Why, the reader may well ask, does Lévi-Strauss consider so important the linking together, through marriage, of the different groups within a society? Why do they *have* to be linked? We can best answer this question by trying to answer another one: Why does he consider matrilateral cross-cousin marriage a step forward in human marriage arrangements? The answer is that he holds generalized exchange to be *better* than restricted exchange from the point of view of the organic solidarity of a society. In restricted exchange the number of sections can increase by powers of two, but as far as marriage is concerned, each section is linked with only one other, and the two swap women directly: there is no "roundaboutness"; whereas in generalized exchange each lineage specializes with respect to two others, from one of which it receives women and to the other of which it gives them. What is more, no lineage can get the women it needs unless the whole ring of marriage transactions works correctly. In Lévi-Strauss's view this makes for the closer integration of the tribe. His words are: "In effect, generalized exchange allows, the group remaining the same in extension and composition, the realization, in the heart of this mechanically stable group, of a greater organic solidarity."[10]

Lévi-Strauss is a French social scientist, and the parentage of his theory is clear. In the language of the turf, it is by Émile Durkheim out of Marcel Mauss's *Essai sur le don*. According to Durkheim in *De la division du travail social*,[11] a society is organically solidary to the extent that its individual members or subgroups are specialists and so dependent on one another, a further implication being that a solidary society is one showing a capacity to maintain itself in the face of disruptive tendencies. While Durkheim is talking for the most part about occupational specialization (the division of labor), Lévi-Strauss is talking about the specialization of one group with respect to others in giving women in marriage, but we believe the two men mean the same thing by *organic solidarity*. For Lévi-Strauss the greater the marriage specialization of each of the kin-groups in a society, the greater the dependence of each upon all, and hence the greater the organic solidarity.

Matrilateral and Patrilateral Cross-Cousin Marriage

We now reach the empirical focus of this paper: the two different forms of unilateral cross-cousin marriage. For the reader will remember that there are *two*, though up to this point in his argument Lévi-Strauss has considered only one of them. Preferred marriage with mother's brother's daughter but not father's sister's daughter is generalized exchange. But how about preferred marriage with father's sister's daughter and not with the other cross-cousin (the patrilateral form)? Just as Lévi-Strauss argues that, from the point of view of organic solidarity, generalized exchange is better than restricted exchange, so he argues that from the same point of view mother's brother's daughter marriage (generalized exchange) is *better* than father's sister's daughter marriage.

It can readily be shown—and Lévi-Strauss does show—that the formal structure created by the patrilateral form is not just the mirror opposite of that created by the matrilateral one. (Compare Figures 2 and 3.) In the latter, the men of B lineage always marry C women—the C's are "givers of women" with respect to the B's—A men always marry B women, and so forth; whereas in the former a B man marries a C woman in one generation, his sister's son marries an A woman in the next, his sister's daughter's son marries a C woman in the third, and so on, the B's being by alternate generations givers and receivers of women with respect to the A's and the C's. The two systems are structurally different, and the difference holds whether the society is matrilineal, as our figures assume, or patrilineal, son and grandson taking, in the latter case, the place of sister's son and sister's daughter's son in the former.

Lévi-Strauss calls father's sister's daughter marriage *discontinuous exchange*. And he asks,

What does this mean? Instead of constituting a global system, as do both bilateral and matrilateral cross-cousin marriage each in its own sphere, marriage with father's sister's daughter is not capable of attaining any other form than a multitude of little closed systems, juxtaposed to one another, without ever realizing a global structure.[12]

MATRILINEAGES

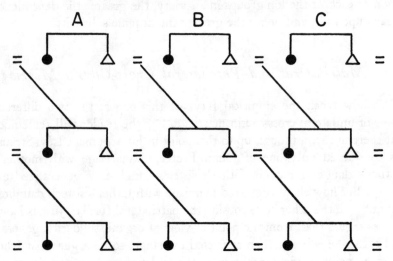

Figure 2. Matrilateral cross-cousin marriage (matrilineal society).

MATRILINEAGES

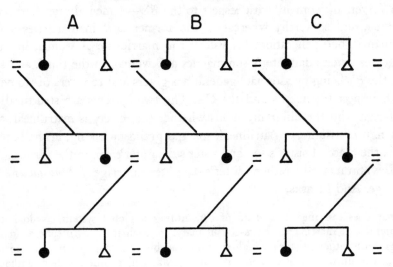

Figure 3. Patrilateral cross-cousin marriage (matrilineal society).

[210]

He finds, moreover, that in his chosen ethnographic area of eastern Asia, the matrilateral form is more common than the patrilateral one. And he goes on to take the stand that it is more common *because it is better* for society. Note his words well:

If then, in the last analysis, marriage with the daughter of the father's sister is less frequent than that with the daughter of the mother's brother, the reason is that the latter not only permits but favors a better integration of the group, while the former never succeeds in creating anything more than a precarious edifice, made of merely juxtaposed materials, obeying no plan of ensemble; and its texture is exposed to the same fragility as that of each of the little local structures of which it is composed.[13]

Are these words anything more than rhetoric? It is true that if, under the patrilateral rule, lineage B gives a woman to lineage A in one generation, it gets a woman back from the A's in the next. Since under the matrilateral rule this cannot happen, one may reasonably argue that exchange in the latter rule is more roundabout, and if roundaboutness creates organic solidarity, and if organic solidarity is good for a society, then the matrilateral form is better than the patrilateral one. This is in fact Lévi-Strauss's argument. On the other hand, father's sister's daughter marriage, just like mother's brother's daughter marriage, requires at least three lineages; any one lineage is linked by marriage to two others in the ring, and the ring can be lengthened indefinitely. On all these counts it meets Lévi-Strauss's requirements for generalized exchange. The only difference is that the men of B lineage, defined either patrilineally or matrilineally, give women alternately to the A's and to the C's instead of always getting them from one and giving them to the other. We might even go on to argue that father's sister's daughter marriage makes for greater organic solidarity, as the specialization in marriage is determined by generation as well as by lineage, and so creates a more intricate intermeshing of groups. We raise this question but we do not insist on it, as our chief criticism of Lévi-Strauss is a far more searching one.

We also concede that there is at least one situation in which mother's brother's daughter marriage is clearly "better" than father's sister's daughter. This is the situation described for the Kachin of upper Burma by Leach.[14] If the lineages of a society differ in social rank, and one of the aspects of the relationship between a superior lineage and a subordinate one is that the former gives women to the latter (or vice versa), then mother's brother's daughter marriage is practicable as a formal structure and father's sister's daughter marriage is not. The latter would destroy the ranking by making any one lineage alternately superior and subordinate to another. But most societies practicing mother's brother's daughter marriage seem not to be stratified in the Kachin manner, and in any event "better" here means "more compatible with other aspects of the social structure" rather than "more creative of organic solidarity"— a very different matter.

A "Final Cause" Theory

Our criticism of Lévi-Strauss goes deeper than anything we have said so far. But before we state our case, let us summarize Lévi-Strauss's, briefly but, we hope, fairly to him. Specialization of groups in their activities makes each dependent on the others. To get what it needs to maintain itself each must exchange with the others the products of the specialized activities. This is Durkheim's organic solidarity of groups within a society. Lévi-Strauss applies the idea to kin-groups and marriage. Women are the most highly valued of scarce goods, and so their exchange is most important in creating organic solidarity. The various rules of preferential marriage, from a simple incest taboo onwards, create exchanges of women between kin-groups, for if my group renounces marriage with its own women, it must get women from other groups. Indeed tribesmen adopt the different rules *in order to* create the exchanges and so the organic solidarity of their societies. Some rules, though, create a higher degree of organic solidarity than others. The more fully each kin-group is dependent, for getting its wives, on all the others, and thus the more "roundabout" the process of exchange, the greater the organic solidarity of the society. If one rule creates more organic solidarity than another, more tribes will adopt it. In the case we are using as a test, mother's brother's daughter marriage creates a higher degree of organic solidarity than father's sister's daughter marriage, and so more societies follow the former than the latter rule.

Like the rest of us, Lévi-Strauss is trying to answer the question: Why is a particular institution, or established norm of conduct, what it is? The answers given to this question have all, at one time or another, been called *functional* theories, but the word *function* has been used in several different senses, sometimes not distinguished from one another even within a single study. As we see it, the chief senses are three:

1. An institution is what it is because it results from the drives or meets the immediate needs of individuals or subgroups within a society. Its function is to meet these needs. We may call this an individual self-interest theory, if we remember that interests may be other than economic. We may also call it Malinowskian functionalism and use Malinowski's theory of magic as an example.[15]

2. An institution is what it is because it meshes with other institutions in a society. This we may call quasi-mathematical functionalism: one institution is a function of others. An illustration might be the relation of matrilateral cross-cousin marriage to the ranking of lineages among the Kachin.

3. An institution is what it is because it is in some sense good for a society as a whole. The latter emphasis is what distinguishes this from an individual self-interest theory. The criterion of the good is often the maintenance of the society in stable equilibrium in the face of what are presumed to be disruptive tendencies: the function of an institution is the part it plays in maintaining societal equilibrium. This we may call Radcliffe-Brownian functionalism, and point to Radcliffe-Brown's theory of magic. But if Radcliffe-Brown asks no more of an institution than that it maintain any old equilibrium, Lévi-Strauss, whose theory falls into this class, goes much further. For him there are, so to speak, better and worse equilibria. An institution is what it is because it is good for a society in the sense of creating organic solidarity, and some institutions are, from this point of view, better than others.

One word about Radcliffe-Brown's functionalism. His position in fact combines theories of the second and third classes:

The *function* of any recurrent activity, such as the punishment of a crime, or a funeral ceremony, is the part it plays in the social life as a whole [class 2 theory], and therefore the contribution it makes to the maintenance of the structural continuity [class 3].[16]

What a lot is implied in that little word *therefore!* Now it is true that, if we know something less than everything about a society, and if, on the grounds of observations however rough, we may reasonably assume the society to be in equilibrium, then we may be able to make certain deductions, in areas not open to direct observation, about the nature of the society's institutions and their relations to one another. By the fact of equilibrium, the institutions and their relations become that much more nearly determinate. This is analogous to, if not as rigorous as, the use of a general equilibrium equation to make up a number of equations equal to the number of unknowns in solving a problem in mechanics. But a society does not *have* to be in equilibrium. Equilibrium is observed or assumed; it is not given automatically by the institutions of a society and their relations; and forces of the first and second classes, which in one balance may establish equilibrium, may in another produce a society changing rapidly, even catastrophically. There is certainly no reason to believe that an institution is what it is just because it helps establish stable equilibrium.

We have no doubt that theories of all three kinds say something true and important about social behavior. An institution like magic may meet individual needs, *and* mesh with other institutions, *and*—at times—contribute to the maintenance of stable equilibrium—all three. We are not forced to choose between Malinowski's and Radcliffe-Brown's approach. We need both. Our quarrel is in fact with scholars who try to explain social behavior with one of these theories alone. In his more *ex cathedra* pronouncements Radcliffe-Brown said the anthropologist is justified in neglecting the personal interest theories, on the grounds that the interests worked to create institutions at some time in the past, and the past is lost to students of societies—like most primitive ones—that have no history. To what extent this position is valid we shall perhaps consider later. Certainly Radcliffe-Brown as a fieldworker was an acute observer of personal interests. His practice was even better than his theory.

When a theory of the third class is used by itself to account for the existence of an institution we shall say that it is, for sociology, a *final-cause* theory. This comes close to being Lévi-Strauss's position: a rule of matrilateral cross-cousin marriage occurs more often than a patrilateral one because it creates a higher degree of organic solidarity for a *society*.

We are not in the least concerned with the question whether organic solidarity is indeed good for a society, nor with the fact that Lévi-Strauss supplies no evidence, independent of the rules themselves, that societies with matrilateral rules are better integrated or indeed better off in any way than societies with patrilateral ones. All we are concerned with is the *nature* of Lévi-Strauss's theory. We argue that, to account for the adoption by a society of a particular institution, it is, in principle, never sufficient to show that the institution is in some sense good for the society, however that good may be defined. The weakness in all such theories was pointed out long ago by Aristotle. In his parable, "the house is there that men may live in it; but it is also there because the builders have laid one stone upon another."[17] Or, no final cause without an efficient cause. Lévi-Strauss's is not an evolutionary theory; it does not argue that the "worse" forms of marriage preceded the "better" in time of origin, but it bears some resemblance nevertheless to the Lamarckian theory of evolution, which held that "higher" animals have evolved from "lower" ones, without citing any mechanism by which this evolution might have taken place: teleology worked without help from nature. Science had no satisfactory theory of evolution until Darwin supplied efficient causes in random variation and the survival of the fittest, and even then an adequate theory of variation had to wait for the geneticists, if indeed we have a fully adequate one even now.

Any theory that will help us make sense of our data—that will redeem them from being *mere* data—is a useful one. If a final-cause theory will do so, we use it for lack of a better.[18] Lamarck's effort was not vain. But the very fact that a final-cause theory *will* order our data should prick us on all the more to find the efficient causes, for nature's efficient causes have a way of playing into the hands of her final ones. If we had no better way of making sense of the data than Lévi-Strauss's, we should have nothing to say against him. As it is, the very success of his effort has stimulated us into playing Darwin to his Lamarck.

Let us be quite clear: we have no doubt that some societies have evolved from good states to better ones. We are not among those that hold civilization no advance. We do believe it idle to say that societies adopted new forms of organization simply because these were better— for the societies—than the old. We must look for the specific conditions that enabled societies to adopt better forms, and this, we believe, requires our turning from functional theories of the third class to functional theories of the first and second.

In the course of trying to make the issue clear, we have not been altogether fair to Lévi-Strauss. We have implied that he has no efficient cause to account for the adoption by some societies of "better" marriage rules—matrilateral cross-cousin marriage rather than bilateral or patrilateral. He does not use, and in this we think him wise, a survival-value theory: we observe today a number of societies following the matrilateral rule because, by reason of having the rule, they were able to survive in competition with other societies. His is a much more powerful, if much more ancient, theory than this. Unlike some anthropologists of earlier generations, he has a high opinion of primitive men—or some of them —as thinkers, and he holds, if we understand him aright, that the members of some societies chose matrilateral cross-cousin marriage because they could "see," in much the same way that Lévi-Strauss himself can "see," that it was better than other forms.[19] He certainly cites many proverbs, current in societies following the matrilateral rule, that imply such recognition. We might argue that no society has trouble finding reasons why its institutions are better than those of others. These are rationalizations, or arguments after the fact. What we should like to have are arguments before the fact—those offered in favor of an institution *before* it was adopted. But since anthropologists have not observed societies in the process of adopting matrilateral cross-cousin marriage, we can hardly ask Lévi-Strauss to cite the debates.

In short, Lévi-Strauss's efficient cause is human intelligence, and this puts at stake nothing less than the nature of social development. We have no doubt that primitive men think rationally about their own societies. We do doubt that intelligent recognition that a certain institution would be good for a society is ever a sufficient—though it may be a necessary—condition for its adoption. If it were, the history of human society would be happier than we observe it to be. In personal behavior we have all groveled with the honest poet who admitted *video meliora proboque, deteriora sequor*. If the problem is one of getting a *society* to adopt a better institution, when a large number of its members must take the risk of pursuing long-run, potential interests competing with short-run, actual ones—and this is precisely the problem with the adoption of matrilateral cross-cousin marriage, as Lévi-Strauss describes it —we know bitterly how difficult the solution is. To account for success, we must bring to light the conditions under which some primitives are not only able to "see" a better institution but actually to attain it. We must also explain why, assuming the same average intelligence among primitive tribes, some are not. Even the Constitution of the United States would never have been adopted if it had not served strong, short-run, personal, even selfish interests. In short we are again, as always, driven back to the arduous task of establishing the immediate determinants of different institutions. A theory of intelligence as the efficient cause, just as much as a pure final-cause theory, drives us back to explanations of the first and second classes.

An Alternative Theory: The Patrilineal Complex

If we find Lévi-Strauss's theory weak, the burden of proof is on us to supply one that will account for the facts more adequately. We have also committed ourselves to supplying a different *kind* of theory from his, one that will not appeal to what we have called a final cause, and that will (1) show the relation between different forms of unilateral cross-cousin marriage and other institutions, and (2) cite adequate individual motivation, aside from intellectual recognition that it is "good" for a society, to account for the adoption of a particular marriage rule. It is fair to say of Lévi-Strauss that he works with a very restricted model of society, a model that hardly includes more than the formal structure, as we have called it above, of lineages and the links between them created by different forms of preferential marriage.[20] For many purposes the use of a highly abstract model is illuminating. In this case, we believe the model is not lifelike enough to serve as a model at all. Using as our crucial test the two different forms of unilateral cross-cousin marriage, we shall try to relate them to aspects of kinship behavior other than those Lévi-Strauss usually takes into consideration.

Now the facts that Lévi-Strauss himself cites at once suggest an hypothesis different from his. Almost all the eastern Asian societies in which he finds mother's brother's daughter marriage preferred are organized in patrilineages. He does not lay any weight on this fact; he concerns himself with linearity, but not with the *kind* of linearity, and it is true that the differences in formal structure between the two forms of unilateral cross-cousin marriage persist whether the societies in question are patrilineal or matrilineal. But we, who are not bound to adopt Lévi-Strauss's model, at once ask ourselves: May not the type of unilateral cross-cousin marriage adopted by a society be associated with the type of linearity of its kin-groups?

What reasons have we for suspecting that such an association exists? We have learned from Radcliffe-Brown in his classic paper, "The Mother's Brother in South Africa,"[21] from Firth in his work on Tikopia,[22] and from Evans-Pritchard, Fortes, Gluckman, and the many other able British anthropologists who have worked in Africa, a good deal about the "patrilineal complex" in everyday kinship sentiment and activity. In a great many patrilineal societies in all parts of the world— just how many we cannot say, as this is a subject to which statistical studies have not yet addressed themselves—jural authority over ego is vested in his father and, more remotely, in his other patrilineal kinsmen of older generations. In these circumstances, a relationship builds up between ego and his father that may be marked on ego's part by admiration but also by respect and constraint, such as is often associated with the subordinate-superior relationship outside of kinship.

As it will play a big part in our argument, let us stop to make clear what we mean by *jural authority*. We shall say that a person has authority over others to the extent that they in fact carry out the wishes, suggestions, orders he addresses to them.[23] But in countless groups from factories to primitive tribes, persons who, by this definition, exercise authority do not exercise jural authority. The classic case is the woman who controls her family, though her husband is its acknowledged head. By *jural authority* we mean, then, legitimate or constituted authority, and a person holds jural authority over others when, according to the stated norms of his group, he has the right to give them orders and they have the duty to obey.[24] As norms must have some correspondence with actual behavior, so *de jure* authority must have some correspondence with *de facto*, and if persons of a particular status in fact exercised chief authority over their groups, regularly and for a long time, we should expect their authority to become jural. Mothers have never been able to establish a legitimate matriarchy only because they have never bossed their families quite regularly enough.

A number of persons may hold jural authority over ego: in a patrilineal society his elder brother and his lineage head as well as his father. When we say that the locus of jural authority over ego in a patrilineal society is his father, we mean that the father is roughly equivalent to what a factory manager would call ego's first-line supervisor. We also imply a comparison. In this case we imply that his father has the recognized right to give orders to ego, and certain other persons do not—notably his mother's brother.

In the patrilineal complex, a relationship somewhat different from the father-son tie grows up between ego and his mother, who meets his compelling needs in infancy, and who is herself at least jurally subordinate to the father. She is a much more warm and nurturant figure. Apparently as a result of the identification of the mother with her brother, who is her protector, and the status of the latter as an older male without jural authority over ego, ego's behavior toward his mother's brother differs sharply from his behavior toward his father. The relationship varies somewhat from one patrilineal society to another. Ego may show great respect for mother's brother, but he also finds in him an intimate older friend, helper, and adviser. As Radcliffe-Brown pointed out, mother's brother in the patrilineal complex tends to become a kind of male mother, and in some societies is called by a word that means just this. The features that appear most often in the relationship seem to be four: (1) absence of jural authority, (2) the giving of help and advice by the mother's brother, as distinguished from orders, (3) frequent interaction, as when ego visits mother's brother from time to time, and (4) considerable freedom, as when either ego or mother's brother is free to use the other's possessions without asking permission.

Let there be no mistake, even about the obvious. In speaking of "the" mother's brother we do not assume that a mother has only one brother or even any brother at all. We mean mother's brother the status, not mother's brother the person, though no doubt when there are many brothers and many sisters, one of the brothers may well be closer than the others to a particular sister's son. Indeed some societies tend to pair off brothers and sisters, each member of such a couple being specially devoted to the other and the other's children.[25]

The data on father's sister in patrilineal societies are much less rich, but they suggest that she tends to become for ego a kind of female father, treated, as she is in Tikopia, with distance and respect.[26] For a fuller discussion of the propositions describing these interpersonal ties among kinsfolk, see G. C. Homans, *The Human Group*.[27] We admit the difficulty, which all novelists have encountered, of describing these ties in precise terms.

We suspect that mother's brother's daughter marriage may be particularly common in patrilineal societies because of the close nature of the tie between ego and mother's brother in these societies. We find in the structure of interpersonal relations the individual motivations, or efficient causes, for the adoption of a particular form of unilateral cross-cousin marriage. The motivations may take many and mixed forms, but they are all predicated on the nature of the ties. As he visits mother's brother often, ego will see a great deal of the daughter: contact will be established. As he is fond of mother's brother, and as mother's brother and his daughter in the patrilineal complex, the Oedipus complex if you will, are themselves particularly close to one another, he will tend to get fond of the daughter. Their marriage will be sentimentally appropriate; it will cement the relationship. Or, if women are indeed scarce and valued goods, and ego is in doubt where he can get one, he will certainly be wise to ask his mother's brother, on whom he already has so strong a sentimental claim.

This latter motive is well documented for the patrilineal Hehe. The Hehe allow other forms of marriage besides cross-cousin marriage, but one-quarter of all marriages are in fact with cross-cousins, real or classificatory, and of cross-cousin marriages four-fifths are with mother's brother's daughter and only one-fifth with father's sister's daughter. One native informant, translated freely, said:

Some people marry their cross-cousins because they realize that they are not of the group with whom marriage is forbidden. A child of an uncle (i.e. a nephew) says, "I shall go and court my cousin, the child of my uncle, because we are related; they will give her to me, they will not refuse me, if my cousin loves me; my uncle will give her to me out of the kindness of his heart [literally 'from a white liver'] because I am the child of his sister."[28]

A similar kind of statement was made about father's sister's daughter marriage, but note that the characteristic patrilineal complex prevails among the Hehe, and the ethnologist says of father's sister: "She is treated with ceremonious respect, to an even greater degree than the uncle."[29]

In stating our argument, we have so far adopted the point of view of a male ego of the younger generation, but the same kinds of motivation might make this form of marriage particularly agreeable to the mother's brother too: he takes care of his beloved daughter by giving her to the man of the younger generation to whom he is sentimentally closest, even closer than he is to his own son. As for the girl, whose views we anthropologists hardly ever consider, whatever the primitives may do, she tends, in the patrilineal complex, to be closer to her father than is his son; through the identification of father and his sister, she would tend to find her elder confidante, outside of the family of orientation, in her father's sister, who is ego's mother. Mother's brother's daughter marriage (father's sister's son marriage from her point of view) is sentimentally appropriate for her too.

Our view that the efficient causes of matrilateral cross-cousin marriage are to be found in interpersonal relationships must now take us back to Lévi-Strauss. He recognizes that a tie between ego and mother's brother, of the kind we have described, exists in many of his patrilineal societies of eastern Asia. But since he tends to think of marriage rules as creating structures complete in themselves, which need not be considered in close relation to other aspects of kinship behavior, he does not lay any great weight on the fact. So far, indeed, as he does consider the role of the mother's brother, he seems to look on it as a consequence of marriage with mother's brother's daughter rather than as a possible cause.[30] But as it is not wholly clear that he takes this position, let us not attribute it to him, but take it up in its own right as an obvious objection to our theory.

The position seems to us untenable for two reasons. First, the special relationship between ego and mother's brother seems to occur more often in patrilineal societies than mother's brother's daughter marriage, and the more general phenomenon can hardly be explained in terms of the less. Second, the position assumes that the mother's brother's role as father-in-law is the primary and governing factor. But the relationship between father-in-law and son-in-law is only less "difficult" than the mother-in-law relationships, and it is hard to see how it could give rise by itself to the characteristic "free and equal" relationship between ego and mother's brother. We argue instead that ego's tie with mother's brother *before* the latter becomes father-in-law is primary in influence as it is in time, and that one good reason why ego might want to marry his daughter is that the established relationship will soften the asperities of an otherwise "difficult" situation.

The reader may also object that we have put our argument in terms of the motives and behavior of individuals, whereas we promised earlier to follow Lévi-Strauss and deal with the various forms of cross-cousin marriage as norms stating the proper, not necessarily the actual be-havior, for many individuals in a society. We hold, of course, that norms are not independent of actual behavior. When the social structures of many kin-groups in a society are similar, which is eminently the case with primitive societies, then many individuals will tend to develop similar sentiments and behavior toward similar kinsmen. For example, many egos will develop similar sentiments and behavior toward their respective mother's brothers. In time such sentiments and behavior will become recognized as the right and proper ones: they will be enshrined in norms. No doubt a norm, once established, has some measure of in-dependent influence, if only because it is then taught to the young. Even then we do not believe that a norm can indefinitely maintain itself in the face of changes in social structure precipitating sentiments and behavior different from those originally enshrined in the norm. We deal with norms for convenience in argument, and because, as we shall see, most ethnographers tell us more about norms than about actual behavior. We admit that the relation between the two is elastic and not rigid, but we also hold that, in the long run and in a first approximation, behavior determines norms.

The Matrilineal Complex

Our theory is of little use unless it applies also to the other form of unilateral cross-cousin marriage—between ego and father's sister's daughter. If the patrilineal complex of relationships is associated with one marriage rule, the idea at once comes to mind that the matrilineal complex is associated with the other. Outside of Australia, Lévi-Strauss pays little attention to matrilineal societies, but of course the best-known of them is the society of the Trobriand Islands. In this society, as Malinowski described it, ego begins life in his father's house, but he belongs to his mother's lineage. His mother's brother holds jural authority over him; as he grows up he spends more and more time in his mother's brother's village, and when he marries his wife joins him there. In these circumstances, the relationship between ego and mother's brother much resembles that between ego and father in the patrilineal complex, and vice versa, for ego and his father are close friends.[31]

Let there, again, be no ambiguity. We are speaking of mother's brother the status, not mother's brother the person. We have said that in the Trobriands mother's brother holds jural authority over ego. A more careful statement would be that, as he grows up, jural authority over ego is normally vested in the head of his subclan, who may well be one of his mother's brothers and who will, in any event, be one of his matrilineal, rather than patrilineal, kinsmen. We always, moreover, imply a comparison: the locus of jural authority is certainly mother's brother *rather* than father.

Moreover, just as there are at least two avunculates—patrilineal and matrilineal—so there are two amitates, and father's sister in the Trobriands plays a very different role from what she does in, for instance, a patrilineal society like Tikopia. Great freedom obtains between ego and herself; they may talk and joke about all matters, sexual or other; sexual intercourse between them is tolerated, and the preferred marriage is with the father's sister's daughter, not the mother's brother's.[32] This form of marriage is carried out in practice more often by members of the chiefly families than by commoners, but unlike some societies we shall mention later, the preference of the two classes is the same. Among the Hopi, another matrilineal society, the relationships between ego, father, mother's brother, and father's sister are described by Eggan in much the same terms as they are among the Trobriands by Malinowski: friendship and freedom to joke on sexual matters obtain between ego and father's sister, and there is some suggestion that in the past father's sister's daughter marriage was practiced.[33] In short, we suggest that the same kinds of motivation that make matrilateral cross-cousin marriage peculiarly appropriate in patrilineal society make patrilateral cross-cousin marriage peculiarly appropriate in matrilineal society. No doubt this motivation will not lead to effective results as often in matrilineal societies as in patrilineal ones. In the latter, ego in getting a wife depends on his ties with a man, his mother's brother; in the former on his ties with a woman, his father's sister, and a woman may well have less power of disposing of her daughter than a man has of his. So long as women are, in general and *de jure*, subordinated to men, matrilineal society can never be the mirror opposite of patrilineal. We believe, nevertheless, that the forces at work will be strong enough in some matrilineal societies to create a preference for father's sister's daughter marriage.

An Hypothesis Stated

When we first presented orally the substance of our present criticism of Lévi-Strauss,[34] we made, on the basis of the argument outlined above, the following prediction.

Hypothesis: *Societies in which marriage is allowed or preferred with mother's brother's daughter but forbidden or disapproved with father's sister's daughter will be societies possessing patrilineal kin-groups, and societies in which marriage is allowed or preferred with father's sister's daughter but forbidden or disapproved with mother's brother's daughter will be societies possessing matrilineal kin-groups.* Let methodological purists note that we made the prediction before we tried to verify it.

The hypothesis invites some explanatory comments. First, it is not an obvious and trivial one, in that it does not follow directly from the common taboo of ego's marriage within his lineage. In neither patrilineal nor matrilineal society is either cross-cousin a member of ego's lineage.

Second, it says nothing about the determinants of unilateral cross-cousin marriage in general, as opposed to rules prescribing marriage with either or neither cross-cousin. *Given* unilateral cross-cousin marriage, it addresses itself to the question: What will determine the adoption of one form of unilateral cross-cousin marriage rather than the other? Third, it deals with the immediate cross-cousins and has nothing to say about more distant ones, such as mother's mother's brother's daughter's daughter.

Fourth, the hypothesis is a deduction from a theory rather than the theory itself. What we may call our general theory holds that the form of unilateral cross-cousin marriage will be determined by the system of interpersonal relations precipitated by a social structure, especially by the locus of jural authority over ego. Because we believe that this locus will be different in patrilineal society from what it is in matrilineal, we predict as a special hypothesis that one kind of unilateral cross-cousin marriage will be associated with patrilineal society, the other kind with matrilineal. For only one reason shall we begin by trying to verify our special hypothesis rather than our general theory: the ethnographic reports usually provide much better data on linearity than on systems of interpersonal relations. Note that we make our prediction in terms of the linearity of kin-groups, not in terms of the linearity of reckoning descent. In the absence of kin-groups that are in some measure corporate bodies, the mere reckoning of descent may mean little structurally. But when unilineal kin-groups are present, we may make a reasonable guess about the locus of jural authority over ego: it will at least lie within ego's own lineage. Even so, the connection between our general theory and our special hypothesis may well turn out to be loose. Our special hypothesis may turn out to be wrong, our general theory remaining right; or, conversely, our special hypothesis may turn out right for the wrong reasons —wrong in the sense of "other than those predicated in the general theory."

Finally, let us restate the differences between Lévi-Strauss's hypothesis and ours. He says that matrilateral cross-cousin marriage will occur in *more* societies than the patrilateral form because the former is *better* than the latter at creating organic solidarity. We say that, better or not, the matrilateral form will occur in patrilineal societies, the patrilateral form in matrilineal ones. Both of these hypotheses could conceivably be true, but it appears that in fact Lévi-Strauss rejects ours. He observes that the Mikir of Assam are organized in patrilineal, patrilocal clans and prefer mother's brother's daughter marriage, and that the nearby Garo are organized matrilineally and matrilocally but also prefer mother's brother's daughter marriage.[35] Both societies possess, in his terms, harmonic regimes. Hence, he says, "One can readily see that the structure of generalized exchange [matrilateral cross-cousin marriage] does not depend at all on linearity [*filiation*] but only on the harmonic character of the regime considered."[36] Because we anticipated this point, we were careful to explain above what Lévi-Strauss means by a harmonic regime. We neither accept nor reject Lévi-Strauss's claim that restricted exchange is associated with dysharmonic regimes. What we do reject is the claim that matrilateral cross-cousin marriage has nothing to do with linearity; we predict, Lévi-Strauss to the contrary, that it will tend to occur in patrilineal societies. If we are to show that our efficient-cause theory is more useful than his final-cause one, we are fortunate in having a problem in which the issue between them is clearly joined. We shall now see how far our hypothesis is verified.

Testing by the Murdock Sample

In testing the hypothesis, we wanted to avoid, if we could, reviewing for ourselves the whole body of ethnographic literature. In these circumstances, the obvious man to ask for help was G. P. Murdock, and we submitted our hypothesis for testing against the data on the sample of 250 societies used in *Social Structure*.[37] Note that we tested on a worldwide basis and did not confine ourselves to Lévi-Strauss's chosen ethnographic area of Australia and eastern Asia. We are much indebted to Murdock for his help, but he must not be held responsible for any of our conclusions. He reported as follows:

1. Societies for which data are lacking on cross-cousin marriage or reported for only one cousin were omitted from the enumeration.

2. In 126 societies of the sample, marriage with either cross-cousin is forbidden or disapproved.

3. In 56 societies of the sample, marriage with either cross-cousin is allowed or preferred.

All of this information was useful in clearing the ground, but was not pertinent to our hypothesis. The next two findings *were* pertinent:

4. In 12 societies of the sample, marriage is allowed or preferred with mother's brother's daughter but forbidden or disapproved with father's

sister's daughter. The societies are: Batak, Lakher, Lhota, Limba, Mbundu, Miwok, Murngin, Rengma, Sema, Thado, Timne, Venda. All of these societies, without exception, have patrilineal kin-groups, although the Murngin and Mbundu have full-fledged double descent (matrilineal as well as patrilineal kin-groups), and the Venda have survivalistic traces of matrilineal descent.

5. In 3 societies of the sample, marriage is allowed or preferred with father's sister's daughter but forbidden or disapproved with mother's brother's daughter. The societies are: Ila, Tismulun, Trobrianders. All three, without exception, have matrilineal kin-groups, the Ila having double descent.

These findings call for some immediate comments. First, if Murdock's sample is at all representative, either form of unilateral cross-cousin marriage must be a rare phenomenon, so that if frequency of occurrence is, as Lévi-Strauss seems to claim, a measure of the "goodness" of an institution, both forms must be fairly "bad." Second, Lévi-Strauss's statement that the matrilateral form is commoner than the patrilateral is confirmed, but the reason seems to be that more patrilineal societies practice unilateral cross-cousin marriage than matrilineal ones. And, third, whether or not one form produces a higher degree of organic solidarity than the other, the fact is that the different forms are associated with differences in the linearity of kin-groups, and, so far as Murdock's sample is concerned, our hypothesis is confirmed.

Retesting with More Societies

In fact it is confirmed all too well. Faced with the findings, one of the authors of this paper felt that they were too good to be true, and insisted on our looking for further examples of unilateral cross-cousin marriage, on the theory that there are no perfect correlations in the field of human behavior. But this decision meant that we had to go to the ethnographic literature ourselves. We doubt that our search has been exhaustive. We got leads from Lévi-Strauss's book, from Murdock, and from others, and we followed them up to the point of diminishing returns, where the importance of this paper did not, in our view, justify more work. But without question there are more societies practicing unilateral cross-cousin marriage than we have discovered.

The decision also meant that we had to face the same problems of

[226]

taxonomy as did Murdock himself. If we are to test the hypothesis, each of its terms should refer to an unambiguously discriminable class of data, and this is not always the case. The word *society* itself is not easy to define. Is an Indian caste a society, and should castes be included in our list? Do the different Naga groups, Lhota, Rengma, and Sema, constitute separate societies? We raise these general questions without answering them, but our practice follows Murdock's. Nor is even the word *marriage* unambiguous. We decided that, even if we lacked other reasons for leaving the Nayar of Malabar off our list, we should reject them on the ground that nothing like marriage, in the sense of husband and wife "living together," exists among the Nayar, at least in that society's classical form.[38] And what do we mean by *unilineal kin-groups*—which raises the problem of double descent? The Mbundu, Murngin, and Venda may recognize matrilineal kin-groups, but what Leach calls the *local descent group*[39]—the core of kinsfolk associated generation by generation with a particular territory—consists in each of these societies of patrilineally-related men. We have had no trouble deciding that these societies are effectively patrilineal. The Ila, we confess, are not so easily handled, and we shall have to take up their case later.

Finally, how do we define *unilateral cross-cousin marriage?* We have chosen to consider only the immediate cross-cousins and not more distant ones. A more important question is whether we take the actual frequencies of the two different forms or what the natives say their preferences are—the official, expressed norms. It would be pleasant, because they would conform to our hypothesis, to include the matrilineal Yao, who formally approve marriage with either cross-cousin but actually marry father's sister's daughter more often than mother's brother's;[40] unpleasant to include the matrilineal Ashanti, who have the same formal rule but marry mother's brother's daughter more often.[41] Apart from our desire to meet Lévi-Strauss so far as possible on his own ground—and he deals regularly with marriage norms—there are so few societies for which we have anything like marriage statistics that we have decided to classify according to formal preferences, as stated by the natives or the ethnographers. Under this rule, neither Yao nor Ashanti appear on our final list. In some societies, moreover, chiefs and other persons of rank follow marriage preferences decidedly different from those of commoners. Thus the heirs of chiefs among the matrilineal Haida often marry mother's brother's daughters for dynastic reasons, while the rule for the masses is father's sister's daughter.[42] When their formal preferences differ from those of commoners, we have decided to eliminate chiefs and the like from consideration, as introducing a complicating variable, that of rank, and we have accordingly moved the Haida from the list of bilateral societies to that of unilateral ones. We have also decided to give ourselves a little more leeway in deciding which societies are really unilateral. Murdock eliminated from his list all societies for which there was information on only one of the two female cross-cousins. Yet there is at least one society for which the ethnographic data show a decided unilateral preference without specifically ruling out the cross-cousin on the other side. We are ready to presume that this society is unilateral and have accordingly included the Garo on our final list. In this we follow Lévi-Strauss, but we differ from him in excluding the Khasi. They allow marriage with either cross-cousin *after the death of father or mother's brother*, respectively, but they tend to disapprove of father's sister's daughter's marriage even then.[43] In our view, their case is ambiguous because they allow unilateral cross-cousin marriage part of the time and forbid it part of the time. Obviously we do not have space to justify our decision in the case of every society, but we are ready to defend ourselves if attacked.

Our final list—final only so long as further relevant societies are not dug out of the literature—is as follows:[44]

1. *Patrilineages—matrilateral form preferred:*
   Altaians and Teleuts, Batak, Gilyak, Gold, Kachin, Karadjeri, Lakher, Lhota, Limba, Lovedu, Mbundu, Mende, Miwok, Murngin, Rengma, Sandawe, Sema, Thado, Timne, Venda, Wik-Munkan (Archer River group), Yir-Yoront.
2. *Patrilineages—patrilateral form preferred:*
   Kandyu, Sherente.
3. *Matrilineages—matrilateral form preferred:*
   Garo, Kaonde, Kaska, Siriono.
4. *Matrilineages—patrilateral form preferred:*
   Haida, Ila, Tismulun, Tlingit, Trobrianders.

If we put the results in a fourfold table, we get Table 1. The general

Table 1

Preferred marriage	Kin-groups	
	Patrilineal	Matrilineal
Mother's brother's daughter	22	4
Father's sister's daughter	2	5

characteristics of this distribution are similar to those of the distribution obtained from the Murdock sample. Unilateral cross-cousin marriage of either kind is still a rare phenomenon. The matrilateral form still is more frequent of occurrence than the patrilateral one, but this still seems to depend, not on the inherent "goodness" of the form, but on the fact that there are more patrilineal societies on our list than matrilineal ones and they tend to prefer the matrilateral form. For, although our perfect correlation has gone, and the six societies in classes 2 and 3 above now constitute exceptions to our hypothesis, the relationship is still in the direction predicted by the hypothesis, and it is still statistically significant. ($P = 0.009$ by Fisher's Exact Test.)[45] Contrary to Lévi-Strauss, linearity *is* a determinant of the form of unilateral cross-cousin marriage. A further question is whether the proportion of patrilineal societies in our list is larger than the proportion in the world at large; that is, whether *even* more patrilineal societies practice unilateral cross-cousin marriage than the number of *all* patrilineal societies, as compared with the number of *all* matrilineal societies, would lead us to expect. Now the matrilineal/patrilineal ratio in Murdock's total sample is 0.45 and in our list 0.375. We got absolutely more patrilineal societies than we had a right to expect. We do not know that we can properly show the difference to be significant, but if it *were* significant it would still suggest that linearity makes a difference to unilateral cross-cousin marriage, in that more patrilineal societies practice either of its forms than do matrilineal ones. Or, in Lévi-Strauss's terms, if the matrilateral form is "good," it is particularly good for patrilineal societies.

Testing the General Theory

The next question is: Do we need to feel discouraged because our predicted correlation did not turn out on retest to be more significant? Can we recapture a really high correlation? There may be a way. The reader will remember that the hypothesis we have just tested was a special deduction from a more general theory, according to which differences in marriage preferences were related to differences in systems of interpersonal relations among kinsfolk. If, in particular, the relation between ego male and mother's brother was "close" and that with father's sister "distant," we expected unilateral cross-cousin marriage, provided it existed at all, to take place with mother's brother's daughter.

If the roles were reversed, we expected marriage with father's sister's daughter. Of course these words "close" and "distant" are only shorthand descriptions of the facts.

We further held that the system would take the first form when father held jural authority over ego, the second when mother's brother held it; that, in short, the locus of jural authority is an important determinant of systems of interpersonal relationships, and these of marriage preferences. Because we further believed that father would be apt to hold jural authority over ego in a society of patrilineal kin-groups, and mother's brother in a society of matrilineal kin-groups, we predicted that mother's brother's daughter marriage would be preferred in the former, father's sister's daughter in the latter. We decided to test our general theory in the form of this special hypothesis, for the reason that ethnographic reports usually contain more adequate information on linearity than on interpersonal relations.

But *some* reports do tell us a little about interpersonal ties, and so the following questions come up: In the societies conforming to our special hypothesis, what evidence is there for the kinds of interpersonal relations we should anticipate from the general theory? Or, were we right for the right reasons? And in the societies that are exceptions to our hypothesis, what evidence is there for the kind of interpersonal relations we should anticipate from the general theory, even though linearity is not as predicted? In particular, is the assumption on which we derived the hypothesis—that the locus of jural authority over ego is the father in all patrilineal societies, the mother's brother in all matrilineal ones —justified in fact? Or, were we wrong for the right reasons? Is, in short, our general theory more adequate than our special hypothesis? To answer this question, we shall have to examine whatever evidence on interpersonal relations exists for societies on our list, particularly evidence on the locus of jural authority over ego and on ego's ties with father, father's sister, and mother's brother.

Patrilineal-Matrilateral Societies (Class 1)

We shall take first the societies that conform to our special hypothesis. For none of the patrilineal-matrilateral societies, except the Murngin and Yir-Yoront, whom we shall consider later, is there reason to suspect that the locus of immediate jural authority over ego lies in any person but his father. For thirteen of these societies—Batak, Gilyak, Karadjeri, Lakher, Lhota, Lovedu, Mbundu, Mende, Murngin, Sema, Venda, and Wik-Munkan—the reported data suggest, in our view, a relationship between ego and mother's brother that has at least some points in common with the relationship in the classic patrilineal complex as it exists, for instance, in Tikopia, and which is the relationship our general theory expected to find associated with mother's brother's daughter marriage. The evidence is perhaps least clear for the Mbundu. In this society, where the local descent groups are patrilineal but dispersed matrilineages are also present, the mother's brother held more jural authority over ego in the past than he does today.[46] As for father's sister, we have information on her from only the Lovedu, Mbundu, Murngin, and Venda, but in every one of these cases she appears in the role we expected from our general theory—a "female father" in a situation where the father is a figure of authority and respect. As for the other societies, we have been unable to consult the Russian sources personally, and the rest do not provide adequate information on interpersonal relationships.

By way of illustration, let us look briefly at interpersonal ties among the Lovedu. Of the father we learn this:

Because he spends most of his time with the men, there is little personal contact between father and young children. . . . The boy finds that his father admonishes him or shows displeasure when he cries and on occasion inculcates manly virtues. The father keeps his distance, yet he becomes the personification of manly ideals, and a boy tries to be like his father. The father has authority, but his authority is never oppressive like that of European fathers, whose children live in much closer contact with them. If a boy has done wrong or let the cattle stray, he will avoid his father by not making an appearance at home till after dark.[47]

Of the father's sister:

Derived from the brother-sister relationship is that of the father's sister, who is accorded honor and respect by the children of the house she has established.

Her role in the patrilineage is that of a priestess.

As for the matrilineal kinsfolk,

The greatest of all bonds between a man and his mother's side of the family is conceived by the Lovedu to be one of love. There is a saying, usually quoted by women, . . . which, freely translated, means, "Love lies on the mother's side of the family; ownership on the father's."

"Ownership," we suspect, refers here to all those jural rights of control that are crucial in determining the respect relationship. Among mother's kin, ego among the Lovedu is particularly close to mother's mother, and his relationship with mother's brother, while friendly, is tinged with respect:

Your mother's brother may be kind to you, but you have to show him respect: if he asks you to go on a message or to help him in the fields, you cannot refuse; while, if he needs you, you may be sent to herd for him or help nurse his small children.

Finally, "the sister's son is a potential son-in-law, who is accorded great honor in the household of his mother's brother." We could indeed state our general theory loosely as: Where a man finds love in one generation, he will find it in the next.

We must now meet an obvious issue head-on. Earlier, we quoted a Hehe informant who said that ego sought mother's brother's daughter in marriage *because* of his close sentimental ties with mother's brother. For none of the present societies do the sources provide explicit statements of this sort. We nevertheless believe that the sentimental tie is a necessary, if not a sufficient, cause of the marriage preference, in the special sense of preceding it in time. We are in no position to demonstrate this, and even if we were, we should expect the "cause" to drop out of explicit recognition by the natives. Without doubt the marriage preference has existed in these societies for some length of time, in the course of which it has become an established norm and linked with aspects of social organization other than the sentimental tie. Among the Lovedu, for instance, it is linked with the transmission of bridewealth. The natives may even come to feel that the system it creates is "good" in the same sense that Lévi-Strauss does. To the norm, to the other linkages, to the advantages, rather than to the sentimental tie, the natives may well refer if asked to account for the marriage preference. From the fact that the nature of the linkages with other institutions varies more from society to society than the sentimental tie itself, we might argue that the latter was the more important, because more nearly universal, determinant: marriage with mother's brother's daughter is found in the presence of the sentimental tie with mother's brother far more often than in that of the transmission of bridewealth. But all we insist on is the sheer association between different forms of unilateral cross-cousin marriage and different systems of interpersonal relations, including different *loci* of jural authority over ego. We believe present association betrays ultimate origin; the history of some institutions is repeated every generation; to some unknown degree the energies that maintain a system are the ones that created it, and to this degree Radcliffe-Brown is wrong in holding that the history of primitive institutions is forever lost to us. We believe this; we do not know that we can prove it, and in any event it becomes irrelevant in the face of the present association of institutions.

The problem of analyzing systems of interpersonal relations is further complicated by the tendency of every kinship system to build its own backfires. Thus if mother's brother has many sister's sons, real or classificatory, competing for his daughter, and he has the power to withhold her from any one of them, this fact might tend to create tension between ego and mother's brother and spoil what might otherwise have been a beautiful friendship. A sentimental tie may create an institution and, in so doing, help poison itself. This may explain why, among the Murngin, ego may be close to mother's brother but is even closer to mother's mother's brother.[48] Indeed we should expect the tie between ego and mother's brother to be most fully friendly in a patrilineal society like Tikopia that does *not* practice mother's brother's daughter marriage.

If, again, the sentimental tie with his mother's brother is very important to ego, he may hesitate to offend mother's brother, which may give the latter *de facto* authority over ego, however little he may have *de jure*. Thus we learn of the Mende, one of the societies of the present class, "In terms of family law, to disobey one's uncle is an even graver offence than disobedience of one's father and may provoke a more serious curse."[49] On this point we are fully in agreement with Radcliffe-Brown's discussion of the mother's brother's curse: "This is sometimes interpreted as though it means that the mother's brother regularly exercises authority over his nephew, and that his authority is greater than that even of a father. I suggest that the proper interpretation is that the mother's brother will be the last person to use his power of cursing, and that it is for this reason that it is feared more than the curse of the father."[50] In accepting this view, we must still admit that these "backfires" add to the ambiguity of interpersonal relations.

We turn last to the difficult case of the Yir-Yoront of the Cape York peninsula, Australia. They are organized in patrilineages, approve marriage with mother's brother's daughter, but forbid it with father's sister's daughter, and thus conform to our special hypothesis.[51] But it is at least doubtful that they also conform to our general theory. Both father and father's sister spoil ego until he is well into manhood—not usual roles for either in the patrilineal complex.[52] Ego's mother is his chief disciplinarian, at least before his adolescence, and shares this role to some extent with mother's brother, to whom ego pays the greatest respect.[53] It is perhaps significant that marriage is uxorilocal, at least for its first years. Our information on this group is inadequate, but if ego's relation to father and father's sister is as described, and if mother's brother is indeed the chief male authority over ego, we should, according to our general theory, have expected to find marriage with father's sister's, not mother's brother's, daughter. In this one society we were right for the wrong reasons.

In a letter to the authors Professor Radcliffe-Brown made a comment that may throw light on interpersonal relations among the Yir-Yoront. In many Australian tribes, he says,

the discipline of very young children is left to the mother and the other women of the horde. A father does not punish and may even not scold his infant children, but if they misbehave he will scold the mother and perhaps give her a blow with a stick. He regards the mother as responsible for misbehavior by very young children. When they are a little older, the father undertakes the education of the boys but leaves the education of the girls to the mother and the women of the horde. But the father behaves affectionately and is very little of a disciplinarian. Discipline for a boy begins when he approaches puberty and is exercised by the men of the horde. The big change comes with the initiation ceremonies when, in some tribes, the father, by a ceremonial (symbolic) action, hands over his son to the men who will carry out the initiation rites. During the initiation period of several years the boy is subjected to rigid and frequently painful discipline by the men other than his father.

This may explain why, among the patrilineal Yir-Yoront, the father is not ego's chief disciplinarian, and the relationship can be an affectionate one. We might therefore expect father's sister's daughter marriage to be sentimentally possible, but among the Yir-Yoront mother's brother's daughter marriage in fact occurs. Why? We might argue as follows. Though chief authority over ego is not exercised by the father, it *is* exercised by the other men of the horde, and in a patrilineal society these are at least men "on the father's side of the family" such as father's brothers—they are ego's patrikin. The patrilineage, if not the father himself, represents authority, and this might still be enough to throw marriage to the mother's side. We raise this as a question. We certainly do not insist on it as an argument, and we shall continue to treat the Yir-Yoront as an exception to our general theory.

Something of the same sort, though apparently in lesser degree, seems to be true of another Australian tribe, the Murngin. Authority over ego is vested in his patrilineage, but ego's own father does not correct him and acts only as a kind of older brother. Since the other interpersonal relations are of the kind we expect in the patrilineal complex, we do not consider the Murngin a full exception to our general theory, as we do so consider the Yir-Yoront.

To sum up the evidence on patrilineal-matrilateral societies: in those societies for which we have any evidence on interpersonal relations and the locus of jural authority over ego, the evidence is that, with the exception of the Yir-Yoront, the societies conform both to our special hypothesis and to our general theory. To this extent, we were right for the right reasons.

Matrilineal-Patrilateral Societies (Class 4)

The other class of societies that conforms to our special hypothesis is the matrilineal-patrilateral one. If our general theory is correct, we should expect to find that jural authority over ego in these societies is vested in his mother's brother, and that he is less "close" to mother's brother, closer to father and father's sister, than he is in the patrilineal complex. This is true, as Malinowski showed, of the Trobrianders, and we have cited the evidence above. Among the Haida, we know that ego, after about the age of ten, goes to live permanently with his mother's brother, who thereafter is in charge of his discipline. Our source tells us little of ego's sentimental ties with mother's brother and father, but father's sister, unlike her counterpart among, for instance, the patrilineal Venda, is a friendly and nurturant figure. Among other things, she nurses ego when he is sick.[54]

As for the Tlingit, neighbors of the Haida on the Northwest Coast, the "ideal" marriage is clearly with father's sister's daughter, though a young man of rank, as among the Haida, may marry mother's brother's daughter. Mother's brother holds jural authority over ego, and the following passage implies a difference, of the expected kind, between ego's attitude to father and to mother's brother:

The father-child tie is one which is stressed on all possible occasions. . . . To address or to refer to a group as "Kagwantan children" brings pleased smiles to their faces. Perhaps it recalls, at least to the men, a carefree childhood in their father's house before they had to submit to the discipline of their uncle in order to prove their manhood and enter upon their matrilineal inheritance.[55]

For the Tismulun, we have no information on interpersonal relations, but one structural fact is especially worth citing. Marriage is permitted and approved between ego and father's sister's daughter *or* mother's brother's daughter's daughter.[56] Since the latter is not by our definition cross-cousin marriage, it does not fall within the scope of our hypothesis. But if the reader will refer to Figure 3, he will note that, in the structure created in a matrilineal society by patrilateral cross-cousin marriage regularly followed, ego's mother's brother's daughter's daughter stands in the relation of father's sister's daughter, i.e., preferred spouse, to ego's own sister's son, i.e., his matrilineal heir.

It might be argued that the Ila do not fall within the scope of our hypothesis because they are not even "effectively matrilineal" in the sense that the Mbundu are effectively patrilineal. According to Smith and Dale,[57] they are organized in exogamous matriclans, and there is some evidence that succession to positions of authority is matrilineal. But the members of a clan are physically dispersed: the core of the lineage does not consist, as it seems to consist in other societies of this class, of a group of matrilineally-related men living in the same place. Instead, the usual residence group consists of "a man, his wives, his married sons, and the latters' children, his unmarried children, and his servants and slaves."[58] Such a local descent group, which is called *lunungu,* might well be considered a patrilineage.

But even if, on these grounds, the Ila should be thrown out of court as far as our special hypothesis is concerned, they fit our general theory well. Smith and Dale are clear that marriage is allowed with father's sister's daughter and not with mother's brother's, and that mother's brother has greater power over ego than father has:

The mother's brother is a person of vast importance, having the power even of life and death over his nephews and nieces, which no other relations, not even the parents have; he is to be held in honor even above the father. This is *avunculi potestas,* which among the Ba-Ila is greater than *patria potestas.*[59]

For the matrilineal-patrilateral societies, the evidence on interpersonal relations and the locus of jural authority is, except for the Trobrianders, scanty, but what there is is all in accordance with our general theory. Once more we were right for the right reasons.

Matrilineal-Matrilateral Societies (Class 3)

Let us now turn to the societies (classes 2 and 3 above) that stand as exceptions to our special hypothesis. If we are honest, we must confess that we are anxious to get rid of them if we may do so with honor—which in this case means showing, that, though they do not conform to our special hypothesis, they do nevertheless conform to our general theory. We shall take first the matrilineal-matrilateral societies.

Although what is at this writing our only printed source on the matrilineal Kaonde—Melland's *In Witch-Bound Africa*—is thoroughly unsatisfactory, it does state clearly that marriage with mother's brother's daughter is "permitted" but with father's sister's daughter prohibited.[60] A letter from Victor Turner of the Rhodes-Livingstone Institute, reporting recent field work among the Kaonde, suggests that their rule is in fact bilateral but for the sake of consistency we shall abide by our printed sources and not throw the Kaonde out of court. Melland says almost nothing about interpersonal relations, except that ego male tends strongly to avoid father's sister and mother-in-law. In short, the Kaonde stand as an exception to our special hypothesis, but we have no evidence whether or not they conform to our general theory—save only for the ego-father's sister tie, which is of the sort expected by our general theory and is very different from the corresponding tie in societies like the Trobrianders and the Haida of the matrilineal—patrilateral class. In another respect, too, the Kaonde differ from the Trobrianders: with the former marriage is uxorilocal, with the latter virilocal.[61] We shall have to deal with residence more thoroughly than we have done so far, and find in it our first hint of the reason why our special hypothesis admitted so many exceptions.

With the Kaska of the Canadian Northwest, we are in a better position. They are organized in two matrilineal "sides" or moieties, the members of neither of which are concentrated in one area, and "the importance of the moiety is slight."[62] Marriage is forbidden with father's sister's daughter, preferred with mother's brother's daughter. As with the Kaonde, marriage is uxorilocal: a man settles down in a log house of his own in the neighborhood of his father-in-law, the household consisting of the married couple, their children, perhaps aged grandparents and orphaned children of kin. And now we come to what, in our eyes, is a crucial point:

Authority in the family is ideally vested in the husband. . . . The authority of the husband is maintained even if the family happens to contain a grandparent. Although under conditions of matrilocal residence, a father may offer advice to his son-in-law, such advice is not given in an authoritative fashion and, once the marriage is established, does not dispute the authority of the husband. The importance of the father is often reflected in the fact that, despite the system of matrilineal moieties, family names follow the patrilineal line.[63]

We are given, moreover, just enough information on mother's brother to suggest that ego's relationship with him resembles what it is in the patrilineal complex, where jural authority is likewise vested in the father:

A woman's brother refers to his sister's daughter as his own child. . . . A reciprocal term is employed between a boy and his mother's brother. It was said to be all right to "talk fun," i.e. refer to salacious matters, with mother's brother. The relationship of a child to its father's sister could not be observed.[64]

The next member of this class is the Siriono, nomad hunters and gatherers of eastern Bolivia. They possess matrilineal extended families. Marriage is forbidden with father's sister's daughter, preferred with mother's brother's daughter.[65] Again, as with the Kaonde and Kaska, marriage is uxorilocal, but when the son-in-law, upon marriage, moves next to his parents-in-law, he may not have to move *far*, as he is apt to be living already in the same house. "An extended family is made up of all females in a direct line of descent, plus their spouses and their unmarried children." And now we come again to the crucial point: "Within the nuclear family, authority is patripotestal. . . . The extended family is generally dominated by the oldest active male. Although his power is not supreme like that of the father in a nuclear family, younger members of the extended family pay heed to his words." We learn nothing of sentimental ties between kinsmen, save for a little more about parents and children: "Between parents and young children there is little reserve. As children grow older, however, they are expected to respect and obey their parents, who treat them roughly in case they do not."[66] This differs greatly from the father-son tie in the Trobriand-type matrilineal complex. Note that under the given conditions—extended families whose persistent core consists of matrilineally-related women, plus uxori-local marriage with mother's brother's daughter—ego is *never*, as he is in the Trobriands, under the jural authority of his mother's brother *before marriage*, but under that of his father. *After marriage* he may come under some slight control by his mother's brother, provided the latter is the oldest active male of the extended family into which ego has married and moved.

We have stretched a point in including the Garos of Assam in our list, because our sources do not indicate that marriage with father's sister's daughter is forbidden or disapproved.[67] But mother's brother's daughter marriage is clearly a preferred form, and in some other re-spects the Garo resemble the Kaska and the Siriono. They are organized in matrilineal exogamous clans;[68] jural authority over ego before mar-riage is certainly vested in the father in the case the latter is a village headman,[69] and we suspect also when he is only head of a household. Uxorilocal marriage is again the rule, and the authority in local groups seems to pass from father-in-law to son-in-law, who, if he marries mother's brother's daughter, will also be the former's sister's son, that is, one of his matrilineal heirs.

In short, the matrilineal-matrilateral societies are clear exceptions to our special hypothesis, but whenever we have information they turn out to conform to our general theory. That is, the locus of jural authority (in the father) and the system of interpersonal relations among kins-folk are what we should expect, according to our general theory, to find associated with mother's brother's daughter marriage. We were wrong for the right reasons.

It should now also be clear why our special hypothesis admitted these exceptions. We derived it from our general theory on the assumption that in matrilineal societies jural authority over ego would always be vested in mother's brother, and this is not the case. That is, we assumed, when we ought to have known better, that there was only one main matrilineal complex—the Trobriand type—whereas in fact there are at least two. In the Trobriand-Haida complex, ego typically goes to live with his mother's brother before marriage and brings his wife to stay with him there: marriage is virilocal. From an early age jural authority over ego is vested in mother's brother, and interpersonal relations are very different from what they are in the patrilineal complex. In the Kaska-Garo complex, ego continues to live with his father until he marries, when he goes to stay at his wife's place: marriage is uxorilocal.

At least until ego marries, jural authority over him is vested in his father, and this is made all the more possible by the fact that the adult males of the mother's—and ego's—matrilineage have moved out. Interpersonal relations much resemble those of the patrilineal complex. The two matrilineal complexes are quite different from one another. We shall return to these differences later.

Patrilineal-Patrilateral Societies (Class 2)

The last and smallest class of exceptions is the patrilineal-patrilateral one. Our printed source on the Kandyu of the Cape York peninsula, Australia, shows them to prefer father's sister's daughter marriage and forbid mother's brother's daughter. In a letter to one of the authors, A. R. Radcliffe-Brown, an authority of especially great weight in the field of Australian kinship, expressed doubt that the Kandyu rule is really patrilateral: a man may marry the daughter of his own father's younger, but not older, sister, and the daughter of a classificatory, but not true, mother's brother. We should probably drop the Kandyu, like the Kaonde, from our list, much to the improvement of our correlation coefficient, since both stand as exceptions to our special hypothesis, but by our principle of respecting the printed sources we shall leave them in.

The only information we are given on interpersonal relations among the Kandyu is not very helpful:

The more extensive hunting grounds of the forest country, and consequent wandering habits of the Kandyu involve a loosening of the close tie with the mother's clan grounds, and a strengthening of the solidarity of the father's clan, a woman being glad to identify herself with her hereditary ground and clan by giving her daughter to her brother's son.[70]

This tells us nothing about the locus of jural authority and almost nothing about interpersonal relations. The Kandyu must remain, like the Kaonde, an unexplained exception to our special hypothesis.

The only other member of this class is an exceptionally interesting one, the Sherente of Brazil, for whom we have much better, though still inadequate, information. The Sherente are organized in patrilineal exogamous moieties, each of which is further divided into three patrilineal exogamous clans, and there is one further clan, fitted only loosely into the moiety organization.[71] The clans are without significance in economic activity, warfare, or religious ceremonial. Households contain nuclear families: parents and children. The effective working groups in hunting, shifting agriculture, and ceremonial are the associations, of which there are four. Each of the four has two leaders, one from each moiety, and each of the leaders directs, in the work of the association, the members that belong to the moiety *other than his own.*[72] About the age of eight, when he becomes of some use at work, a boy joins one of the associations, and generally he is *"kept from joining his father's organization."*[73] At the same time, he leaves his father's house for a special association hut for bachelors.[74]

Note that although this society is formally patrilineal, jural authority over ego male is not, after an early age, vested in his father, but in one of the leaders of his association. Even if his father belongs to the same association, which is not generally the case, ego is not bossed by him but by an older member of the other moiety, who must therefore belong to ego's mother's moiety. His boss might be his mother's brother, though he might also be his father's sister's husband. In short, this may be a patrilineal society, but it is not a patripotestal one.

Marriage is, after the first year, patrilocal. It is permitted with father's sister's daughter but not with mother's brother's daughter. This is perfectly compatible with the existence of two exogamous patrilineal moieties and six exogamous patrilineal clans. But our source also says: "There seems to be a tendency to marry close matrilineal kin so long as the prohibited degrees are avoided," and cites an example of marriage with mother's brother's daughter's daughter, who was a member of the loosely-linked seventh clan.[75] We have noted above the structural connection between father's sister's daughter marriage and mother's brother's daughter's daughter marriage.

Of interpersonal ties we learn little, and that little has to do with girls, whereas most ethnographic reports tell us chiefly about the ties of men. Girls belong to women's associations, which have no economic significance, and girls do not leave home to live in a special hut. Up to the age of six,

. . . there is little punishment; but a change occurs as soon as the mother begins to employ her daughter in the household, where she is made especially to tend younger siblings and the kitchen. Then the women frequently bawl at their daughters and beat them in a manner that would horrify any Timbira mother. I have also seen a father strike his daughter because she disobeyed her mother. Incidentally, similar treatment is meted out to boys of this age. . . . I was told that paternal and maternal uncles were equally esteemed, but concrete example suggest that only a girl's maternal uncle plays a significant part. . . . He distributes food among the members of the name-conferring society when his niece gets her name, and in return obtains decorations for her. He leads his niece to her bridegroom and dissolves an untenable marriage by bringing her back from her husband's to her father's house. He allows a virgin the formal choice between wedlock and the wanton's state, and in case of premarital defloration calls the culprit to account.[76]

Note that, with father's sister's daughter marriage, this bridegroom to whom mother's brother leads his sister's daughter is the mother's brother's own son. And does this account suggest that mother's brother has jural authority over a girl, as he might well have over a boy, if they belonged to the same association and mother's brother was one of its leaders?

Both the Kandyu and the Sherente are exceptions to our special hypothesis. For the Kandyu we do not have the information to say whether or not they conform to our general theory. The Sherente conform in a negative sense: authority over ego *is not*, after an early age, vested in his father, which is what we should expect from the theory. We cannot say that it *is* positively vested in his mother's brother, but only that, as a member of one of the actual working groups of this society, ego is at least bossed by a member of his mother's moiety.

To sum up our findings on all four classes: among those societies on our list for which we have some information on interpersonal relations and the locus of jural authority, there is only *one* that stands as a true exception to our general theory—the Yir-Yoront of the patrilineal-matrilateral class. Specifically, the following is a highly significant proposition: *Societies in which marriage is allowed or preferred with mother's brother's daughter but forbidden or disapproved with father's sister's daughter will be societies in which jural authority over ego male, before marriage, is vested in his father or father's lineage; and societies in which marriage is allowed or preferred with father's sister's daughter but forbidden or disapproved with mother's brother's daughter will be societies in which jural authority over ego male, before marriage, is vested in his mother's brother or mother's brother's lineage.*

A Classification of Local Descent Groups

In determining whether the societies on our list conformed to our general theory, we have learned more about their social organization than just their linearity and marriage rules. Some of these facts fit so well into a classification made by Murdock of types of *clans*,[77] and by Leach of what he calls *local descent groups*,[78] that we are encouraged to discuss the classification briefly. In most primitive societies we observe kin-groups each of which occupies a particular territory generation after generation. How is the continuity of such groups maintained? In particular, what rules of descent and residence determine what category of persons shall form the continuing core of such groups? We also observe that certain persons exercise authority over others in these groups. What rules determine succession to authority?

Two rules that seem, in practice, to be often obeyed are the following:

1. The continuing core of the local group consists of persons of the same sex and the same lineage.

2. Authority is transmitted from men to men of the same local group and lineage.

Murdock and Leach, each in his own way, suggest that the main possibilities of constituting local descent groups according to these rules are three:

A. *Patrilineages with Patrilocal (Virilocal) Residence at Marriage.* Under these circumstances, the continuing core of the local group consists, generation by generation, of *patrilineally-related men* (fathers and sons). The women of the lineage move out, the women of other lineages move in, at marriage. Authority is transmitted from father to son, and there is no problem in following the rule of transmission, as both men, throughout life, are members of the same local group. For men, this is a zero-move type of society. This class seems to include most of our patrilineal-matrilateral societies (Class 1). We shall want to ask ourselves why this solution is adopted far more frequently than the others.

B. *Matrilineages with Avunculocal (Virilocal) Residence at Marriage.* Here the continuing core of the local group consists of *matrilineally-related men* (mother's brothers and sister's sons). The daughters of the men move out, the women of other lineages move in, at marriage. Authority is transmitted from mother's brother to sister's son, but there is a problem in following the rule of transmission, which is solved by the sister's son moving from his father's to his mother's brother's local group before marriage. For men, this is a one-move (before marriage) type of society. This class seems to include most of our matrilineal-patrilateral societies (Class 4), with the exception of the Ila.

The Trobrianders meet the requirements of this class under all conditions except one, but that one is particularly interesting to us. If ego marries father's sister's daughter, he may be allowed to remain in his father's village, which is also the village associated with his father's matrilineage, including father's sister and her daughter. Then only does the "closeness" of father and son, in a society in which jural authority over ego is vested in mother's brother, overcome the rule of avunculocal residence.

C. *Matrilineages with Matrilocal (Uxorilocal) Residence at Marriage.* Here the continuing core of the local group consists of *matrilineally-related women* (mothers and daughters). The men of the lineage move out, the men of other lineages move in, at marriage. Authority is transmitted from father-in-law to son-in-law, and there is an obvious problem in following the rule of transmission. It can be solved by mother's brother's daughter marriage, in which case father-in-law and son-in-law are also mother's brother and sister's son. That is, they are men who, when the transmission of authority takes place, sometime between the marriage of the latter and the death of the former, are members of the same local group and the same lineage, though the lineage is different from that of the women who form the constituting core of the local group. For men, this is a one-move (at marriage) type of society. This class seems to include most of our matrilineal-matrilateral societies (Class 3). In these societies, mother's brother's daughter marriage is, so to speak, overdetermined: it is appropriate to the system of interpersonal relations, and it also satisfies the rule for succession to authority.

By symmetry in a fourfold table, in which we know the characteristics of three of the classes, we might in theory expect a fourth class, to wit:

D. *Patrilineages with Amitalocal (Uxorilocal) Residence at Marriage.* Murdock and Leach believe that societies truly of this class do not exist. Certainly our patrilineal-patrilateral societies (Class 2) do not belong to it, both being patrilineal-patrilocal. But we can state what characteristics such societies should have if they did exist, and in so stating understand why they do not. The continuing core of the local group should consist of *patrilineally-related women* (father's sisters and brother's daughters). The men of the lineage should move out, the men of other lineages should move in, at marriage. Authority should be transmitted from father to son, and on considerations of pure symmetry, without regard for the locus of jural authority, father's sister's daughter marriage should be the rule, if unilateral cross-cousin marriage took place at all.

Unhappily, theoretical possibilities in this case run into practical difficulties. In a local group whose core was formed by patrilineally-related women, there would be a serious problem in following the rule of transmission of authority. It can be shown that, under the given conditions, unlike those of the matrilineal-matrilocal societies (Class C), father-in-law cannot also be of the same lineage as son-in-law and of the same local group at the time of transmission of authority. Neither father's sister's daughter marriage nor mother's brother's daughter marriage would allow him to be both. Mother's brother's daughter marriage would allow ego after marriage to live in the same local group as his father, who would not, of course, be father-in-law too. But if ego, in his early years, resides with his father in almost all societies, the local group that ego would be born into would also be the one he married into. He would be *already there*. Or if he moved out, like the Trobriand young man, before marriage, he would have to move back at marriage. Presumably authority would be transmitted from father to son, but this, taken together with the persistent association of each with the same local group, would have the tendency to turn such societies, if they ever existed, into patrilineal-patrilocal ones (Class A). If it ever came into being, the life-expectancy of a patrilineal-amitalocal society, as such, would be short. Interestingly enough, the theoretical requirements of a patrilineal-amitalocal society could be met if the marriage rule was that ego married father's sister's daughter who was also mother's brother's daughter. This would make the society one of Kariera type, which is effectively, as we should expect, patrilineal-patrilocal. These structural difficulties and instabilities go far to explain why societies of the patrilineal-amitalocal class do not seem to exist.

In this last section, we have tried to put our three largest classes (1, 3, and 4) of societies practicing unilateral cross-cousin marriage into a wider framework of types of social organization, and to show why our smallest class (patrilineal-patrilateral, Class 2) must be made up of real "sports." We know enough of the Sherente to see that they have a very unusual kind of social organization.

In the course of this examination, we have also had reason to remember Lévi-Strauss's statement that unilateral cross-cousin marriage of either kind would be found associated with what he called harmonic regimes.[79] We have no difficulty in agreeing that societies of Classes A and C above are harmonic regimes in Lévi-Strauss's terms; they are patrilineal-patrilocal and matrilineal-matrilocal respectively, and when they practice unilateral cross-cousin marriage they adopt the matrilateral form. Whether the societies of Class B, the matrilineal—avunculocal ones practicing the patrilateral form, are also harmonic in Lévi-Strauss's terms is not so clear. For him a regime is harmonic if "the rule of residence is the same as the rule of filiation."[80] We might argue that the Trobrianders have a harmonic regime because ego belongs to the same lineage as his mother's brother and goes to live with mother's brother when he grows up. We might also argue that the Trobrianders were matrilineal-patrilocal, in that ego belongs to the same lineage as his mother but certainly does not continue to live where she does. In short, what Lévi-Strauss means by either *residence* or *filiation* is not unambiguous enough to deal with the Trobriand case. We might also argue that no society in the world is effectively dysharmonic. In any event, Lévi-Strauss uses harmony and dysharmony to separate unilateral societies from bilateral ones. We are interested only in distinguishing between the two kinds of unilateral rules and have nothing to say about bilateral ones. Lévi-Strauss's further statement that the matrilateral rule depends only on the harmonic character of the regime and has nothing to do with linearity we have already shown to be correct only if we neglect to compare the *number* of patrilineal societies following the rule with the number of matrilineal ones. The rule is in fact heavily associated with patriliny.

Conclusion

Let us now sum up what we believe we have accomplished in this paper.

We took our departure from a criticism of Lévi-Strauss's *Les structures élémentaires de la parenté*, using a study of the two forms of unilateral cross-cousin marriage as a test of his theory. In the place of two crucial statements of his, we adopted different hypotheses. These statements were that (*a*) the adoption of the matrilateral form (mother's brother's daughter marriage) had nothing to do with the linearity of a society, and (*b*) more societies would practice the matrilateral form than the patrilateral (father's sister's daughter marriage), because the former was better than the latter at creating organic solidarity in the society. We argued instead that (*a*) linearity was indeed a determinant and that the matrilateral form would tend to be found in patrilineal societies, the patrilateral in matrilineal ones (our special hypothesis), and (*b*) the "goodness" of the form (in Lévi-Strauss's sense) was not a determinant and that the choice of form would be determined by the locus of jural authority over ego and the consequent pattern of interpersonal relations among kinsmen (our general theory). We expected to find one locus and pattern in patrilineal societies, another in matrilineal ones. We then proceeded to test our hypotheses by a cross-cultural survey.

By means of this survey, we have shown a significant correlation between the linearity of societies and their rules of unilateral cross-cousin marriage. Mother's brother's daughter marriage is the rule in patrilineal societies, father's sister's daughter in matrilineal ones significantly more often than the matrilateral type in matrilineal societies, the patrilateral type in patrilineal ones. That is, we have produced evidence in favor of our special hypothesis. As far as our list of societies is concerned, we have shown that Lévi-Strauss was wrong in arguing that linearity had nothing to do with the form of unilateral cross-cousin marriage, but the discovery of a few more unilateral societies might conceivably upset our correlation.

In the course of examining other data on the societies on our list, we have shown a far more significant correlation between the locus of jural authority over ego and the rule of unilateral cross-cousin marriage. From our general theory we argued that, if the locus of jural authority over ego, before marriage, is his father, then, provided unilateral cross-cousin marriage is allowed at all, the matrilateral form will be the rule, and if the locus of jural authority over ego, before marriage, is his mother's brother, the patrilateral form will be the rule. Among those societies on our list for which we have evidence on the locus of authority, there is only one exception to this hypothesis—the Yir-Yoront —though the Sherente conform to it only in part: father's sister's daughter marriage is the rule, and father is *not* the locus of jural authority over ego. It will take the discovery of many exceptional societies to upset this hypothesis.

We have also come to understand why our special hypothesis received less significant support than this more general one. In at least one formally patrilineal society—the Sherente—jural authority over ego is not vested in the father, and in several matrilineal societies—the matrilocal ones—authority is not vested in mother's brother but in father. If anyone wants to say that we, like Lévi-Strauss, are now arguing that linearity has nothing to do with unilateral cross-cousin marriage, we shall accept the criticism, provided he adds that we believe *potestality* has a great deal to do with it. Potestality is a far better predictor than linearity.

Our general theory did more than predict a relation between the locus of jural authority over ego and the form of unilateral cross-cousin marriage: it also explained why this relation should exist. It argued that the locus of jural authority in father or mother's brother would be an important determinant of ego's sentimental ties with kinsfolk. In the former case, father and father's sister would be sentimentally "distant" from ego, mother's brother "close." And in the latter case, mother's brother would be "distant," father and father's sister "close." Authority discourages intimacy, or "there is a separation made between jural relations and relations of personal attachment."[81] We further argued that ego would tend to seek as his wife the daughter of the member of the older generation, outside his nuclear family, with whom he had formed the closest attachment, and that that person in turn would have good sentimental reasons for giving the daughter to ego. Not only the locus of jural authority, but also, in all the societies on our list for which we have information on these matters, except always the Yir-Yoront, the interpersonal ties have been of the type predicted. We have produced evidence in favor of our general theory. If this paper has anything to add to anthropology, it is less its negative contribution—the criticism of Lévi-Strauss—than its positive ones—further evidence that authority is an important determinant of social behavior, that jural ties tend to be segregated from affectionate ones, and that sentiment plays its part in marriage in primitive societies as well as in modern Western ones. None of these propositions is surprising, but none has received the emphasis it deserves.

Lévi-Strauss argues that mother's brother's daughter marriage occurs in more societies than does father's sister's daughter marriage because the former is "better" for a *society*, as creating a higher degree of organic solidarity. That is, he gives what we have called a *final-cause* type of explanation for the frequency of the matrilateral form. This form is indeed the more common, and we should give Lévi-Strauss full credit for being correct, did we not believe that it is more common, not for Lévi-Strauss's reasons, but rather because societies in which jural au-

[248]

thority over ego is vested in father are more numerous than those in which it is vested in mother's brother. In the locus of authority and the personal, sentimental interests it precipitates we have provided an *efficient-cause* type of explanation. Note that the facts on which we have based our theory are just the ones to which Lévi-Strauss pays least attention. He has little to say about what we have called "interpersonal relations" and less about authority. We believe that the forces he exiled have returned to undo him, and that his model of social behavior is too formal and abstract.

More soberly, we do not argue that Lévi-Strauss's final cause theory is right or that it is wrong, but only that it is now unnecessary. We have been able to point out some of the other features of social systems and individual behavior that determine the adoption of the patrilateral or the matrilateral form of unilateral cross-cousin marriage, whether or not one is "better" than the other. Or, to put the matter another way, our theory will predict *what* societies will adopt *what* form, and Lévi-Strauss's theory will not. But remember that we have never claimed to specify all the determinants of the phenomena. For one thing, we have not tried to explain why some societies have a unilateral rule of either form and others do not. That is the next task, and a big one. We suspect empirically, without being able to explain why it should be the case, that unilateral cross-cousin marriage is especially likely to occur in societies where lineage is important but the number of members of any lineage living close together in the same place is small.

For obviously no theory will explain everything: something must always be accepted as given. In the case of our theory, a critic may well say:

Granted you have shown that matrilateral marriage occurs more often than patrilateral, not because it is better, but because there are more patripotestal societies than avuncupotestal ones. This latter fact remains to be explained; you have only shifted the issue to new ground, and a final-cause theory may still be valid if *patria potestas* is in some sense better than *avunculi potestas*.

We should then argue, though we should not be able to prove our case, that it may indeed be better, but not necessarily in the sense of "better for a society as an organic whole." Consider the fact that in our list there are just twice as many patrilineal-patrilocal-patripotestal societies as all the others put together. These are societies the core of whose local groups consists of fathers and sons, generation after generation, and in which men need not leave their old homes either before or at marriage.

If men are, in general, of higher status than women in all societies, and if the effectiveness of the men is increased by preserving from early childhood their association with the same hunting grounds or the same farm land, then the patrilineal-patrilocal-patripotestal organization may well be better than other forms of organization, as serving both social and economic interests. The organization is more convenient for the men and their local groups, and for this reason may be adopted more often than other forms. But this is very different from saying it is better for society as an organic whole. Pursuing their interests, men create social structures, which then create new interests, and so on. Some of these structures may indeed turn out to be better for society as a whole than others, and thus indirectly serve the interests of individuals. But we doubt that the final cause alone is ever a sufficient condition for the existence of an institution.

POSTSCRIPT:

FIVE YEARS LATER

THIS is not the place to make a new study of unilateral cross-cousin marriage. At the same time, the reprinting of this paper allows me to consider some of the developments in the study of the subject that have taken place since its original publication.

First, as to new data. From the field reports available to us at the time we wrote the paper, we believed that the matrilineal, matrilateral Garo, while certainly an exception to our original hypothesis, conformed nevertheless to our general theory, since jural authority over a boy appeared to be vested in his father. Recent field work has shown that, on the contrary, jural authority is vested in the mother's brother, and so the Garo must now stand as an exception to our general theory too.[1]

Other new data have given us more comfort. A paper by Needham has argued that *prescriptive* marriage with father's sister's daughter does not exist, a prescriptive rule being one that absolutely requires a man to marry one of a particular class of women.[2] Whether or not Needham's argument is correct, it does not affect ours, for we did not limit ourselves to prescriptive rules, but included all "allowed or preferred" ones.

Yet in the course of working out his argument he reviewed all the cases he could find of patrilateral cross-cousin marriage, and thus drew our attention to several cases that were unknown or unavailable to us. Two of them are Indian castes, and both are matrilineal, which would add support to our original hypothesis, had we not, perhaps wrongly, ruled Indian castes out of our list of societies. Having once ruled them out, we cannot for our convenience bring them back in now.

But a third case Needham considers does qualify as a "society"—the Pende of the former Belgian Congo—and it turns out to be an instructive one. The Pende were described in a pamphlet published in the same year as our paper.[3] They constitute a society of our Class 4, resembling in many ways the Trobrianders. The most visible unit of Pende society is a small, localized matrilineage (*jigo*) of about four generations in depth, its principle of continuity on the ground being a succession of mother's brothers and their sisters' sons. This means that a boy as he grows up generally leaves his father's *jigo* and joins that of his mother's brother, and, when he marries, his wife joins him there. A boy may choose to stay in his father's *jigo* for the latter's lifetime, but even if he does, he cannot inherit any of his father's economic rights in the *jigo*. The preferred marriage *par excellence* links a man with his father's sister's daughter, and so the Pende clearly conform to our original hypothesis.

What is more important, they appear also to conform to our general theory. First, it is clear that the mother's brother (*lemba*) and not the father holds jural authority over ego: "That the child belongs chiefly to his matrilineage and to the *lemba* is shown by the fact that only the *lemba* can beat him or administer severe correction to him, and formerly could sell him."[4] Second, the characteristic sentiments toward father and mother's brother respectively that we should expect from this locus of jural authority are in fact reported: "While bonds of economic solidarity link the Mu-Pende to his matrilineage and to his *lemba*, his mother's brother, bonds of spiritual solidarity link him to his father and his paternal ancestors."[5] Again, one of the songs the Pende children sing contains the words: "If my *lemba* dies it's nothing; if my father dies, then my heart is sad."[6] Third, the father's sister is called by a term meaning "female father,"[7] the father himself being in a "warm and close" relation with ego. And fourth, when Pende are asked why they prefer marriage with the father's sister's daughter, they usually say something like: "Because we want to see once more the face of our fathers," which apparently means to return the father's seed to the father's lineage.[8] The sentimental reference seems clear.

Seldom has so short a paper as ours aroused so much controversy, and my next job is to comment on a few of the issues raised. Naturally Lévi-Strauss himself had something to say in reply to our criticism of his work. One of his statements concerns our use of statistics:

In support of their thesis, according to which the matrilateral form of marriage should be a function of patrilinearity, they [Homans and Schneider] invoke statistical correlations that do not prove much. In effect, the patrilineal societies are many more in number than the matrilineal ones; what is more, the matrilateral form of marriage itself occurs more often than the patrilateral one. If then the distribution were a matter of chance, one might expect that the number of societies characterized by the association: patrilinearity and matrilateral marriage, would be higher than that of the others, and the correlation invoked by my critics would be empty of significance.[9]

This argument is simply wrong. The statistical test used—Fisher's Exact Test—allows for the fact that there are more patrilineal than matrilineal societies, more matrilateral ones than patrilateral. To assert that it does not betrays a lack of elementary knowledge of statistical method. Or, as two other commentators point out: "It appears that he [Lévi-Strauss] has not taken the trouble to find out what we measure by significance tests."[10]

Lévi-Strauss goes on to argue that there is no necessary "logical connection" between the linearity of a society and its form of unilateral cross-cousin marriage. Unfortunately the truth of statements about human behavior is not settled by logic but by fact, and the fact is that there *is* a connection, logical or not. He ends by finding our argument unacceptable on doctrinaire grounds—because it rests on "psychological considerations"; and he says he had hoped "that ethnology had finally gotten away from these old habits" (*vieux errements*)—presumably bad old habits.

Our argument certainly does rest on psychological considerations—there is no blinking that fact—but what adds irony to Lévi-Strauss's accusation is that his own argument does so too. I shall call psychological any explanation in the social sciences that relies on propositions about the behavior of men as men, as members of a species rather than just as members of a particular society. Thus our explanation of our correlations is psychological in that it relies, among other things, on a proposition that men, as men, have some tendency to fear, avoid, and feel some constraint in the presence of, persons placed in authority over them. In the same way, Lévi-Strauss's explanation of the fact that the matrilateral form of marriage occurs in a larger number of societies than does the patrilateral one relies, as we showed, on the proposition that men as men have some tendency to recognize a particular institution as in some way good for their societies and to adopt it for that reason. True, his is a different kind of psychological explanation from ours—and naturally we believe that some psychological explanations are better than others—but it is no less psychological in relying on presumed characteristics of the behavior of men as members of a species. Indeed it is my belief that all explanations of human behavior ultimately turn out to be psychological in this sense.[11]

To George P. Murdock we owed the first and all-too-successful test of our original hypothesis. After the publication of his *Social Structure*,[12] he worked for some years to develop a better-designed ethnographic sample of the societies of the world and one that should include a much larger number of societies. In 1957 he published a paper presenting his results and, among other things, testing our original hypothesis with his new sample. His conclusion was this: "Examination of Table 3 will reveal that these authors are correct in ascribing matrilateral preferences primarily to patrilineal societies and patrilateral preferences to matrilineal societies." The correlation is highly significant: $p = 0.001$ by chi-square test. But Murdock went on to say: "The worldwide incidence of such preferences, however, is so low as to cast some doubt on the validity of the theoretical interpretation advanced."[13]

Murdock did not advance an alternative theoretical explanation of his own, nor did he say what kind of doubt might be cast, but it is not hard to guess what it might be. Many patripotestal societies display the characteristic warm and close relation between a man and his mother's brother. Yet only a few of them prefer marriage with mother's brother's daughter; most of them prohibit marriage with any first cousin. If interpersonal relations were all that important, why should not more of these societies prefer matrilateral cross-cousin marriage? Our only answer to this hypothetical argument must be that we never claimed interpersonal relations were all that important. Certainly we never argued that they were the only determinants of marriage rules. On the contrary, it looks as if they could have a decisive effect only in special circumstances. If we survey the full range of data on the rules of marriage, it will be clear to us that their most important determinant is some force—we are not altogether sure of its nature—that tends to prevent marriage with any first cousin whatever: the majority of societies follow this rule.[14] What the special conditions are that allow the general rule to be broken in favor of one of the two cross-cousins we do not know. The best guess is still the one we made in our paper: it looks as if unilateral cross-cousin marriage were apt to occur in societies where unilinearity is important and fairly strict; but where the number of members of any given lineage living in one place is, for one reason or another, small; and where a number of these small lineages live closely interspersed. In any case, only if conditions favoring some kind of unilateral cross-cousin marriage exist can interpersonal relations be decisive in determining which form is preferred. In short, we argue that the types of interpersonal relations we have been interested in are, in determining marriage rules, normally masked by more powerful forces and can only tip the scales under special circumstances. This kind of situation often emerges in scientific work.

A paper by Berting and Philipsen is the latest on the subject of unilateral cross-cousin marriage that has appeared up to the time when this is being written. In this paper the authors review both the data and the theories of Lévi-Strauss, Leach,[15] and ourselves. Using a somewhat longer list of societies than ours, one that includes later field reports, they confirm statistically both our original hypothesis and our more general one that associates the form of marriage with the locus of jural authority. They show, as we did, that the correlations can hardly have occurred by chance. And they go on to say:

The conclusion must be that of the three theories . . . , Homans and Schneider's theory is supported most by the facts, in the sense that we have been able to make hypotheses derived from their ideas accessible to empirical indications and that we have been able to show the predicted statistical relations between these indications. In other words: the results shown by the tables are there and have to be interpreted. However, the question is whether Homans and Schneider's explanation gives full satisfaction.[16]

This passage makes an important point. As far as their sheer empirical power to predict the data is concerned, our original hypothesis has now been confirmed twice (Murdock, Berting and Philipsen) and our general hypothesis once (Berting and Philipsen) by anthropologists working independently of ourselves. Our hypotheses have survived far closer scrutiny than most hypotheses get in anthropology. The results are there; they are not lightly to be dismissed. And yet our explanation of the hypotheses, that is to say, the reasoning by which we derived them, may still turn out to have been wrong. We may still have been right for the wrong reasons: stranger things have happened in science.

Berting and Philipsen have many other sensible things to say; I shall mention here only one point that I disagree with. They claim that our theory is based on the assumption of "romantic love," the view that men choose their wives for love alone, rather than for property, status, or the like.[17] There is some excuse for their believing that we make this assumption, but our most careful statement shows we do not:

We find in the structure of interpersonal relations the individual motivations, or efficient causes, for the adoption of a particular form of unilateral cross-cousin marriage. The motivations may take many and mixed forms, but they are all predicated on the nature of the ties.[18]

For example, the Pende say that they prefer to marry father's sister's daughter "so that they can see again the face of the father." This explanation does not imply anything about romantic love, but it is certainly predicated on a certain kind of interpersonal relation between a man and his father.

For the benefit of any scholar who may be interested in disproving or refuting our theory, let me finally point out the many strategies open to him in trying to accomplish that result. First, he may be able to undermine our statistical correlations by finding enough new cases that go against our hypotheses or by showing in a sufficient number of cases that we classified the data wrongly. We may, for instance, have called a society patripotestal when it was really avuncupotestal. We were certainly wrong about the Garo, and we may have been wrong about others, though the men who have retested our hypotheses have generally agreed with our classifications. Second, he may be able to show that our correlations were matters of chance after all. True, the statistical tests show that the correlations are unlikely to have occurred by chance, but the unlikely does sometimes happen. To show that it did in this case, our refuter will have to provide, in the special circumstances of each of the societies in question, an explanation of its marriage rules that is different from ours and different from society to society, and the sum of these explanations will nevertheless just happen to generate our correlations. Third, he may be able to discover a general theory different from ours, from which he can derive empirically testable hypotheses that take account of a larger amount of the variation in the data than ours do now. This would be the most interesting thing for him to do, for he would not merely refute our theory but put a better one in its place.

What I think is more likely to happen than any of these things is that someone will develop a theory that, taken together with ours, will predict the data better than ours will alone. Indeed I think this is almost bound to happen, but if it does, it will not refute our theory but supplement it. Or, if you like, our theory will supplement the new one.

15

The Strategy

of Industrial

Sociology

People who write about methodology often forget that it is a matter of strategy, not of morals. There are neither good nor bad methods, but only methods that are more or less effective under particular circumstances in reaching objectives on the way to a distant goal. For this reason a general, in science as in warfare, is lost if his thinking is rigid. He must be a master of timing; what has served him well in the past may get in his way now. He must have more than one weapon in his armory and know when to change one for another.

In this spirit I propose to consider not just the methods but the strategy of industrial sociology: what its goal is; how the campaign has gone so far; what ideas and methods have been followed and why; what changes in ideas and methods have been followed and why; what changes in ideas and methods will probably be necessary in the future. I emphasize both ideas and methods. Our present difficulties may spring from our not having examined carefully enough the relation between the two.

There can be only one final goal for industrial sociology as for sociology at large—a system of equations which defines the relations between

Reprinted from *American Journal of Sociology*, 54 (1949), 330–337, by permission of the University of Chicago Press, publisher of the *Journal*. Copyright 1949 by the University of Chicago.

variables, time being one, and by means of which it is possible to predict the changing behavior of single human groups and account for the differences between groups.[1] If we had such a system of equations, the similarities and differences between groups would not be statistical. There would be neither "exceptional" groups nor "random" variations in group characteristics but only different solutions of the system of equations.[2]

It is quite likely that this goal cannot be reached; that we cannot get the necessary quantitative data and do not have the mathematical tools for dealing with them if we did. Yet a lesser goal is no more conceivable for sociology than it is for other sciences. This is our maximum objective. As prudent strategists we shall no doubt also have a minimum one and be satisfied to reach it. But, if we do not try for the most, we shall not get even the least.

So far as he is trying to reach the maximum objective, an industrial sociologist is not just an expert on industrial organization; he is an expert on human organization. There is a difference. Does he warm his heart at the uniqueness of the field? Then he is no industrial sociologist as I shall use the term. Does he, on the other hand, take the fact that he works in industry as an incident and ask himself always what group life in industry has in common with group life everywhere? Does he draw no line between industrial and family sociology, between rural and urban sociology, and recognize that, unless methods are devised by which an industrial group and a farm family are no longer treated as different in kind, the study of neither will advance much further? Then he is an industrial sociologist because he is a plain sociologist first. Of course, he will work long and hard in factories in intimate contact with workingmen, and he will act as consultant to industrial executives. This is his job. But his skill here will develop only if he holds to his high purpose: fundamental research on the characteristics of human groups.

What the strategy of industrial sociology has been in the past can be brought out by examining some of the broad differences in behavior between certain industrial sociologists, on the one hand, and certain social psychologists, on the other. I am interested in the kinds of behavior the two groups take for granted when they are in their shirt sleeves and not in what they say when they are trying to be precise and careful. The traits of each group make up a syndrome: they are all related. No doubt it is easy to make the differences too sharp; to state is to overstate. And they are getting significantly smaller. But at the beginning and to establish a talking-point, I can afford to be crude.

I speak of certain social psychologists and industrial sociologists. I do not mean every man in these groups. For the purposes of this paper, and these alone, social psychologists are experimentalists, attitude scalers, and public opinion pollers. The activities differ and yet have something in common. In the same way, the industrial sociologists described here are the men trained in the traditions of Elton Mayo and the Western Electric research. No prejudice is implied in this choice; I cannot make the contrast I want unless I narrow the field.

A study of the differences between the two groups serves a minor as well as a major purpose. Industrial sociologists, faced with the rising prestige of the social psychologists, are in danger of losing morale. They know that their methods are considered sloppy by some of their colleagues in social science, and they begin to wonder whether they picked up the methods by chance, as an accident of working in a particular field, or adopted them as a logical move in a grand strategy. They need reassurance that it was not an accident.

At any rate, the chief observed differences of behavior are the following:

1. Industrial sociologists are always working in the "field"; social psychologists less often so. This is one of the great glories of industrial sociology. Some social scientists will do any mad thing rather than study men at firsthand in their natural surroundings. An industrial sociologist is ready to study human behavior instead of the various statistical results of human behavior, and he is rewarded with trouble. The problem of establishing and maintaining the kind of relation with his subjects without which he cannot begin to do his job is always paramount with him. The interviewer for a poll, as he rings the next doorbell, is faced with no such task. For the industrial sociologist, moreover, it is not just a question of doing his job but of what job he is going to do. Will he try to get what he wants from the field, or will he take what the field is willing to offer? The social psychologist assumes that there is a difference between the two; the industrial sociologist, that there is none, that the things he demands are just the things that the field, sooner or later, will supply. Opinion surveyors often find that "questions which appear satisfactory when they are written turn out to be too difficult or ambiguous, or they unexpectedly set off irrelevant trains of thought on the part of the respondents."[3] An industrial sociologist assumes that nothing is irrelevant; that everything in time fits into a

context. So doing, he is making a virtue of necessity, for his willingness to welcome whatever comes along makes it possible for him to maintain his relations with people. He is not pressing them for anything.

2. Industrial sociologists are likely to use the methods of participant observation and nondirective interviewing; social psychologists, the classic controlled experiment and the questionnaire. The industrial sociologist must always be thinking how to keep up good relations with his subjects over long periods of time. It is no wonder that he finds that participant observation and nondirective interviewing are the best methods he can use, at least in the beginning. They meet the conditions he has set for himself. But if they are positive helps in maintaining relations, they also have implications for the kind of data he collects and the way he uses the data. Working with these methods in a factory —and the same thing holds for a community study—he will get information in scraps on a whole series of topics. It is simply not economical to stick to one and neglect the others. Think what he would waste! He must have a set of mental pigeonholes and accumulate matter slowly in each one. His hypotheses are tested by the accumulation.

The social psychologist, on the other hand, is, even when in the field, working for only a short time with any one subject or group, and he wants only certain definite kinds of information from them. For these and other reasons which we shall go into later, his methods must be different. Nevertheless, the two approaches are beginning to converge. The social psychologist's "open-ended" interview is an example; another is the practice of pretesting questionnaires in interviews that are much less fully directed. For their part, sociologists have used experiment in industry. But the differences in emphasis remain.

3. Industrial sociologists are always studying social organization; social psychologists less often so. For instance, social psychologists, concerned as they are with statistical reliability, try to get their data from a standardized sample of a population. I am quite sure that sampling methods can be used in studying social organization. The problem does not lie in sampling itself but in the way the sample is set up. In practice the poller standardizes his sample in such matters as age, sex, income, occupation, marital status, and religious affiliation, that is to say in the matters on which he can get information from the census. Some of these are causes or results of organization, but they are not organization. The poller studies populations and can get many interesting results by doing so. But the industrial or community sociologist wants to study

[260]

groups. He can do much with sampling methods, provided that the sample is based on information other than that which the census and similar sources provide. Suppose, in a study of opinion in a neighborhood, we interviewed members of every tenth family in each street or a certain number of families in every income class. This would be a characteristic, though simplified, modern sampling procedure. But suppose that, instead, we worked out first the groups in the neighborhood whose members often visit one another, and then interviewed a certain number of people in each group. Our sample could still be made statistically reliable, and it would have the advantage of showing us the relation, if any existed, between opinion and everyday social interaction in the neighborhood. This the more conventional sample might or might not do—we could not be sure. Of course, we should not go to work in this way unless we were interested in the relation between opinion and social interaction. But this is just the kind of question that industrial sociologists are interested in, and it is well to recognize that conventional sampling cannot help them answer it. The information on which the new sampling must be based cannot be got from the census or, in industry, from the usual personnel data. It can be got only by methods seldom used by pollers. For reasons of this kind, I believe that in many of the fields of social science progress in the future will come through using several different methods together.

Accumulating material on many topics, as he must when working in the field with his special methods, the industrial sociologist finds that his intellectual illumination comes from relating the different topics to one another. For him there is nothing that exists in itself; there are only relations between things. When we speak of social organization, we mean this fact of relatedness. Suppose a sociologist goes to southern California to study prejudice toward Japanese-Americans. He will not be able to study prejudice alone. If he uses the methods already mentioned, he will find that, whether he likes it or not, he is studying a society in which prejudice is only one element. He will also find that his illumination on the subject of prejudice itself comes from relating it to other aspects of the daily life of the community. This the social psychologist has a hard time seeing, not because he is a boob—he is anything but that—but because his experience has been different. He is used to "fixing" things so that people will talk on some one topic such as prejudice. Recently, in the study of influence, the two approaches—that of the social psychologist and that of the industrial or community sociologist—are beginning to come together, as they are in other ways.[4] For the study of influence is the study of how opinion gets to be what it is: the relation of opinion to other aspects of social organization.

This preoccupation with organization explains why an industrial sociologist is likely to study the single instance, or case, in contrast with the social psychologist, who wants many instances, the more the better. In the laboratory and in the field, the latter wants to get a sample large enough to give him significant quantitative results. The former is not worried about the size of his sample, because he is, as we shall see, not much worried about proof, but his chief reason for focusing on the "case" is of another kind. He feels that the study of organization in general is best begun by the study of some one organization: a group or plant. Of course I have used the word "instance" ambiguously. The instance that the industrial sociologist has in mind is the single group. He does not rule out a population of many observations of the group.

4. Industrial sociologists are concerned with discovery more than with proof. It is true that preoccupation with proof can have strange results. It affects the choice of questions to be studied. Investigators seize on hypotheses just because they can be given quantitative demonstration, although a problem does not become more significant by being easy to handle elegantly. We should make what is important mathematical and not what is mathematical important. Nevertheless, the criticism that industrial sociologists are too little concerned with rigorous demonstration is often well taken. They could do much more, even with the protocols of nondirective interviews, in the way of quantitative analysis. They should be more aware of mathematics, though not necessarily the mathematics of statistics alone. The fact is that they are much stronger on insight into the many factors of their problems than they are on demonstrating beyond doubt the precise influence of these factors. But here I touch on one of the philosophical differences between industrial sociology and social psychology, and I must go more slowly.

Modern industrial sociology starts with the Relay Assembly Test Room at the Hawthorne Plant of the Western Electric Company. Whatever else this experiment proved—if you dignify it with the name of experiment—it proved at least that other kinds of things besides the physical conditions of work can affect the output of a group of girls. Proving this was proving something. Yet I sense in some of my colleagues a feeling that the experiment was somehow wrong: it should not have happened. The sample was not large enough for statistical re-liability, or an insufficient analysis of the figures was made, or nobody calculated the residual variance. After all, it must be possible to show a relation between rest pauses and output, if only the other factors affecting output are adequately controlled.

It depends on what you want of an experiment and when you want it. Social psychologists are preoccupied with demonstrating the relation between two variables when the other variables that come into the con-crete phenomenon are controlled. If possible, the control is built into the setup of the experiment. Individuals may be selected who are alike in one or more ways. But, beyond a certain point, the control must be statistical; if enough instances are taken, the effects of other variables can be treated as random.

But this is not the only thing that one may ask of an experiment, nor always the most important. One may also ask for illumination. This idea that there is only one way of going to work will be the ruin of our science. I have no doubt that a new experiment can be designed that will show a relation between rest pauses and output, other variables controlled. Perhaps it has already been designed and carried through. But I doubt if this could have been done before we had some idea what the variables to be controlled are. Some of them were revealed by the very Relay Assembly Test Room experiment that my colleagues feel was improperly designed. (Of course there are people who now say that they knew of the presence of these variables all the time, but there is no evidence in the experimentation before the Hawthorne studies that they took them into practical account.) If, moreover, in the interests of greater "control," the experiment had been designed differently— if, for instance, a larger number of girls had been included—it is not hard to believe that some of the group effects revealed by the experiment would have been obscured. I do not say that it was planned to produce these effects, but it did so just the same, and Mayo was the kind of man who could make his mistakes work for him. He did not have a single hypothesis and give up when he could not prove it. He was flex-ible, and flexibility is the mark of the strategist.

In short, if you are at an early stage in the development of a science and want to discover what the main factors are that come into a phe-nomenon, you welcome experiments like the Relay Assembly Test Room. These I call *experiments of light*. If you are at a late stage in the development of a science and want to know the relation between two variables, you welcome controlled experiments. These I call *experiments of proof*. The first suggest something new; the second demonstrate what you are already pretty sure of. I fail to see why one is more "scientific" than the other. The idea that the controlled experiment is the only method comes, I think, from the seventeenth century. When the first great advances in physical science were then being made, the configurations studied could be treated as if they involved only a small number of variables. Only in the last fifty years have we begun to tackle complicated problems, and we have only just begun to ask whether a single method is still adequate for success.

5. Social psychologists are concerned with a single hypothesis or topic at a time; industrial sociologists with a social system. With this admitted overstatement, I think that I am getting close to the heart of the differences between the two. Working in the field, where he has to take information as it comes, using methods that will help him get it on these terms, preoccupied intellectually with the large number of factors that come into the phenomena, the industrial sociologist accumulates material on many topics simultaneously. He finds also that his enlightenment comes from relating these topics to one another, from discovering the facts of social organization. In these circumstances it is no wonder that he is preoccupied with a conceptual scheme, that is, not just the concrete social system but the conceptual social system. It provides him with the mental pigeonholes he needs and some notion of the relations between the materials in them, and it will help him to new discovery if he does not let it altogether master his thinking.

To illustrate: A colleague suggested that we study the effects of the various wage-incentive plans in American factories. To what extent do they increase output, efficiency, and worker satisfaction? He had in mind getting whatever quantitative data were available from a large number of plants on such matters as output, costs, efficiency, composition of work force, and absenteeism, and seeing whether any of these items could be correlated with variations in incentive payment plans. He assumed that the sample would have to be relatively large to make the results reliable.

The colleague was not familiar with the field. The industrial sociologists I know would hardly have considered making such a study. But we have a right to ask why. A decision that is a matter of feeling must sooner or later be defended. In this case it would not be based on the judgment that my colleague's plan would not get anywhere; it might get quite far. The real problem, like most strategic problems, is one of economy. With what methods can one probably get most for the effort expended? The most superficial in-plant studies have taught the industrial sociologist that incentive payment plans almost never work in the way they are supposed to work and that it is often hard to be sure just what effects they do have. Read even the published material on such well-known wartime plants as Jack and Heintz and Lincoln Electric and learn what very different combinations of wage plans, working conditions, and administrative practices can provide high satisfactions for certain kinds of workers, at certain times, and under certain conditions. Not any single factor but a large number in balance make the difference between satisfaction and dissatisfaction. Finally, the statistics that are readily available, the kind that my colleague would have to work with if he were studying enough plants to make his sample a good one from his point of view, simply do not bear on what in-plant research shows to be decisive. The question is, then, whether more enlightenment is achieved by getting, for a few plants, some crude notion of the balance of many factors than by getting, for many plants, the correlations of a few factors, not necessarily the most important.

The final goal we have set ourselves is the system of equations that describes the behavior of many different groups. Social psychologists, like the colleague I have mentioned, want to approach the problem by establishing, one by one, the single equations as they apply to many different groups. Industrial sociologists want to approach it by establishing the solutions of the system of equations in successive single groups. At the risk of overstating, it might be said that the former works on the single equation in many groups; the latter on the system of equations in the single group.

The choice of approaches is again, I suspect, a matter of strategy. Which one is likely to yield greater results for a given amount of effort under particular circumstances? We do not know, but the important point is that a choice is possible. There is more than one way.

It may be that the industrial sociologist's way is not always bad strategy. Remember Pareto's dictum:

It is only the knowledge, even if very vague, very imperfect, of the system of equations that allows us to have any knowledge of the relations [between the factors *A*, *B*, *C*, . . . that come into the phenomena] and of their evolution. Most authors do not take any account of it, and even ignore its existence, but that does not prevent their train of thought from having this system as a premise, even if they are not aware of the fact.[5]

Pareto had plenty of experience, in economics and sociology, with the problems of systems.

At any rate, the methods and ideas of industrial sociology are not chance products. They are consistent with a certain kind of approach to the general problem, and they are mutually consistent: they themselves form a system. They have a rationale as part of a grand strategy.

This is the stage that industrial sociology has reached at the present time: identification of the variables and some rough notion of their relations in particular cases. Now a new stage opens that demands new methods, and in it we are not going to make progress unless we are again ready to be flexible. The adepts of the controlled experiment are not the only people that may be rigid. The clinicians run the same risk. In the future it will not be enough to be a sensitive soul, who has a feeling for the "total situation." What, in detail, is the nature of the totalness? It will not be enough to emphasize the "social" factors at the expense of the "economic." As I watch industrial sociologists, I think I see that they are beginning to discover, in each new situation, the same kinds of things over and over again. They need procedures that will give them something on which they can build, so that they will not find themselves beginning at the beginning every time. Continuing to collect "cases" will lead only to boredom unless there are specific methods by which cases can be shown to differ in the degree they possess the things that appear in each case.

This is as much as to say that the industrial sociologist, on his way to the ultimate goal, will move from a study of the social system as it is exemplified in single groups toward a study of the system as it is exemplified in many groups, including groups changing in time, just as the social psychologist will move from a study of single equations toward a study of a system of equations. The methods and ideas of the two will converge as they approach the goal from different directions. For the industrial sociologist this means that his methods must become more quantitative. If the differences between solutions of the social system are differences in the values of variables present in all, he must have means, however crude, of measuring the values. He must have methods of measuring aspects of nonverbal as well as verbal behavior. They must also be comparable from group to group. The physicist was able to make progress when he could, for instance, measure pressure in one thermodynamic system by the same method as he measured it in another, when the measures were quantitative, and when he could show that pressure, so measured, varied with volume and temperature.[6] On the other hand, a new insistence on quantitative methods does not mean that the industrial sociologist will necessarily turn to the classic controlled experiment. I can conceive that he might make most progress, at least in the beginning of the new stage, by making experiments in which he changed, or was able to follow a change in, one aspect of an industrial group and then watched how all the other aspects changed. I only insist that he should try to measure the changes.

Modern physics has recognized the close and mutual relation between methods and concepts. A careful criticism of our methods of measuring space and time led to changes in our ideas of space and time. In somewhat the same way, a criticism of our methods in industrial sociology leads to a criticism of our concepts, and vice versa. As our methods become more quantitative and more comparable from group to group, so our concepts will become more analytical. At the moment they are hopelessly taxonomic, like *caste* and *class*, or composite, like *status*.

Let us examine the case of *status*, a word that is certainly often heard in the discussions of industrial sociologists. I call the concept composite, because as it is ordinarily used it includes most of the following subconcepts: (a) position in a system of communication or interaction; (b) work actually done by a person in that position; (c) evaluation of the position and of the person occupying it (high or low status); (d) a verbal description of the behavior proper to a person occupying the position (usually called the *role*); and (e) some notion that departure from the proper behavior would bring some form of punishment. Thus the idea of status includes the ideas of *position, interaction, activity, sentiment, ideology,* and *control.* Now if we examine what we actually do when we determine and describe a person's status, we shall find that we state the facts under several of the subconcepts. We do not observe status directly; we do observe interactions, activities, verbal descriptions of proper forms of behavior, etc. Moreover, when we talk about changes in status, we are in fact talking about changes in interactions, activities, and the rest. What is much more important, if we think of status as a unitary concept, we prevent ourselves from seeing that, for instance, as activities change, so do interactions and sentiments. We prevent ourselves from seeing the relations between variables. *Status* is, in fact, a second-order abstraction. The analytical concepts that we need will come, at first, from the first-order abstractions, that is, from the concepts that are names for classes of direct observations of behavior. And the clear recognition that these are in fact the things we observe will encourage us to develop better methods of observing them. It will encourage us, above all, to make our methods more fully quantitative.

What, then, is the use of *status*? It has, I think, little use in the study of small groups, from which a great deal of our progress will come, but much, on the contrary, in the kind of study of societies as wholes that Talcott Parsons makes. Where a fine-grained analysis is impossible, status sums up compactly a large number of facts. Of course, I am taking status as only one illustration. A full discussion of taxonomic, composite, and analytical concepts would require a book in itself.

Let industrial sociology, then, remain true to its founders by its insistence on intimate, firsthand acquaintance with the facts in the field, by its eagerness to discover all the factors that may have a bearing on the phenomena, and by its awareness of the total situation. But let it never be complacent, never satisfied, that these excellences are enough. Let it prepare to make a dynamic study of varied and changing configurations by developing its quantitative measures of important variables and by refining its analytical concepts. Then, if it keeps flexible too, it will be equipped at all points for grand strategy.

16

The Strategy

of Small-Group

Research

SMALL-GROUP research is newly rooted in the cranny between individual psychology, on the one hand, and sociology and social anthropology, disciplines devoted to the study of large-scale societies, on the other. The relation of his field of investigation to kindred fields must sooner or later be a matter of concern to a scholar, and as a sociologist who has worked in the small-group area, I must at some time concern myself with its relations to the science of society. Nevertheless I am going to argue that we "small-group men" should not, at this moment, worry about our foreign relations. The rest of this essay will be given over to explaining in just what sense—and it is not common sense—I mean this.

When I say "should not," my ends are theoretical and not practical, my problems strategic and not moral. If I am interested in changing small-group behavior as a means, let us say, of increasing productivity in industry, then I must, of course, concern myself with the sociology of the larger organizations. With a thoughtless swish of the tail they may wreck my handiwork. But if I am the general of the research

Read at a symposium on "Sociological and Anthropological Perspectives on Small-Group Research" at the annual convention of the American Psychological Association, Cleveland, Ohio, September 5, 1953; not previously published.

[269]

army of social science, and my mission is theoretical—to establish systems of general propositions about human behavior—and my problem strategic—the economical use of scarce means, including manpower—then I say to my division of small-group research, "At this point in the battle, attack on your own front. Do not worry about your flanks. You will contribute more to sociology, anthropology, yes, and to psychology too, in the long run, and they will contribute more to you, if you worry very little about them now." I am assuming that strategy and tactics are largely problems of *timing*. I am also assuming that we cannot be sure beforehand what strategy will turn out to be wise. We can only back our best judgment.

I say all this in full recognition that small-group research did not, in the recent past, develop in independence of sociology and psychology. Theoretical interests are no more conscious than other motives, but if the interests of the sociologists who took up small-group research had been made fully explicit, they might have been stated as follows: "We have a vague notion of a social system. Could we not establish more rigorously and completely the propositions of such a system if we used for our data small societies rather than large ones? We should gain simplification by scale, with the incidental opportunity to make experiments and more nearly exhaustive observations." In small-group research, the sociologists sought, I believe, theoretical clarification.

But if small-group research was a branch of sociology or of psychology in the past, it does not follow that, as a matter of strategy, it should not now and for some little time to come act as if it were an independent subject. Rather, having plunked for theory, we must both play our choice for what it is worth and accept the bounds it imposes. Now the process of theoretical clarification has, it seems to me, two aspects. On the one hand, it creates a more and more complete system of analytical propositions—or, in the long run, equations—describing the behavior of a body of phenomena. On the other hand, it specifies more and more clearly those kinds of data that do not get explication in the body of propositions but are treated simply as givens or boundary conditions. I think the distinction I make is that between the variables of a system of equations and its parameters, but I am too intuitive a mathematician to be sure.

The distinction between the propositions and the givens is more clearly made in economics than in other social science fields. In that science, for instance, a person's scale of valuation of goods is taken as given: it receives no explication in the formal propositions, which describe only what follows when this and other such things are fixed at certain points.[1] Now it is the essence of strategy as of all choice that you do not get something for nothing, and the price of a complete system of propositions within a field is the specified renunciation of what lies outside it, whose influences are taken as given at the boundary. As the most fully developed of the social sciences, economics has both exploited the advantages of this strategy and paid its price most fully. That is why we feel so ambivalent about economics.

My hunch is that in small-group research we should, if only for the time being, adopt the strategy of economics, but this at once raises, in the relations between this field and both psychology and sociology, problems of two kinds, which proceed directly from my distinction between the propositions and the givens. The first is the problem of reductionism: To what extent are the propositions of small-group research deducible, as special cases, from some more general system in one of the other disciplines? And the second is the problem of the status of the givens: To what extent are the givens of small-group research the variables of other disciplines? I shall take these problems up in order, still developing a strategic doctrine, which means I am no more interested in the final form of a science than in the best way to get there.

I call myself an ultimate psychological reductionist—horrible phrase —because I have faith that the propositions of small-group research— when we have them—will be found deducible from a general psychology of behavior—when we have *it*. But to confess I am an ultimate reductionist is not to say I am a proximate one. In my capacity as strategist, I argue instead that reduction, in the long run, is best served by avoiding it for the time being. Or, better avoid reducing until you know what you've got to reduce—and what to reduce it *to*.

In my support, I can only cite the history of science, as I understand it. As practitioners of new sciences, I think we have more to learn from the early strategies of the physical sciences than from their more or less completed forms today. If we get enchanted by the latter, we shall try to go too far, too soon, and probably in the direction of unsuitable models. At any rate, to take one example, Willard Gibbs was able, in 1901, to show that the propositions of thermodynamics were directly deducible from his more general statistical mechanics. I doubt that he would have been able to do so if thermodynamics had not been, for a quarter-century, fairly complete at its own level of generalization.

(And I confess that if someone asks me to define "own level of generalization," I shall not be able to do so any more than I can define a cow. I can only point to what I believe to be the animal.)

Accordingly, to take now an example from the small-group field, if one of us finds that, when two groups are in rivalry, the frequency of hostile interaction to the other group is greatest among low-status members, *because* the latter feel most insecure socially and so must prove their identification with their own group by displaying conspicuously their hostility to the other, my reaction is as follows.[2] Let us state in its most general form the finding itself, that is, the first half of the statement, but let us not insist for the moment on the explanation, in terms of insecurity, contained in the second half. Let us keep the latter in the back, rather than the front, of our minds, even if we believe it in the long run to be valid. Let us not reduce to personality psychology too soon, for if we do, the finding itself will tend in practice to be lost and not take its place in a system of propositions at its own level of generality. I have the impression that isolated findings tend to get attracted as satellites to some more developed body of theory. I do not want the propositions discovered by small-group research to be attracted, one here and one there, to different points on the body of personality psychology. I want them first attracted to one another.

It is the system and not the isolated proposition that we want, in the end, to reduce. Perhaps Bacon had this in mind when he said that propositions should be held merely positive and not referred to a cause, or Newton when he said, "I do not deal in explanations." *Hypotheses non fingo* is, indeed, a rule of strategy, not of final truth. In Newton's time, his propositions could not be deduced from some more general formulation, and, to put it mildly, were none the worse for that. In light-hearted moments I have thought that, if some of our present social science theorists had lived in Newton's time, they would have been bound to speak of his laws as "mere empirical generalizations." If no truth is final, let us seek truth before finality.

By the same token, I do not think that we who work on small groups should be in any hurry to show that the propositions, largely unstated to be sure, of the sociology of larger organizations follow, under appropriate assumptions, from our own; though some such attempt will have to be made sooner or later.

I turn now to the second problem, that of the status of the givens. Those easiest to recognize and accept as such illustrate the problem most clearly. Ten families live in ten different flats in an apartment building. The means of access to the flats are so laid out that they set different initial probabilities for social contact between any one of the families and each of the others. These initial probabilities *given,* then what I believe to be one of the most important propositions about small groups takes over, so to speak. Stated loosely, this proposition is: the more frequent the interaction between persons, the greater their friendliness. As a result, the families nearest one another in functional distance are particularly apt to become friends.[3] Note that different givens might have produced different concrete results, the proposition remaining the same. It was to take care of differences in the givens that I introduced what I call the *external system* into the conceptual scheme of my book, *The Human Group.*[4]

In this example, I believe the status of the givens—architectural layout—is the same as that of the individual schedules of valuation in economics, and we do not find it hard to accept their escaping from explication by our science. In other cases, acceptance is not so easy, and we yearn to make our parameters variables. In a certain department of a factory, I find that different persons get different pay, and that these differences tend to establish initial differences in rank (status). At this point, a number of propositions about small groups may take over, one of which is this: the more nearly equal to one another in status are the members of a group, the more often they will interact with one another in leisure-time activities, such as going to coffee. Here the pay differential and the fact that high pay gets high valuation in our culture are simply givens from the point of view of the analysis of the group. They are determined by forces outside the group, the one by the company and the union, the other by the Western culture in which we all share. But since we are social scientists, and since a company and a culture are social phenomena, we find it harder to accept these givens as such than we do the physical facts of architecture.

I think the same considerations hold good for a question that has begun to exercise some minds: whether the propositions describing the behavior of groups in our culture apply to groups in other cultures. I have no doubt that when we start to do small-group research in other cultures we shall have to introduce into our equations parameters representing cultural differences, which I think turn out to be differences in the past histories of the societies in question. But that the general forms of the equations will differ I very much doubt. If they did, we should not be able to make the successful cross-cultural predictions about kinship behavior that we make already.[5] I hold the heretical belief—heretical because it sounds like common sense—that cat nature or crow nature may differ from human nature, but that human nature is the same the world over—it only manifests itself in different circumstances. And even if the propositions *were* different in different cultures, I should not let this worry me. It has often been held against American psychology that it is a psychology of the college sophomore. I think the charge ambiguous. Given the strategic problem, I had rather work for a systematic psychology of the sophomore than for a comparison of the sophomore with the Navaho shepherd without the system on either side.

I assume that some of us have made a choice: to try to get theoretical clarification of a social system by working with data simplified at least by scale. Strategically, I think the choice was wise, and we should follow it up; accepting its limitations in order to exploit its advantages. Just as we renounce, for the moment, reductionism, so we should, again for the moment, fight off the temptation to turn our parameters into variables, even if our ultimate mission includes both. Instead we should more and more clearly specify our parameters—our givens—for what they are, and stop there. Are we so proud that we cannot accept and renounce? Are we interested in the relations between small-group research and other social science fields? Let us learn from economics. In making clear its relations to sociology and psychology, economics has, in my view, done far better by specifying what it takes as givens for its own system than it has by trying to bring the data of the other social sciences within its system. We outsiders can learn more from the classicists than from the institutionalists. If you are trying to relate one field to another, it helps to mark the boundary between them. Don't relate until you know what you're relating to. Or, to put the matter still more crudely, if anyone says that my argument amounts to a plea for doing well one thing at a time, I shall accept this too, though it boils me down a bit. Let other social scientists follow what strategies they please: this is the one for us in small groups.

The specification of the givens entails our stating the propositions themselves in more and more rigorous and explicit form. The two processes interact. I am often accused of not adequately hedging my own propositions with limiting conditions, but it is often true also that, until a proposition is stated in general terms, you cannot see what its givens are. I suggest a new categorical imperative: state your findings as if they were laws governing all human behavior—for they may turn out to be just that. It is because I am sure we are fast developing in small-group research a single system of propositions at the same level of generality that I hate to see us distracted by premature reductionism or "variablizing."

Some of us will have the devil's own time admitting that the system is indeed single. One trouble is that the propositions tested in small-group research are stated in almost as many different languages as there are investigators. One man speaks of *communication* when the other uses *interaction*. But when I trace my way down the semantic chains from the words to the operations performed in research, I become satisfied that the different words often refer to the same kind of operation, and that some propositions different in verbal form are identical in substance. That identical propositions have been tested by different investigators is one of the strongest grounds for confidence that small-group research can be a science. But the identities can be a source of growth only if we recognize them, which means that we must carry through the semantic analysis more often than we do now. Small-group research is developing a frontier where more and more research is done, advancing more and more subtle hypotheses and employing more and more delicate methods, but the frontier is hollow; the land behind it, which should consist of established propositions, is burnt-over, not consolidated. Codification of established results in a single language should follow step by step behind our advances, or our field will sooner or later cease to grow, because it has nothing to grow *from*. Unhappily a specialist in codification is not highly rewarded in informal academic status; the whole American tradition in social science research is against him. Who, moreover, can be trusted with codification, and whose language will he use? Investigators are reluctant to give up their terms if these form part of a higher-order theoretical system from which, they hold, the hypotheses they test have been deduced. If the test is satisfactory, the whole theory also is satisfactory, the implication seems to be. But there may be two kinds of theory: one is, so to speak, a scaffolding for investigation, the other is simply an economical way of summing up the results of investigation. I am sure that this is an important strategic problem. I am also sure that it is far from solution.

Another difficulty about formulating a single system of propositions in small-group research is that the propositions standing most in need of codification are just the ones that sound most like common sense.

We should expect this to be the case. People have direct experience of human behavior as they do not of molecular behavior, and it would it would be surprising indeed if some of the propositions of small-group research bore no correspondence with common sense. But the role of a scientist, which until lately was that of a physical scientist, is discovery, and the obvious, by definition, cannot be *discovered*. Under the compulsion of his role, the social scientist is on the lookout for the strange; he is a little reluctant to find the object in plain sight—which means the object may be effectively lost. Or if he does find the purloined letter he is at pains to hide it again as a "culturally-defined object of deviant cathexis." But fear of public opinion or even of their colleagues' opinion was not always a characteristic of scientists in the past, and unless we are ready to codify common sense in rigorous terms we shall not be able to draw the conclusions that are not common sense.

To turn briefly, at the end, from foreign relations to wholly domestic affairs, I do not think that, within small-group research, any serious problem arises because some of us call ourselves "sociologists" and some "psychologists," or because some of us work on "natural" groups in places like factories and some on "experimental" groups in social-relations laboratories. No doubt the latter have advantages in precision of observation and in systematic variation, the former in studying conditions not easily reproduced in laboratories. And no doubt the givens of the organizational circumstances or the experimental situation are inadequately specified by both parties. A discussion group has a very different given in the shape of assigned task from a group working on physical production—and this fact is not always recognized. I myself am guilty of talking about *the* human group. But if we are careful to specify our different givens, the propositions we discover will, I am persuaded, take their places within a single system. In the unity of our propositions lies our unity as a group.

Such a process of clarification will allow us to bring closer together the work of two kinds of investigator: those who try to establish the truth of a single proposition, or small number of propositions, by experimental and statistical manipulation of the data from more than one group, and those who try to determine the validity of a system of propositions as applied to a single group, which they may not be able to manipulate experimentally. Single propositions tested in many groups as against many propositions tested in single groups—the distinction between the statisticians and the "case study men" can be made sharper

[276]

in words than it is in fact. The reconciliation of the two approaches may take a long time in practice, but the first step toward it is the clear recognition by all concerned of what is after all a truism of mathematics: a single system of general propositions (equations), under givens fixed for any one case but varying from case to case, admits of an enormous number of different solutions. For our field, these solutions are single concrete group structures.[6]

In this sense only I mean it, when I say that we should not worry about psychological, sociological, or anthropological perspectives on small-group research. Create an adequate system, and its perspectives will take care of themselves. In the cathedral many men are building, our own pier must go up before the arches can meet.

17

Social

Behavior

as Exchange

The Problems of Small-Group Research

THIS essay will hope to honor the memory of Georg Simmel in two different ways. So far as it pretends to be suggestive rather than conclusive, its tone will be Simmel's; and its subject, too, will be one of his. Because Simmel, in essays such as those on sociability, games, coquetry, and conversation, was an analyst of elementary social behavior, we call him an ancestor of what is known today as small-group research. For what we are really studying in small groups is elementary social behavior: what happens when two or three persons are in a position to influence one another, the sort of thing of which those massive structures called "classes," "firms," "communities," and "societies" must ultimately be composed.

As I survey small-group research today, I feel that, apart from just

Reprinted from *American Journal of Sociology*, 63 (1958), 597–606, by permission of the University of Chicago Press, publisher of the *Journal*. Copyright 1958 by the University of Chicago. The number in which this article appeared was devoted to the memory of Georg Simmel. The ideas put forward in the article are treated at much greater length in G. C. Homans, *Social Behavior: Its Elementary Forms* (New York: Harcourt, 1961).

keeping on with it, three sorts of things need to be done. The first is to show the relation between the results of experimental work done under laboratory conditions and the results of quasi-anthropological field research on what those of us who do it are pleased to call "real-life" groups in industry and elsewhere. If the experimental work has anything to do with real life—and I am persuaded that it has everything to do—its propositions cannot be inconsistent with those discovered through the field work. But the consistency has not yet been demonstrated in any systematic way.

The second job is to pull together in some set of general propositions the actual results, from the laboratory and from the field, of work on small groups—propositions that at least sum up, to an approximation, what happens in elementary social behavior, even though we may not be able to explain why the propositions should take the form they do. A great amount of work has been done, and more appears every day, but what it all amounts to in the shape of a set of propositions from which, under specified conditions, many of the observational results might be derived, is not at all clear—and yet to state such a set is the first aim of science.

The third job is to begin to show how the propositions that empirically hold good in small groups may be derived from some set of still more general propositions. "Still more general" means only that empirical propositions other than ours may also be derived from the set. This derivation would constitute the explanatory stage in the science of elementary social behavior, for explanation *is* derivation.[1] (I myself suspect that the more general set will turn out to contain the propositions of behavioral psychology. I hold myself to be an "ultimate psychological reductionist," but I cannot know that I am right so long as the reduction has not been carried out.)

I have come to think that all three of these jobs would be furthered by our adopting the view that interaction between persons is an exchange of goods, material and nonmaterial. This is one of the oldest theories of social behavior, and one that we still use every day to interpret our own behavior, as when we say, "I found so-and-so rewarding"; or "I got a great deal out of him"; or, even, "Talking with him took a great deal out of me." But, perhaps just because it is so obvious, this view has been much neglected by social scientists. So far as I know, the only theoretical work that makes explicit use of it is Marcel Mauss's *Essai sur le don*, published in 1925, which is ancient as social science goes.[2] It may be that the tradition of neglect is now changing and that, for instance, the psychologists who interpret behavior in terms of transactions may be coming back to something of the sort I have in mind.[3]

An incidental advantage of an exchange theory is that it might bring sociology closer to economics—that science of man most advanced, most capable of application, and, intellectually, most isolated. Economics studies exchange carried out under special circumstances and with a most useful built-in numerical measure of value. What are the laws of the general phenomenon of which economic behavior is one class?

In what follows I shall suggest some reasons for the usefulness of a theory of social behavior as exchange and suggest the nature of the propositions such a theory might contain.

An Exchange Paradigm

I start with the link to behavioral psychology and the kind of statement it makes about the behavior of an experimental animal such as the pigeon.[4] As a pigeon explores its cage in the laboratory, it happens to peck a target, whereupon the psychologist feeds it corn. The evidence is that it will peck the target again; it has learned the behavior, or, as my friend Skinner says, the behavior has been reinforced, and the pigeon has undergone *operant conditioning*. This kind of psychologist is not interested in how the behavior was learned: "learning theory" is a poor name for his field. Instead, he is interested in what determines changes in the rate of emission of learned behavior, whether pecks at a target or something else.

The more hungry the pigeon, the less corn or other food it has gotten in the recent past, the more often it will peck. By the same token, if the behavior is often reinforced, if the pigeon is given much corn every time it pecks, the rate of emission will fall off as the pigeon gets *satiated*. If, on the other hand, the behavior is not reinforced at all, then, too, its rate of emission will tend to fall off, though a long time may pass before it stops altogether, before it is *extinguished*. In the emission of many kinds of behavior the pigeon incurs *aversive stimulation*, or what I shall call "cost" for short, and this, too, will lead in time to a decrease in the emission rate. Fatigue is an example of a "cost." Extinction, satiation, and cost, by decreasing the rate of emission of a particular kind of behavior, render more probable the emission of some other kind of behavior, including doing nothing. As a statement of the propositions of behavioral psychology, the foregoing is, of course, inadequate for any purpose except my present one.

We may look on the pigeon as engaged in an exchange—pecks for corn—with the psychologist, but let us not dwell upon that, for the behavior of the pigeon hardly determines the behavior of the psychologist at all. Let us turn to a situation where the exchange is real, that is, where the determination is mutual. Suppose we are dealing with two men. Each is emitting behavior reinforced to some degree by the behavior of the other. How it was in the past that each learned the behavior he emits and how he learned to find the other's behavior reinforcing we are not concerned with. It is enough that each does find the other's behavior reinforcing, and I shall call the reinforcers—the equivalent of the pigeon's corn—*values*, for this, I think, is what we mean by this term. As he emits behavior, each man may incur costs, and each man has more than one course of behavior open to him.

This seems to me the paradigm of elementary social behavior, and the problem of the elementary sociologist is to state propositions relating the variations in the values and costs of each man to his frequency distribution of behavior among alternatives, where the values (in the mathematical sense) taken by these variables for one man determine in part their values for the other.[5]

I see no reason to believe that the propositions of behavioral psychology do not apply to this situation, though the complexity of their implications in the concrete case may be great indeed. In particular, we must suppose that, with men as with pigeons, an increase in extinction, satiation, or aversive stimulation of any one kind of behavior will increase the probability of emission of some other kind. The problem is not, as it is often stated, merely, what a man's values are, what he has learned in the past to find reinforcing, but how much of any one value his behavior is getting him now. The more he gets, the less valuable any further unit of that value is to him, and the less often he will emit behavior reinforced by it.

The Influence Process

We do not, I think, possess the kind of studies of two-person interaction that would either bear out these propositions or fail to do so. But we do have studies of larger numbers of persons that suggest that they may apply, notably the studies by Festinger, Schachter, Back, and their associates on the dynamics of influence. One of the variables they work with they call *cohesiveness*, defined as anything that attracts people to take part in a group. Cohesiveness is a value variable; it refers to the degree of reinforcement people find in the activities of the group. Festinger and his colleagues consider two kinds of reinforcing activity: the symbolic behavior we call "social approval" and activity valuable in other ways, such as doing something interesting.

The other variable they work with they call *communication* and others call *interaction*. This is a frequency variable; it is a measure of the frequency of emission of valuable and costly verbal behavior. We must bear in mind that, in general, the one kind of variable is a function of the other.

Festinger and his co-workers show that the more cohesive a group is, that is, the more valuable the sentiment or activity the members exchange with one another, the greater the average frequency of interaction of the members.[6] With men, as with pigeons, the greater the reinforcement, the more often is the reinforced behavior emitted. The more cohesive a group, too, the greater the change that members can produce in the behavior of other members in the direction of rendering these activities more valuable.[7] That is, the more valuable the activities that members get, the more valuable those that they must give. For if a person is emitting behavior of a certain kind, and other people do not find it particularly rewarding, these others will suffer their own production of sentiment and activity, in time, to fall off. But perhaps the first person has found their sentiment and activity rewarding, and, if he is to keep on getting them, he must make his own behavior more valuable to the others. In short, the propositions of behavioral psychology imply a tendency toward a certain proportionality between the value to others of the behavior a man gives them and the value to him of the behavior they give him.[8]

Schachter also studied the behavior of members of a group toward two kinds of other members, "conformers" and "deviates."[9] I assume that conformers are people whose activity the other members find valuable. For conformity is behavior that coincides to a degree with some group standard or norm, and the only meaning I can assign to *norm* is "a verbal description of behavior that many members find it valuable for the actual behavior of themselves and others to conform to." By the same token, a deviate is a member whose behavior is not particularly valuable. Now Schachter shows that, as the members of a group come to see another member as a deviate, their interaction with him—communication addressed to getting him to change his behavior—goes up, the faster the more cohesive the group. The members need not talk to the other conformers so much; they are relatively satiated by the conformers' behavior: they have gotten what they want out of them. But if the deviate, by failing to change his behavior, fails to reinforce the members, they start to withhold social approval from him: the deviate gets low sociometric choice at the end of the experiment. And in the most cohesive groups—those Schachter calls "high cohesive-relevant" —interaction with the deviate also falls off in the end and is lowest among those members that rejected him most strongly, as if they had given him up as a bad job. But how plonking can we get? These findings are utterly in line with everyday experience.

Practical Equilibrium

At the beginning of this paper I suggested that one of the tasks of small-group research was to show the relation between the results of experimental work done under laboratory conditions and the results of field research on real-life small groups. Now the latter often appear to be in practical equilibrium, and by this I mean nothing fancy. I do not mean that all real-life groups are in equilibrium. I certainly do not mean that all groups must tend to equilibrium. I do not mean that groups have built-in antidotes to change: there is no homeostasis here. I do not mean that we assume equilibrium. I mean only that we sometimes *observe* it, that for the time we are with a group—and it is often short—there is no great change in the values of the variables we choose to measure. If, for instance, person A is interacting with B more than with C both at the beginning and at the end of the study, then at least by this crude measure the group is in equilibrium.

Many of the Festinger-Schachter studies are experimental, and their propositions about the process of influence seem to me to imply the kind of proposition that empirically holds good of real-life groups in practical equilibrium. For instance, Festinger *et al.* find that, the more cohesive a group is, the greater the change that members can produce in the behavior of other members. If the influence is exerted in the direction of conformity to group norms, then, when the process of influence has accomplished all the change of which it is capable, the proposition should hold good that, the more cohesive a group is, the larger the number of members that conform to its norms. And it does hold good.[10]

Again, Schachter found, in the experiment I summarized above, that in the most cohesive groups and at the end, when the effort to influence the deviate had failed, members interacted little with the deviate and gave him little in the way of sociometric choice. Now two of the propositions that hold good most often of real-life groups in practical equilibrium are precisely that the more closely a member's activity conforms to the norms the more interaction he receives from other members and the more liking choices he gets from them too. From these main propositions a number of others may be derived that also hold good.[11]

Yet we must ever remember that the truth of the proposition linking conformity to liking may on occasion be masked by the truth of other propositions. If, for instance, the man that conforms to the norms most closely also exerts some authority over the group, this may render liking for him somewhat less than it might otherwise have been.[12]

Be that as it may, I suggest that the laboratory experiments on influence imply propositions about the behavior of members of small groups, when the process of influence has worked itself out, that are identical with propositions that hold good of real-life groups in equilibrium. This is hardly surprising if all we mean by equilibrium is that all the change of which the system is, under present conditions, capable has been effected, so that no further change occurs. Nor would this be the first time that statics has turned out to be a special case of dynamics.

Profit and Social Control

Though I have treated equilibrium as an observed fact, it is a fact that cries for explanation. I shall not, as structural-functional sociologists do, use an assumed equilibrium as a means of explaining, or trying to explain, why the other features of a social system should be what they are. Rather, I shall take practical equilibrium as something that is itself to be explained by the other features of the system.

If every member of a group emits at the end of, and during, a period of time much the same kinds of behavior and in much the same frequencies as he did at the beginning, the group is for that period in equilibrium. Let us then ask why any one member's behavior should persist. Suppose he is emitting behavior of value A_1. Why does he not let his behavior get worse (less valuable or reinforcing to the others) until it stands at $A_1-\Delta A$? True, the sentiments expressed by others toward him are apt to decline in value (become less reinforcing to him), so that what he gets from them may be $S_1-\Delta S$. But it is conceivable that, since most activity carries cost, a decline in the value of what he emits will mean a reduction in cost to him that more than offsets his losses in sentiment. Where, then, does he stabilize his behavior? This is the problem of social control.[13]

Mankind has always assumed that a person stabilizes his behavior, at least in the short run, at the point where he is doing the best he can for himself under the circumstances, though his best may not be a "rational" best, and what he can do may not be at all easy to specify, except that he is not apt to think like one of the theoretical antagonists in the *Theory of Games*. Before a sociologist rejects this answer out of hand for its horrid profit-seeking implications, he will do well to ask himself if he can offer any other answer to the question posed. I think he will find that he cannot. Yet experiments designed to test the truth of the answer are extraordinarily rare.

I shall review one that seems to me to provide a little support for the theory, though it was not meant to do so. The experiment is reported by H. B. Gerard, a member of the Festinger-Schachter team, under the title "The Anchorage of Opinions in Face-to-Face Groups."[14] The experimenter formed artificial groups whose members met to discuss a case in industrial relations and to express their opinions about its probable outcome. The groups were of two kinds: high-attraction groups, whose members were told that they would like one another very much, and low-attraction groups, whose members were told that they would not find one another particularly likable.

At a later time the experimenter called the members in separately, asked them again to express their opinions on the outcome of the case, and counted the number that had changed their opinions to bring them into accord with those of other members of their groups. Then a paid participant entered into a further discussion of the case with each member, always taking, on the probable outcome of the case, a position opposed to that taken by the bulk of the other members of the group to which the person belonged. The experimenter counted the number of persons shifting toward the opinion of the paid participant.

[285]

Table 1. *Percentage of Subjects Changing toward Someone in the Group*

	Agreement	Mild disagreement	Strong disagreement
High attraction	0	12	44
Low attraction	0	15	9

Table 2. *Percentage of Subjects Changing toward the Paid Participant*

	Agreement	Mild disagreement	Strong disagreement
High attraction	7	13	25
Low attraction	20	38	8

The experiment had many interesting results, from which I choose only those summed up in Tables 1 and 2. The three different agreement classes are made up of people who, at the original sessions, expressed different degrees of agreement with the opinions of other members of their groups. And the figure 44, for instance, means that, of all members of high-attraction groups whose initial opinions were strongly in disagreement with those of other members, 44 per cent shifted their opinion later toward that of others.

In these results the experimenter seems to have been interested only in the differences in the sums of the rows, which show that there is more shifting toward the group and less shifting toward the paid participant in the high-attraction than in the low-attraction condition. This is in line with a proposition suggested earlier. If you think that the members of a group can give you much—in this case, liking—you are apt to give them much, in this case, a change to an opinion in accordance with their views—or you will not get the liking. And, by the same token, if the group can give you little of value, you will not be ready to give it much of value. Indeed, you may change your opinion so as to depart from agreement even further, to move, that is, toward the view held by the paid participant.

So far so good, but, when I first scanned these tables, I was less struck by the difference between them than by their similarity. The same classes of people in both tables showed much the same relative propensities to change their opinions, no matter whether the change was toward the group or toward the paid participant. We see, for instance, that those who change least are the high-attraction, agreement people and the low-attraction, strong-disagreement ones. And those who change most are the high-attraction, strong-disagreement people and the low-attraction, mild-disagreement ones.

How am I to interpret these particular results? Since the experimenter did not discuss them, I am free to offer my own explanation. The behavior emitted by the subjects is opinion and changes in opinion. For this behavior they have learned to expect two possible kinds of reinforcement. Agreement with the group gets the subject favorable sentiment (acceptance) from it, and the experiment was designed to give this reinforcement a higher value in the high-attraction condition than in the low-attraction one. The second kind of possible reinforcement is what I shall call the "maintenance of one's personal integrity," which a subject gets by sticking to his own opinion in the face of disagreement with the group. The experimenter does not mention this reward, but I cannot make sense of the results without something much like it. In different degrees for different subjects, depending on their initial positions, these rewards are in competition with one another: they are alternatives. They are not absolutely scarce goods, but some persons cannot get both at once.

Since the rewards are alternatives, let me introduce a familiar assumption from economics—that the cost of a particular course of action is the equivalent of the foregone value of an alternative[15]—and then add the definition: Profit = Reward − Cost.

Now consider the persons in the corresponding cells of the two tables. The behavior of the high-attraction, agreement people gets them much in the way of acceptance by the group, and for it they must give up little in the way of personal integrity, for their views are from the start in accord with those of the group. Their profit is high, and they are not prone to change their behavior. The low-attraction, strong-disagreement people are getting much in integrity, and they are not giving up for it much in valuable acceptance, for they are members of low-attraction groups. Reward-less-cost is high for them, too, and they change little. The high-attraction, strong-disagreement people are getting much in the way of integrity, but their costs in doing so are high, for they are in high-attraction groups and thus foregoing much valuable acceptance by the group. Their profit is low, and they are very apt to change, either toward the group or toward the paid participant, from whom they think, perhaps, they will get some acceptance while maintaining some integrity. The low-attraction, mild-disagreement people do not get much in the way of integrity, for they are only in mild disagreement with the group, but neither are they giving up much in acceptance, for they are members of low-attraction groups. Their rewards are low; their costs are low too, and their profit—the difference between the two—is also low. In their low profit they resemble the high-attraction, strong-disagreement people, and, like them, they are prone to change their opinions, in this case, more toward the paid participant. The subjects in the other two cells, who have medium profits, display medium propensities to change.

If we define profit as reward less cost, and if cost is value foregone, I suggest that we have here some evidence for the proposition that change in behavior is greatest when perceived profit is least. This constitutes no direct demonstration that change in behavior is least when profit is greatest. But if, whenever a man's behavior brought him a balance of reward and cost, he changed his behavior away from what got him the less profit, there might well come a time when his behavior would not change further. That is, his behavior would be stabilized, at least for the time being. So far as this were true for every member of a group, the group would have a social organization in equilibrium.

I do not say that a member would stabilize his behavior at the point of greatest conceivable profit to himself, because his profit is partly at the mercy of the behavior of others. It is a commonplace that the short-run pursuit of profit by several persons often lands them in positions where all are worse off than they might conceivably be. I do not say that the paths of behavioral change in which a member pursues his profit under the condition that others are pursuing theirs are easy to describe or predict; we can readily conceive that in jockeying for position they might never arrive at any equilibrium at all.

Distributive Justice

Yet practical equilibrium is often observed; thus some further condition may make its attainment, under some circumstances, more probable than would the individual pursuit of profit left to itself. I can offer evidence for this further condition only in the behavior of subgroups and not in that of individuals. Suppose that there are two subgroups, working close together in a factory, the job of one being somewhat different from that of the other. And suppose that the members of the first complain and say: "We are getting the same pay as they are. We ought to get just a couple of dollars a week more to show that our work is more responsible." When you ask them what they mean by "more responsible," they say that, if they do their work wrong, more damage can result, and so they are under more pressure to take care.[16] Something like this is a common feature of industrial behavior. It is at the heart of disputes not over absolute wages but over wage differentials—indeed, at the heart of disputes over rewards other than wages.

In what kind of proposition may we express observations like these? We may say that wages and responsibility give status in the group, in the sense that a man who takes high responsibility and gets high wages is admired, other things equal. Then, if the members of one group score higher on responsibility than do the members of another, there is a felt need on the part of the first to score higher on pay too. There is a pressure, which shows itself in complaints, to bring the *status factors*, as I have called them, into line with one another. If they are in line, a condition of *status congruence* is said to exist. In this condition the workers may find their jobs dull or irksome, but they will not complain about the relative position of groups.

But there may be a more illuminating way of looking at the matter. In my example I have considered only responsibility and pay, but these may be enough, for they represent the two kinds of thing that come into the problem. Pay is clearly a reward; responsibility may be looked on, less clearly, as a cost. It means constraint and worry—or peace of mind foregone. Then the proposition about status congruence becomes this: If the costs of the members of one group are higher than those of another, distributive justice requires that their rewards should be higher too. But the thing works both ways: If the rewards are higher, the costs should be higher too. This last is the theory of *noblesse oblige*, which we all subscribe to, though we all laugh at it, perhaps because the *noblesse* often fails to *oblige*. To put the matter in terms of profit: though the rewards and costs of two persons or the members of two groups may be different, yet the profits of the two—the excess of reward over cost—should tend to equality. And more than "should." The less-advantaged group will at least try to attain greater equality, as, in the example I have used, the first group tried to increase its profit by increasing its pay.

I have talked of distributive justice. Clearly, this is not the only condition determining the actual distribution of rewards and costs. At the
same time, never tell me that notions of justice are not a strong influence on behavior, though we sociologists often neglect them. Distributive
justice may be one of the conditions of group equilibrium.

Exchange and Social Structure

I shall end by reviewing almost the only study I am aware of that
begins to show in detail how a stable and differentiated social structure
in a real-life group might arise out of a process of exchange between
members. This is Peter Blau's description of the behavior of sixteen
agents in a federal law-enforcement agency.[17]

The agents had the duty of investigating firms and preparing reports
on the firms' compliance with the law. Since the reports might lead to
legal action against the firms, the agents had to prepare them carefully,
in the proper form, and take strict account of the many regulations that
might apply. The agents were often in doubt what they should do, and
then they were supposed to take the question to their supervisor. This
they were reluctant to do, for they naturally believed that thus confessing to him their inability to solve a problem would reflect on their competence, affect the official ratings he made of their work, and so hurt
their chances for promotion. So agents often asked other agents for help
and advice; though this was nominally forbidden, the supervisor usually let it pass.

Blau ascertained the ratings the supervisor made of the agents; he also
asked the agents to rate one another. The two opinions agreed closely.
Fewer agents were regarded as highly competent than were regarded as
of middle or low competence; competence, or the ability to solve technical problems, was a fairly scarce good. One or two of the more competent agents would not give help and advice when asked, and so received
few interactions and little liking. A man that will not exchange, that will
not give you what he has when you need it, will not get from you the
only thing you are able to give him in return, in this case, your regard.

But most of the more competent agents were willing to give help,
and of them Blau says:

A consultation can be considered an exchange of values: both participants
gain something, and both have to pay a price. The questioning agent is en-

abled to perform better than he could otherwise have done, without exposing his difficulties to his supervisor. By asking for advice, he implicitly pays his respect to the superior proficiency of his colleague. This acknowledgment of inferiority is the cost of receiving assistance. The consultant gains prestige, in return for which he is willing to devote some time to the consultation and permit it to disrupt his own work. The following remark of an agent illustrates this: "I like giving advice. It's flattering, I suppose, if you feel that others come to you for advice.[18]

Blau goes on to say: "All agents liked being consulted, but the value of any one of very many consultations became deflated for experts, and the price they paid in frequent interruptions became inflated."[19] This implies that, the more prestige an agent received, the less was the increment of value of that prestige; the more advice an agent gave, the greater was the increment of cost of that advice, the cost lying precisely in the foregone value of time to do his own work. Blau suggests that something of the same sort was true of an agent who went to a more competent colleague for advice: the more often he went, the more costly to him, in feelings of inferiority, became any further request. "The repeated admission of his inability to solve his own problems . . . undermined the self-confidence of the worker and his standing in the group."[20]

The result was that the less competent agents went to the more competent ones for help less often than they might have done if the costs of repeated admissions of inferiority had been less high and that, while many agents sought out the few highly competent ones, no single agent sought out the latter much. Had they done so (to look at the exchange from the other side), the costs to the highly competent in interruptions to their own work would have become exorbitant. Yet the need of the less competent for help was still not fully satisfied. Under these circumstances they tended to turn for help to agents more nearly like themselves in competence. Though the help they got was not the most valuable, it was of a kind they could themselves return on occasion. With such agents they could exchange help and liking, without the exchange becoming on either side too great a confession of inferiority.

The highly competent agents tended to enter into exchanges, that is, to interact, with many others. But, in the more equal exchanges I have just spoken of, less competent agents tended to pair off as partners. That is, they interacted with a smaller number of people, but interacted often with these few. I think I could show why pair relations in these more equal exchanges would be more economical for an agent than a wider distribution of favors. But perhaps I have gone far enough. The final pattern of this social structure was one in which a small number of highly competent agents exchanged advice for prestige with a large number of others less competent; and in which the less competent agents exchanged, in pairs and in trios, both help and liking on more nearly equal terms.

Blau shows, then, that a social structure in equilibrium might be the result of a process of exchanging behavior rewarding and costly in different degrees, in which the increment of reward and cost varied with the frequency of the behavior, that is, with the frequency of interaction. Note that the behavior of the agents seems also to have satisfied my second condition of equilibrium: the more competent agents took more responsibility for the work, either their own or others', than did the less competent ones, but they also got more for it in the way of prestige. I suspect that the same kind of explanation could be given for the structure of many "informal" groups.

Summary

The current job of theory in small-group research is to make the connection between experimental and real-life studies, to consolidate the propositions that empirically hold good in the two fields, and to show how these propositions might be derived from a still more general set. One way of doing this job would be to revive and make more rigorous the oldest of theories of social behavior—social behavior as exchange.

Some of the statements of such a theory might be the following. Social behavior is an exchange of goods, material goods but also nonmaterial ones, such as the symbols of approval or prestige. Persons that give much to others try to get much from them, and persons that get much from others are under pressure to give much to them. This process of influence tends to work out at equilibrium to a balance in the exchanges. For a person engaged in exchange, what he gives may be a cost to him, just as what he gets may be a reward, and his behavior changes less as profit, that is, reward less cost, tends to a maximum. Not only does he seek a maximum for himself, but he tries to see to it that no one in his group makes more profit than he does. The cost and the value of what he gives and of what he gets vary with the quantity of what he gives and gets. It is surprising how familiar these propositions are; it is surprising, too, how propositions about the dynamics of exchange can begin to generate the static thing we call "group structure" and, in so doing, generate also some of the propositions about group structure that students of real-life groups have stated.

" In our unguarded moments we sociologists find words like "reward" and "cost" slipping into what we say. Human nature will break in upon even our most elaborate theories. But we seldom let it have its way with us and systematically follow up what these words imply.[21] Of all our many "approaches" to social behavior, the one that sees it as an economy is the most neglected, and yet it is the one we use every moment of our lives—except when we write sociology.

18

Small

Groups

THE field of investigation in the social sciences that has come to be called the study of small groups is not, in my view, properly so called. Small groups are not *what* we study, but *where* we often study it, as I shall presently try to show.

If you will look at the behavior that students of small groups actually investigate, you will find that it has the following characteristics. First, at least two men are in face-to-face contact, each behaving toward the other in ways that reward or punish him and therefore influence his behavior. Second, the rewards or punishments that each gets from the behavior of the other are direct and immediate rather than indirect and deferred. And third, the behavior of the two men is determined in part by something besides their conformity to institutional rules or roles. Indeed it is this noninstitutional aspect that small-group research is most interested in; and so I prefer to speak of what we study as informal, subinstitutional, or elementary social behavior.

Why then is it in fact called behavior in small groups? Consider two kinds of social network. In an *open* network Person A is in contact with Person B, who is in turn in contact with C, but C is not in contact with A —that is why we call it an open network. In a *closed* network A is in

Delivered as a talk on a radio program called "Forum—The Arts and Sciences in Mid-Century America," broadcast by The Voice of America, 1959; published as a pamphlet, Washington: U.S. Information Agency, 1961.

contact with *B*, who is in contact with *C*, but *C* is now also in contact with *A*—that is why we call it a closed network. Since elementary social behavior obviously occurs in networks of both kinds, while only the closed network makes a real group, it is wrong to speak of our subject as if it were limited to small-group behavior. On the other hand, it is often practically convenient to study elementary social behavior through observations made on small groups, for in them a number of people are interacting with one another in the same place within the same span of time, so that a single observer can economically collect many of the data he requires. It is this practical advantage that has determined the name of our field.

Now let us look at an example of elementary social behavior. Two clerks are assigned to the same sort of job in an office.[1] That is, both are expected to obey the same institutional rules. But one of them is not very competent at his work. Should he ask his supervisor for help, he would confess his incompetence and perhaps hurt his chances for promotion; so he goes instead to the other clerk, who is more competent than he is himself, and asks help from him. The other helps him and thus rewards him; and he in turn rewards the other by thanking him, by praising him, by rendering him what I shall call *esteem*. Accordingly we may look on the behavior of the two clerks toward one another, indeed we may look on all social behavior, as an exchange of goods; the causes, the nature, and the consequences of the exchange are examples of the sort of thing small-group research studies.

The boundary of a field of investigation is the line between its *explicanda*—the phenomenon it undertakes to explain and ultimately to predict—and the things it does not undertake to explain but simply accepts as given. The behavior of the two clerks cannot be understood without reference to the institution, the office, to which both belong. For one thing, the help the first clerk gets from the other would have no value to him unless he were assigned to a certain kind of job. Nor can it be understood without reference to much more general cultural rules, for instance, the expectation that a man should thank whoever does him a favor. But the student of elementary social behavior does not undertake to explain why the institutional and cultural rules should be what they are. There are other social scientists to do that. What he does undertake to answer are questions like the following: Given that both clerks have learned the institutional rules, what determines whether one gets help from the other? What determines how much help he asks for and how much he gets? What determines how much esteem he gives to the other? The student of elementary social behavior takes the institutional framework of exchange as given and constant, and studies the variables entering into the process of exchange itself. He may secondarily be interested in the effect of the informal exchange on the success of the institution—on how, for instance, the informal exchange of advice may make the office better able to accomplish its assigned task.

At this point the listener may say to himself: "In different groups, in different societies, men exchange very different things. In one group they may exchange help for social approval; in another group they may exchange jokes for laughter. How can such things as joking and clerical help be measured along the same dimensions and so explained by the same theory?" The answer is that, from one point of view, they are indeed incomparable. But from another point of view—and this is the point of view of the student of elementary social behavior—the two are comparable because both are activities given by one man to another in variable *quantities* or frequencies, and both have variable *values; that is,* they are more or less rewarding to the man who receives them. Since the quantity and value of activities given by one man to another affect the quantity and values of the activities the other returns, the study of interpersonal exchange is the study of interpersonal influence. Note that *quantity* and *value* are also the variables of elementary economics —but this is hardly surprising, since economics too is concerned with exchange.

It should be clear that by this definition much human behavior is elementary social behavior; or better, that elementary social behavior is one aspect of all social behavior. Indeed their behavior in face-to-face contact with others is the thing men are most familiar with, which makes it hard for us social scientists to explain why we study it. Laymen will necessarily find that many of the true propositions about it are obvious; and exceptions to some of the propositions that are not obvious will necessarily occur to them, not realizing that an exception need not disprove a proposition though it certainly calls for adding new propositions to a theory. The situation is as if the particles whose social behavior in the atom the physicist describes were able to talk back and tell him his propositions were either obvious or too abstract.

The interest in the study of small groups came from two different directions and from two different disciplines. Early in this century the psychologists, studying individual behavior, became interested in phenomena like *social facilitation*—the curious fact that men do some kinds of work better when they are in the presence of others, even when the others do not communicate with them in any way, than when they are alone. From there it was a short step for the new subdiscipline of social psychology to study the effect on men's behavior of more direct and explicit social influence brought to bear on them, including the influence of their immediate companions. In this field the most important recent contribution has been that of Kurt Lewin, his students, and his students' students.[2]

The sociologists' interest in small groups was a little different. Their tradition was more theoretical than the psychologists'. They were obsessed with imitating the more advanced sciences and formulating general propositions from which a variety of empirical ones might be logically deduced under specified conditions. But if a theory as it matures takes a more and more deductive form, men do not arrive at it deductively. They arrive at it by induction from the very empirical propositions that the theory will ultimately explain. Some sociologists despaired of developing such a theory for large social units like national states. But small social units, those whose members were few in number, were another matter. In such units an investigator could make the detailed and comprehensive observations of social behavior, on which alone the empirical propositions could be reliably based. Moreover a very great number of such units were available for comparison, control, and even experimentation. As some of these sociologists used to say, they wanted to work with a unit small enough so that they could see all the way around it. More than by anything else their eyes were opened to these possibilities by the small-group studies made by Elton Mayo and his associates in the Western Electric researches—even though the Western Electric researches were designed as studies of American industry and not of elementary social behavior as such.[3]

I emphasize that the interest in small groups has been, at least on the part of the sociologists, primarily intellectual. True, the field does have, or may turn out to have, practical applications—in making the committees and other discussion groups that proliferate in our society more effective, in helping industrial workers become both more productive and more interested, in improving the new practice of group psychotherapy. But it is not the applications that most intrigue the sociologist. On the contrary, what he says is this: "Better a good theory in an unimportant field than a bad theory in an important one. Theory comes first." He likes small groups because they will let him pull off the kind of stunt he most enjoys. I must be honest about his values, even if it leads you to question them.

Speaking for myself, I doubt that the intellectual interest has been misplaced. The study of elementary social behavior occupies a strategic central position among the social sciences. On one side, it links up with behavioral psychology, which has been concerned with the effects of reward and punishment in changing the behavior of the higher animals. On another, it links with elementary economics, which is concerned, like itself, with exchange—the special but important form of exchange that occurs in an organized market. And finally, it is obviously and closely linked with standard sociology, or the study of institutions, for subinstitutional behavior is always becoming institutional—we need only remember that institutional Christianity began with a small group—and subinstitutional behavior is always modifying in actual practice the behavior called for by institutional norms. If we are to attain any intellectual understanding of social behavior, it is a good bet to begin here.

True to their different traditions, the psychologists once tended to study elementary social behavior through laboratory experiments on groups artificially formed, while the sociologists concentrated on observational (field) studies of what they were pleased to call real-life small groups in industry and elsewhere. There is no reason to believe that the findings reached under the two different conditions are inconsistent with one another, though the sociologists are perhaps better at discovering what needs study and the psychologists at studying it rigorously. As time has gone on, these distinctions between the two disciplines have gotten blurred, and today in the study of elementary social behavior it is hard to tell the two apart.

So far I have spent my time defining the field of research in elementary social behavior and showing why social scientists are interested in it. I have made no survey of the substantive findings in the field, nor have I room to do so. Instead I shall end with an illustration. I shall put before you a couple of characteristic empirical propositions, and then suggest how a student of elementary social behavior would undertake to explain them. I claim no greater practical importance for the illustration than I do for the field as a whole.

Suppose, then, that several persons are able to associate freely with one another, subject only to the limitations imposed by tasks they must carry out together. They may be fellow members of a class at school;

or, as above, they may be clerks working together in the same office. In such circumstances, different investigators have observed in several different groups the two phenomena that will concern us. In the first place, in connection with the tasks performed in common, some members of the group receive from other members a larger number of expressions of esteem than others do. Thus, in the office I have used as an illustration, some of the clerks get more esteem than others do. They receive not only more expressions of esteem but more communications in general; and the clerks that stand highest in esteem are relatively few in number. In short, the members of the group become ranked in esteem or, if you like, in status, though the word *status* is perhaps best reserved for the rank a man has formally received in an institution.

In the second place, outside the sphere of common tasks and inside what I shall call for convenience leisure-time activities, the distribution of expressions of approval and other communications among the members is different from, though still related to, what it is in the sphere of work. In leisure, members of the group tend to express liking for, and to associate with, other members who are their equals in esteem more often than they do with either their social superiors or inferiors. In having lunch or coffee or in visiting after hours, our clerks are apt to associate with other clerks who are their social equals in the office. These two findings can be reproduced under laboratory conditions, and something like them is familiar in the social experience of many of us.[4] The question now is how a student of elementary social behavior would explain them.

First to be explained are the differences in esteem in the work-situation. A member who is both able and willing to provide others with a service that many of them want but few are able to supply can get from them in return a more valuable reward than another member can get from supplying a less rare and less valuable service. Naturally the service need not be morally admirable, or such as the rest of us mortals would enjoy, so long as the other members do in fact find it both rare and rewarding. This principle, which applies to ordinary market exchange, such as the exchange of money for physical goods, applies to any social exchange. It applies, for instance, to the exchange of help for esteem in our office. The few clerks who are so experienced and skillful in their jobs that they are able and willing to give the other clerks badly needed help and advice are the clerks that get most esteem from their fellows. We need not expect them to bargain consciously over the terms of exchange of help for esteem; we need only point to the kind of service they supply. The persons who provide rare and rewarding services for other members are the persons who manage somehow or other, by conscious or unconscious processes, to enjoy high esteem in informal groups. In short, something much like the old law of supply and demand explains why the members of a group are differentiated in esteem and why the members held in highest esteem are few.

We must next explain why members equal in esteem tend to associate with one another in their leisure-time, and this will take us a little longer. In the office, both parties to the exchange, besides getting rewards—esteem for the few, help for the many—also incur costs. In our economics as in ordinary economics, their costs are the alternative rewards they give up, or forego, while they are exchanging help for esteem. What does each party give up? The skillful clerk, who helps the others, gives up the time he could otherwise have spent on doing his own work. That is clear enough, but it is much less clear what cost is incurred by the unskillful clerk who gets the help. Students of elementary social behavior believe that his cost lies precisely in his confessing, as he does when he asks for help, that he is in this respect a social inferior.

How much cost he incurs is determined by another explanatory principle, which Aristotle enunciated long ago, and which we now call the principle of *status congruence*. If one man is equal to another in all respects but one, which is in doubt, he will feel sorry if he is not equal in that one too: his inferiority in that will be incongruent with his equality in the others. But if, on the other hand, he is inferior in all respects but one, he will not feel so sorry if he is inferior in that one too: his inferiority in that will be congruent with his inferiority in the others. To go to another man and ask for help is to confess oneself his inferior in skill. If one clerk is equal to another in the outward trappings of status (for instance, the same pay and seniority), then going to the other to ask for help will tend to bring him down in his social world, and this will be a cost to him. But if he has less pay and seniority than the other to begin with, then asking for help will not bring him down in the world, but will only confirm him in his present position of social inferiority, and so it will not cost him much. In short, it will cost an equal more to ask another equal for a service, and to give him esteem in return, than it will for an inferior to ask a superior.

The costs of each party to the exchange also increase with the amounts of help and approval they exchange. The skillful clerk, who gives help, takes more and more time from his own work, and accordingly what time he has left becomes more and more valuable to him. And the clerk who asks for more and more help confesses his social inferiority to an ever greater degree. Therefore, the longer the exchange goes on, the more reason both parties have for breaking it off and for working alone or entering into a new kind of exchange with a different person.

Let us now ask what the unskillful clerk needs in the way of a new kind of exchange. By giving the skillful clerk esteem in return for the help he has himself received, he has made the other his social superior, and he has himself incurred social costs in so doing. The people with whom he can still enter into exchange without incurring further costs in inferiority are, in the nature of the case, the clerks who are still his social equals, clerks, that is, who provide no services at work superior to those he can provide for himself. For this reason, he is little motivated to approach them for assistance in the work-situation; indeed to do so would, as we have seen, put his equality with them in jeopardy. Therefore, he is more likely to seek them out in the nonwork situation, the sphere of leisure or "social" life in the narrow sense of the word *social*. There he can exchange with them activities that are indeed rewarding, for now that the skillful clerk has helped him take care of the problems he encountered in his work, he will welcome companionship of another sort. But the activities he shares with his new companions must not be the kind in which he can be made inferior: they must be activities in which he can return the same sort of reward as he gets—activities that in fact run all the way from exchanging jokes to exchanging hospitality. In such exchanges the English-speaker is apt to say that he feels able to "be himself"—which means precisely that in them he runs no risk of being judged inferior, since his partners are in no position so to judge him. It is for reasons like this that people tend, in the sphere of leisure, to associate with, and to express liking for, other people who are their equals in esteem in the sphere of work.

In this way a theory of elementary social behavior as an exchange of rewarding and costly activities is able to explain the two merely empirical propositions that we started with. The theory would not be interesting if it explained only these two, but it will account for others which I have not time to go into here. I do not claim that I have given the full explanation. For one thing, I have not asked why the superior should avoid the inferior on social occasions, as the inferior does *him*.

Nor do I argue that ordinary men or, better, the novelists of manners, whose domain we have invaded, could not have come up with an explanation much like ours. On the contrary, men have always explained their behavior by pointing to what it gets them and what it costs them. That ours is an explanation of the same sort I claim as one of its positive advantages. Modern social science has gone far out of its way to show that common-sense explanations are incorrect, and it has ended by painting a picture of man that men cannot recognize. We students of elementary social behavior are not out to destroy common sense but to make explicit and general the wisdom it embodies.

Nor, finally, are the phenomena we have dealt with of great importance by practical standards. But remember this: what men have come to value in science is not only the practical importance of its subject matter but also the intellectual power of its methods. As long as men value the explanation and ultimately the prediction of any phenomena by the methods called scientific, they must value the study of elementary social behavior, for within its own modest field it will explain and, at least crudely, predict. So far, it has been more successful in attaining these ends than has the study of larger social units. This is the claim that may be made for it—and it is a purely intellectual one.

Notes

Chapter 1

1. R. K. Merton, *Social Theory and Social Structure* (rev. ed.; New York: The Free Press, 1957), p. 9.

2. Vilfredo Pareto, *Traité de Sociologie Générale* (Paris, 1917).

3. Vilfredo Pareto, *Les systèmes socialistes* (Paris, 1926).

4. C. P. Curtis and G. C. Homans, *An Introduction to Pareto* (New York: Knopf, 1934).

5. See G. C. Homans and O. T. Bailey, *The Society of Fellows* (Cambridge, Mass.: Harvard University Press, 1948).

6. See especially F. J. Roethlisberger and W. J. Dickson, *Management and the Worker* (Cambridge, Mass.: Harvard University Press, 1939).

7. See W. L. Warner and P. S. Lunt, *The Social Life of a Modern Community* (New Haven: Yale University Press, 1941).

8. Elton Mayo, *The Social Problems of an Industrial Civilization* (Boston: Harvard Business School, 1945).

9. Frederick Seebohm, *The English Village Community* (London, 1883).

10. G. C. Homans, *English Villagers of the Thirteenth Century* (Cambridge, Mass.: Harvard University Press, 1941).

11. Sir George W. Cox and E. H. Jones, *Popular Romances of the Middle Ages* (London, 1880).

12. See Reginald Lennard, "The Economic Position of the Domesday Sokemen," *Economic Journal*, 57 (1947), 179–195.

13. See W. G. Hoskins, *The Making of the English Landscape* (London, 1955), p. 38.

14. H. M. Chadwick, *The Origin of the English Nation* (Cambridge, 1907).

15. B. E. Siebs, *Grundlagen und Aufbau der altfriesischen Verfassung* (Breslau, 1933).

16. C. M. Arensberg and S. T. Kimball, *Family and Community in Ireland* (Cambridge, Mass.: Harvard University Press, 1941).

17. Bronislaw Malinowski, *Magic, Science and Religion and Other Essays* (New York: The Free Press, 1948), p. 14.

18. A. R. Radcliffe-Brown, *Structure and Function in Primitive Society* (New York: The Free Press, 1952), p. 180.

19. A. R. Radcliffe-Brown, *Taboo* (Cambridge, 1939).

20. D. F. Aberle *et al.*, "The Functional Prerequisites of a Society," *Ethics*, 60 (1950), 100–111.

21. Bronislaw Malinowski, *The Father in Primitive Psychology* (London, 1927).

22. Raymond Firth, *We, the Tikopia* (New York: Macmillan, 1936), pp. 138–234.

23. Émile Durkheim, *Les règles de la méthode sociologique* (Paris, 1927), p. 125.

24. Radcliffe-Brown, *Structure and Function in Primitive Society*, pp. 15–31.

25. G. C. Homans, *The Human Group* (New York: Harcourt, 1950), pp. 190–280.

26. Claude Lévi-Strauss, *Les structures élémentaires de la parenté* (Paris, 1949).

27. Merton, *op. cit.*, pp. 71n, 82.

28. See C. G. Hempel, "The Function of General Laws in History," in P. Gardiner (ed.), *Theories of History* (New York: The Free Press, 1959), pp. 344–356.

29. B. M. Selekman, S. K. Selekman, and S. H. Fuller, *Problems in Labor Relations* (2d ed.; New York: McGraw-Hill, 1958), pp. 626–666.

30. A. N. Whitehead, *Science and the Modern World* (New York: Macmillan, 1929).

31. Percy Bridgman, *The Logic of Modern Physics* (New York: Macmillan, 1927).

32. E. D. Chapple, "Measuring Human Relations," *Genetic Psychology Monographs*, 22 (1940), 3–147.

33. G. C. Homans, "A Conceptual Scheme for the Study of Social Organization," *American Sociological Review*, 12 (1947), 13–26.

34. G. C. Homans, *The Human Group* (New York: Harcourt, 1950).

35. W. F. Whyte, *Street Corner Society* (Chicago: University of Chicago Press, 1943).

36. G. P. Murdock, *Social Structure* (New York: Macmillan, 1949).

37. A good example of codification is J. G. March and H. A. Simon, *Organizations* (New York: Wiley, 1958).

38. Gardner Lindzey (ed.), *Handbook of Social Psychology* (Reading, Mass.: Addison-Wesley, 1954).

39. See especially R. B. Braithwaite, *Scientific Explanation* (Cambridge, 1953).

40. Talcott Parsons, *Essays in Sociological Theory, Pure and Applied* (New York: The Free Press, 1949), p. 17.

41. Merton, *op. cit.*, p. 5.

42. Talcott Parsons, "General Theory in Sociology," in R. K. Merton, L. Broom, and L. S. Cottrell, Jr. (eds.), *Sociology Today* (New York: Basic Books, 1959), pp. 4–16.

43. Quoted in Merton, *Social Theory and Social Structure*, p. 113.

44. Quoted in M. Rukeyser, *Willard Gibbs* (New York: Doubleday, 1942), p. 232.

45. Francis Bacon, *Novum Organum*, Aphorism XLVIII.

46. Ernst Mach, *The Science of Mechanics*, trans. by T. J. McCormack (LaSalle, Ill.: Open Court, 1942), pp. 155, 190.

47. Especially B. F. Skinner, *Science and Human Behavior* (New York: Macmillan, 1953).

48. G. C. Homans, *Social Behavior: Its Elementary Forms* (New York: Harcourt, 1961).

49. C. I. Barnard, *The Functions of the Executive* (Cambridge, Mass.: Harvard University Press, 1938), p. xiii.

Chapter 2

1. See especially F. J. Roethlisberger, *Management and Morale* (Cambridge,

Mass.: Harvard University Press, 1941),
pp. 109–113.

Chapter 3

1. One good one is W. F. Whyte,
*Human Relations in the Restaurant In-
dustry* (New York: McGraw-Hill,
1948), pp. 33–46.
2. See G. C. Homans, *The Human
Group* (New York: Harcourt, 1950),
p. 140.
3. This method, plus the distances at
which observations were made, pre-
cluded accurate recording of *origina-
tions* and *receipts* of interaction. I could
only see *which persons* were interacting.
4. This interpretation is essentially
the same as the "status equilibrium"
theory of E. Benoit-Smullyan, "Status
Types and Status Interrelations," *American Sociological Review*, 9 (1944),
151–161. See also G. E. Fenchel, J. H.
Monderer, and E. L. Hartley, "Subjective Status and the Equilibrium Hypothesis," *Journal of Abnormal and Social
Psychology*, 46 (1951), 476–479.

Chapter 4

1. See F. J. Roethlisberger and W.
J. Dickson, *Management and the Worker*
(Cambridge, Mass.: Harvard University
Press, 1939).
2. All names are fictitious but faithful to ethnic background.
3. See G. C. Homans, *The Human
Group* (New York: Harcourt, 1950),
especially Chaps. 4 and 5.
4. $P = 0.024$ by Fisher's Exact Test;
population divided into those above the
median and those below on each variable.
5. R. F. Bales, "The Equilibrium
Problem in Small Groups," in Talcott

Parsons, R. F. Bales, and E. A. Shils,
*Working Papers in the Theory of Ac-
tion* (New York: The Free Press, 1953),
pp. 146–147.
6. Homans, *op. cit.*, pp. 244–248.
7. Claude Bernard, *Introduction à
l'Étude de la Médicine Expérimentale*
(Paris, 1952), p. 113.
8. See especially Elton Mayo, *The
Social Problems of an Industrial Civilization* (Boston: Harvard Business School,
1945), Chap. 5.

Chapter 5

1. *Politics*, Book III, Chap. 9; R.
McKeon (ed.), *The Basic Works of
Aristotle* (New York: Random House,
1941), p. 1187.
2. Bertrand de Jouvenel, *De la sou-
veraineté* (Paris, 1955), p. 195.
3. E. Benoit-Smullyan, "Status Types
and Status Interrelations," *American
Sociological Review*, 9 (1944), 151–
161.
4. Gerhard Lenski, "Status Crystallization," *American Sociological Review*, 19 (1954), 405–413.
5. Stuart Adams, "Social Climate and
Productivity in Small Military Groups,"
American Sociological Review, 19
(1954), 421–425.
6. F. J. Roethlisberger, *Management
and Morale* (Cambridge, Mass.: Harvard University Press, 1941), pp. 34–
35.
7. Lenski, *op. cit.*
8. See A. Zaleznik, C. R. Christen-
sen, and F. J. Roethlisberger, *The Motivation, Productivity, and Satisfaction
of Workers* (Boston: Harvard Business
School, 1958), pp. 291–321.
9. See especially A. R. Radcliffe-
Brown, "On Joking Relationships,"
Structure and Function in Primitive

Society (New York: The Free Press, 1952), pp. 90–116.

10. Zaleznik, *et al., op. cit.*, pp. 148, 156–157, 359–361.

11. Adams, *op. cit.*

Chapter 6

1. N. Balchin ("Mark Spade"), *How to Run a Bassoon Factory and Business for Pleasure* (London: Hamish Hamilton, 1950), p. 219.

Chapter 7

1. G. M. Trevelyan, *English Social History* (New York: Longmans, 1942).

2. K. Z. Lorenz, *King Solomon's Ring* (New York: Crowell, 1952).

3. E. Devons, "The Role of the Myth in Politics," *The Listener*, June 21, 1956.

Chapter 9

1. William Harrison, *Description of England*, ed. F. J. Furnivall (The New Shakspere Society), I, 259. See also p. 237.

2. See Frederick Seebohm, *Tribal Custom in Anglo-Saxon Law*, p. 36, quoting *Ancient Laws of Wales*, II, 693.

3. See A. Birnie, "Ridge Cultivation in Scotland," *Scottish Historical Review*, XXIV, 194 ff. There are ways of plowing ridges other than the one described.

4. The custom of the Germans in having a certain amount of land around their houses struck Tacitus by its contrast with the customs of the Italians in building their houses against each other, wall to wall. (*Germania*, Chap. 16.)

5. E. Gutch, *Folklore of the North Riding of Yorkshire* (*York and the Ainsty*), p. 338; M. C. Balfour and N. W. Thomas, *Folklore of Northumberland*, p. 122.

6. See Elton Mayo, *Human Problems of an Industrial Civilization* (New York: Macmillan, 1933); F. J. Roethlisberger and W. J. Dickson, *Management and the Worker* (Cambridge, Mass.: Harvard University Press, 1939).

7. W. I. Thomas and Florian Znaniecki, *The Polish Peasant in Europe and America* (Chicago, 1918), I, 174.

Chapter 10

1. Some of the useful authorities are: H. L. Gray, *English Field Systems*; D. C. Douglas, *The Social Structure of Medieval East Anglia* (Oxford Studies in Social and Legal History, Vol. IX); J. E. A. Jolliffe, *Pre-Feudal England: The Jutes*; G. C. Homans, *English Villagers of the Thirteenth Century*.

2. G. C. Homans, *English Villagers of the Thirteenth Century* (Cambridge, Mass.: Harvard University Press, 1941), p. 111.

3. *Ibid.*, p. 112.

4. See J. E. A. Jolliffe, *Pre-Feudal England: The Jutes*.

5. See the evidence for partible inheritance in Norfolk at the end of the twelfth century in *Feet of Fines for the County of Norfolk, 1199–1202*, ed. B. Dodwell (Pipe Roll Soc., Vol. XXVII, 1952).

6. Reginald Lennard, "The Economic Position of the Domesday Villani," *Economic Journal*, 56 (1946), 244–261; and "The Economic Position of the Domesday Sokemen," *Economic Journal*, 57 (1947), 179–195.

7. The prevalence in Domesday of tenure in *parage* in the Jutish area of southern Hampshire suggests that the Jutes set up their joint-family organization there too.

8. R. G. Collingwood and J. N. L. Myres, *Roman Britain and the English Settlements* (2d ed.; Oxford, 1937).

9. Lennard, *op. cit.* "Domesday" is William the Conqueror's great land register of 1086.

10. Homans, *op. cit.*, pp. 121–159.

11. K. H. Connell, *Population of Ireland: 1750–1845* (Oxford: Oxford University Press, 1950); C. M. Arensberg and S. T. Kimball, *Family and Community in Ireland* (Cambridge, Mass.: Harvard University Press, 1941).

12. See, among other possible examples, the custumal of Ogbourne St. George, Wilts., in M. Chibnall (ed.), *Select Documents of the English Lands of the Abbey of Bec* (Camden Soc., 3d ser., Vol. LXXIII, 1951), pp. 29–36.

13. Marc Bloch, "The Rise of Dependent Cultivation and Seigniorial Institutions," in J. H. Clapham and E. Powers (eds.), *The Cambridge Economic History of Europe*, I, 264.

14. *Ibid.*, p. 264.

15. *Ibid.*, pp. 260–271.

16. See Raymond Firth, *We, the Tikopia* and *Primitive Polynesian Economy*, and the various books by Bronislaw Malinowski about the Trobriands, particularly *Coral Gardens and Their Magic*.

17. M. Bloch, *op. cit.*, p. 261. For the ambiguous position of the lord, see Homans, *op. cit.*, pp. 339–349.

Chapter 11

1. R. H. C. Davis, "East Anglia and the Danelaw," *Transactions of the Royal Historical Society*, 5th ser., 5 (1955), 23–39.

2. P. H. Blair, *An Introduction to Anglo-Saxon England* (Cambridge, 1956), p. 7.

3. M. Ashdown, *English and Norse Documents Relating to the Reign of Ethelred the Unready* (Cambridge, 1930), p. 138.

4. R. H. Hodgkin, *A History of the Anglo-Saxons* (Oxford, 1952), Chap. 1.

5. H. L. Gray, *English Field Systems* (Cambridge, Mass.: Harvard University Press, 1915), especially pp. 305–354.

6. For East Anglian tenements see especially D. C. Douglas, *Medieval East Anglia*, Oxford Studies in Social and Legal History, Vol. IX (Oxford, 1927), pp. 17–67; subsequently referred to as Douglas, *East Anglia*. Besides the *tenmanloth*, a *ninemaendale* appears in the 1222 Ely extent of Wisbech: B. M. Cotton MS, Tiberius B II, fol. 147.

7. *Feet of Fines for the County of Norfolk, 1199–1202*, ed. B. Dodwell (Pipe Roll Soc., New ser., Vol. XXVII, 1952), p. xxiii. A "fine" or "final concord" is the record of the settlement of a suit "out of court."

8. For East Anglian inheritance see Sir Frederick Pollock and F. W. Maitland, *History of English Law* (2d ed.,), II, 270; H. L. Gray, *op. cit.*, p. 337; G. C. Homans, "Partible Inheritance of Villagers' Holdings," *Economic History Review*, 8 (1937), 48–56; G. C. Homans, *English Villagers of the Thirteenth Century* (Cambridge, Mass.: Harvard University Press, 1941), pp. 109–132; B. Dodwell, *op. cit.*, pp. xxxvi–xl; *The Kalendar of Abbot Samson of Bury St. Edmunds and Related Documents*, ed. R. H. C. Davis (Camden Soc., 3d ser., Vol. LXXXIV, 1954), pp. xxxi, xxxiii; subsequently referred to as *Kalendar*.

9. *Kalendar*, pp. 97, 135. Socage is a free, nonmilitary tenure.

10. For example, Douglas, *East Anglia*, Appendix, No. 52.

11. P. R. O. Court Rolls, S.C. 2, 204/22, memb. 6.

12. G. C. Homans, "The Rural Sociology of Medieval England," *Past and Present*, No. 4 (1953), p. 35. Reprinted as Chap. 10 of this present work.

13. *Feet of Fines of the Seventh and Eighth Years of the Reign of Richard I* (Pipe Roll Soc., Vol. XX, 1896), p. 76.

14. In a survey of 1291 of lands of the Prior of Norwich in Martham, Norfolk; see W. Hudson, "Manorial Life," *History Teachers' Miscellany*, I, 161.

15. *Register of the Abbey of St. Benet of Holme*, ed. J. R. West (Norfolk Record Soc.), I, 169; F. M. Stenton, "St. Benet of Holme and the Norman Conquest," *English Historical Review*, 37 (1922), 225–235.

16. *Kalendar*, p. 52; *Rotuli Hundredorum*, I, 527, 529.

17. W. Hudson, "Three Manorial Extents of the Thirteenth Century," *Norfolk Archaeology*, XIV, 46.

18. *Rotuli Hundredorum*, I, 498, 517. The "suit" here is the duty to attend at the hundred court.

19. Davis, *op. cit.*

20. Douglas, *East Anglia*, pp. 52–59. The geld is a land tax.

21. D. C. Douglas, "Fragments of an Anglo-Saxon Survey from Bury St. Edmunds," *English Historical Review*, 43 (1928), 376–383.

22. *Documents Illustrative of the Social and Economic History of the Danelaw*, ed. F. M. Stenton (British Academy: Records of the Social and Economic History of England and Wales Vol. V), pp. lxviii–lxix; for the 12-carucate hundred in the Danelaw, see pp. lxiii ff.

23. G. C. Homans, "Partible Inheritance of Villagers' Holdings," *Economic History Review*, 8 (1937), 51–52.

24. Douglas, *East Anglia*, pp. 197–198.

25. Sir Frederick Pollock and F. W. Maitland, *History of English Law*, 2d ed., I, 532, 580. The "view of frankpledge" was an inquest to determine whether all adult men belonged to those groups, in theory of ten men each, whose members were jointly responsible for their obedience to the law, and which were called "tithings" or "frankpledges." The capital pledge was the headman of a tithing.

26. Douglas, *East Anglia*, p. 194.

27. *Kalendar*, p. 44.

28. Douglas, *East Anglia*, p. 198.

29. *Rotuli Hundredorum*, I, 50.

30. *Leet Jurisdiction in the City of Norwich*, ed. W. Hudson (Seldon Soc., Vol. V, 1891).

31. *Ibid.*, p. xxvi.

32. Cited, *ibid.*, p. xxi.

33. For the ferding see *Victoria County History: Suffolk*, I, 358; *Register of the Abbey of St. Benet of Holme*, ed. J. R. West (Norfolk Record Soc.), I, 169; *Kalendar*, pp. xxix, 24, 65–68.

34. O. S. Anderson, "The English Hundred-Names," *Lunds Universitets Arsskrift*, N. F., Avd 1, 30 (1934), 91.

35. R. H. C. Davis, "East Anglia and the Danelaw," *Transactions of the Royal Historical Society*, 5th ser., 5 (1955), 39.

36. *Kalendar*, pp. xxxii–xlvii. Tenants in socage are sokemen.

37. Douglas, *East Anglia*, pp. 48–49.

38. *Victoria County History: Suffolk*, I, 369, 372.

39. B. E. Siebs, *Untersuchungen zur Deutschen Staats- und Rechtsgeschichte*, Vol. 144 (Breslau, 1933); subsequently referred to as Siebs.

40. Siebs, pp. 18–31.

41. Siebs, pp. 33–35.
42. Siebs, pp. 39–40.
43. Siebs, p. 37.
44. Siebs, p. 37.
45. Siebs, pp. 18, 31–32.
46. Siebs, pp. 3–13, 22.
47. Siebs, pp. 32, 116.
48. S. Fairbanks, *The Old West Frisian Skeltana Riucht* (Cambridge, Mass.: Harvard University Press, 1939), p. 113; subsequently referred to as *Skeltana Riucht.*
49. Siebs, p. 32.
50. Siebs, pp. 122–127 and maps at end.
51. Siebs, pp. 32–33.
52. Siebs, pp. 135–136.
53. For example: *Cartularium Monasterii de Rameseia* (Rolls Series), III, 285; W. Hudson, "Traces of Primitive Agricultural Organization as Suggested by a Survey of the Manor of Martham, Norfolk (1101–1292)," *Transactions of the Royal Historical Society*, 4th ser., I, 36; "The archaic word used for a full villeinage tenement deserves notice. It is always written *eruing*. The letters in the ms. are very carefully formed. Once or twice the form *erving* is used."
54. Siebs, p. 118.
55. K. von Richthofen, *De Lex Frisionum* (Leeuwarden, 1886), p. 113; Siebs, p. 119.
56. Siebs, pp. 112–113.
57. Siebs, p. 117.
58. Douglas, *East Anglia*, p. 221.
59. *Ibid.*, p. 28.
60. *Domesday Book*, Vol. II, fol. 130b; cited in Sir Paul Vinogradoff, *English Society in the Eleventh Century*, p. 104. "Soke and sake" is a duty to attend at court.
61. Siebs, pp. 88–96; Fairbanks, *Skeltana Riucht*, p. 27.
62. F. Lot, *Naissance de la France* (Paris, 1948), p. 74.
63. *Register of the Abbey of St. Benet of Holme*, ed. J. R. West (Norfolk Record Soc., 1932), I, 22, 115; II, 218.
64. B. M. Cotton MS, Tiberius B II, fols. 188–191; see Douglas, *East Anglia*, p. 63.
65. *English Historical Documents, c. 500–1042*, ed. Dorothy Whitelock (New York: Oxford University Press, 1955), pp. 357–358. Note that only in these laws is *leodgyld* used to mean wergild. That is, in Kent, *leod* means "man."
66. Fairbanks, *Skeltana Riucht*, p. 99.
67. Siebs, pp. 41–47.
68. Siebs, p. 50.
69. *Kalendar*, pp. xvi–xxv, 26; note Pulham, above, and *Rotuli Hundredorum*, II, 147, 150.
70. *A New English Dictionary on Historical Principles, s.v.* "leet," "lathe"; Richard Cleasby, Gudbrand Vigfusson, and Sir W. A. Craigie, *An Icelandic-English Dictionary on Historical Principles* (Oxford, 1957), *s.v.* "leith."
71. Siebs, pp. 49, 62; for the larger Frisian political units see pp. 61–76, 94–96.
72. See Table II at the end of Siebs.
73. For the 12 leets of Thingoe see *Kalendar*, p. xvii; for *thing* and *howe* in Frisian see Fairbanks, *Skeltana Riucht*, pp. 33, 100, etc.
74. M. Bloch, "The Rise of Dependent Cultivation and Seigniorial Institutions," in J. H. Clapham and E. Power (eds.), *Cambridge Economic History of Europe*, I, 264.

Chapter 12

1. Richard Baxter, *Reliquiae Baxterianae*, ed. M. Sylvester (London, 1696), p. 30.

2. Charles E. Banks, "English Sources of Emigration to the New England Colonies in the Seventeenth Century," Massachusetts Historical Society, *Proceedings*, 60 (1927), 366–371. Unfortunately Banks is not as explicit as he ought to be in stating what material his statistics are based on, but he implies that it is the lists of passengers sailing for New England, which were kept at all English ports. A large part of these are lost, but a number survive, mostly of the year 1635, in which numerous sailings occurred. They indicate the English residence of the emigrants.

3. The best discussion of the geographical distribution of the clothing industry is that of Ephraim Lipson, *History of the Woollen and Worsted Industries* (London, 1921), pp. 220–255.

4. Thomas Fuller, *The Church History of England*, ed. J. S. Brewer (Oxford, 1845), II, 287.

5. *Victoria County History: Dorset* (London, 1908), II, 360.

6. See G. A. Moriarty, "Social and Geographic Origins of the Founders of Massachusetts," in A. B. Hart, *Commonwealth History of Massachusetts* (New York, 1927), I, 57 ff.

7. Edward Johnson, *Wonder-Working Providence of Sions Saviour in New England*, ed. W. F. Poole (Andover, 1867), p. 129.

8. See F. Walker, *Historical Geography of Southwest Lancashire before the Industrial Revolution* (Manchester: Chetham Society, 1939).

9. Lipson, *op. cit.*, p. 101; Astrid Friis, *Alderman Cockayne's Project and the Cloth Trade* (London, 1927).

10. Lipson, *op. cit.*, p. 109; Friis, *op. cit.*, p. 384.

11. *Calendar of State Papers: Domestic* [hereinafter *Calendar*], *1619–1623* (London, 1858), *passim*.

12. *Ibid.*, p. 346.

13. *Acts of the Privy Council of England, 1621–1623* (London, 1932), p. 190.

14. *Calendar, op. cit.*, p. 410.

15. *Calendar, 1629–1631* (London, 1860) and *1631–1633* (London, 1862), *passim*.

16. *Calendar, 1631–1633*, p. 14.

17. *Calendar, 1637* (London, 1868), p. 64.

18. J. T. Adams, *The Founding of New England* (Boston, 1921), pp. 121 ff.

19. Lord Francis Hervey (ed.), *Suffolk in the XVII Century: The Breviary of Suffolk by Robert Reyce, 1618* (London, 1902), p. 57.

20. *John White's Planters' Plea* (facsimile), ed. M. H. Saville (Rockport, Mass., 1930), p. 17.

21. *Calendar of State Papers: Colonial, 1574–1660* (London, 1911), p. 266.

22. *Winthrop Papers*, Collections of the Massachusetts Historical Society (Boston, 1929—).

23. See C. H. Pope, *The Pioneers of Massachusetts* (Boston, 1900), pp. 523–524.

24. G. M. Trevelyan, *England in the Age of Wycliffe* (London, 1929), Chap. 8.

25. *Victoria County History: Suffolk* (London, 1911), II, 32.

26. C. H. Haskins, *Studies in Medieval Culture* (London, 1929), p. 198. Falstaff's remark (*Henry IV, Part I*, Act II, scene 4): "I would I were a weaver; I could sing psalms or anything," may spring from a contemporary belief that clothworkers were likely to be Puritans in religion. But it may

refer to nothing more than a weavers' custom of singing at their work. See also Ben Jonson, *The Silent Woman*, Act III, scene 2.

Chapter 13

1. A. R. Radcliffe-Brown, *Taboo* (Cambridge: Cambridge University Press, 1939). His views are most prominently stated elsewhere in *The Andaman Islanders* (Cambridge: Cambridge University Press, 1933).
2. See *Magic, Science and Religion* in J. Needham (ed.), *Science, Religion and Reality*; *Coral Gardens and Their Magic*; and *Foundations of Faith and Morals* (Riddell Memorial Lectures).
3. The word *anxiety* is used here in its ordinary common-sense meaning. This use is not to be confused with the psychoanalytic one, though of course the two are related.
4. *Science, Religion and Reality*, p. 32.
5. *Ibid.*, p. 38.
6. Radcliffe-Brown, *Taboo*, p. 25.
7. R. R. Willoughby, *Magic and Cognate Phenomena: An Hypothesis*, in C. Murchison (ed.), *Handbook of Social Psychology*, p. 471.
8. *Science, Religion and Reality*, p. 82.
9. Radcliffe-Brown, *Taboo*, p. 33.
10. *Ibid.*, p. 41.
11. I. Hogbin, *Law and Order in Polynesia* (London: Christophers, 1934), p. xxxviii. The introduction is by Malinowski.
12. Radcliffe-Brown, *Taboo*, p. 35.
13. *Ibid.*, p. 39.
14. W. I. Thomas and Florian Znaniecki, *The Polish Peasant in Europe and America* (Chicago, 1918), I, 174.
15. W. L. Warner, *A Black Civili-*

zation (New York: Harper, 1937), p. 410.

Chapter 14

1. Claude Lévi-Strauss, *Les structures élémentaires de la parenté* (Paris: Presses Universitaires de France, 1949); hereafter called *Structures*.
2. A. R. Radcliffe-Brown, *Structure and Function in Primitive Society* (Glencoe: The Free Press, 1952), pp. 15–31. The paper was originally published in 1924.
3. A good summary of Lévi-Strauss's book, with some useful criticism, is J. P. B. de Josselin de Jong, *Lévi-Strauss's Theory on Kinship and Marriage: Mededelingen van het Rijkmuseum voor Volkenkunde, No. 10* (Leiden, 1952).
4. Lévi-Strauss, *Structures*, p. 64.
5. *Ibid.*, p. 65.
6. One of the few examples is that of the Bedouin and other groups influenced through Islam by Bedouin custom.
7. Lévi-Strauss, *Structures*, p. 274.
8. *Ibid.*, p. 270.
9. *Ibid.*, p. 271.
10. *Ibid.*, p. 548.
11. Émile Durkheim, *De la division du travail social* (Paris, 1893), Chap. 3, sec. 4.
12. Lévi-Strauss, *Structures*, p. 553.
13. *Ibid.*, p. 558.
14. E. R. Leach, "The Structural Implications of Matrilateral Cross-Cousin Marriage," *Journal of the Royal Anthropological Institute*, 81 (1951), 23–55.
15. For a discussion of Malinowski's and Radcliffe-Brown's theories of magic, see G. C. Homans, *The Human Group* (New York: Harcourt, 1950), pp. 321–330.

16. Radcliffe-Brown, *Structure and Function in Primitive Society*, p. 180.

17. Quoted in D. W. Thompson, *On Growth and Form* (New York: Macmillan, 1948), p. 6.

18. See R. B. Braithwaite, *Scientific Explanation* (Cambridge, 1953), pp. 319–341.

19. Lévi-Strauss, *Structures*, pp. 558–566.

20. See Leach, *op. cit.*, p. 53.

21. Radcliffe-Brown, *op. cit.*, pp. 15–31.

22. Raymond Firth, *We, the Tikopia* (New York: Macmillan, 1936).

23. This is a Barnardian definition of authority. See C. I. Barnard, *The Functions of the Executive* (Cambridge, Mass.: Harvard University Press, 1938), Chap. 12.

24. For a discussion of jural relations, see A. R. Radcliffe-Brown, "Introduction," in A. R. Radcliffe-Brown and D. Forde (eds.), *African Systems of Kinship and Marriage* (New York: Oxford University Press, 1950), p. 11.

25. I. Schapera, "Kinship and Marriage among the Tswana," Radcliffe-Brown and Forde (eds.), *African Systems* . . . , p. 142.

26. Firth, *op. cit.*, pp. 209–210; Radcliffe-Brown, *op. cit.*, p. 26.

27. Homans, *op. cit.*, pp. 230–280.

28. G. G. Brown, "Hehe Cross-Cousin Marriage," in E. E. Evans-Pritchard, Raymond Firth, Bronislaw Malinowski, and I. Schapera (eds.), *Essays Presented to C. G. Seligman* (London, 1934), p. 28.

29. *Ibid.*, p. 35.

30. Lévi-Strauss, *Structures*, pp. 531–535.

31. See especially Bronislaw Malinowski, *The Father in Primitive Psychology* (London, 1927), and *Sex and Repression in Savage Society* (London, 1927).

32. Bronislaw Malinowski, *The Sexual Life of Savages in North-Western Melanesia* (London, 1952), pp. 81, 450–451.

33. Fred Eggan, *The Social Organization of the Western Pueblos* (Chicago: University of Chicago Press, 1950), pp. 39–41; M. Titiev, "The Problem of Cross-Cousin Marriage among the Hopi," *American Anthropologist*, New ser., 40 (1938), 105–111.

34. At a session of the anthropological section of the American Association for the Advancement of Science, December 28, 1951.

35. Lévi-Strauss, *Structures*, pp. 332–333.

36. *Ibid.*, p. 334.

37. G. P. Murdock, *Social Structure* (New York: Macmillan, 1949).

38. E. K. Gough, "Changing Kinship Usages in the Setting of Political and Economic Change among the Nayars of Malabar," *Journal of the Royal Anthropological Institute*, 82 (1952), 73–74.

39. Leach, *op. cit.*, pp. 24–25.

40. J. C. Mitchell, *The Yao Village* (Manchester, 1956).

41. Meyer Fortes, "Kinship and Marriage among the Ashanti," in Radcliffe-Brown and Forde (eds.), *African Systems* . . . , p. 279.

42. G. P. Murdock, "Kinship and Social Behavior among the Haida," *American Anthropologist*, New ser., 36 (1934), 364.

43. P. T. R. Gurdon, *The Khasis* (London, 1914), p. 78.

44. Our chief sources for these societies are those cited in G. P. Murdock, *Social Structure*, plus the following: Altaians and Teleuts: N. P. Dryenkova, "Klassifikatsionnaya sistema i brachnye

normy a altaitsev i teleut," in L. Ya. Shternberg (ed.), *Sbornik materialov po svad'be i semeino-rodovoyu stroyu narodov S.S.S.R.* (Leningrad, 1926), Vol. I; Gilyak: L. Ya. Shternberg, *Sem'ia i rod* (Leningrad, 1933); Gold: O. Lattimore, *The Gold Tribe, "Fishskin Tatars" of the Lower Sungari* (Memoirs of the American Anthropological Association, No. 40, 1933); Kachin: E. R. Leach, *The Political Systems of Highland Burma* (London, 1953); Karadjeri: A. P. Elkin, "Social Organization of the Kimberley Division, Northwestern Australia," *Oceania*, 2 (1932), 296–333; Lovedu: E. J. Krige and J. D. Krige, *The Realm of a Rain-Queen* (London, 1943); Mbundu: G. M. Childs, *Umbundu Kinship and Character* (Oxford, 1949); Mende: K. L. Little, *The Mende of Sierra Leone* (London, 1951); Sandawe: O. Dempwolff, *Die Sandawe* (Hamburg, 1916); Wik-Munkan: U. McConnel, "The Wik-Munkan and Allied Tribes of the Cape York Peninsula, N.Q., Part III," *Oceania*, 4 (1934) 310–367; Yir-Yoront: L. Sharp, "The Social Organization of the Yir-Yoront Tribe, Cape York Peninsula; Part I: Kinship and the Family," *Oceania*, 4 (1934), 404–431; Kandyu: U. McConnel, "Social Organization of the Tribes of the Cape York Peninsula," *Oceania*, 10 (1940), 434–455; Sherente: C. Nimuendajú, *The Serente*, trans. R. H. Lowie (Los Angeles: The Southwest Museum, 1942); Garo: A. Playfair, *The Garos* (London, 1909); Kaska: J. H. Honigmann, *Culture and Ethos of Kaska Society*, Yale University Publications in Anthropology, No. 40 (New Haven, 1946); Kaonde: F. H. Melland, *In Witch-Bound Africa* (London, 1923); Siriono: A. R. Holmberg, *Nomads of the Long Bow: The Siriono of Eastern Bolivia*, Institute of Social Anthropology, Smithsonian Institution, Publication No. 7 (Washington, 1950); Ila: A. I. Richards, "Some Types of Social Structure among the Central Bantu," in Radcliffe-Brown and Forde (eds.), *African Systems* . . . , pp. 207–251; Tlingit: F. de Laguna, "Some Dynamic Forces in Tlingit Society," *Southwestern Journal of Anthropology*, 8 (1952), 1–12. We have had to rely on friends for information from the Russian sources.

45. R. A. Fisher, *Statistical Methods for Research Workers* (10th ed.; Edinburgh, 1946), p. 96 ff.

46. G. M. Childs, *Umbundu Kinship and Character* (Oxford, 1949), pp. 44–45.

47. E. J. Krige and J. D. Krige, *The Realm of a Rain-Queen* (London, 1943), pp. 70–84.

48. W. L. Warner, *A Black Civilization* (New York: Harper, 1937), p. 99.

49. K. L. Little, *The Mende of Sierra Leone* (London, 1951), p. 110.

50. Radcliffe-Brown, "Introduction," in Radcliffe-Brown and Forde (eds.), *African Systems* . . . , p. 37.

51. L. Sharp, "The Social Organization of the Yir-Yoront Tribe, Cape York Peninsula. Part I: Kinship and the Family," *Oceania*, 4 (1934), 412.

52. *Ibid.*, p. 415.

53. *Ibid.*, p. 426.

54. G. P. Murdock, "Kinship and Social Behavior among the Haida," *American Anthropologist*, New ser., 36 (1934), 363–364.

55. F. de Laguna, "Some Dynamic Forces in Tlingit Society," *Southwestern Journal of Anthropology*, 8 (1952), 11–12.

56. A. B. Deacon, "Notes on Some Islands of the New Hebrides," *Journal*

of the Royal Anthropological Institute, 59 (1929), 483.

57. E. W. Smith and A. M. Dale, *The Ila-Speaking Peoples of Northern Rhodesia* (London, 1920).

58. A. I. Richards, "Some Types of Social Structure among the Central Bantu," in Radcliffe-Brown and Forde (eds.), *African Systems* . . . , p. 239.

59. Smith and Dale, *op. cit.,* I, 319–320.

60. F. H. Melland, *In Witch-Bound Africa* (London, 1923), pp. 62–63.

61. *Ibid.,* p. 57.

62. J. H. Honigmann, *Culture and Ethos of Kaska Society,* Yale University Publications in Anthropology, No. 40 (New Haven, 1946), p. 131.

63. *Ibid.,* pp. 124–125.

64. *Ibid.,* p. 129.

65. A. R. Holmberg, *Nomads of the Long Bow: The Siriono of Eastern Bolivia,* Institute of Social Anthropology, Smithsonian Institution, Publication No. 7 (Washington, 1950), pp. 54, 81–83.

66. *Ibid.,* pp. 49–57.

67. A Playfair, *The Garos* (London, 1909); T. C. Hodson, "The Garo and Khasi Marriage Systems Contrasted," *Man in India,* 1 (1921), 106–127; J. K. Bose, "The Nokrom System of the Garos of Assam," *Man,* 36 (1936), 44–46.

68. Playfair, *The Garos,* p. 64.

69. *Ibid.,* p. 73.

70. U. McConnel, "Social Organization of the Tribes of the Cape York Peninsula," *Oceania,* 10 (1940), 437–438.

71. C. Nimuendajú, *The Serente,* trans. R. H. Lowie (Los Angeles: The Southwest Museum, 1942), pp. 16–22.

72. *Ibid.,* p. 12, italics ours.

73. *Ibid.,* p. 43.

74. *Ibid.,* p. 50.

75. *Ibid.,* p. 26.

76. *Ibid.,* pp. 57–58.

77. Murdock, *Social Structure,* pp. 69–71.

78. Leach, *loc. cit.*

79. Lévi-Strauss, *Structures,* p. 274.

80. *Ibid.,* p. 271.

81. Radcliffe-Brown, "Introduction," in Radcliffe-Brown and Forde (eds.), *African Systems* . . . , p. 78.

Postscript: Five Years Later

1. R. Burling, "Garo Avuncular Authority and Matrilateral Cross-Cousin Marriage," *American Anthropologist,* 60 (1958), 743–749.

2. R. Needham, "The Formal Analysis of Prescriptive Patrilateral Cross-Cousin Marriage," *Southwestern Journal of Anthropology,* 14 (1958), 199–219.

3. R. P. L. de Sousberghe, "Structures de parenté et d'alliance d'après les formules Pende," *Académie royale de Sciences coloniales: Classe des Sciences morales et politiques, Mémoires* Vol. 4, fasc. 1 (Brussels, 1955).

4. *Ibid.,* p. 31.

5. *Ibid.,* p. 27.

6. *Ibid.,* p. 34.

7. *Ibid.,* p. 40.

8. *Ibid.,* p. 48.

9. Claude Lévi-Strauss, *Anthropologie structurale* (Paris, 1958), pp. 344–345.

10. J. Berting and H. Philipsen, "Solidarity, Stratification, and Sentiments," *Bijdragen tot de taal-, landen Volkenkunde,* 116 (1960), 55–80, 66.

11. This is the position called "methodological individualism"; see J. W. N. Watkins, "Historical Explanation in the Social Sciences," in P. Gardiner (ed.), *Theories of History* (New

York: The Free Press, 1959), pp. 503–514.

12. G. P. Murdock, *Social Structure* (New York: Macmillan, 1949).

13. G. P. Murdock, "World Ethnographic Sample," *American Anthropologist*, 59 (1957), 664–687.

14. *Ibid.*, p. 687.

15. E. R. Leach, "The Structural Implications of Matrilateral Cross-Cousin Marriage," *Journal of the Royal Anthropological Institute*, 81 (1951), 23–55.

16. Berting and Philipsen, *op. cit.*, p. 67.

17. *Ibid.*, p. 76.

18. See above, p. 255.

Chapter 15

1. For a discussion of the general problem see Vilfredo Pareto, *Traité de sociologie générale* (Paris, 1917), sec. 2022, n.1.

2. Kurt Lewin makes this point in a paper that bears strongly on the present topic, "The Conflict between Aristotelian and Galilean Modes of Thought in Contemporary Psychology," *A Dynamic Theory of Personality* (New York: McGraw-Hill, 1935), p. 23.

3. E. E. Maccoby and R. R. Holt, "How Surveys Are Made," in T. M. Newcomb, E. L. Hartley *et al.* (eds.), *Readings in Social Psychology* (New York: Holt, 1947), p. 589.

4. See P. F. Lazarsfeld, B. Berelson, and H. Gaudet, *The People's Choice* (New York: Duell, Sloane & Pearce, 1944).

5. Pareto, *loc. cit.*

6. See C. M. Arensberg, "Industry and the Community," in S. D. Hoslett (ed.), *Human Factors in Management* (Parkville: Park College Press, 1946),

p. 292. This paper, reprinted from *American Journal of Sociology*, 48 (1942), 1–12, is, like the Lewin paper cited above, one of the most important papers bearing on the present subject.

Chapter 16

1. See Lionel Robbins, *The Nature and Significance of Economic Science* (London, 1948), pp. 33, 126–127.

2. Muzafer Sherif, "A Preliminary Experimental Study of Inter-Group Relations," in J. R. Rohrer and M. Sherif (eds.), *Social Psychology at the Crossroads* (New York: Harper, 1951), p. 420.

3. Leon Festinger *et al.*, *Social Pressures in Informal Groups* (New York: Harper, 1950), pp. 33–59.

4. G. C. Homans, *The Human Group* (New York: Harcourt, 1950).

5. See especially G. P. Murdock, *Social Structure* (New York: Macmillan, 1949).

6. See "The Conflict between Aristotelian and Galilean Modes of Thought in Contemporary Psychology," in Kurt Lewin, *A Dynamic Theory of Personality* (New York: McGraw-Hill, 1935), pp. 1–42; and G. C. Homans, "The Strategy of Industrial Sociology," *American Journal of Sociology*, 54 (1949), 330–337 (reprinted as Chap. 15 of this present work).

Chapter 17

1. See R. B. Braithwaite, *Scientific Explanation* (Cambridge, 1953).

2. Translated by I. Cunnison as *The Gift* (New York: The Free Press, 1954).

3. In social anthropology D. L. Oliver is working along these lines, and I

owe much to him. See also T. M. Newcomb, "The Prediction of Interpersonal Attraction," *American Psychologist*, 11 (1956), 575–586.

4. B. F. Skinner, *Science and Human Behavior* (New York: Macmillan, 1953).

5. *Ibid.*, pp. 297–329. The discussion of "double contingency" by Talcott Parsons and E. A. Shils could easily lead to a similar paradigm. See *Toward a General Theory of Action* (Cambridge, Mass.: Harvard University Press, 1951), pp. 14–16.

6. K. W. Back, "The Exertion of Influence through Social Communication," in Leon Festinger *et al.* (eds.), *Theory and Experiment in Social Communication* (Ann Arbor: Research Center for Dynamics, University of Michigan, 1950), pp. 21–36.

7. S. Schachter *et al.*, "An Experimental Study of Cohesiveness and Productivity," *Human Relations*, 4 (1951), 229–238.

8. Skinner, *op. cit.* p. 100.

9. S. Schachter, "Deviation, Rejection, and Communication," *Journal of Abnormal and Social Psychology*, 46 (1951), 190–207.

10. Leon Festinger *et al.*, *Social Pressures in Informal Groups* (New York: Harper, 1950), pp. 72–100.

11. For propositions holding good of groups in practical equilibrium see G. C. Homans, *The Human Group* (New York: Harcourt, 1950); and H. W. Riecken and G. C. Homans, "Psychological Aspects of Social Structure," in Gardner Lindzey (ed.), *Handbook of Social Psychology* (Reading, Mass.: Addison-Wesley, 1954), II, 786–832.

12. See Homans, *op. cit.*, pp. 244–248; and R. F. Bales, "The Equilibrium Problem in Small Groups," in A. P. Hare, E. F. Borgatta, and R. F. Bales (eds.), *Small Groups* (New York: Knopf, 1953), pp. 450–456.

13. Homans, *op. cit.*, pp. 281–301.

14. H. B. Gerard, "The Anchorage of Opinions in Face-to-Face Groups," *Human Relations*, 7 (1954), 313–325.

15. G. J. Stigler, *The Theory of Price* (rev. ed.; New York: Macmillan, 1952), p. 99.

16. G. C. Homans, "Status among Clerical Workers," *Human Organization*, 12 (1953), 5–10. Reprinted as Chap. 3 of this present work.

17. Peter M. Blau, *The Dynamics of Bureaucracy* (Chicago: University of Chicago Press, 1955), pp. 99–116.

18. *Ibid.*, p. 108.

19. *Ibid.*, p. 108.

20. *Ibid.*, p. 109.

21. But see N. Morse, *Satisfactions in the White-Collar Job* (Ann Arbor: Survey Research Center, University of Michigan, 1953), pp. 115–127.

Chapter 18

1. See P. M. Blau, *The Dynamics of Bureaucracy* (Chicago: University of Chicago Press, 1955), pp. 99–200.

2. See especially Kurt Lewin, *Field Theory in Social Science*, ed. Dorwin Cartwright (New York: Harper, 1951).

3. See especially F. J. Roethlisberger and W. J. Dickson, *Management and the Worker* (Cambridge, Mass.: Harvard University Press, 1939).

4. See G. C. Homans, *Social Behavior* (New York: Harcourt, 1961), pp. 145–164, 316–335.

Index

Functionalism (*Cont.*)
  of Parsons, 43
  See also Anthropology

Garo society, 224–225, 228, 239–240, 250, 255
Gaudet, H., 315
Gavelkind inheritance, 148, 153, 180
Generalized exchange (*see* Exchange)
Geographical factors, of field systems, 16–18, 129
Gerard, H. B., 285, 316
Germanic society, 21, 31
  in England, 19
  and Friesland, 20
  and land systems, 131
Gibbs, W., 46, 271
Gilyak society, 228, 231
Givens, 274–275, 276–277
  in economics, 270–271
  status of, 272–273
Gough, E. K., 312
Gray, H. L., 159, 306, 307
Great Leets, 167, 168, 173
Group psychotherapy, 297
Group structure, 293
Groups, attraction, 285–287
Gurdon, P. T. R., 312
Gutch, E., 306

Haida society, 227–228, 235, 237, 239
Hamlets, 148
Hare, A. P., 316
Harmonic regimes, 206–207, 225, 245–246
Harrison, W., 128, 308
Hartley, E. L., 305
Haskins, C. H., 191, 310–311
Hehe society, 220, 232
Hempel, C. G., 304
Henderson, L. J., 10, 23, 37, 38, 47
Heran (*see* Ethelings)
High-attraction groups (*see* Groups)
High producer, among cash posters, 89
Historian, economic, 16, 157
  method of, 14
History, 40
  categories of, 145–146
  in curriculum, 106
  economic interpretation of, 16–17, 18, 130
  and functionalism, 35
  social, 10–22, 114, 145–146
  and sociology, 1, 11–12, 13, 145, 146–147
  theory for, 34
Hodgkin, R. H., 307
Hodson, T. C., 314

Hogbin, I., 311
Holmberg, A. R., 313, 314
Holt, R. R., 315
Homans, G. C., 202 n, 219
  criticized, 252
  hypotheses of, 223, 229–230, 247, 254, 255, 303, 304, 305, 306, 307, 308, 311, 312, 315, 316
  proposition of jural authority of, 242
Honigman, H., 313, 314
Hopi society, 223
Hoskins, W. G., 303
Hostility, among cash posters, 82–83, 86
"Houses," East Anglian, 162–163
Hudson, W., 308, 309
Human Group, The, 31, 39, 40, 42, 219, 273
Hundreds, 169
  as court, 175
  Frisian, 177–179
  long, 172
  official, 165, 167, 179
  small, 165, 167, 168, 180, 181

Ila society, 226, 227, 228, 236, 243
Incest prohibition, and preferential mating, 203, 212
Income, and status congruence, 96
  as status factor, 96–97
Industrial behavior (*see* Behavior, in industry)
Industrial sociology (*see* Sociology, industrial)
Industrial studies, 35, 257–268
  See also Western Electric research
Inheritance, Frisian, 177
  impartible, 15, 153, 156
  land, 14–15
  partible, 15, 151, 153, 156, 161, 162, 165, 170, 172–173
  rules of, 151–152, 154, 160–161, 180
  women and, 161–162
  See also Gavelkind inheritance
Institutions, and behavior, 23, 146, 298
  defined, 34
  determination of character, 212–213
  dysfunction of, 26
  Frisian, in East Anglia, 158–181
  function of, 24, 26, 27
  interrelation of, 22, 23, 150
  repetition of, 233
  and social organization, 25
Intellectualism, attitude toward, 122, 123, 124
Intelligence, as efficient cause, 216
Interaction, 281
  among cash posters, 80–85, 87
  defined, 37–38, 39

Ranking, basis of, 71
Rationalization, 200
  of magic, 195
Reciprocity, defined, 57
  problem of, 51, 55–57
Records, historical, need for, 19–20
  See also Court rolls
Reductionism, 271, 274, 275
Relay Assembly Test Room, experiment in, 262–263
Religion, and anxiety, 141
  and calendar, 142
  and industrial society, 190–191
  and medieval farming, 141
  Radcliffe-Brown's views on, 192
  Roman, 140, 141
  See also Ritual; Sociology
Religious sociology (*see* Sociology)
Rengwa society, 226, 228
Residence, 246
  uxorilocal, 237, 238, 239
    amitalocal, 244–245
    matrilocal, 244
  virilocal, 237, 239
    avunculocal, 243–244
    patrilocal, 243
Responsibility, among clerical workers, 73
  of commanding officer, 52, 55–56, 60
  of ledger clerks, 92
  as status factor, 93, 97, 289
Restricted exchange (*see* Exchange)
Reward, 287–288, 292, 298
  esteem as, 295–296, 299
Richards, A. I., 313, 314
Richthofen, K. von, 309
Riecken, H. W., 42, 316
Rites, magical, 193–194
Ritual, and anxiety, 24–25, 198–199
  and human collaboration, 7
  magic, 193, 195
  in Middle Ages, 141
  primary, 200
  religious, 141, 193, 195
  secondary, 200
  theory of, 192
Robbins, L., 315
Roethlisberger, F., 7, 97, 100, 303, 304–305, 306, 316
Rotation of crops, 134, 135, 139, 140
  in East Anglia, 160
Rukeyser, M., 304

Salic Law, 161
Sampling methods, 260–261

Samson, Abbott, 161, 164, 165, 168
Saxons, in southern England, 19, 21, 150
Schachter, S., 282–284, 285, 316
Schapera, I., 312
Schneider, D., 32, 202 n, 254, 255
  criticized, 252
Schumpeter, J., 5
Science, history of, 3
  intellectual power of, 302
  process of, 105
  strategies of, 271
  usefulness of, 104–105
Sections (*see* Kin groups)
Seebohm, F., 11, 303, 306
Selekman, B. M., 35, 304
Selekman, S. K., 304
Self-government, medieval, 136
Sema society, 226, 228, 231
Seniority, as status factor, 93
Sentiment, in primitive marriage, 231, 248, 255
  See also Interpersonal relations
Settlements, scattered, 129, 130, 131
Sharp, L., 313
Sheep farming, in East Anglia, 15, 16, 17, 157
Sherente society, 228, 240–242, 245, 247
Sherif, M., 315
Shils, E. A., 305, 316
Shternberg, L. Y., 313
Siebs, B. E., 171, 173, 174, 179, 303, 308, 309
Simon, H. A., 304
Siriono society, 228, 239
Skinner, B. F., 47, 248, 304, 316
Small-group behavior (*see* Behavior; Distributive justice; Equilibrium; Social control)
Small-group research, 262–263
  on cash posters, 75–90
  on clerical status, 61–74
  goal of, 283
  Homans' interest in, 36, 39–42, 47–48
  interest in, 296–297
  among law-enforcement agents, 290–292
  problems of, 278–280
  on small warship, 50–60
  strategy of, 41, 269–277
  theory in, 292
  See also Status congruence
Small groups, study of, 9, 36, 48, 124
Small warship, morale on, 51
  as small group, 50–60
Smith, E. W., 236, 314
Socage, 147, 161
Social anthropology (*see* Anthropology)